T0202906

Communications
in Computer and Information Science   1938

Rationale

The CCIS series is devoted to the publication of proceedings of computer science conferences. Its aim is to efficiently disseminate original research results in informatics in printed and electronic form. While the focus is on publication of peer-reviewed full papers presenting mature work, inclusion of reviewed short papers reporting on work in progress is welcome, too. Besides globally relevant meetings with internationally representative program committees guaranteeing a strict peer-reviewing and paper selection process, conferences run by societies or of high regional or national relevance are also considered for publication.

Topics

The topical scope of CCIS spans the entire spectrum of informatics ranging from foundational topics in the theory of computing to information and communications science and technology and a broad variety of interdisciplinary application fields.

Information for Volume Editors and Authors

Publication in CCIS is free of charge. No royalties are paid, however, we offer registered conference participants temporary free access to the online version of the conference proceedings on SpringerLink (http://link.springer.com) by means of an http referrer from the conference website and/or a number of complimentary printed copies, as specified in the official acceptance email of the event.

CCIS proceedings can be published in time for distribution at conferences or as post-proceedings, and delivered in the form of printed books and/or electronically as USBs and/or e-content licenses for accessing proceedings at SpringerLink. Furthermore, CCIS proceedings are included in the CCIS electronic book series hosted in the SpringerLink digital library at http://link.springer.com/bookseries/7899. Conferences publishing in CCIS are allowed to use Online Conference Service (OCS) for managing the whole proceedings lifecycle (from submission and reviewing to preparing for publication) free of charge.

Publication process

The language of publication is exclusively English. Authors publishing in CCIS have to sign the Springer CCIS copyright transfer form, however, they are free to use their material published in CCIS for substantially changed, more elaborate subsequent publications elsewhere. For the preparation of the camera-ready papers/files, authors have to strictly adhere to the Springer CCIS Authors' Instructions and are strongly encouraged to use the CCIS LaTeX style files or templates.

Abstracting/Indexing

CCIS is abstracted/indexed in DBLP, Google Scholar, EI-Compendex, Mathematical Reviews, SCImago, Scopus. CCIS volumes are also submitted for the inclusion in ISI Proceedings.

How to start

To start the evaluation of your proposal for inclusion in the CCIS series, please send an e-mail to ccis@springer.com.

Sergio Nesmachnow · Luis Hernández Callejo
Editors

Smart Cities

6th Ibero-American Congress, ICSC-Cities 2023
Mexico City and Cuernavaca, Mexico, November 13–17, 2023
Revised Selected Papers

 Springer

Editors
Sergio Nesmachnow ⓘ
Universidad de la República
Montevideo, Uruguay

Luis Hernández Callejo ⓘ
Universidad de Valladolid
Soria, Soria, Spain

ISSN 1865-0929   ISSN 1865-0937 (electronic)
Communications in Computer and Information Science
ISBN 978-3-031-52516-2   ISBN 978-3-031-52517-9 (eBook)
https://doi.org/10.1007/978-3-031-52517-9

This Springer imprint is published by the registered company Springer Nature Switzerland AG
The registered company address is: Gewerbestrasse 11, 6330 Cham, Switzerland

Paper in this product is recyclable.

Preface

This CCIS volume presents selected articles from the 6th edition of the Iberoamerican Congress on Smart Cities (ICSC-Cities 2023), held from November 13 to November 17, 2023 in Mexico City and Cuernavaca, México, in a mixed modality, with presential and on-line talks and article presentations. This event continues the successful five previous editions of the congress, held in Soria, Spain in 2018 and 2019, Costa Rica in 2020, Cancún, Mexico, in 2021, and Cuenca, Ecuador, 2022.

The main goal of ICSC-Cities 2023 was to provide a forum for researchers, scientists, teachers, decision-makers, postgraduate students and practitioners from different countries in IberoAmerica and worldwide to share their current initiatives related to Smart Cities. Articles in this volume address four relevant topics (Computational intelligence and urban informatics for smart cities, Internet of things, Optimization, smart production, and smart public services, and Smart monitoring and communications) covering several areas of research and applications.

The main program consisted of three round tables, 72 oral presentations and 8 poster presentations from international speakers, highlighting recent developments in areas related to smart cities. Over three hundred distinguished participants from 30 countries gathered presentially or virtually for the congress. The Program Committee of ICSC-Cities 2023 received 94 manuscripts. 72 submissions were accepted for oral presentation and the best 19 whose contents are within Computer and Information Science areas were selected to be published in this CCIS volume. All articles have undergone a careful single-blind peer-review process by at least three subject-matter experts before being selected for publication.

We would like to express our deep gratitude to all the contributors to ICSC-Cities 2023, to the congress organizers, and to the authors and reviewers for their endeavors that made the paper reviewing process efficient and easy. We also thank the participants of the congress, our institutions, and all readers of this CCIS volume.

December 2023

Sergio Nesmachnow
Luis Hernández Callejo

Organization

General Chairs

Sergio Nesmachnow	Universidad de la República, Uruguay
Luis Hernández Callejo	Universidad de Valladolid, Spain
Pedro Moreno Bernal	Universidad Autónoma del Estado de Morelos, Mexico
Ponciano Jorge Escamilla Ambrosio	Instituto Politécnico Nacional, Mexico

Publication Chairs

Luis Hernández Callejo	Universidad de Valladolid, Spain
Sergio Nesmachnow	Universidad de la República, Uruguay
Pedro Moreno Bernal	Universidad Autónoma del Estado de Morelos, Mexico
Diego Rossit	Universidad Nacional del Sur, Argentina
Carlos E. Torres	Tecnológico Nacional de México/CENIDET, Mexico
Rodrigo Porteiro	UTE, Uruguay

Submission and Conference Management Chair

Santiago Iturriaga	Universidad de la República, Uruguay

Local Organization Chairs

Ponciano Jorge Escamilla Ambrosio	Instituto Politécnico Nacional, Mexico
Pedro Moreno Bernal	Universidad Autónoma del Estado de Morelos, Mexico

Program Committee Chairs

Luis Hernández Callejo	Universidad de Valladolid, Spain
Sergio Nesmachnow	Universidad de la República, Uruguay
Pedro Moreno Bernal	Universidad Autónoma del Estado de Morelos, Mexico
Diego Rossit	Universidad Nacional del Sur, Argentina
Carlos E. Torres	Tecnológico Nacional de México/CENIDET, Mexico
Rodrigo Porteiro	UTE, Uruguay

Program Committee

Abdelkarim Bouras	Annaba University, Algeria
Abigail Parra	Universidad Autónoma del Estado de Morelos, Mexico
Adrian Toncovich	Universidad Nacional del Sur, Argentina
Adriana Correa-Guimaraes	Universidad de Valladolid, Spain
Alberto López Casillas	Diputación de Ávila, Spain
Alberto Redondo	Universidad de Valladolid, Spain
Alejandro Valencia-Arias	Universidad Señor de Sipán, Peru
Alessandra Bussador	Universidade Federal da Integração Latino-Americana, Brazil
Alex Adiels Cano Heredia	Universidad de Quintana Roo, Mexico
Alexander Vallejo Díaz	Instituto Tecnológico de Santo Domingo, Dominican Republic
Alicia Martinez	Centro Nacional de Investigación y Desarrollo Tecnológico, Mexico
Ana Carolina Olivera	Universidad Nacional de Cuyo-CONICET, Argentina
Ana Ruiz	Universidad San Jorge, Spain
Ana Sánchez	Centro Nacional de Investigación y Desarrollo Tecnológico, Mexico
Andrei Tchernykh	CICESE Research Center, Mexico
Andrés Adolfo Navarro Newball	Pontificia Universidad Javeriana, Colombia
Andres Felipe Fuentes Vasquez	Pontificia Universidad Javeriana, Colombia
Ángel Hernández Jiménez	CEDER-CIEMAT, Spain
Ángel L. Zorita Lamadrid	Universidad de Valladolid, Spain
Angela Ferreira	Polytechnic Institute of Bragança, Portugal
João Coelho	Polytechnic Institute of Bragança, Portugal
Yahia Amoura	Polytechnic Institute of Bragança, Portugal
Antonella Cavallin	Universidad Nacional del Sur, Argentina

Antonio Mauttone	Universidad de la República, Uruguay
Antonio Muñoz	University of Malaga, Spain
Araceli Ávila	Instituto Tecnológico Superior de Perote, Mexico
Armando Huicochea	Universidad Autónoma del Estado de Morelos, Mexico
Beatriz Martinez	Universidad Autónoma del Estado de Morelos, Mexico
Begoña González Landin	Universidad de Las Palmas de Gran Canaria, Spain
Belén Carro	Universidad de Valladolid, Spain
Benjamín Álvarez Alor	Centro Nacional de Investigación y Desarrollo Tecnológico, Mexico
Bernardo Pulido-Gaytan	CICESE Research Center, Mexico
Carlos Barroso-Moreno	Universidad Europea de Madrid, Spain
Carlos Enrique Torres Aguilar	Universidad Juárez Autónoma de Tabasco, Mexico
Carlos Meza Benavides	Anhalt University of Applied Sciences, Germany
Carlos Miguel Jiménez-Xaman	Universidad Autónoma de San Luis Potosí, Bolivia
César Varela	Centro Nacional de Investigación y Desarrollo Tecnológico, Mexico
Christian Cintrano	Universidad de Málaga, Spain
Claudio Paz	Universidad Tecnológica Nacional, Argentina
Claudio Risso	Universidad de la República, Uruguay
Cristina Sáez Blázquez	Universidad de Salamanca, Spain
Daniel H. Stolfi	University of Luxembourg, Luxembourg
Daniel Morinigo-Sotelo	Universidad de Valladolid, Spain
Daniel Rossit	Universidad Nacional del Sur-CONICET, Argentina
David Balladares	Universidad Juárez Autónoma de Tabasco, Mexico
David Peña Morales	Universidad de Cádiz, Spain
Deyslen Mariano	Instituto Tecnológico de Santo Domingo, Dominican Republic
Diego Alberto Godoy	Universidad Gastón Dachary, Argentina
Diego Arcos-Aviles	Universidad de las Fuerzas Armadas, Ecuador
Diego Rossit	Universidad Nacional del Sur-CONICET, Argentina
Edgar Vazquez Beltran	Universidad de Sonora, Mexico
Edgar Vicente Macias Melo	Universidad Juárez Autónoma de Tabasco, Mexico
Edith Gabriela Manchego Huaquipaco	Universidad Nacional de San Agustín de Arequipa, Peru

Joao Coelho	Polytechnic Institute of Bragança, Portugal
Jonathan Muraña	Universidad de la República, Uruguay
Jorge Arturo Del Ángel Ramos	Universidad Veracruzana, Mexico
Jorge De La Cruz	Aalborg Universty, Denmark
Jorge López-Rebollo	Universidad de Salamanca, Spain
Jorge Mario Cortés-Mendoza	Universidad Politécnica de Amozoc, Mexico
Jorge Luis Cerino Isidro	Universidad Juárez Autónoma de Tabasco, Mexico
José Alberto Hernández	Universidad Autónoma del Estado de Morelos, Mexico
José Ángel Morell Martínez	Universidad de Málaga, Spain
Jose Ignacio Morales Aragonés	Universidad de Valladolid, Spain
José Ramón Aira	Universidad Politécnica de Madrid, España
Jose-Alfredo Jimenez-Alvarez	Instituto Tecnológico Superior de Perote, Mexico
Juan Carlos Martínez Serra	Universidad UTE, Ecuador
Juan Chavat	Universidad de la República, Uruguay
Juan Espinoza	Universidad de Cuenca, Ecuador
Juan Manuel Ramírez Alcaraz	Universidad de Colima, Mexico
Juan Moises Mauricio Villanueva	Universidade Federal da Paraíba, Brazil
Juan Paul Ayala Taco	Universidad de las Fuerzas Armadas, Ecuador
Juan Pavón	Universidad Complutense de Madrid, Spain
Juan R. Coca	Universidad de Valladolid, Spain
Karla María Aguilar Castro	Universidad Juárez Autónoma de Tabasco, Mexico
Leonardo Cardinale	Instituto Tecnológico de Costa Rica, Costa Rica
Lilian Obregon	Universidad de Valladolid, Spain
Lorena Parra	Universitat Politècnica de València, Spain
Lucas Mohimont	Université de Reims, France
Lucas Spierenburg	Technology University of Delft, The Netherlands
Luis Enrique Ángeles Montero	Universidad Juárez Autónoma de Tabasco, Mexico
Luis G. Montané Jiménez	Universidad Veracruzana, Mexico
Luis Hernández Callejo	Universidad de Valladolid, Spain
Luis Manuel Navas Gracia	Universidad de Valladolid, Spain
Luis Marrone	Universidad Nacional de La Plata, Argentina
Luis Omar Jamed Boza	Universidad Veracruzana, Mexico
Luis Tobon	Pontificia Universidad Javeriana Cali, Colombia
Manuel Gonzalez	Universidad de Valladolid, Spain
Marcin Seredynski	E-Bus Competence Center, Luxembourg
María Clara Tarifa	Universidad Nacional de Río Negro-CONICET, Argentina
Maria Teresa Cepero	Universidad Veracruzana, Mexico

Mariana Coccola	Universidad Tecnológica Nacional-CONICET, Argentina
Mariano Frutos	Universidad Nacional del Sur-CONICET, Argentina
Mario Andrés Paredes Valverde	ITS de Teziutlán-TecNM, Mexico
Mario Carbono de la Rosa	Universidad Nacional Autónoma de México, Mexico
Mario Hernandez Dominguez	Instituto Tecnológico de Monterrey, Mexico
Mario Limon	Universidad Autónoma del Estado de Morelos, Mexico
Máximo Méndez Babey	Universidad de Las Palmas de Gran Canaria, Spain
Miguel Angel Che Pan	Instituto Tecnológico Superior de Perote, Mexico
Miguel Ángel Juárez Merino	Universidad Nacional Autónoma de México, Mexico
Miguel Aybar	Instituto Tecnológico de Santo Domingo, Dominican Republic
Miguel Davila	Universidad Politécnica Salesiana del Ecuador, Ecuador
Miguel Quimbayo	University of Tolima, Colombia
Miguel-Ángel Muñoz-García	Universidad Politécnica de Madrid, Spain
Monica Alonso	University Carlos III de Madrid, Spain
Mónica Montoya Giraldo	CIDET, Colombia
Muhyettin Sirer	DEMIR Enerji, Turkey
Nestor Rocchetti	Universidad de la República, Uruguay
Noelia Uribe-Perez	Tecnalia Research & Innovation, Spain
Olalla García Pérez	Universidad Europea de Madrid, Spain
Oscar Duque-Perez	Universidad de Valladolid, Spain
Oscar Izquierdo	CEDER-CIEMAT, Spain
Outmane Oubram	Universidad Autónoma del Estado de Morelos, Mexico
Pablo Daniel Godoy	Universidad Nacional de Cuyo, Argentina
Pablo Vidal	Universidad Nacional de Cuyo-CONICET, Argentina
Paula de Andrés Anaya	Escuela Politécnica Superior de Ávila, Spain
Paula Guerra	Kennesaw State University, USA
Paula Peña-Carro	CEDER-CIEMAT, Spain
Pedro Moreno Bernal	Universidad Autónoma del Estado de Morelos, Mexico
Pedro Piñeyro	Universidad de la República, Uruguay
Ponciano Jorge Escamilla-Ambrosio	Instituto Politécnico Nacional, Mexico
Rafael Rosa	Universidad de la República, Uruguay

Ramiro Martins	Polytechnic Institute of Bragança, Portugal
Rasikh Tariq	Tecnológico de Monterrey, Mexico
Raúl Alberto López Meraz	Universidad Veracruzana, Mexico
Renato Andara	Universidad Nacional Experimental Politécnica Antonio José de Sucre, Venezuela
Renzo Massobrio	Universidad de la República, Uruguay
Ricardo Beltran-Chacon	Centro de Investigacion en Materiales Avanzados, Mexico
Roberto Flores	Universidad Autónoma del Estado de Morelos, Mexico
Roberto Ramirez	Alemania
Roberto Villafafila	Universitat Politècnica de Catalunya, Spain
Rodrigo Alonso-Suárez	Universidad de la República, Uruguay
Rodrigo Porteiro	Universidad de la República, Uruguay
Rogelio Vargas Lopez	Universidad Autónoma de Guadalajara, Mexico
Roger Castillo Palomera	Universidad Juárez Autónoma de Tabasco, Mexico
Rui Pedro Lopes	Polytechnic Institute of Bragança, Portugal
Ryszard Edward Rozga Luter	Universidad Autónoma Metropolitana Unidad Lerma, Mexico
Samanta López Salazar	Centro Nacional de Investigación y Desarrollo Tecnológico, Mexico
Santiago Iturriaga	Universidad de la República, Uruguay
Sara Gallardo-Saavedra	Universidad de Valladolid, Spain
Sebastian Montes de Oca	Universidad de la República, Uruguay
Sergio Nesmachnow	Universidad de la República, Uruguay
Silvia Soutullo	CEDER-CIEMAT, Spain
Susana del Pozo	Universidad de Salamanca, Spain
Teodoro Calonge	Universidad de Valladolid, Spain
Thania Guadalupe Lima Tellez	Universidad de Sonora, Mexico
Valentín Cardeñoso-Payo	Universidad de Valladolid, Spain
Verônica de Menezes Nascimento Nagata	Universidade do Estado do Pará, Brazil
Veronica Gonzalez	Universidad Autónoma del Estado de Morelos, Mexico
Vicente Canals	Universidad de las Islas Baleares, Spain
Vicente Leite	Polytechnic Institute of Bragança, Portugal
Víctor Alonso Gómez	Universidad de Valladolid, Spain
Zakaryaa Zarhri	Universidad Autónoma del Estado de Morelos, Mexico

Contents

Internet of Things

Computational Intelligence and Urban Informatics for Smart Cities

Innovative Informatic Approaches for Smart Cities

Urban Informatics for Smart Cities

Methodology to Obtain Traffic Data and Road Incidents Through Maps Applications

Ernesto De la Cruz-Nicolás(✉) ⓘ, Alicia Martínez-Rebollar ⓘ,
Hugo Estrada-Esquivel ⓘ, and Odette Alejandra Pliego-Martínez ⓘ

National Institute of Technology of Mexico /CENIDET, Interior Street Internado Palmira S/N,
Palmira Neighborhood, 62490 Cuernavaca, Morelos, Mexico
{d21ce090,alicia.mr,hugo.ee,d21ce092}@cenidet.tecnm.mx

Abstract. The increase of vehicular traffic and road incidents in large cities is usually the cause of road congestion, which generates several problems to citizens such as: loss of time in city transfers, health problems associated to pollution, and high fuel costs among others. Map applications are one of the most accessible mechanisms for obtaining, in real time traffic data and road incidents in a city, however each data provider provides different processes to obtain traffic and road incidents. At the present time there are various sources of traffic and incident data, however, there is a lack of architectures, guides, or methodologies that allow developers to obtain updated and real-time traffic data in cities, so the user must search and intuit the process to follow to obtain the information. This paper aims to propose a methodology that allows the user to be correctly guided to obtain traffic data and road incidents from the different map applications on the market.

Keywords: Map applications · Traffic congestion · Road incidents

1 Introduction

Traffic and road incident data are crucial for any software application that deals with planning routes between two points in the city [17], whether to help a driver find the shortest route to reach their destination or to Provide information to users about road incidents found on the selected route [18]. Some of the possibilities in the use of traffic data are to make a history of the road networks with the greatest road congestion to be evaluated by frustrated and happy users after having completed the journey, recognition of mobility patterns, data analysis using statistical techniques [19]. Among other activities. In the literature it is possible to find different techniques for extracting traffic data and road incidents through image and video processing, tweet analysis, remote sensing, sensor analysis, data sets from government portals, among others. Nowadays there are mapping applications that make it easy to obtain temporal and spatial data from tweets, images, sensors and surveys [20].

There are several mapping applications that provide an API (Application Programming Interface) to obtain traffic and road incident data, each with unique characteristics, such as a set of variables that describe the characteristics of traffic and road incidents, and

S. Nesmachnow and L. Hernández Callejo (Eds.): ICSC-Cities 2023, CCIS 1938, pp. 3–17, 2024.
https://doi.org/10.1007/978-3-031-52517-9_1

providing answers. In JSON (Java Script Object Notation) or XML (Extensible Markup Language) format. According to Dashboard Analysis [1], there are various map applications responsible for extracting information about cartographic data (Fig. 1). Here Maps takes first place, second is Google Maps, third is TomTom Traffic, fourth is Amap and fifth is Mapbox. This categorization is based on the number of services and capabilities that each platform offers: in the case of Here Maps, it offers various services such as: Here Anonymizer, Here Consent Manager, EV Routing, ISA Map, etc.

However, the process for collecting traffic data and road incidents differs between different mapping applications. The objective of this research work is to present a methodology that guides developers in the processes and activities required to obtain traffic data and road incidents through the use of map applications. The proposed methodology aims to provide a framework that guides the developer in the execution of the data collection methods required in research work related to traffic analysis and prediction [21].

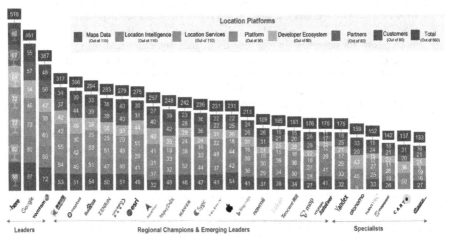

Fig. 1. Location Platform Vendor Scorecard 2021 report analyzing more than 25 leading location platform vendors and mapping using the proprietary CORE (Competitive, Rankings & Evaluation) framework.

2   Related Works

In the analysis of the state of the art it is possible to find different approaches that start from a set of data obtained from some traffic data source.

In the work carried out by [2], active lane management and control are investigated using connected and automated vehicles in a mixed traffic environment. In this work, traffic data collection is performed by active traffic management systems, lane management systems, and connected and automated vehicle systems.

In the work carried out by [3], an analytical model was developed to quantify the efficiency of the collection of traffic data using instrumented vehicles. For this work, the collection of traffic data was carried out using sensors and radars. The research presented in [4] presents a social Internet of Things smart city solution for traffic and pollution control in Cagliari city. In this research, the collection of mobility data is carried out through a monitoring network based on sensors and devices placed in public transport, with the aim of monitoring in real time the most sensitive areas of traffic congestion.

The work carried out by [5] consisted of the analysis of a real case study of a social smart city for public and private mobility. The collection of traffic data from cars, trains and bicycles was carried out using the Internet of Things paradigm. The research carried out by [6] consisted of a critical review of urban traffic accidents using GIS (Geographic Information System) type applications. In this work, the data collection of urban traffic accidents was carried out using ArcGIS software. The research proposal of [7] consisted of a method to extract information from road structures effectively and accurately to provide tourist navigation experience and accurate geographic information. The data collection of road structures was carried out using high resolution remote sensing in gray scale. The work carried out by [8] consisted in carrying out the analysis of the prediction of the geographical location of people using machine learning algorithms. Location data collection was done using location data from Twitter messages, to obtain latitude and longitude of the position. The work carried out by [9] is in charge of identifying the traffic signs in the road infrastructure, collecting data from those obtained through cloud of points obtained from the images. The research carried out by [10] consisted of collecting data from drivers based on facial recognition, the above was to identify the driver's behavior as the cause of traffic congestion. The research work carried out by [11] is a research that is characterized by forecasting the traffic dynamics, collecting data for the forecast, which is done by mining Twitter messages. The work carried out by [12] presents an overview of the prediction of traffic accidents through learning algorithms, which are a cause of road congestion and shows a compendium of the most used data sources. The research work carried out by [13] uses data from social networks to detect the conditions of the road infrastructure and traffic based on communication between users. The research done by [14] focuses on the extraction of images of accidents, foggy places and collision places to form a traffic database. With the data they train algorithms for the prediction of traffic congestion. Research work by [15] uses mobile devices to collect traffic data over large geographic regions. The data collected is used in simulations to analyze the proportions of vehicles in certain areas and determine if it is a traffic congestion.

3 Methodology for Obtaining Traffic Data and Road Incidents

The proposed methodology for obtaining traffic data and road incidents in geographical areas of interest through the use of map applications is made up of five phases (Fig. 2).

The five phases that make up the proposed methodology are described below:

a) Phase of selection of the map application: it consists of selecting the map application to obtain traffic data and road incidents using the characteristics proposed in this research work. Following, some elements that should be considered when selecting a mapping application are presented:

- Scheme for obtaining data: this refers to the scale used by the map application to obtain traffic data and road incidents. The most popular shapes are: linear,

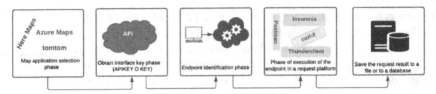

Fig. 2. Methodology for obtaining traffic and incident data using map applications.

polygons and circles, however not all applications offer the same shapes to obtain data.

- Real-time updating: this refers to the fact that data provided can be captured in real-time or they are historical data stored in a database. Some applications explicitly indicate the type of data provided while others do not indicate it, so it is unknown for the users if the data provided is real-time or historical.
- Developer section: some of the applications have a developer section, this section provides the necessary instructions to obtain data and its corresponding use or analysis.
- Additional services: Mapping applications can offer data analytics, debugging, regression, and statistical inference services.

b) Phase for obtaining the interface key (APIKEY or KEY): consists of visiting the official web site of the map application and locating the section where the APIKEY or KEY is offered for free or for a fee. It is necessary to follow, in an orderly manner, the steps indicated by the application provider to obtain the APIKEY or KEY. The relevant elements to obtain an APIKEY are the following:

- Service provider registration: data providers require registration for the creation of a developer account.
- Pricing plan: all map applications offer a pricing section on their Web portal, as well as free levels that they offer with certain limitations.
- APIKEY Generation: Map applications have a developer control panel. This panel has sections and instructions to generate the number of API KEYs offered by each map application.
- Documentation and examples: The APIKEY provider provides documentation that includes examples of how to make data requests with the generated APIKEY.
- Use limits: Providers establish limits on the number of requests according to the type of data, which can be per day, week or month.

c) Phase of endpoint identification (data request URL): each map application defines a set of endpoints to obtain data. This phase consists of identifying the section of each map application where the endpoints are listed, and also identifying the endpoint elements described in the official documentation of the map application to properly request traffic data and road incidents. For the endpoint the following elements must be considered:

- Endpoint URL: syntax of the URL that contains the elements of the request: URL of the server, geographic coordinates of the location where the data will be extracted, types of data to be extracted and access key.
- HTTP request method: This refers to the HTTP request method to obtain traffic data and road incidents.
- Endpoint Parameters: This describes the query parameters to the endpoint URL to understand the customization of the request. These parameters can include information such as location, date, time, type of traffic data, among others.
- Response format: when making the data request with the endpoint, the response can be provided in different formats such as JSON, XML, CSV, among others.

d) Phase of execution of the endpoint in a request platform: it consists of executing the endpoint of the map application through a request platform. To do this, the platform to execute the endpoint need to be selected based on the endpoint characteristics.
e) Phase of storing the result of the request in a file or in a database: it consists of serializing the information in a set of records and attributes to store them in a file or in a database.

The implementation details of each of the phases of the proposed methodology is presented below.

4   Implementation of the Methodology for Obtaining Traffic Data and Road Incidents Through Map Applications

In this section, a case study is implemented in which the five phases of the proposed methodology for obtaining traffic data and road incidents of geographical areas using map applications are described.

4.1   Phase of Selection of Map Application

In the selection phase of the map application, various characteristics can be considered to make a comparison between them and choose the appropriate application according to the context of the problem to be solved.

Table 1 shows the characteristics proposed to compare applications, as well as the comparison of 10 data applications using these characteristics. The features used are described below:

1. Traffic: This feature indicates whether the application offers the option to extract traffic data in real-time. This is a service provided by mapping applications to provide real-time traffic data using a RESTful API. Traffic data is provided in the following ways:

- Flow segment data: this provides information on speed, road type, free flow, jam factor from the pair of geographic coordinates (latitude and longitude).
- Raster flow tiles: Provide m x n pixel information showing traffic flow. Traffic flow is represented in the three basic colors (green, yellow and red) to indicate the speed of traffic on different road segments.

- Vector Flow Tiles: Provides traffic flow information packaged vector-shaped square sections called vector tiles. Each of the boxes includes a predefined collection of road shapes with traffic flow data.

2. Incidents: this feature indicates if the application offers the option of extracting data on traffic incidents in real time. Map applications offer the service of road incidents in real time through a RESTful API. Road incident data is provided in the following ways:

- Incident Details: Provides information about road incidents that fall within a user defined bounding box.
- Raster incident mosaics: the services offer information on road incidents in images of m x n pixels. Road incident mosaics are represented by color to indicate the magnitude of the road incident on a road segment.
- Vector Incident Tiles: Mapping applications offer vector-packaged traffic incident data. Each vector includes a predefined collection of road shapes with traffic incident data.

3. API: This feature indicates if the application offers an API to extract data from the map application. In order to verify if the map application offers an API KEY, it is necessary to consider the following aspects:

- Explore the developers section to identify the process that is required to obtain API KEYs for the different services it offers.
- Search the developer documentation to find details about the KEY API, including usage examples.
- Analyze the terms and conditions associated with the use of the KEY API to be aware of usage limits, restrictions and fees if applicable.
- Verify the number of transactions offered for each type of plan.

4. Free plan: this characteristic indicates if the application offers the option of obtaining a free API, which allows extracting the information at no cost. At this point it is necessary to identify the benefits provided by the free plan such as: number of requests daily, weekly or monthly, need for a credit card to make payments, identify if it is possible that with the free data you can develop commercial applications, technical support offered and finally, the type of data offered.

5. JSON data type: This feature indicates if the application offers the option to extract traffic data in JSON format. To do this, the following aspects must be considered:

- Review the website documentation to determine the structure of the endpoint. In the endpoint results section, it is necessary to identify the different formats of the results, which can be XML, JSON, KML or GEOJSON.
- Review the JSON structure parameters of the endpoint to identify the parameter where the JSON format type should be set.

6. Image type data: this feature indicates if the application offers the option of extracting traffic data in image format.

Table 1 shows that several applications share many of the proposed characteristics, however the information provided by each map application in terms of traffic and road

Table 1. Comparative table between map applications.

Maps app	Traffic	Incidents	API	Free plan	JSON type data	Image data
Here Maps	Yes	Yes	Yes	Yes	Yes	Yes
Google Maps	Yes	Yes	Yes	No	Yes	Yes
Tom Tom	Yes	Yes	Yes	Yes	Yes	Yes
Amap	No	No	No	No	No	No
Mapbox	Yes	No	Yes	Yes	Yes	Yes
Baidu	Yes	No	Yes	Yes	Yes	Yes
Zenrin	Yes	No	No	No	Yes	Yes
Nvr Info	Yes	Yes	No	No	No	No
Esri	Yes	No	No	No	Yes	Yes
AzureMaps	Yes	Yes	Yes	Yes	Yes	Yes

incidents differ in the fields. Therefore, it is important to analyze each map application in terms of the information provided according to the problem to be solved. For this case study, Here Maps was chosen to exemplify traffic data and road incidents.

4.2 Phase to Obtain the Interface Key (APIKEY O KEY)

The process to obtain the interface key is done by following these steps:

a) Locate the official page of the map application using a web browser. In this case, the official page of Here Maps is https://developer.here.com/

b) Locate the APIKEY section: once the official page of the map application is located, it is necessary to navigate through the sections of the portal and locate the APIKEY. Figure 3 shows the API's section where the APIKEY can be obtained for the Here Maps.

Fig. 3. Section of the map application where the APIKEY can be obtained.

c) Registration on the portal to obtain the APIKEY: the APIKEY section requests registration on the portal to obtain the APIKEY. It is important to comment that all map applications require registration for the corresponding access. Figure 4 shows the filling out of a registration form in the case of Here Maps.

Fig. 4. Form for the creation of an Account in Here maps.

Once the registration for the creation of an account in Here Maps has been completed, the account must be verified using the email provided in the registration (Fig. 5).

Fig. 5. Email verification provided in Here Maps.

4.3   Phase of Endpoint Identification

In order to request real-time traffic data through the map application, it is necessary to access the platform and locate the endpoint or URL address to which the requests are sent. All map applications provide multiple endpoints, but it is important to locate the right endpoint to extract traffic information. The endpoint that is used to download the real-time traffic data for the Here Maps example is the following:

https://data.traffic.hereapi.com/v7/flow?locationReferencing=shape&in=bbox:-99. 188511,19.276095,99.150781,19.298058&apiKey=xxxxxxxxxxxxxxxxxxxxxxxxx.

The endpoint to extract information on road incidents in Here Maps is the following:
https://data.traffic.hereapi.com/v7/incdents?in=bbox:99.20575,19.29684,99.09908, 1.35957&locationReferencing = olr&apiKey = xxxxxx.

The endpoint are composed by the following elements:

a) Server: refers to the map application server domain, in this case https://data.traffic. hereapi.com
b) Version: in the endpoint it is important to indicate its version, in the case of Here Maps used in this paper is version 7.
c) Type of information: refers to the type of information to be extracted. In case that traffic data need to be extracted, the flow tag is used. In case that road incidents need to be extracted, incident tag is used.
d) Bbox: is the acronym for Bounding Box and this refers to the geographical area from which traffic data is required to be obtained.
e) ApiKey: this refers to the access key to the Here Maps server to obtain traffic data.

4.4   Phase of Execution of the Endpoint in a Request Platform

Once the endpoint has been defined, its functionality must be verified through a request platform. In the market there are several request platforms such as: Postman, Thunderclient, Swagger, Insomnia, Sandbox among others. In this case, Thunderclient was used as the platform to verify the functionality of the traffic data collection endpoint, as shown in Fig. 6.

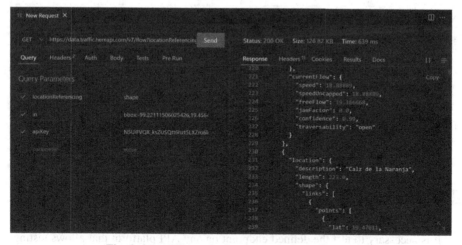

Fig. 6. Here Maps endpoint test to obtain traffic data.

As a result of the traffic data endpoint request, a response is obtained in JSON format with the traffic status of the streets that are in the previously indicated bounding box. The variables provided by the endpoint are presented in Table 2 and Table 3.

Table 2. Description of the variables returned from the traffic data endpoint (part 1), the description was taken from the documentation of [16].

Variable	Description
sourceUpdated	Date and time the data is extracted
results	Set of streets monitored to obtain traffic data
location	Dataset of the monitored street
description	Name of the street
length	Length in meters of the street
shape	Set of geographic coordinates of the street
links	Set of segments that make up the street
points	Set of coordinates of each segment
lat	Geographic coordinate latitude
lng	Geographic coordinate longitude
length	Length in meters of the street segment
currentFlow	Current flow rate

Table 3. Description of returned variables from the endpoint of traffic data (part 2), the description was taken from the documentation of [16].

Variable	Description
speed	Expected speed along the roadway; this speed did not exceed the legal speed limit for the street
speedUncapped	Expected speed along the roadway; this speed could exceed the legal speed limit for the street
freeFlow	Reference speed along the road when no traffic is present
jamFactor	Provides a value for the amount of traffic on the road. The value is between 0.0 and 10.0
confidence	It is a normalized value between 0.0 and 1.0 with the following meaning: $0.7 < confidence <= 1.0$
Traversability	Passability describes whether you can drive on the road

It is necessary to test the defined endpoint on any API platform that allows testing and iterating any API. In this case Thunderclient was used as shown in Fig. 7.

As a result of the request from the endpoint for road incident data, a response was obtained in JSON format with the status of the incidents of the streets that are in the

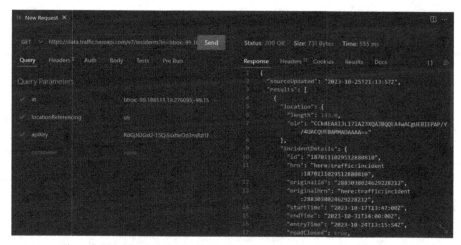

Fig. 7. Here Maps endpoint test to obtain data on road incidents.

bounding box that was provided. Some of the variables provided by the map application are shown in Table 4.

Table 4. Variables returned by the road incident endpoint, the description was taken from the documentation of [16].

Variable	Description
length	Incident length
incidentDetails	Detail of the incident
originalId	Id of the incident
roadClosed	Closed street status
criticality	Level of criticality of the incident
type	Incident type
description	Description of the incident

In the phase, a procedure is proposed to save the results provided by the execution of the traffic endpoint or road incidents:

a) Serialize the JSON provided by the traffic or road incident endpoint as follows: data = response.json(), where the response variable contains the traffic or road incident data.

b) Iterate the serialized variable through any cycle statement of any programming language, this is to extract the value of each key from Fig. 8 and Fig. 9 shows a fragment of the iteration of the JSON file provided by the endpoint of traffic and road incidents.

```
for i in range (len(data['results'])):
    speed=data['results'][i]['currentFlow']['speed']
    speedUncapped=data['results'][i]['currentFlow']['speedUncapped']
    freeFlow=data['results'][i]['currentFlow']['freeFlow']
    jamFactor=data['results'][i]['currentFlow']['jamFactor']
    confidence=data['results'][i]['currentFlow']['confidence']
```

Fig. 8. Iteration of the JSON file traffic dataset provided by the endpoint.

```
for i in range(len(dataincidencias["results"])):
    longitudincidencia=dataincidencias["results"][i]["location"]["length"]
    idincidencia=dataincidencias["results"][i]["incidentDetails"]['originalId']
    callecerrada=dataincidencias["results"][i]["incidentDetails"]['roadClosed']
    nivelincidencia=dataincidencias["results"][i]["incidentDetails"]['criticality']
    calleincidencia=dataincidencias["results"][i]["incidentDetails"]['description']['value']
    descripincidencia=dataincidencias["results"][i]["incidentDetails"]['summary']['value']
```

Fig. 9. Iteration of the set of road incidents in the JSON file provided by the endpoint.

4.5   Save the Request Result to a File or to a Database

The results obtained through the incident and traffic request endpoints can be converted into a data frame as shown in the code fragments made in Python in Fig. 10 and Fig. 11, in CSV or EXCEL files, see Fig. 12. They are also stored in a NoSQL database due to the volume of data, see Fig. 13. Information stored in any format can be used by machine learning algorithms or other computational techniques for prediction, forecasting or classification of vehicular mobility.

```
def getTraffic(bbox,apikeytraffic):
    reqUrl="https://data.traffic.hereapi.com/v7/flow?locationReferencing=shape&in=bbox:"+bbox+"&apiKey="+apikeytraffic
    response = requests.get(reqUrl)
    datatraffic = response.json()
    traffic=pd.DataFrame()
    for i in range (len(datatraffic['results'])):
        location=pd.DataFrame.from_dict([datatraffic['results'][i]['location']])
        currentflow=pd.DataFrame.from_dict([datatraffic['results'][i]['currentFlow']])
        location_currentflow=pd.concat([location,currentflow],axis=1)
        traffic=pd.concat([traffic,location_currentflow],axis=0,ignore_index=True)
    return traffic
```

Fig. 10. Endpoint traffic data converted into a data frame.

```
def getIncidents(bbox,apikeyincidents):
    reqUrl="https://api.tomtom.com/traffic/services/5/incidentDetails?key="+apikeyincidents+"&bbox="+bbox
    +"&fields={incidents{type,geometry{type,coordinates}}}&language=en-GB&t=1111&timeValidityFilter=present"
    response = requests.get(reqUrl)
    dataincidents = response.json()
    #JSON processing code is missing to convert it to a dataframe
    incidents=pd.DataFrame(dataincidents)
    return incidents
```

Fig. 11. Endpoint incident data converted to a data frame.

```
traffic.to_excel("traffic.xlsx")
traffic.to_csv("traffic.csv")

incidents.to_excel("incidents.xlsx")
incidents.to_csv("incidents.csv")
```

Fig. 12. Traffic and incident data frame data exported to EXCEL or CSV.

```
def insertTraffic_Incidents(collection,dataframe_traffic_or_incidents):
    collection.insert_many(dataframe_traffic_or_incidents.to_dict('records'))
```

Fig. 13. The traffic and incident data frame data inserted into a NOSQL type handler.

5 Findings of the Research

The proposed methodology provides a set of phases that is need to follow in order to obtain traffic data and road incidents in real time through any map application through a provided APIKEY. The first finding found was the flexibility that map applications provide in providing traffic data and road incidents in different dimensions or areas from the national, state, municipal, neighborhood, block, and street perspectives, among other desired dimensions. The second finding found consists of the diversity of fields offered by traffic-related map applications, which are the following: sourceUpdated, results, location, description, length, shape, links, points, lat, lng, length, currentFlow, speed, speedUncapped, freeFlow, jamFactor, confidence and traversability; Likewise, the fields related to road incidents were the following: length, incidentDetails, originalId, roadClosed, criticality, type, description. Having a variety of characteristics in traffic information and road incidents helps in carrying out various research activities such as analysis, prediction and forecast with the aim of finding solutions to existing mobility problems. Finally, a set of features is proposed in this research to select the map application, it is important to mention that certain features are shared in a similar way between the applications, this allows researchers to experiment with the use of various map applications for traffic extraction and road incidents and compare the results.

6 Conclusions and Future Work

One of the limitations of research on vehicular traffic in cities is obtaining data, which are considered the raw material for the development of analyzes and proposals for new mobility models. Maps applications are a new source of traffic data that can be used to generate mobility data sets at various times and magnitudes.

The methodology proposed in this research work allows developers to take full advantage of map applications in the task of obtaining traffic data and road incidents in real time from geographical areas of interest in Mexico City. There are currently no detailed guides to use mapping applications to capture real-time traffic in specific areas of a city.

The use of the methodology proposed in this paper will allow developers to create datasets with historical data and incidents of the city that can be used for the analysis of the occurrence of patterns of incidents and road accidents in CDMX, as well as the development of indicators of vehicular mobility that allow quantifying the degree of traffic congestion.

Acknowledgments. This research was supported by Project TecNM 17329.23-P.

References

1. Sharma, M.: Counterpoint (2023). https://www.counterpointresearch.com/maintains-loc ation-platform-leadership-ahead-google-tomtom/
2. Khattak, Z., Smith, B., Fontaine, M., Ma, J., Khattak, A.: Active lane management and control using connected and automated vehicles in a mixed traffic environment. Transp. Res. Part C Emerg. Technol. **139**, 1–44 (2022). https://doi.org/10.1016/j.trc.2022.103648
3. Cao, P., Xiong, Z., Liu, X.: An analytical model for quantifying the efficiency of traffic-datacollection using instrumented vehicles. Transp. Res. Part C emerg. Technol. **136**(4), 103558 (2022). https://doi.org/10.1016/j.trc.2022.103558
4. Fadda, M., Anedda, M., Girau, R., Pau, G., Giusto, D.: A social internet of things smart city solution for traffic and pollution monitoring in Cagliari. IEEE Internet Things J. **10**(3), 2373–2390 (2023). https://doi.org/10.1109/JIOT.2022.3211093
5. Anedda, M., Fadda, M., Girau, R., Pau, G., Giusto, D.: A social smart city for public and private mobility: a real case study. Comput. Netw. **220**, 109464 (2023). https://doi.org/10.1016/j.comnet.2022.109464
6. Aghasi, N.H.: Application of GIS for urban traffic accidents: a critical review. J. Geog. Inf. Syst. **11**, 82–96 (2019). https://doi.org/10.4236/jgis.2019.111007
7. Wang, G., Ma, C., Liang, X.: Application of road extraction from high-resolution remote sensing images in tourism navigation and GIS. Wirel. Commun. Mob. Comput. **2022**, 1–8 (2022). https://doi.org/10.1155/2022/2422030
8. Utomo, B., Rizal, M.: A systematic literature review of machine learning to predict location in social media. In: 2022 6th International Conference on Information Technology, In-formation Systems and Electrical Engineering (ICITISEE), pp. 1–6 (2022). https://doi.org/10.1109/ICI TISEE57756.2022.10057871
9. Zhang, F., Zhang, J., Xu, Z., Tang, J., Jiang, P., Zhong, R.: Extracting traffic signage by combining point clouds and images. Sensors **23**(4), 2062 (2022). https://doi.org/10.3390/s23 042262
10. Qian, X., Yaxin, H.: Feature extraction of driver in traffic image based on wavelet critical threshold denoising method. In: Chinese Control and Decision Conference (CCDC), pp. 5707–5710 (2019).https://doi.org/10.1109/CCDC.2019.8832828
11. Yao, W., Qian, S.: From Twitter to traffic predictor: next-day morning traffic pre-diction using social media data. Transp. Res. Part C Emerg. Technol. **124**, 102938 (2021). https://doi.org/10.1016/j.trc.2020.102938
12. Gutierrez-Osorio, C., Pedraza, C.: Modern data sources and techniques for analysis and fore-cast of road accidents: a review. J. Traffic Transp. Eng. **7**(4), 432–446 (2020). https://doi.org/10.1016/j.jtte.2020.05.002
13. Yu, L., Li, D.: Road-related information mining from social media data: a joint relation extraction and entity recognition approach. Buildings **13**(1), 104 (2023). https://doi.org/10.3390/buildings13010104
14. Mounica, B., Nithya, B.S., Rakshitha, N., Sirisha, M.: Traffic analysis using image processing. Int. J. Comput. Sci. Mob. Comput. **10**(7), 39–45 (2021). https://doi.org/10.47760/ijcsmc.2021.v10i07.006
15. Holmgren, J., Fredriksson, H., Dahl, M.: Traffic data collection using active mobile and stationary devices. Procedia Comput. Sci. **177**, 49–56 (2020). https://doi.org/10.1016/j.procs.2020.10.010

16. Here Maps: Here maps developer (2023). https://developer.here.com/documentation/exa mples/rest/traffic/traffic-incidents
17. Mesquitela, J., Elvas, L., Ferreira, J., Nunes, L.: Data analytics process over road accidents data—a case study of Lisbon city. ISPRS Int. J. Geo-Inf. **11**(2), 143 (2022). https://doi.org/ 10.3390/ijgi11020143
18. Chand, A., Jayesh, S., Bhasi, A.: Road traffic accidents: an overview of data sources, analysis techniques and contributing factors. Mater. Today Proc. **47**, 5135–5141 (2021). https://doi. org/10.1016/j.matpr.2021.05.415
19. Shepelev, V., Aliukov, S., Nikolskaya, K., Shabiev, S.: The capacity of the road network: data collection and statistical analysis of traffic characteristics. Energies **13**(7), 1765 (2020). https://doi.org/10.3390/en13071765
20. Gutierrez-Osorio, C., Pedraza, C.: Modern data sources and techniques for analysis and fore-cast of road accidents: a review. J. Traffic Transp. Eng. (English Edition) **7**(4), 432–446 (2020). https://doi.org/10.1016/j.jtte.2020.05.002
21. Rahman, M., Nower, N.: Attention based deep hybrid networks for traffic flow prediction using google maps data. In: ICMLT 2023: Proceedings of the 2023 8th International Conference on Machine Learning Technologies, pp.74–81 (2023). https://doi.org/10.1145/3589883.358 9894

Detection of Suboptimal Conditions in Photovoltaic Systems Integrating Data from Several Domains

Leonardo Cardinale-Villalobos$^{(\boxtimes)}$ (ID), Luis D. Murillo-Soto (ID),
Efrén Jimenez-Delgado (ID), and Jose Andrey Sequeira (ID)

Costa Rica Institute of Technology, San Carlos, Costa Rica
{lcardinale,lmurillo,efjimenez}@tec.ac.cr
http://www.tec.ac.cr

Abstract. Researchers have been exploring methods to detect suboptimal conditions in photovoltaic (PV) modules, such as visual inspection, electrical analysis, and thermography. Each method has its advantages and limitations. To enhance the accuracy and efficiency of detecting these conditions, this research proposed an integrated Internet of Things (IoT) platform called the Multi-method system (MMS). This platform combines Infrared Thermography (IRT), visual inspection using RGB image processing, and electrical analysis. The MMS enables automated data capture, analysis, and remote accessibility. To validate the system, an experiment was conducted at the Costa Rica Institute of Technology. The MMS effectively detected suboptimal conditions due to soiling, partial shading, and short circuits. The system achieved a sensitivity of 0.97%, an accuracy of 0.98%, and a precision of 100%. This project functions as a proof of concept, in this case limited to a fixed location and for specific suboptimal conditions, however, it represents a solution with potential for industrial use. The research contributes to advancing PV system reliability and performance monitoring in Smart Cities, offering implications for improving solar energy efficiency and reducing maintenance costs.

Keywords: Internet of things platform · Photovoltaic · Fault Detection Technique · CNN · Deep Learning

1 Introduction

In recent years, multiple solutions for diagnosing photovoltaic (PV) systems have been proposed, including visual, electrical, thermographic analysis. However, each method has its limitations, highlighting the need for new alternatives, supported by AI techniques [1], and also combining techniques for better results [2]. Moreover, for efficient implementation, AI automation can enhance effectiveness by eliminating human errors, making the process more efficient and reliable [3].

© The Author(s), under exclusive license to Springer Nature Switzerland AG 2024
S. Nesmachnow and L. Hernández Callejo (Eds.): ICSC-Cities 2023, CCIS 1938, pp. 18–32, 2024.
https://doi.org/10.1007/978-3-031-52517-9_2

To addresses the problem, this paper proposed an Internet of Things (IoT) platform called the Multi-method system (MMS), integrating IRT, visual inspection and electrical analysis. IRT and visual data were processed using AI models, while the electrical analysis employs the Least Significance Difference (LSD) algorithm [4]. Visual analysis (RGB analysis) was implemented processing images from a traditional camera. The MMS automates data capture, analysis, and remote accessibility, processed using AI models. The research validates the system through experiments inducing controlled soiling, partial shading, and short circuits in a real PV installation. The results demonstrate that IoT solutions, specifically the proposed MMS, significantly improve the efficiency of detecting suboptimal conditions in PV modules. The system enhances sensitivity, accuracy, and precision, offering both detection and localization of faults. These findings have crucial implications for PV installation managers and maintenance companies, showcasing the potential of IoT technology and AI for automatic and intelligent solutions in diagnosing PV installations and addressing the growing need for efficient suboptimal condition detection in the context of Smart Cities.

This document is organized as follows: Sect. 2 presents a theoretical framework of this area, followed by the materials and methods used in the research (Sect. 3); then, Sect. 4 shows the results and their discussion, ending with the conclusions in Sect. 5.

2 Framework

This section provides an overview of the recent scientific literature related to the detection of suboptimal conditions in PV modules, with the aim of identifying the existing research and development requirements in this field. The section is subdivided in the analysis of: a) IRT, b) RGB and c) electrical.

In recent studies, IRT has emerged as a prominent technique for identifying suboptimal conditions in PV modules. Researchers have leveraged the thermal imaging capabilities of IRT to detect issues such as hot spot formation, module defects, and electrical failures within PV systems. The literature highlights the importance of IRT in non-invasively assessing the thermal performance of PV modules, thereby improving overall system efficiency. Regarding to Red-Green-Blue (RGB) imaging for suboptimal condition detection in PV modules, recent research has explored the potential of RGB images, typically captured by drones or ground-based cameras, to identify visual anomalies and physical defects in solar panels. This includes the identification of cracks, soiling, corrosion, and other visible issues that may affect the performance of PV modules. Integrating machine learning algorithms with RGB imagery has shown promise in automating the detection process. The research around electrical analysis to detect suboptimal conditions in PV sytems, recently have focused on detecting issues such as electrical mismatch, bypass diode failures, and inverter problems. Advanced monitoring systems and data analytics have played a crucial role in improving the detection and diagnosis of electrical anomalies within PV modules.

2.1 Detection of Hot Spot by IRT

The need to detect suboptimal conditions in PV modules has generated extensive research on using IRT in combination with advanced processing and AI techniques. In [5], an IRT method that involves a linear iterative segmentation technique is proposed. The image is preprocessed, followed by the extraction of statistical information. The author proposed continuing with further tests to refine the algorithm's performance and enhance its accuracy.

The authors [6,7] evaluate the application of IRT image preprocessing techniques for fault detection, finding promising results and suggesting further experimental investigation for their combination with AI for fault identification.

In [8], a framework for real-time automated monitoring is presented, targeting the analysis of unprocessed video data acquired via drone cameras. The framework combines image processing with statistical machine-learning methodologies. The project was validated and has been made accessible to other professionals. It employed Transform Invariant Low-rank Textures (TILT) and Edge detection for image processing, while the detection and localization of hot spots were accomplished through Robust Principal Component Analysis (RPCA).

The research [1] conducts a comprehensive literature review focusing on methodologies for diagnosing large-scale PV systems, with a dedicated section for (IRT) analysis. The study analyzed 11 articles highlighting the utilization of unmanned aerial vehicle (UAV) to implement this technique, along with image processing and AI methods for information analysis. The study's conclusion emphasizes that improvements are needed to render the technology more efficient, accurate, agile, and cost-effective.

2.2 Detection of Suboptimal Conditions by RGB Analysis

The early detection of issues in solar panels is a vital challenge. The utilization of images in RGB and thermal spectra captured by drones promises a holistic and detailed view of PV installations. The application of Convolutional Neural Networks (CNNs), specifically based on the YOLOv5 architecture, enables precise and efficient detection of solar panels in the images. However, to overcome inherent detection accuracy limitations, computer vision techniques are implemented that accurately separate the panels from their backgrounds. The classification phase is addressed using an EfficientNet classifier trained on a synthetic dataset. This allows categorizing the panels as "normal" or "anomalous", with the latter grouped into four categories: "cell", "multi-cell", "diode", and "multi-diode" [9]. The obtained results underscore the potential of drones in identifying and classifying issues in solar panels and emphasize the need for accurate models for effective solar park management.

In the context of PV array mapping and detection, there has been a growing interest in applying deep learning techniques to accurately and efficiently identify solar energy systems in aerial imagery. The approach proposed in [10], aligns with this trend. Utilizing fully supervised convolutional neural networks, particularly the modified variant of the UNet network incorporating depthwise-separable convolutions, presents a significant advancement in PV array detection. This methodology addresses the pressing need to accurately estimate the energy generated by these arrays in urban areas. Given the limited resolution of the utilized images, constrained to 0.3 m or less, the network's ability to precisely segment and classify arrays based on their shapes and sizes is crucial. Compared to previous approaches, this proposed model demonstrates a noteworthy enhancement in segmentation accuracy, underscoring its efficacy in identifying PV arrays in high-resolution images. Furthermore, its efficiency in terms of parameters and complexity bolsters its applicability in real-world scenarios.

2.3 Detection of Suboptimal Conditions by Electrical Analysis

Fault detection using electrical variables such as power, voltage, and current are studied in [11,12]; several approaches are used to detect faults; however, we classify into six main areas: a) power loss analysis [13], b) signal processing and statistical methods [14], c) frequency analysis and reflectometry [15], d) machine learning techniques [16], e) electrical current-voltage measurements and health indicators [17,18], f) comparison between measured variables and PV models [19]. This work uses a mixed approach combining one statistical method and the PV systems' output power analysis. The selection is based on the fact that no physical model nor indicators were required to detect faults; the detection is based on the majority criterion calculated statistically, as we explain in the next subsection.

Least Significance Difference Analysis. The implemented algorithm is based on the Least Significant Difference (LSD) test [20], which determines if a difference between two averages is statistically significant. The concept behind this algorithm is founded on the idea that PV installations with "identical" conditions, i.e., same location, same inverters, arrays' power, similar ambient temperature, and irradiance, would have similar output power and, therefore, equivalent average power. The aforementioned concept makes it possible to detect failures when one output power is statistically less than the majority [4].

3 Materials and Methods

3.1 Site Description

The project was developed at the Tecnológico Local San Carlos campus in Costa Rica, 10°32' latitude and 84°31' longitude. The system was located in such a way as to achieve a correct capture of thermal images as stated in [21]. The camera was placed at a distance of 10.66 m from the PV array, at an angle of 50° with respect to the plane of the modules (see Fig. 1.a). The PV arrays used to evaluate the system were composed of polycrystalline modules of 12 modules in series each (see Fig. 1.b).

Fig. 1. a) Location of the fault detection system camera with respect to the PV array under analysis. b) PV installation used for the research. Arrays 1, 3 and 5 are polycrystalline of 12 modules each

3.2   Architecture Description

The implemented system integrates three suboptimal condition detection methods: IRT, RGB, and LSD. The system described in [22] was used for IRT analysis. It acquires temperature information with a FLIR VUE PRO R336 radiometric camera and environmental information with two Raspberry PI 4 microcontrollers, and the information processing is done on a server. The RGB analysis is done by acquiring images with an Argom CAM40 camera controlled by the same Raspberry Pi 4 as the thermal camera. The processing of the information is done on the same server recently mentioned. The LSD analysis is done by acquiring information from the Raspberry Pi 4, which is processed on the same server. The Fig. 2 shows a system architecture diagram.

The server has an AMD Ryzen 5 2600 six-core processor, 8 GB DDR4 2400 MHz RAM, GeForce GTX 1050 Ti graphics card, and runs the Ubunto 22.04.2 LTS operating system. Table 1 shows the principal characteristics of the instrumentation used for the system.

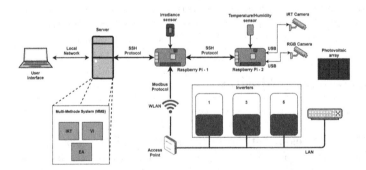

Fig. 2. Schematic diagram of the architecture of the Multi-method system for detection of suboptimal conditions.

Table 1. Characteristics of sensor used in the project.

Device	Parameter	Value
IRT camera Flir VUE PRO R 336	HFOV x VFOV	25º x 1954º
	Focal length	13.00 m
	Resolution	336 × 256
	Accuracy	∓ 5° C
	Thermal sensitivity	40 mK
RGB Camera Argom CAM40	Resolution	1920 × 1080p
	Focal length	4 mm
	Lens Size	14 mm
	Optical length	22.5 mm
	Viewing depth	107º
	Sensor	1/3" CMOS
	FOV	60–120º Horizontal
DHT11 Humidity sensor and temperature sensor	Temperature range	0°C to 50°C
	Humidity range	20% to 90%
	Accuracy	±1°C and ±1%
Spectron 210 Irradiance sensor	Irradiation range	0 to 1500 W/m^2

The proposed system executes each of the three suboptimal condition detection techniques and from the output of these, generates the system diagnosis; resulting in a more reliable response.

3.3   Criteria Used for Detection of Suboptimal Conditions

This section outlines the criteria employed by each technique to ascertain the presence of suboptimal conditions. Each of the techniques is automatic and yields a binary response: "Condition Detected" (D) or "Condition Not Detected" (ND).

IRT. The detection of hot spots from IRT took as a reference that a temperature delta of 10°C is required when there is an irradiance of at least 700 W/m^2 [23]. However, due to the highly variable weather conditions at the site, the AI hot spot detection system for irradiances higher than 300 W/m^2 developed by [22] was used.

This system is based on the temperature analysis of each pixel of the PV array, which identifies a reference panel as a healthy panel in the array (lower temperature difference between pixels), then identifies the pixel with the highest temperature in the other panels and compares it with the highest temperature of the healthy panel. Additionally, the analysis considers the real-time values of the site's relative humidity, ambient temperature, and irradiance.

RGB. The images are input into the CNN [24] as an array of pixels, the value of which is indicative of the light intensity of the point.

The process of classifying suboptimal conditions used YOLO to label three states: - Panel_sucio1 (non-uniform soiling type 1, S1), Panel_sucio2 (non-uniform soiling type 2, S2), and Panel_limpio (non-fault condition, NF), involves a series of crucial steps. To begin with, it was necessary to gather a dataset containing a total of 439 images of solar panels in various conditions. Among these images, 307 were allocated for training, 88 for validation, and 44 for testing. Each image was labeled with one of the three mentioned classes: "Panel_sucio1", "Panel_sucio2", and "Panel_limpio". This involves setting the parameters of the neural network, such as the network size and learning rate, as well as other aspects related to the training process.

LSD. The implemented algorithm based on the LSD Test compares the average output power of the inverters {1,3,5} using hypothesis tests. When one average power is statistically different from the others, the algorithm points out that the different average belongs to a PV array with a suboptimal condition. This algorithm takes only five samples per inverter to calculate the average, and the sampling rate is one sample per second. This small time window ensures low fluctuations in irradiance and ambient temperature. This means that a time's window of five seconds ensures the ambient conditions are similar in the three adjacent PV arrays.

The steps of the algorithm were explained in detail in [4]; however, they can be summarized as follows.

Calculus of the average output power. From each inverter, using a moving window of size five, the average of the power is calculated using (1),

$$\bar{p}_i = \Sigma_{k=1}^{5} \mathbf{P}\left[k, i\right]/5. \tag{1}$$

where $\mathbf{P}$ is a matrix where power data is stored from all the inverters and, i, j represent the inverter's number and k the samples. The hypothesis tests analyze the data to see if it accepts or rejects the Null Hypothesis (H^0). This is formulated as in equation (2),

$$\begin{aligned} \mathbf{H}_{i,j}^{0} &: \bar{p}_i = \bar{p}_j \\ \mathbf{H}_{i,j}^{1} &: \bar{p}_i \neq \bar{p}_j \\ \alpha &= 0.05 \\ \forall i, j \in \{1, 2, 3\}, |i \neq j. \end{aligned} \tag{2}$$

Determining which PV array is affected by fault is done by pairwise comparisons. The number of comparisons is defined by $n(n-1)/2$, where $n = 3$ is the number of PV installations. For this paper, the computer analyzes just 3 comparisons. The results of the comparisons are stored in a square matrix of size n, called **Alarm**$[\cdot]$, which records the binary results with the following conditions,

$$\mathbf{Alarm}[i,j] = \begin{cases} True & \text{if } H_{i,j}^1 \\ False & \text{if } H_{i,j}^0 \end{cases}, \quad \forall i,j \in \{1,2,3\}, |i \neq j. \tag{3}$$

Finally, the detection of the fault event in the $i-th$ PV array occurs when it generates $(n-1)$ true alarms. This can be formulated as follows,

$$\mathbf{Fault}[i] = \wedge_{j=1}^{n-1} \mathbf{Alarm}[i,j], \quad \forall i,j \in \{1,2,3\}, |i \neq j, \tag{4}$$

this last equation allows it to locate that the $i-th$ PV array has statistically abnormal behavior with respect to the other arrays analyzed. Notice that the **Fault**$[\cdot]$ vector has a size of (1×3), and the symbol $\wedge$ represents the logical AND function.

Performance Reference Criteria. To assess the efficacy of each technique employed by the system, we introduced an additional suboptimal condition detection method as a reference. This reference method establishes a baseline, defining a suboptimal condition as one that results in a power decrease of at least 4% [25]. To implement this, array 5 was designated as the reference (representing normal conditions), and the output power of array 1 was compared to that of array 5. If the power output of array 1 was 4% or lower than that of array 5, it was considered indicative of a suboptimal condition; otherwise, array 1 was deemed to be operating normally.

3.4   System Validation

To validate the system's performance, an experiment was conducted to analyze the responses of each fault detection technique and the complete system. Given the specific requirements of the evaluated detection methods, arrays 1, 3, and 5 were used (see Fig. 1.b); as the LSD method requires the involvement of three arrays. Suboptimal conditions were intentionally induced in array 1 (experiment factors), including two types of non-uniform soiling (S1 and S2), partial shading (PS), and a short circuit in the PV module (E, as an electrical fault). Each of these conditions (referred to as "treatments") was applied independently, randomly positioned within the array, and repeated nine times. Additionally, we established a non-fault (NF) treatment as a reference, in which the array operated normally, using the tests previously developed in [2]. A total of 45 tests were analyzed in the experiment (experimental units); each treatment was individually applied, and the binary output of the system and each method was recorded.

To ensure the thermal equilibrium required by the IRT method, diagnoses were conducted after 15 min of applying the treatment, following the recommendations provided in [26].

The results were analyzed using inferential statistics from a quantitative and descriptive approach, evaluating the sensitivity, accuracy, precision, and F1 score related to the receiver operating characteristic (ROC) analysis described by [27].

4   Results and Discussion

This section includes the results of the investigation and the analysis of the results. The analysis of the performance of the MMS and for each technique separately was considered.

4.1   General System Performance

The experiment was conducted between 3 and 12 of September 2023. During the tests, the weather was clear with irradiance between 305 and 1195 W/m^2; in addition, with the reference method, it was possible to verify that all the applied treatments generated a decrease in power of at least 4%.

The parameters corresponding to each method's confusion matrices were obtained From the tests performed (Fig. 3). The Fig. 3 shows a visual comparison of the results for each method; for example, for the TP parameter, the highest bar was for the MMS, indicating that it was able to detect the highest number of suboptimal conditions that were effectively suboptimal. Then, considering that: 1) Sensitivity = TP / (TP + FN), 2) Accuracy = (TP + TN)/(TP+TN+FP+FN), 3) Precision = TP / (TP + FP), and 4) F1score = 2TP / (2TP + FP + FN), the parameters associated with the ROC test were obtained (Fig. 3.a).

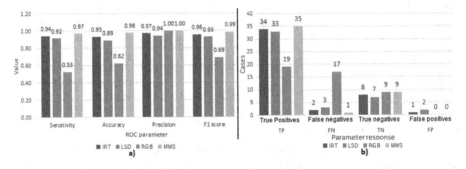

Fig. 3. Results obtain from the experiment: a) confusion matrix parameters, b) receiver operating characteristic parameters

As seen in Fig. 3.b, the best performing method was the MMS, achieving a sensitivity of 0.97, an accuracy of 0.98, a precision of 1, and an F1 score of 0.99. IRT had very close results in all parameters, followed by LSD, and the lowest performance was by RGB. This proves experimentally that the combination of methods will generate a better detection of suboptimal conditions than the use of a single technique. The performance of the IRT and RGB technique varies with those found in [2, 28], because in the previous investigations, the diagnosis of each test was made manually, while in this case, it was done automatically using AI. Therefore, the performance in this case is closely related to each technique's training. In this case, the RGB algorithm was being tested for the first time, having a limited data set that did not include the PS condition (generating a lower performance). At the same time, the IRT had been previously validated with satisfactory results [22].

It should be noted that although one of the methods had a lower performance (RGB), this did not affect the good performance of the MMS. Considering that in this case, only four types of suboptimal conditions were evaluated and in practice, we can find more than 25 related to the PV modules [11], and that each technique performs correctly detecting specific conditions, this suggests that the proposed system will perform well in the presence of other types of suboptimal conditions (or faults), even if each method used specializes in detecting certain types of faults; this remains to be demonstrated experimentally.

The satisfactory results of the automatic MMS, demonstrate the possibilities of automating processes through IoT solutions, enabling their application in smart cities for PV systems diagnostics.

4.2 Methods Performance

The LSD technique achieved a good performance (with an F1 score of 0.93). Considering that this is the one with the lowest implementation cost, not requiring auxiliary equipment (cameras and sensors), nor a previous training process of an AI, this technique could be an alternative to be used as a stand-alone technique; however, it must be remembered that this technique does not have the possibility of locating the suboptimal condition; situation that is required to be able to attend the PV installation. Considering that IRT and RGB can locate the faults, it is required to combine the techniques for agile maintenance.

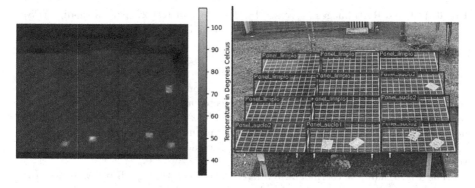

Fig. 4. IRT and RGB images processed by the MMS for test 1, inducing soiling type 1 (S1). IRT and RGB detected the suboptimal condition. Modules where suboptimal conditions were detected are marked in red. (Color figure online)

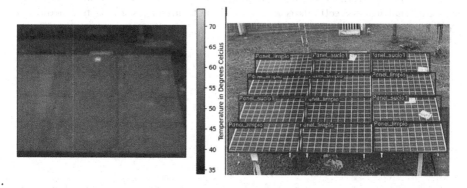

Fig. 5. IRT and RGB images processed by the MMS for test 2, inducing soiling type 2 (S2). IRT and RGB detected the suboptimal condition. Modules where suboptimal conditions were detected are marked in red. (Color figure online)

Figures 4, 5, and 6 show an example of the images processed by the MMS for some of the induced treatments (suboptimal conditions). Table 2 shows the information processed by the LSD technique for the same induced treatments.

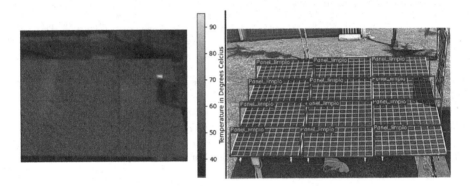

Fig. 6. IRT and RGB images processed by the MMS for test 27, partial shading (PS). IRT and RGB detected the suboptimal condition. IRT detected and RGB not detected the suboptimal condition.

As can be seen in Fig. 4. The induced soiling conditions (green leaves) generated temperature gradients that in this case were detected as hot spots by the IRT technique; in addition, the RGB technique also detected modules with soiling. However, the latter detected two modules with soiling erroneously; this indicates a risk that this technique could eventually generate false positives, which could be improved by increasing the training dataset.

The Fig. 5 shows a thermogram where the temperature gradients were less evident, however, the system was still able to detect that there was a soling condition (bird droppings). Regarding the RGB technique, the behavior of the previous case is repeated, in this case erroneously identifying one module with soiling.

From the results of table 2 it is clearly observed that, for the power values measured in array 1 for the cases in which a suboptical condition was induced, a decrease was generated that was correctly detected by the LSD technique; a situation that did not occur in the control cases (normal conditions).

Table 2. Examples of power measurements used by the LSD technique for some type of suboptimal condition applied in the experiment. All cases presented detected a suboptimal condition.

TEST	Condition	Measure	Power array 1 [W]	Power array 3 [W]	Power array 5 [W]
1	S1 (Soling) green leaves	1	2420	2964	3035
		2	2416	2962	3035
		3	2416	2959	3035
		4	2418	2959	3034
		5	2409	2958	3025
2	S2 (Soling) bird droppings	1	2559	3137	3329
		2	2683	3176	3336
		3	2781	3203	3205
		4	2869	3175	3102
		5	2890	3103	3131
27	PS (Partial Shading)	1	2120	2439	2490
		2	2125	2439	2489
		3	2130	2435	2487
		4	2128	2439	2485
		5	2129	2438	2492

Analyzing the performance of the RGB technique, without considering the PS treatment (because it was not trained to detect this condition), the model has demonstrated the ability to classify the other conditions. The results are summarized in Tables 3 and 4. The performance obtained indicates that the model is precise and effective in its task. These results are highly encouraging and confirm that the YOLO model is highly effective in the task of classifying suboptimal conditions of solar panels in images. Its ability to detect, locate, and correctly label panels in these conditions demonstrates its utility in applications related to the maintenance and monitoring of solar installations, where precision and reliability are crucial. It remains for future research to train the network to detect partial shading and other types of conditions.

Table 3. YOLO evaluation results

Metric	Value
mAP	97.8%
Precision	95.6%
Recall	93.9%

Table 4. YOLO classification results

Class	Value
all	98%
No_Fault(NF)	99%
Soiling_1 (S1)	98%
Soiling_2 (S2)	97%

4.3 System Limitations

The proposed fault detection method presented in this research has the limitation that it takes images from a fixed location. In reality, they are possibly taken with a drone from different orientations, which could affect the performance of the image-based techniques. Additionally, the results of the IRT and RGB techniques were limited by their training, which, in this case, is in the initial stage. The training data set should be increased to improve performance; for example, the RGB method is not yet trained to detect partial shadows. Also, the materials used to induce soiling conditions do not represent the variability of colors and shapes that leaves or bird droppings may have in reality, limiting the possibility of detecting real conditions using the RGB method. Finally, system performance is an indicator associated with the types of suboptimal conditions evaluated. For other types of suboptimal conditions, the results may vary.

5 Conclusions

The research was able to prove experimentally, in a quantitative approach, that the combination of techniques achieved the maximum detection of suboptimal conditions, reaching an F1 score of 0.99, compared to the individual application of IRT, LSD and RGB, which reached an F1 score of 0.96, 0.93 and 0.69, respectively. The high performance of the MMS was achieved even including a technique that obtained a lower performance (RGB). The results obtained correspond to the detection of particular suboptimal conditions, however, due to the nature of these conditions, the results serve as a reference for other cases; detailed experimental analysis for other types of conditions is an aspect to be considered for future research.

The results suggest that finding a high-performance technique such as LSD may be sufficient to detect suboptimal conditions without the need for more complex systems that combine techniques, however, the combination of techniques can improve diagnosis, for example, by enabling fault localization (with RGB or IRT), which is becoming more accessible every day due to technological innovation in IoT systems.

The results of this research are closely related to the characteristics of the experiment. It is important in future research to evaluate the cost-benefit of such a system, expanding the range of suboptimal conditions and ideally under real conditions. Finally, the results demonstrate the ability of current technologies to develop IoT solutions with AI to automate with high accuracy and effectiveness vital tasks in Smart Cities; in this case, the maintenance management of PV installations for an efficient and better use of renewable energy resources.

Funding Information. This work was fully funded by the Instituto Tecnológico de Costa Rica (TEC) through the project "Identificación de Fallas en Instalaciones Solares Fotovoltaicas", funding number 1360051. TEC was supported by State of Costa Rica as one of the public estate universities. The funders had no role in study design, data collection and analysis, decision to publish, or preparation of the manuscript.

References

1. Navid, Q., Hassan, A., Fardoun, A.A., Ramzan, R., Alraeesi, A.: Fault diagnostic methodologies for utility-scale photovoltaic power plants: a state of the art review. Sustainability **13**, 1629 (2021)
2. Cardinale-Villalobos, L., Meza, C., Méndez-Porras, A., Murillo-Soto, L.D.: Quantitative comparison of infrared thermography, visual inspection, and electrical analysis techniques on photovoltaic modules: a case study. Energies **15**, 1841 (2022)
3. Waqar Akram, M., Li, G., Jin, Y., Chen, X.: Failures of photovoltaic modules and their detection: a review. Appl. Energy **313**, 118822 (2022)
4. Murillo-Soto, L.D., Meza, C.: Photovoltaic array fault detection algorithm based on least significant difference test. In: Figueroa-García, J.C., Garay-Rairán, F.S., Hernández-Pérez, G.J., Díaz-Gutierrez, Y. (eds.) WEA 2020. CCIS, vol. 1274, pp. 501–515. Springer, Cham (2020). https://doi.org/10.1007/978-3-030-61834-6_43
5. Jamuna, V., Muniraj, C., Periasamy, P.S.: Fault detection for photovoltaic panels in solar power plants by using linear iterative fault diagnosis (LIFD) technique based on thermal imaging system. J. Electr. Eng. Technol. **18**, 3091–3103 (2023)
6. Kirubakaran, V., et al.: Infrared thermal images of solar PV panels for fault identification using image processing technique. Int. J. Photoenergy **2022**, 1–10 (2022)
7. Pathak, S.P., Patil, S.A.: Evaluation of effect of pre-processing techniques in solar panel fault detection. IEEE Access **11**, 72848–72860 (2023)
8. Wang, Q., Paynabar, K., Pacella, M.: Online automatic anomaly detection for photovoltaic systems using thermography imaging and low rank matrix decomposition. J. Qual. Technol. **54**, 503–516 (2022)
9. Terzoglou, G., Loufakis, M., Symeonidis, P., Ioannidis, D., Tzovaras, D.: Employing deep learning framework for improving solar panel defects using drone imagery In: 2023 24th International Conference on Digital Signal Processing (DSP), pp. 1–5 (2023)
10. Mujtaba, T., ArifWani, M.: Photovoltaic solar array mapping using supervised fully convolutional neural networks. In: 2021 8th International Conference on Computing for Sustainable Global Development (INDIACom), pp. 98–103 (2021)
11. Madeti, S.R., Singh, S.: A comprehensive study on different types of faults and detection techniques for solar photovoltaic system. Sol. Energy **158**, 161–185 (2017)
12. AbdulMawjood, K., Refaat, S.S., Morsi, W.G.: Detection and prediction of faults in photovoltaic arrays: a review. In: 2018 IEEE 12th International Conference on Compatibility, Power Electronics and Power Engineering (CPE-POWERENG 2018), pp. 1–8. IEEE (2018)
13. Chouder, A., Silvestre, S.: Automatic supervision and fault detection of PV systems based on power losses analysis. Energy Convers. Manage. **51**(10), 1929–1937 (2010)
14. Vergura, S., Acciani, G., Amoruso, V., Patrono, G.: Inferential statistics for monitoring and fault forecasting of PV plants. In: 2008 IEEE International Symposium on Industrial Electronics, pp. 2414–2419. IEEE (2008)

15. Takashima, T., Yamaguchi, J., Otani, K., Oozeki, T., Kato, K., Ishida, M.: Experimental studies of fault location in PV module strings. Sol. Energy Mater. Sol. Cells **93**(6–7), 1079–1082 (2009)

16. Youssef, A., El-Telbany, M., Zekry, A.: The role of artificial intelligence in photovoltaic systems design and control: a review. Renew. Sustain. Energy Rev. **78**, 72–79 (2017)

17. Silvestre, S., Kichou, S., Chouder, A., Nofuentes, G., Karatepe, E.: Analysis of current and voltage indicators in grid connected PV (photovoltaic) systems working in faulty and partial shading conditions. Energy **86**, 42–50 (2015)

18. Murillo-Soto, L.D., Meza, C.: Detection criterion for progressive faults in photovoltaic modules based on differential voltage measurements. Appl. Sci. **12**(5), 2565 (2022)

19. Chouder, A., Silvestre, S.: Analysis model of mismatch power losses in PV systems. J. Solar Energy Eng. 131, 024504 (2009)

20. Montgomery, D.C.: Design and analysis of experiments. John Wiley & Sons (2017)

21. Cardinale-Villalobos, C., Rimolo-Donadio, L., Meza, R.: Solar panel failure detection by infrared UAS digital photogrammetry: a case study. Int. J. Renew. Energy Res. (IJRER) **10**(3), 1154–1164 (2020)

22. Cardinale-Villalobos, L., et al.: IoT system based on artificial intelligence for hot spot detection in photovoltaic modules for a wide range of irradiances. Sensors **23**, 6749 (2023)

23. International Energy Agency: review of failures of photovoltaic modules. Tech. Rep, July, International Energy Agency (2014)

24. Chen, L., Li, S., Bai, Q., Yang, J., Jiang, S., Miao, Y.: Review of image classification algorithms based on convolutional neural networks. Remote Sens. **13**(22), 4712 (2021)

25. Acciani, G., Falcone, O., Vergura, S.: Typical defects of PV-cells. In: IEEE International Symposium on Industrial Electronics, pp. 2745–2749 (2010)

26. International Energy Agency, Review on infrared and electroluminescence imaging for PV field applications. Tech. Rep., Photovoltaic Power Systems Programme (2018)

27. Pintea, S., Moldovan, R.: The receiver-operating characteristic (ROC) analysis: fundamentals and applications in clinical psychology. J. Cogn. Behav. Psychother. **9**(1), 49–66 (2009)

28. Cardinale-Villalobos, L., Meza, C., Murillo-Soto, L.D.: Experimental comparison of visual inspection and infrared thermography for the detection of soling and partial shading in photovoltaic arrays. In: Nesmachnow, S., Hernández Callejo, L. (eds.) ICSC-CITIES 2020. CCIS, vol. 1359, pp. 302–321. Springer, Cham (2021). https://doi.org/10.1007/978-3-030-69136-3_21

Characterization of Household Electricity Consumption in Uruguay

Pablo Llagueiro[1], Rodrigo Porteiro[2] , and Sergio Nesmachnow[1]($\boxtimes$)

[1] Facultad de Ingeniería, Universidad de la República, Montevideo, Uruguay
{pablo.llagueiro,sergion}@fing.edu.uy
[2] UTE, Montevideo, Uruguay
rporteiro@ute.com.uy

Abstract. This article presents a study to characterize the electricity consumption in residential buildings in Uruguay. Understanding residential electricity consumption is a relevant concept to identify factors that influence electricity usage, and allows developing specific and custom energy efficiency policies. The study focuses on two home appliances: air conditioner and water heater, which represents a large share of the electricity consumption of Uruguayan households. A data-analysis approach is applied to process several data sources and compute relevant indicators. Statistical methods are applied to study the relationships between different relevant variables, including appliance ownership, average income of households, and temperature, and the residential electricity consumption. A specific application of the data analysis is presented: a regression model to determine the consumption patterns of water heaters in households. Results show that the proposed approach is able to compute good values for precision, recall and F1-score and an excellent value for accuracy (0.92). These results are very promising for conducting an economic analysis that takes into account the investment cost of remotely controlling water heaters and the benefits derived from managing their demand.

Keywords: residential electricity consumption · smart grid · computational intelligence

1 Introduction

Residential electricity consumption accounts for a significant share of the total electricity consumption worldwide. Globally, the percentage of electricity used in residential buildings for heating, cooling, lighting, electric appliances, and other residential activities is about 30% of the total energy consumption [10]. This figure varies depending on several factors, including the climate and average

This research was developed within a joint research project between Universidad de la república, the National Supercomputing Centar (Cluster-UY), and the national electricity company UTE.

S. Nesmachnow and L. Hernández Callejo (Eds.): ICSC-Cities 2023, CCIS 1938, pp. 33–47, 2024.
https://doi.org/10.1007/978-3-031-52517-9_3

temperature, the population density, the availability of different energy sources, energy efficiency measures, electricity policies for the residential sector, and also because of cultural practices.

In this context, the characterization of residential electricity consumption is crucial for effective energy planning. Relevant reasons for characterizing residential electricity consumption include: i) energy planning and management, since understanding residential electricity consumption patterns allows policymakers and energy utilities to anticipate and meet the growing energy demands of households, ensuring a reliable and efficient power supply; ii) load forecasting, which is crucial for providing stability to the power grid by predicting peak demand periods, appropriately planning for capacity expansions, and efficiently allocating resources to balance supply and demand; iii) development of targeted energy efficiency programs and campaigns, focusing on identified areas with higher energy utilization, to promote energy conservation and the participation on programs to buy and use energy-efficient household appliances, to improve energy efficiency and sustainability; iv) demand-side management, encouraging consumers to change their behavior regarding electricity usage to optimize the operation of the power grid by taking informed decisions to reduce energy waste, shift usage to off-peak hours, and participate in demand response programs; and v) integration of renewable energy sources at the residential level, maximizing self-consumption, reduce the dependence on the electricity grid, and contribute with to surplus energy generated by solar panels or wind turbines.

In this line of work, this article presents a characterization of residential electricity consumption for the real case study of residential households in Uruguay. A data-analysis approach [15] is applied to study the consumption of two important home appliances: air conditioner and water heater. These appliances account for a significant share of the electricity residential consumption in Uruguay. Several data sources are analyzed to compute relevant indicators and statistical methods are applied to study the relationships between residential electricity consumption and different variables, including appliance ownership, average income of households, and temperature. A regression model to determine the consumption patterns of water heaters in households is developed as a specific application of the data analysis performed.

The experimental evaluation of the proposed regression model is performed over a set of 49929 total consumption curves and water heater consumption curves with daily horizon and fifteen-minute frequency corresponding to 82 consumers. Results show that the proposed approach is able to compute good values for precision, recall and F1-score (0.58, 0.62 and 0.60 respectively), and an excellent value for accuracy (0.92).

The article is organized as follows. Section 2 describes the problem of characterizing household electricity consumption and reviews relevant related work. Section 3 describes the data sources and the proposed approach for data analysis in the case study of Uruguay. The results of the data analysis are reported in Sect. 4. A relevant application of the analysis for determining the consumption of residential water heaters is described and reported in Sect. 5. Finally, Sect. 6

presents the conclusions of the research and formulates the main lines for future work.

2   Household Electricity Consumption Characterization

This section describes the addressed problem and reviews relevant related works.

2.1   Problem Description

The problem of characterizing household electricity consumption refers to understanding and describing the patterns and behavior of electricity usage within residential households. The characterization includes quantifying the electricity consumed, identifying factors that influence consumption, analyzing the temporal variations and trends in usage patterns, and studying the electricity consumption of different devices [4]. The goal is to gain insights into the factors that contribute to energy consumption, such as family size and occupancy patterns, socio-economic factors, appliance usage, and lifestyle choices. This information is useful to help citizens for energy efficiency improvements, participation in demand response programs, and the development of effective energy management strategies that can lead to important savings in the electricity bill.

The characterization of household electricity consumption is important for energy providers, policymakers, and consumers themselves. It allows for better understanding of energy usage patterns, facilitates the development of more accurate load forecasting models, enables the design of targeted energy conservation programs, and supports the optimization of energy distribution and generation systems.

Beyond the complexities of modeling the behavior of citizens, the characterization of electricity consumption in households is also hard due to the difficulties of obtaining accurate and detailed consumption data. Not all households have smart meters that provide real-time data. Furthermore, many times the granularity of the available data on electricity usage is not high enough, making it difficult to precisely characterize electricity consumption patterns.

To overcome the aforementioned challenges, utilities, energy agencies, and researchers employ various methods, including surveys, smart metering, and data analytics, to collect and analyze data on household electricity consumption. These approaches help in understanding consumption patterns, identifying energy-saving opportunities, and developing targeted strategies to promote energy efficiency in residential areas.

2.2   Related Work

Several recent articles have studied the characterization of energy consumption in residential households [1, 2, 7–9, 13, 19, 25, 26].

Amayri et al. [3] applied interactive learning used to identify the usage patterns of flexible appliances, including water heater. Then, a Random Forest classifier was applied to determine the ON times of flexible appliances and a K-means clustering algorithm is utilized to evaluate the flexibility of each appliance. The proposed approach computed high accuracy results for the characterization, based solely on aggregated electricity consumption data.

Liu et al. [14] studied energy utilization prediction techniques at different time scales, building, and types of consumption. The study emphasized the importance of data preprocessing for enabling predictions at different time scales, and feature extraction as a key factor for characterization and prediction of energy consumption.

Previous studies [4,5,12] applied pattern consumption similarities for dis-aggregating household electricity consumption. Computational intelligence was applied for characterizing and dissagregating residential electricity consumption [11]. Computational models are useful for energy demand management [16], demand response [17], and the characterization of electricity usage in the industry [22,23]. Intelligent methods [20,21] were applied to develop an index for demand management of electric water heaters. Extra Trees and linear regressions were used to estimate water utilization and temperature. The index accurately captured the effect on temperature over real scenarios [6]. Neural networks obtained high classification accuracy to determine the intensive usage of air conditioner in households [24]. By accurately identifying households with intensive air conditioner usage, targeted strategies can be implemented to encourage energy efficiency and optimize energy consumption.

By enabling the characterization of residential electricity consumption, this article contributes with valuable insights for demand-side management, energy efficiency programs, and electric grid optimization. It offers a practical solution for understanding and leveraging the use of appliances in the residential sector, even in situations where detailed appliance-level data is not available.

3   Data Analysis for the Characterization of Household Electricity Consumption in Uruguay

This section describes the analysis for the proposed characterization.

3.1   Description of the Proposed Approach and Data Sources

The analysis primarily centers around two key appliances: the air conditioner and the water heater. These appliances contribute more than 50% of the households electricity consumption in Uruguay [6]. Moreover, both appliances are widely prevalent in the majority of households.

Several data sources were considered for the analysis:

– A survey performed by UTE to determine relevant electricity consumption information. The survey was performed in June 2021 to 18070 residential consumers in many locations in Uruguay. Relevant questions include:
  1. 'How many air conditioners do you have in your home?

2. 'Do you use any other equipment for heating?'
3. 'Do you use air conditioning in winter?'
4. 'Do you use air conditioning in summer?'
5. 'How many square meters built does your home have?'

- A partial table associating consumers to smart meters, provided by UTE.
- A partial table describing some features of consumers regarding tariff, approximate geolocation data, contracted electrical power, provided by UTE.
- Socio-economical information from the Continuous Household Survey (ECH), year 2022, provided by National Statistics Institute (INE-ECH 2022). The ECH dataset includes 528 fields, including the total household income, the number of people in the household, and the number of air conditioner appliances.
- Geographical information in shapefile format, provided by INE.
- Weather information (average temperature, average maximum temperature in January, average minimum temperature in July) for 16 weather stations in the country, from Uruguayan Institute of Meteorology.

3.2   Methodology

The applied methodology involved three stages: i) data cleansing, grouping, and adding new data from existing ones; ii) geographical characterization and clustering; and iii) computation/assessment of relevant indicators.

Data Cleansing and Grouping. Several transformation and corrections were applied to improve the quality and usefulness of the information provided by the consumers survey by UTE, including:

- Renaming columns to eliminate confusing characters, with the aim of facilitating the understanding and analysis of the data.
- Removing duplicate responses of the same consumer. The number of responses was reduced from 18299 to 18070, eliminating duplicated data.
- Filling null values in heating data and in the question about the presence of air conditioner in each household, allowing to have a coherent and complete response for all records.
- Replacing not-a-number values with 0 where a numerical value was required, for a uniform treatment of the data and avoiding misscalculations.
- Replacing text responses with shorter, clearer strings, eliminating confusing or unnecessary characters to facilitate the interpretation of data.
- Generation of new columns to represent different types or sources of heating. The text from multiple choice questions was processed, identifying the different types or sources mentioned in each answer and assigning the value 1 to the corresponding column.

The data cleaning and transformation actions performed on the UTE Survey contributed to improving the quality of the available information and preparing it for subsequent analysis and use in related applications. Additional data cleansing processes were performed over the temperature series, e.g., reviewing missing data and applying interpolation to determine the average temperature values for those departments that do not have a weather station installed.

Geographical Characterization and Clustering. For the geographical characterization, polygons of departments of Uruguay were added to the data, corresponding to the geographical boundaries for the specific areas of interest.

The geolocalization also performed the merge between the data from the consumer survey, the table matching consumers to smart meters, and the table describing features of consumers. While smaller geographical areas may provide more granular insights, departments provide meaningful information about temperature patterns, utilization of electric appliances, and trends across the region. Geolocation data were also added to the consumers dataset.

Computation of Relevant Indicators. For the analysis of consumers characteristics and their association with electricity use, several investigations were conducted. The following associations were explored:

1. Association between air conditioner ownership and its relationship with other heating devices:
   - Proportion of homes with full air conditioner holding (both cooling and heating capabilities) compared to those without.
   - Proportion of homes with air conditioner that also have other heating devices, and vice versa.
2. Analysis of declared air conditioner use:
   - General use of air conditioner (never, winter only, summer only, both).
   - Declared hours of air conditioner use based on days of the week and season.
   - Declared hours of use based on whether or not consumers have other heating devices.
   - Routine use of air conditioner between different stations or geographical areas.
3. Association between air conditioner ownership and household characteristics:
   - air conditioner ownership based on the number of cohabitants in the home.
   - Average number of air conditioner units according to the number of cohabitants.
4. Association between air conditioner ownership and household area:
   - air conditioner ownership based on household area categorized into four bands.
   - Average number of air conditioner units according to household area.
5. Association between heating type and air conditioner ownership: type of heating device used based on whether consumers own or do not own air conditioner units.

In the analysis of the ECH data, several steps were taken to incorporate additional information and investigate regression models, including:

1. The temperature series were added to the ECH data, from the same source used in the UTE survey. The time series is useful to examine relationships between temperature and other variables in the dataset.

2. The average number of equipment (heating/cooling devices) per home was calculated based on department, to help understanding the equipment distribution across different areas.
3. The average income per department was determined. This information provides insights into the economic characteristics of different areas.
4. Study of linear regression models with income (air conditioner ownership vs. average income), to analyze how average income influences air conditioner ownership.
5. Study of linear regression models with income and temperature (air conditioner ownership / average income ∪ temperature).
6. Study of linear regression models with income and rescaled temperature (air conditioner ownership / average income ∪ rescaled temperature). Since the previous analysis did not yield satisfactory results, the time series was rescaled to facilitate the interpretation and analysis of temperature values. Each temperature value (average, average maximum in January, average minimum in July) was linearly rescaled considering minimum and maximum values.

The analysis of linear regression models contributes to the understanding of the relationship between air conditioner ownership, average income of households, and temperature variables.

4   Results and Analysis

The main results of the data analysis are reported in this section.

4.1   Appliances Ownership and Utilization

Regarding air conditioner appliances, 76.3% of the surveyed households (11287) have at least one air conditioner. Within them, 70.3% also have another heating appliance and 29.7% only use air conditioner. Water heaters are significantly more present in Uruguayan households: 95% of the households have at least one water heater. Air conditioner is used both in winter and summer in 70.1% households. Figure 1 reports the use of air conditioner equipment (hours) in summer and winter for weekdays and weekends.

In summer, the mode of use is 2 to 3 h a day during weekdays and bimodal on weekends (between 2 and 3, and longer than 5 h). In winter, two situations stand out for weekdays: non-use of air conditioner and using it from 2 to 3 h a day; adding another mode of use on weekends. The zero-hour bars correspond to air conditioner owner who only uses them in the opposite extreme season, or not at all.

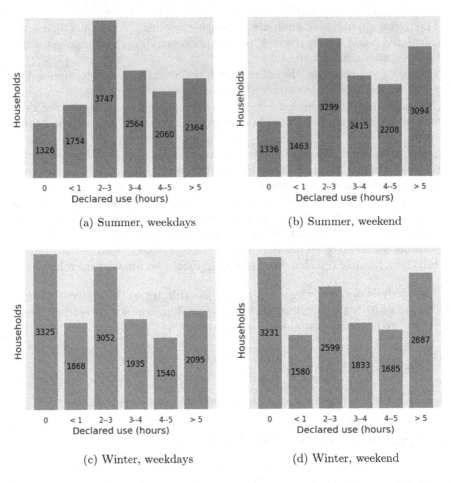

(a) Summer, weekdays

(b) Summer, weekend

(c) Winter, weekdays

(d) Winter, weekend

Fig. 1. Histograms of air conditioner use in summer and winter for weekdays and weekends

4.2 Ownership and Geographic Characterization

Figure 2 presents the percentage of households that have an air conditioner appliance, broken by the number of cohabitants in the household.

A clear trend is shown: the percentage of air conditioner ownership is lower for single-inhabitant households (64.9%) and the percentage continuously increase up to four cohabitants. Then, the air conditioner ownership decrease until a minimum of 60% for households with eight or more cohabitants. Both the average household income and the average maximum temperature of the area (departament) are positively associated with the ownership of air conditioner equipment.

A similar relationship is verified between the number of air conditioner owned and the number of cohabitants in the household, with just a slight decrease for six, as shown in Fig. 3.

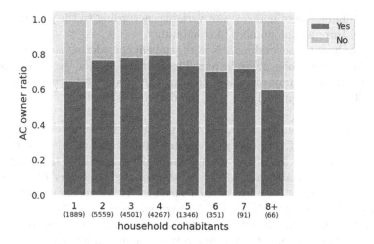

Fig. 2. Air conditioner ownership, by cohabitants

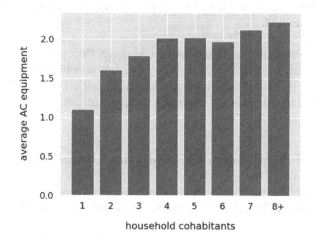

Fig. 3. Number of air conditioner owned, by cohabitants

4.3   Correlations with ECH Data

This subsection describes the statistical analysis to study the correlations of the number of appliances (air conditioner and water heater) with data from ECH.

Methodology. Statistical data exploration experiments were performed using the Ordinary Least Squares linear regression model provided by the `statsmodels` Python module. Several linear regression models were studied to estimate the probability of owning an air conditioner and a water heater appliance.

For air conditioner, eight models were studied, considering successive refinements based on the most significant indicators, rescaling of temperatures, the successive elimination of non-relevant variables according to the p-value and the final control through the number of cohabitants.

For water heaters, several models were studied, considering standard, instantaneous, and at least one water heater. The best models for the entire data set were identified. A dummy variable indicating the border status of a department with Brazil is used to model and split the data into subsets.

Air Conditioner. Minimum and maximum temperatures were non-relevant after rescaling. The selected variables were income×1000 (average household income in thousands pesos ∼ 25 USD), average annual temperature (rescaled to the interval [0,1]) and cohabitants. Model A6 showed slightly better results and its lower intercept clarifies the effect of each variable. Although the intercept for A6 is negative, it is offset by 'cohabitants' (always equal or greater than one), and its coefficient has the same magnitude as the intercept. The sign of each coefficient of a linear probability model is associated with the increase in the probability of the exogenous variable. Thus, using air conditioner equipment was shown to be related to higher average incomes, higher average temperatures, and the number of household members.

Water Heater. Proximity to Brazil was the variable that presented the greatest (positive) correlation with the ownership of instantaneous heaters. Then, to a lesser extent, INSE had a (negative) correlation. Considering only the cases with proximity to Brazil, the average minimum temperature also showed a (positive) correlation.

5   Practical Application: Classifying Use of Water Heaters

This section describes a highly relevant application: determining the usage of the electric water heaters in a household based on the total household consumption.

5.1   Motivation

A tool that provides the functionality of detecting the usage of electric water heaters is essential for implementing active demand management plans from the electric company to its consumers. To apply this technique, water heaters that can interrupt the electrical supply to the heater are needed. Installing these devices entails a significant investment for the electric company, so a thorough analysis that allows for the determination of water heaters usage for each consumer is crucial when deciding which households to invest in.

According to the data available for this study, only a small subset of water heaters are sub-metered. A tool capable of detecting the usage profile of the water heaters for any household with smart meter (even its absence) is essential. With this tool, simulations of active demand management for different groups of water heaters could be performed. Using the results of this simulations, an economic analysis that considers usage profiles, investment costs, and the cost of discomfort associated with implementing management strategies [20] would allow determining the optimal set of water heaters to consider and the economic benefit it would yield.

Determining the usage of the water heater based on consumption provide an approximation of the water heater usage profile for each household with a smart meter. Currently, in Uruguay, 72% of residential consumers have smart meters, and 89% have water heaters. Therefore, determining the presence and usage profile of the water heater in 72% of residential users would provide information about 64% of them. This represents approximately 1,000,000 households that consume 35% of the total energy demanded in Uruguay. Considering that the energy used for water heaters represents 30% of household consumption, the use of water heaters for demand management of households with smart meters would potentially affect 10% of the energy consumed in Uruguay, approximately 1200 GWh in a year.

5.2   Training and Validation Data

The available data was pre-processed as described in Subsect. 3.2 to obtain the dataset for training the classifier. The total daily consumption curve is used as input, without taking into account consumer-specific data. This curve contains 24 h of fifteen-minute interval data, therefore, 96 data points of average power. The labels used for classification consist of 96 binary variables, one for each interval, representing whether the water heater is on or off during that interval.

From the data described in Sect. 3, days with incomplete information were excluded. The result of this pre-processing consists of a matrix with 49929 d of data from the considered consumer set. Each row of the matrix contains a total of 192 data points: 96 data points with the average power in the interval and 96 binary data points indicating whether the water heater is on during the interval. The binary labels for classification were generated by observing the continuous water heater consumption curve per minute, as follows: if the water heater reports less than 200 W in the fifteen minute interval, the binary label for that interval was set to 0; otherwise the binary label was set to 1.

A subset of 10% randomly chosen days were taken as testing set. On the remaining 90%, a 10–fold cross–validation was conducted, where in each fold, the set was split into 80% for training and 20% for validation.

The applied Linear Regression model was developed in Python, using the libraries Tensorflow and Keras. The executions were carried out in the National Supercomputing Center [18].

5.3   The Proposed Classifier

Considering that the instantaneous power of an electric water heater is highly relevant within the total consumption for any residential consumer, it is deemed that a standard classifier using the training data described Sect. 5.2 can suffi-ciently capture the presence of the water heater in each time interval. A linear regression was employed to address this problem using a threshold of 0.5 to determine the binary label, as standard practice.

5.4   Results

The evaluation of the classifier was performed on the testing set. Figure 4 shows the confusion matrix obtained from the evaluation of the classifier on the testing set. The evaluation of the four standard learning metrics yielded: accuracy = 0.92, precision = 0.58, recall = 0.62 and F1-score = 0.60.

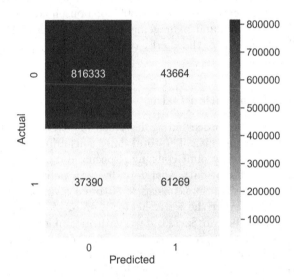

Fig. 4. Resulting confusion matrix for the classifier

The obtained results are appropriate for conducting an economic analysis as mentioned in Sect. 5.1. Since the dataset is imbalanced (the number of intervals without water heater usage is approximately 90% of the total), accuracy is not the most appropriate measure to consider alone. However, the values of the other three metrics are around 0.6 and along with the reported accuracy of 0.92, constitutes an appropriate outcome considering that the aim of the classifier is to approximate the water heater usage curve in order to analyze which intervals should be actively managed for demand control.

6   Conclusions and Future Work

This article presented a characterization study of the ownership and use of two appliances that have a significant impact on the electricity consumption of Uruguayan households: air conditioner and water heater. The analysis considered the geographical, economic, sociodemographic and climatic factors of

Uruguay, which were confirmed to be relevant. Statistical models were developed to determine the linear relationship between appliances ownership and the studied variables.

A model to estimate air conditioner and water heater ownership was proposed to adjust long-term consumption forecasts of households. As a relevant application, a linear regression-based classifier was also proposed to estimate real-time water heater usage. The combined models approach enables accurate future projections of the general ownership and use of these appliances. Moreover, it can enhance the very short-term prediction of household-level electricity demand. Another valuable features of this approach are the low cost of its implementation and its non-intrusive nature. Consumption data from 82 households and their water heater were used. The main results demonstrated the effectiveness of the proposed approach, yielding accuracy values of 0.92 and accurate values of precision, recall, and F1-score.

The main lines for future work include expanding the analysis considering more complex statistical models, to improve the estimation of the ownership of these appliances and their use in real time. Ownership data can most likely be improved by working with the complete 2023 census data for Uruguay (not yet available). Another line of future work is the implementation of more complex models for the calcification problem, such as Neural Networks, Random Forest, or Support Vector Machines, using more data to improve the classification accuracy.

References

1. Ahmed, R., Sreeram, V., Mishra, Y., Arif, M.: A review and evaluation of the state-of-the-art in PV solar power forecasting: techniques and optimization. Renew. Sustain. Energy Rev. **124**, 109792 (2020). https://doi.org/10.1016/j.rser.2020.109792
2. Alkhayat, G., Mehmood, R.: A review and taxonomy of wind and solar energy forecasting methods based on deep learning. Energy AI **4**, 100060 (2021). https://doi.org/10.1016/j.egyai.2021.100060
3. Amayri, M., Silva, C., Pombeiro, H., Ploix, S.: Flexibility characterization of residential electricity consumption: a machine learning approach. Sustain. Energy, Grids Netw. **32**, 100801 (2022). https://doi.org/10.1016/j.segan.2022.100801
4. Chavat, J., Nesmachnow, S.: Analysis of residential electricity consumption by areas in Uruguay. In: Nesmachnow, S., Hernández Callejo, L. (eds.) ICSC-CITIES 2020. CCIS, vol. 1359, pp. 42–57. Springer, Cham (2021). https://doi.org/10.1007/978-3-030-69136-3_4
5. Chavat, J., Nesmachnow, S., Graneri, J.: Non-intrusive energy disaggregation by detecting similarities in consumption patterns. Revista Facultad de Ingeniería Universidad de Antioquia (2020). https://doi.org/10.17533/udea.redin.20200370
6. Chavat, J., Nesmachnow, S., Graneri, J., Alvez, G.: ECD-UY, detailed household electricity consumption dataset of Uruguay. Scientific Data **9**(1) (2022). https://doi.org/10.1038/s41597-022-01122-x
7. Chen, C., Duan, S., Cai, T., Liu, B.: Online 24-h solar power forecasting based on weather type classification using artificial neural network. Sol. Energy **85**(11), 2856–2870 (2011). https://doi.org/10.1016/j.solener.2011.08.027

8. Chupong, C., Plangklang, B.: Forecasting power output of PV grid connected system in Thailand without using solar radiation measurement. Energy Procedia **9**, 230–237 (2011). https://doi.org/10.1016/j.egypro.2011.09.024

9. Ding, M., Wang, L., Bi, R.: An ANN-based approach for forecasting the power output of photovoltaic system. Procedia Environ. Sci. **11**, 1308–1315 (2011). https://doi.org/10.1016/j.proenv.2011.12.196

10. Energy Information Administration: international energy outlook (2021). https://www.eia.gov/outlooks/ieo/tables_side_xls.php. Accessed 3 July 2023. Washington, DC: U.S. EIA

11. Esteban, M., Fiori, I., Mujica, M., Nesmachnow, S.: Computational intelligence for characterization and disaggregation of residential electricity consumption. In: Nesmachnow, S., Hernández Callejo, L. (eds.) ICSC-CITIES 2020. CCIS, vol. 1359, pp. 58–73. Springer, Cham (2021). https://doi.org/10.1007/978-3-030-69136-3_5

12. Fraccanabbia, N., Gomes, R., Molin, M.D., Rodrigues, S., dos Santos, L., Cocco, V.: Solar power forecasting based on ensemble learning methods. In: International Joint Conference on Neural Networks. IEEE (2020). https://doi.org/10.1109/ijcnn48605.2020.9206777

13. Iheanetu, K.: Solar photovoltaic power forecasting: a review. Sustainability **14**(24), 17005 (2022). https://doi.org/10.3390/su142417005

14. Liu, H., Liang, J., Liu, Y., Wu, H.: A review of data-driven building energy prediction. Buildings **13**(2), 532 (2023). https://doi.org/10.3390/buildings13020532

15. Massobrio, R., Nesmachnow, S.: Urban mobility data analysis for public transportation systems: a case study in Montevideo. Uruguay Appl. Sci. **10**(16), 5400 (2020). https://doi.org/10.3390/app10165400

16. Muraña, J., et al.: Negotiation approach for the participation of datacenters and supercomputing facilities in smart electricity markets. Program. Comput. Softw. **46**(8), 636–651 (2020). https://doi.org/10.1134/s0361768820080150

17. Muraña, J., Nesmachnow, S.: Simulation and evaluation of multicriteria planning heuristics for demand response in datacenters. SIMULATION **99**(3), 003754972110200 (2021). https://doi.org/10.1177/00375497211020083

18. Nesmachnow, S., Iturriaga, S.: Cluster-UY: collaborative scientific high performance computing in Uruguay. In: Torres, M., Klapp, J. (eds.) ISUM 2019. CCIS, vol. 1151, pp. 188–202. Springer, Cham (2019). https://doi.org/10.1007/978-3-030-38043-4_16

19. Pedro, H., Coimbra, C.: Assessment of forecasting techniques for solar power production with no exogenous inputs. Sol. Energy **86**(7), 2017–2028 (2012). https://doi.org/10.1016/j.solener.2012.04.004

20. Porteiro, R., Chavat, J., Nesmachnow, S.: A thermal discomfort index for demand response control in residential water heaters. Appl. Sci. **11**(21), 10048 (2021). https://doi.org/10.3390/app112110048

21. Porteiro, R., Chavat, J., Nesmachnow, S., Hernández-Callejo, L.: Demand response control in electric water heaters: evaluation of impact on thermal comfort. In: Nesmachnow, S., Hernández Callejo, L. (eds.) ICSC-CITIES 2020. CCIS, vol. 1359, pp. 74–89. Springer, Cham (2021). https://doi.org/10.1007/978-3-030-69136-3_6

22. Porteiro, R., Hernández-Callejo, L., Nesmachnow, S.: Electricity demand forecasting in industrial and residential facilities using ensemble machine learning. Revista Facultad de Ingeniería Universidad de Antioquia 102, 9–25 (2020). https://doi.org/10.17533/udea.redin.20200584

23. Porteiro, R., Nesmachnow, S., Hernández-Callejo, L.: Short term load forecasting of industrial electricity using machine learning. In: Nesmachnow, S., Hernández

Callejo, L. (eds.) ICSC-CITIES 2019. CCIS, vol. 1152, pp. 146–161. Springer, Cham (2020). https://doi.org/10.1007/978-3-030-38889-8_12

24. Porteiro, R., Nesmachnow, S., Moreno-Bernal, P., Torres-Aguilar, C.E.: Computational intelligence for residential electricity consumption assessment: detecting air conditioner use in households. Sustain. Energy Technol. Assess. **58**, 103319 (2023). https://doi.org/10.1016/j.seta.2023.103319

25. Theocharides, S., Alonso, R., Giacosa, G., Makrides, G., Theristis, M., Georghiou, G.: Intra-hour forecasting for a 50 MW photovoltaic system in Uruguay: baseline approach. In: IEEE $46^{t}h$ Photovoltaic Specialists Conference. IEEE (2019). https://doi.org/10.1109/pvsc40753.2019.8980756

26. Zang, H., Cheng, L., Ding, T., Cheung, K.W., Wei, Z., Sun, G.: Day-ahead photovoltaic power forecasting approach based on deep convolutional neural networks and meta learning. Int. J. Electr. Power Energy Syst. **118**, 105790 (2020). https://doi.org/10.1016/j.ijepes.2019.105790

Visual Analytic of Traffic Simulation Data: A Review

Christopher Almachi[✉][ID], Rolando Armas[ID], and Erick Cuenca[ID]

Yachay Tech University, Urcuquí 100119, Ecuador
{christopher.almachi,tarmas,ecuenca}@yachaytech.edu.ec
http://www.yachaytech.edu.ec

Abstract. In the contemporary world, transportation is one of the foremost necessities for modern society, particularly within urban locales. Effective traffic management and planning represent indispensable tasks to maintain a seamless traffic flow and reduce congestion. To achieve this objective, traffic simulation data plays a pivotal role by furnishing intricate insights into traffic patterns, vehicle positions, events, and other pertinent aspects of a specific area. The visualization of traffic simulation data assumes paramount importance, serving as a vital tool for comprehending this information and making informed decisions. This paper provides a comprehensive review of the state of the art regarding web-based visualization techniques focused on traffic data provided by simulators, especially Multi-Agent Transport Simulation (MATSim). In addition, it will shed light on the most commonly employed features designed to facilitate the temporal analysis of traffic data, encompassing movement and congestion patterns. These resources hold significant potential for transport planners and traffic management professionals in creating web-based visualizations.

Keywords: Data visualization · Traffic data · Simulation

1 Introduction

Traffic congestion has become a worldwide phenomenon derived from the high density of the growing population and the excessive use of public and private vehicles [3]. The same causes large queues of cars and prevents free movement for long periods in highly demanded areas, making traffic systems a fundamental part of human life and significantly influencing the quality of life. For this reason, the collection of traffic data in cities has become a subject of urban planning studies for planners and engineers. Different sensors collect and analyze such data to visualize the vehicle's behavior daily or on demanding days [4]. However, planners opt for alternative solutions when traffic flow optimization is required in cities without data collection mechanisms. It is here where urban transport simulation plays a crucial role in understanding and improving mobility in urban areas, by creating trajectories, which are a representation of the route that a vehicle follows over time.

S. Nesmachnow and L. Hernández Callejo (Eds.): ICSC-Cities 2023, CCIS 1938, pp. 48–60, 2024.
https://doi.org/10.1007/978-3-031-52517-9_4

Tools such as Multi-Agent Transport Simulation (MATSim), Simulation of Urban MObility (SUMO), and Multimodal Traffic Simulation Software (VISSIM) allow simulations in large scenarios, identifying the transport agents involved and describing particular characteristics that could have an impact on traffic [8]. They simulate traffic flow under different conditions in a controlled environment [24]. However, the computer's resources limit the simulators' performance capability, which affects the fluidity of the simulations, advanced visualization functionalities, and the integration of external tools. Moreover, the complexity of the data format and the challenges associated with visualizing large volumes of data also contribute to the limitations of simulators [15, 21, 24]. Transportation management researchers and practitioners must improve interpreting and communicating simulation results effectively. Adequate visualization of transportation simulation results is crucial for understanding and visualizing traffic dynamics, assessing the impact of transportation policies, and communicating results to stakeholders [1].

This article aims to present and analyze the current state of traffic data visualizations generated from simulators, focusing on MATSim. This review intends to expand the understanding of the relevance and impact of data visualization in the traffic context. Furthermore, this review is intended to serve as a useful tool for examining existing projects and, at the same time, inspire ideas for the development of a traffic data visualization tool for MATSim outputs.

2 Theoretical Framework

This section will delve into the fundamental theoretical foundations underpinning research related to traffic data visualization. Throughout this exploration, we will shed light on the crucial importance of visualizing traffic data, clarify the key components of the data, and introduce advanced simulation tools such as MATSim. Additionally, we will present a compelling rationale for delving into the research problem at hand.

2.1 Traffic Data

Traffic congestion on highways can often be caused by poor road planning or design, which wastes time and money for drivers and passengers. On several occasions, traffic has led to aggression among drivers [23]. A visualization system for urban transport can provide better traffic control and guidance of the different routes in a given sector [29], being necessary for the traffic simulation for a development based on sustainability [23].

Real Traffic Data. Data sets generated and collected by monitoring devices installed in vehicles or along roads, such as GPS [17], vehicle sensors [3], or video and image tracking monitors [14], are called real traffic data. Driver behavior patterns can be identified by collecting data on everyday traffic to detect risky situations and prevent accidents. Early warning systems, navigation applications, real-time maps, and driver assistance technologies that improve road safety and allow users to avoid congestion and reach their destination faster and more efficiently can be developed with this data [4].

Simulation Traffic Data. Understanding and controlling the movement of vehicles on highways, in cities, and other transportation infrastructures often requires using traffic simulation data. The ability to replicate or build new roads or modify existing roads allows engineers to predict how vehicles will behave in various scenarios [26]. This information aids in cost-effective infrastructure design optimization and helps to guarantee the efficiency and safety of future structures. Simulations are crucial instruments for well-informed decision-making in the planning and administration of transportation [11].

2.2   Traffic Simulations Tools

Traffic simulation tools are software or applications designed to model and analyze the flow of vehicles on highways, streets, and transportation systems [22]. There are various tools for traffic simulation, including MATSim[1], VISSIM[2] and SUMO[3]. However, this study will focus more on the data from the MATSim [24] since it is an open-source simulation framework widely used to model multi-agents (people, vehicles). It focuses on making autonomous decisions about their trips, routes, and modes of transportation. This makes it highly configurable and complete for effective visualization [15].

2.3   MATSim Dimensions

The data generated from MATSim provide different output results that store the traffic behavior, such as events, counts, facilities, households, networks, persons, plans, trips, vehicles, etc. Among these, we will highlight two: network and event dimensions. These will be presented below.

Network. This file contains the representation of the transportation network in the simulated environment. As shown in Fig. 1, the network file includes information about the roads, streets, intersections, and connections between nodes in the modeled transportation system. In addition, it contains geospatial and topological data describing the location and connectivity of transport routes, such as nodes, links, link types, capacity, speed limits, and other relevant attributes. Its use is essential, as it defines the infrastructure over which agents (vehicles) move [24].

---

[1] https://www.matsim.org/.

[2] https://www.ptvgroup.com/en/products/ptv-vissim.

[3] https://eclipse.dev/sumo/.

```
<nodes>
    <node id="1000916573" x="724210.0883466646" y="9680394.5530272" >
    </node>
    <node id="1000916592" x="724280.914322159" y="9680457.326553036" >
    </node>
</nodes>

<links>
    <link id="1005493150004f" from="1162464733" to="1162464562" length="203.6683087"
        freespeed="4.16667" capacity="600.0" permlanes="1.0" oneway="1" modes="car" >
        <attributes>
            <attribute name="origid" class="java.lang.Long">100549315</attribute>
            <attribute name="type" class="java.lang.String">residential</attribute>
        </attributes>
    </link>
</links>
```

Fig. 1. Network file sample from MATSim.

Events. This file records a sequence of events during the simulation. These events can include agent movements, destination arrivals, collisions, speed changes, and more [9]. As shown in Fig. 2, each entry represents a specific event with detailed information, such as the time, the agent involved, and the geospatial coordinates at which it occurred [24]. This file is valuable for post-simulation analysis. It allows examination of agent behavior, identification of traffic flow problems, congestion assessment, and detailed investigations of transportation system performance.

```
<event time="16886.0" type="left link" link="5329917980002f" vehicle="1810" />
<event time="16886.0" type="entered link" link="5329917980002r" vehicle="1810" />
<event time="16930.0" type="left link" link="5329917980002r" vehicle="1810" />
<event time="16930.0" type="entered link" link="899646210008r" vehicle="1810" />
<event time="16953.0" type="left link" link="899646210008r" vehicle="1810" />
```

Fig. 2. Event file sample from MATSim.

2.4   Data Visualization

Data visualization techniques allow users to reveal patterns and trends in data through graphical representations [25]. It can transform complex data into actionable data in an intelligent, logical, and efficient way for optimizing the analysis of large amounts of data [20]. This will improve both information understanding and decision-making [3]. Data visualization combines machine intelligence with human intelligence through an intuitive visual interface, giving rise to what is known as visual analytics [8].

As described in [13], visual analytics is a discipline that aims to handle huge data sets of information by combining them with applications that enable strong automatic analysis and achieve correct human visual analytics. Figure 3 shows the visual analytics process, meaning it must go through exploration processes. The processes are iterative, allowing identification and improvement of the model at each step until the correct visualization is achieved.

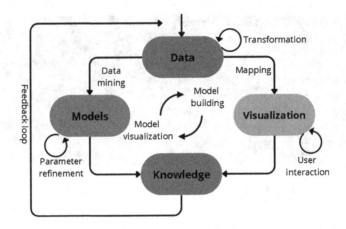

Fig. 3. Visual analysis process automated [13].

On the other hand, according to a conceptual pipeline put forward by [8], traffic data visualization typically includes four data states: raw data, processed data, visual symbols, and visualization. As previously mentioned, there are various ways to access raw data. The pre-processed data includes multivariate, spatiotemporal, spatial, and temporal features. The data are then transformed visually into symbols with the proper layout and design, including map plots, line graphs, and dot plots. Finally, the visual metaphors and symbols are assembled into various kinds of visualization, including color images, infographics, animation, and video, and mapped with various visual channels. Enabling user interaction with visual symbols and visual mapping types.

2.5   Traffic Data Features

Existing traffic visualization applications and visual analysis systems are analyzed according to the tasks employed. For this reason, we must define five relevant aspects for data analysis: time, space, spatiotemporal, multivariate, and velocity.

Time. Time is an essential dimension in traffic data. As mentioned [24], it captures information about how traffic flow and user behavior change over time. Also, it can be broken down into time intervals, such as seconds, minutes, hours, days, and more. Analyzing traffic over time allows users to identify congestion patterns, peak times, and seasonal trends [2].

Space. Space in traffic data is essential for understanding traffic events and behaviors' location and geographic distribution [8]. In other words, it refers to the physical location of traffic events, such as vehicles, intersections, roads, streets, public transport stops, and other infrastructure elements. Traffic data records the precise geographic position of these elements to map the transportation network [24].

Spatio-temporal. Spatio-temporal in traffic simulation data refers to the representation of traffic evolution over time and space [1]. Traffic simulation models use spatio-temporal data to predict and analyze traffic behavior in different situations. Spatio-temporal is used in a trajectory like a coordinate system, in which the spatial geographic information is mapped using the plane created by the X, Y, or latitude, longitude [2].

Multivariate. Refers to the action of several objects or entities moving simultaneously or in parallel [1]. This means that several elements are changing position or displacement simultaneously and in a coordinated or independent manner. Traffic simulation refers to coordinating multiple vehicles or transportation events moving simultaneously on a network of roads, routes, or transportation lines [22].

Velocity. It is one of the essential characteristics in traffic simulation data and plays a critical role in understanding and efficiently managing vehicle flow in simulated transportation networks [1]. This measure reflects the velocity of vehicles traveling along roads and streets in a simulation environment.

3 Related Work

In this section, we will show previous work related to traffic data visualization in more detail. In addition, the methodology used for collecting these papers is explained, and finally, the articles are presented. Remember that articles have been classified as real scene and simulation data. Table 1 shows the authors' names, the article's purpose, the classification of real and simulated traffic data, relevant characteristics taken for visualization, and finally, the origin of these data, either from collection or simulation systems.

3.1 Methodology

For this study, a search was conducted to identify scientific papers using real and simulation-generated scenario traffic data. The investigation was performed in recognized databases, including Google Scholar, Scopus, and IEEE, using the Boolean method. The Boolean method improves searches' efficiency and accuracy, allowing you to find more relevant results and valuable sources [10]. Therefore, the keywords used for the search included "data traffic", "simulation" and "data visualization". In addition, it is essential to note that the study focused on articles published between 2013 and 2023. In the end, a complete set of 15 articles explicitly addressing traffic data visualization was obtained.

For the selection of articles in our study, we prioritized including those that specifically addressed the topic of traffic data visualization. This allowed us to focus on research to achieve an effective and understandable representation of traffic-related data, a fundamental aspect of traffic management and decision-making. Therefore, the search included articles that used traffic data from real situations and simulations, especially MATSim, which allowed contrasting different approaches in the implementations. Moreover, a detailed analysis of the features of traffic data that the authors highlighted and considered critical in developing visualizations was carried out.

3.2   Real Scenario Data Visualizations

Let's start with the articles that used real data to generate analysis visualizations. Carter *et al.* [4] develops a web application that remotely monitors some intersections of traffic lanes within Michigan (see Fig. 4a). The application's main purpose is to take Basic Safety Message (BSM) data and use it to simulate vehicle activity and connectivity as it travels through intersections. Then, in 2019, Pi *et al.* [17] proposes to extract vehicle flows from traffic data such as GPS trajectory and Vehicle Detector data from Open Street Map (OSM) (see Fig. 4b). They found the changes in vehicle flow using information theory entropy and constructed count curves (N-curve) that can quantify the vehicle flow in the congestion zone, thus predicting the traffic using a neural network. They developed a dashboard to analyze all the data generated. In the same year, Lee *et al.* [14] presented an interactive visual analysis system to explore, monitor, and predict traffic congestion using data from dedicated short-range communications (DSRC) vehicle detectors (see Fig. 4c). The visualization uses Volume-Speed Rivers (VSRivers) graphs that present traffic volumes and speeds. Achieving the usefulness of your system in the field of traffic management.

However, moving a little out of the context of vehicle traffic and moving to ships. Scheepens *et al.* [19] achieves a visualization of traffic flow directions from the Vassel database using a particle system on a density map (see Fig. 4d). The user can interact by extracting traffic flows using an original widget that allows selecting an area intuitively and filtering it in a range of directions and additional attributes. Finally, Petrovska *et al.* [16] proposes a real-time traffic congestion visualization and analysis tool that uses live traffic data and historical data to estimate congestion. The tool uses Google Maps and social travel information embedded in some maps to visualize congestion.

3.3   Simulation Data Visualizations

Now, articles related to traffic data from the different simulation tools will be presented. Erath and Fourie [9] proposed a dashboard in which MATSim generated data from Singapore's smart cards and analyzed using Tableau, a business analysis software (see Fig. 5a). The team created relational tables in Tableau to interactively aggregate and visualize the data. By analyzing traffic data visually, they could make more effective decisions. Piris *et al.* [18] have designed a

Table 1. Summary of state of the art, the main authors of the articles, the purposes of their research, the types of data used, the features of the traffic data required for the analysis (t = time, s = space, x = temporal-space, m = multivariate, v = velocity) and the source of the data they used in their respective studies.

Paper	Purpose	Traffic	t	s	x	m	v	Data
Carter et al. [4]	Traffic monitoring	Real scenario	✓		✓		✓	Basic Safety Message
Pi et al. [17]	Simulation and prediction		✓	✓			✓	OSM trajectories
Lee et al. [14]	Monitoring and prediction		✓		✓	✓	✓	DSRC data
Scheepens et al. [19]	Trajectories visualization		✓			✓	✓	Vassel trajectory
Petrovska et al. [16]	Traffic analysis and visualization		✓		✓	✓		Google Maps
Xu et al. [28]	Visualization of large-scale traffic	Simulation	✓	✓				VISSIM and SUMO
Xu et al. [27]	Traffic pattern analysis		✓		✓		✓	
Jung et al. [12]	Selection and visualization		✓				✓	
Erath and Fourie [9]	Trajectory analysis and visualization		✓					MATSim data
Charlton et al. [6]	Visualization taxi routes		✓	✓	✓	✓		
Piris et al. [18]	Generation of simulation of data		✓	✓	✓			
Charlton and Laudan [5]	Trajectory analysis and visualization		✓	✓	✓	✓		
Miranda and Arruda [15]	Generation of simulation data		✓	✓	✓			
Charlton and Sana [7]	Visualization of large-scale		✓	✓	✓	✓		
Strippgen [21]	Real-time display		✓	✓	✓	✓		

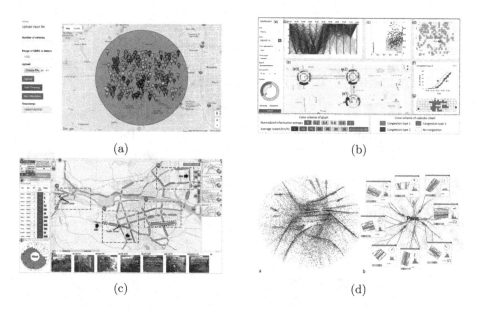

(a)   (b)

(c)   (d)

Fig. 4. Visualizations generated with real data. (a) Show an interface of the simulator with a high density of nodes [4], (b) Dashboard visual cause analytics system for traffic congestion [17], (c) Map view on dashboard [14], (d) Overview of traffic flows over the Paris area [19].

web-based tool to streamline handling traffic data for utilization with the MAT-Sim simulator. This application simplifies the tasks of inputting data, extracting results, and interpreting the information required for MATSim simulations (see Fig. 5b). Moreover, it can generate the essential files needed for future agent simulations. Additionally, they have provided a repository and an instructional guide to assist users in effectively utilizing the system. In other research, Jung *et al.* [12] explored the potential of employing an open-source real-time web platform that connects simulation outcomes with visual display interfaces (see Fig. 5c). In this context, they employed the microtraffic simulation tool VISSIM to achieve this integration. The data is then visually represented based on both time-related and spatial attributes, forming the structure of the interactive dashboard. Users can effectively analyze and predict traffic conditions through this intuitive visualization platform. Also, Charlton *et al.* [6] introduced a distinctive online data visualization portal specifically designed for researchers and public transportation entities who advocate for advancing taxi-sharing initiatives (see Fig. 5d). This portal is tailored for utilizing MATSim data. It offers interactive features, including visual representations of agent (taxi) movements that are color-coded based on passenger counts and the origins and destinations of trip requests. It also provides insights into variations in road and passenger traffic volumes compared to a reference scenario, among other functionalities.

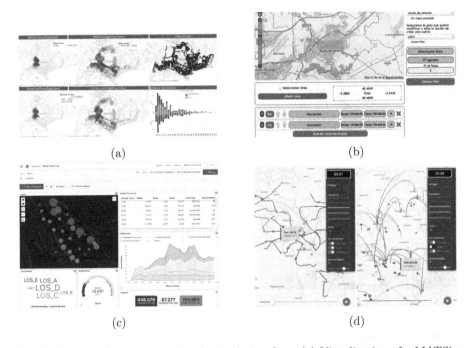

(a)

(b)

(c)

(d)

Fig. 5. Visualizations generated with simulation data. (a) Visualization of a MATSim simulation in Tableau about the number of public transport users [9]. (b) The initial screen of the visualization tool in the description of the plans [18]. (c) Dashboard interface created in elastic [12]. (d) Dynamic response transit system (DRT) animation, vehicles, routes, and destinations [6].

In 2021, Xu *et al.* [27] offers an energy analysis approach to understand vehicle energy consumption patterns in response to varying traffic signal phases at multiple intersections along a major transportation corridor. An interactive visualization dashboard allows transportation planners to explore and analyze these energy consumption patterns. One year later, Xu *et al.* [28] introduced a web-based tool designed to facilitate storing, sharing, and presenting extensive traffic simulation data (see Fig. 6a). This application has been seamlessly integrated into the real-time mobility communication and control system known as RyThMiCCS. To showcase its capabilities, the authors utilized simulation results obtained from VISSIM and SUMO as examples. Similarly, Charlton and Laudan [5] devised an online viewing platform for MATSim results that operates entirely over the web. After conducting numerous initial experiments with various web technologies, they developed a client/server platform design (see Fig. 6b). In this design, they leveraged the advanced UI capabilities of modern browsers on the front end while relying on back-end server processing for more CPU-demanding tasks. Miranda and Arruda [15] developed an approach for acquiring and handling data about input details within a granular model, utilizing the identical simulation tool as previously mentioned. They further showcased an illustrative scenario within the Brasilia region, the capital of Brazil. The processed informa-

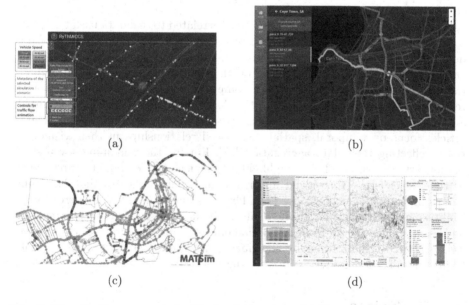

(a)

(b)

(c)

(d)

Fig. 6. Visualizations generated with simulation data. (a) The user interface includes controls for selecting traffic simulation scenarios and animating traffic flow [28]. (b) Transit routes explorer displays all transit routes and allows the user to see which routes serve in specific links [5]. (c) OTFVis was used to visualize a simulation of morning peak-hour traffic in Brasilia [15]. (d) Web application dashboard where indicated vehicle animation, area data, and basic graphical analysis [7].

tion encompassed the road infrastructure and a synthetic population, followed by a subsequent analysis of the area and examination of the traffic data (see Fig. 6c). In another article, Charlton and Sana [7] introduced a fresh web-based, open-source, and adaptable data visualization system tailored explicitly to facilitate extensive transportation simulations like MATSim and ActivitySim. This platform generates diverse interactive charts, maps, animations, and analytical dashboards, frequently valuable in transportation (see Fig. 6d). Finally, Strippgen [21] describes the design and operation of OTFVis, a data visualizer that allows real-time visualization of large amounts of information generated by traffic simulations. OTFVis uses layers to optimize performance and minimize the amount of data sent and has a user interface that allows the selection of predefined queries or the creation of custom queries.

4   Discussion

Real traffic data provides a solid reference to ensure that any simulation model approximates real-world traffic behavior. In turn, using traffic simulation data can help detect anomalies and unexpected events in the future. This broad perspective allowed us to contrast and analyze different approaches to data visualization, considering the variability and specific characteristics of traffic data in various situations.

On the one hand, we identified five articles related to real data used for monitoring, prediction, and visualization purposes. Despite diverse data sources, these data present distinctive characteristics focused on time, spatio-temporal, multi-variability, and speed. Concentrating on these features underscores the importance of capturing the dynamics and complexity inherent to traffic control in real-world environments [14]. On the other hand, we found ten simulation-related articles, three of which employ simulators such as VISSIM and SUMO. These articles focus on temporal, spatial, and speed relationships in their visualizations, reflecting their data aggregation [27]. Finally, the remaining seven simulation articles use MATSim, highlighting particularly relevant features, such as time, space, time-space, and multivariability. This indicates that MATSim details individual agent behavior [24]. This information presents numerous possibilities and challenges for traffic analysis. Visualizing traffic data is crucial in addressing issues arising from large-scale data [8]. Furthermore, we will achieve well-generated visualizations by recognizing traffic data characteristics and following visualization analytic processes such as [13].

5   Conclusions

This work presents the differences between the various simulation and data visualization articles, allowing us to identify patterns and trends in the importance of certain aspects of traffic data, contributing to a deeper understanding of how researchers approach visualization in this domain. Visual analytics can perform various tasks, such as accident control, route optimization, and traffic jam prevention. However, most data collection and generation systems work with already generated data. In other words, they are not constantly updated.

Combining the best practices of traffic data visualization is an extensive task that benefits the development of cities and towns. In this context, the approaches presented in this work highlight the results obtained, especially using MATSim data. Several works have successfully aligned visual analytic workflows to create web-based applications that allow users to interact with this data interactively. As a future work, an interconnected visualization system using online traffic data from different sources would be proposed.

Acknowledgment. The authors express their gratitude to the Data Science and Analytics (DataScienceYT) group at Yachay Tech University for their assistance during the development of this work.

References

1. Andrienko, G., Andrienko, N., Bak, P., Keim, D., Wrobel, S.: Visual Analytics of Movement. Springer, Heidelberg (2013). https://doi.org/10.1007/978-3-642-37583-5
2. Andrienko, N., Andrienko, G., Gatalsky, P.: Exploratory spatio-temporal visualization: an analytical review. J. Vis. Lang. Comput. **14**(6), 503–541 (2003)
3. Bachechi, C., Po, L., Rollo, F.: Big Data analytics and visualization in traffic monitoring. Big Data Res. **27**, 100292 (2022)
4. Carter, N., et al.: Developing mobility and traffic visualization applications for connected vehicles. arXiv preprint arXiv:1811.11012 (2018)
5. Charlton, B., Laudan, J.: Web-based data visualization platform for MATSim. Transp. Res. Rec. **2674**(10), 124–133 (2020)
6. Charlton, W., Leich, G., Kaddoura, I.: Open-source web-based visualizer for dynamic-response shared taxi simulations. Procedia Comput. Sci. **184**, 728–733 (2021)
7. Charlton, W., Sana, B.: SimWrapper, an open source web-based platform for interactive visualization of microsimulation outputs and transport data. Procedia Comput. Sci. **220**, 724–729 (2023)
8. Chen, W., Guo, F., Wang, F.Y.: A survey of traffic data visualization. IEEE Trans. Intell. Transp. Syst. **16**(6), 2970–2984 (2015)
9. Erath, A., Fourie, P.J.: Interactive analysis and decision support with MATSim. In: The Multi-agent Transport Simulation MATSim, pp. 253–258. Ubiquity Press (2016)
10. Hammer, P.L., Rudeanu, S.: Boolean Methods in Operations Research and Related Areas. Springer, Heidelberg (2012). https://doi.org/10.1007/978-3-642-85823-9
11. Islam, M., Jin, S.: An overview of data visualization. In: 2019 International Conference on Information Science and Communications Technologies (ICISCT), pp. 1–7. IEEE (2019)
12. Jung, J., Oh, T., Kim, I., Park, S.: Open-sourced real-time visualization platform for traffic simulation. Procedia Comput. Sci. **220**, 243–250 (2023)
13. Kohlhammer, J., Keim, D., Pohl, M., Santucci, G., Andrienko, G.: Solving problems with visual analytics. Procedia Comput. Sci. **7**, 117–120 (2011)

14. Lee, C., et al.: A visual analytics system for exploring, monitoring, and forecasting road traffic congestion. IEEE Trans. Vis. Comput. Graph. **26**(11), 3133–3146 (2019)
15. Miranda, D., Arruda, F.: Method for simulating a MATSim multi-agent activity-based transport model in developing countries, July 2019
16. Petrovska, N., Stevanovic, A.: Traffic congestion analysis visualisation tool. In: 2015 IEEE 18th International Conference on Intelligent Transportation Systems, pp. 1489–1494. IEEE (2015)
17. Pi, M., Yeon, H., Son, H., Jang, Y.: Visual cause analytics for traffic congestion. IEEE Trans. Vis. Comput. Graph. **27**(3), 2186–2201 (2019)
18. Piris, C., et al.: Estudio y desarrollo de una aplicación web para la generación y tratamiento de datos del simulador MATSIm (2013)
19. Scheepens, R., Hurter, C., Van De Wetering, H., Van Wijk, J.J.: Visualization, selection, and analysis of traffic flows. IEEE Trans. Vis. Comput. Graph. **22**(1), 379–388 (2015)
20. Shakeel, H.M., Iram, S., Al-Aqrabi, H., Alsboui, T., Hill, R.: A comprehensive state-of-the-art survey on data visualization tools: research developments, challenges and future domain specific visualization framework. IEEE Access **10**, 96581–96601 (2022)
21. Strippgen, D.: OTFVis: MATSim's open-source visualizer. In: The Multi-Agent Transport Simulation MATSim, pp. 225–234 (2016)
22. Taplin, J.: Simulation models of traffic flow. In: The 34th Annual Conference of the Operational Research Society of New Zealand, New Zealand (1999)
23. Ullah, M.R., Khattak, K.S., Khan, Z.H., Khan, M.A., Minallah, N., Khan, A.N.: Vehicular traffic simulation software: a systematic comparative analysis. Pakistan J. Eng. Technol. **4**(1), 66–78 (2021)
24. Axhausen, K.W., Horni, A., Nagel, K.: The Multi-Agent Transport Simulation MATSim. Ubiquity Press (2016)
25. Wang, K., Liang, M., Li, Y., Liu, J., Liu, R.W.: Maritime traffic data visualization: a brief review. In: 2019 IEEE 4th International Conference on Big Data Analytics (ICBDA), pp. 67–72. IEEE (2019)
26. Waraich, R.A., Charypar, D., Balmer, M., Axhausen, K.W.: Performance improvements for large-scale traffic simulation in MATSim. In: Helbich, M., Jokar Arsanjani, J., Leitner, M. (eds.) Computational Approaches for Urban Environments. GE, vol. 13, pp. 211–233. Springer, Cham (2015). https://doi.org/10.1007/978-3-319-11469-9_9
27. Xu, H., Berres, A., Wang, C.R., LaClair, T.J., Sanyal, J.: Visualizing vehicle acceleration and braking energy at intersections along a major traffic corridor. In: Proceedings of the Twelfth ACM International Conference on Future Energy Systems, pp. 401–405 (2021)
28. Xu, H., Wang, C., Berres, A., LaClair, T., Sanyal, J.: Interactive web application for traffic simulation data management and visualization. Transp. Res. Rec. **2676**(1), 274–292 (2022)
29. Zhang, H.S., Zhang, Y., Li, Z.H., Hu, D.C.: Spatial-temporal traffic data analysis based on global data management using MAS. IEEE Trans. Intell. Transp. Syst. **5**(4), 267–275 (2004)

Optimization, Smart Industry, and Smart Public Services

Harnessing Computer Science to Drive Sustainable Supply Chains Facing Resilience Organizational Complexity

Pablo Guerrero-Sánchez[1](✉) , Belem Hernández-Jaimes[1] ,
José Guerrero-Grajeda[3] , Víctor Pacheco-Valencia[2] ,
Rosa Álvarez-González[4] , and Felipe Bonilla-Sánchez[1]

[1] Faculty of Accounting, Administration and Informatics, Autonomous University
of the State of Morelos, Cuernavaca, Morelos, Mexico
pablodbk@gmail.com, belem.hernandezjai@uaem.edu.mx, fbonilla@uaem.mx
[2] Science Research Center, Autonomous University of the State of Morelos,
Cuernavaca, Morelos, Mexico
[3] Science Faculty, National Autonomous University of Mexico, Mexico City, Mexico
grajeda@ciencias.unam.mx
[4] Mathematical and Computational Modeling, National Autonomous University
of Mexico, Mexico City, Mexico
rosa.alvarez@uacm.edu.mx

Abstract. In an era of increasing complexity, where sustainability has become a pressing global concern, the role of computer science in supply chain in managing has never been crucial. With limited resources, growing populations, and environmental degradation, businesses and industries are compelled to adopt sustainable practices. Fortunately, advancements in computer science offer innovative solutions to address the complexities of supply chains, enabling companies to achieve sustainability goals while minimizing environmental impact and maximizing efficiency. This article explores the intersection of sustainability, computer science, supply chains, and complexity, highlighting the transformative potential of this multidisciplinary approach. Modern supply chains face numerous sustainability challenges, including resource depletion, greenhouse gas emissions, waste generation [1], and social issues such as labor rights [28]. The complexity of global supply networks exacerbates these challenges, as companies must track and manage a multitude of interconnected processes, stakeholders [23], and geographic locations. Moreover, the need for timely and accurate data, efficient decision-making, and effective risk management further amplifies the difficulty of achieving sustainable supply chains. The objective of this article is to lay the foundations for the construction of a heuristic optimization model that will be developed from the elements raised. The methodology involves the construction of a heuristic optimization model, exploring complex dynamic elements with a simple example of Monte Carlo simulation, with the objective of analyzing processes.

Keywords: Optimization · Complexity · Supply chains · Computer modeling

S. Nesmachnow and L. Hernández Callejo (Eds.): ICSC-Cities 2023, CCIS 1938, pp. 63–76, 2024.
https://doi.org/10.1007/978-3-031-52517-9_5

1   Introduction

Supply chain resilience is the operational capacity to not only restore, but also strengthen an interrupted supply network, making it more robust than its previous state [4]. This resilience develops as companies prove their ability to resist, adapt, and recover from disruptions, all while ensuring the fulfillment of customer demands and maintaining the performance of the supply chain to achieve sustainability goals [11].

The COVID-19 pandemic has demonstrated the intricate interconnections of supply, demand, and logistics infrastructure in our modern world [22]. It is, therefore, essential to examine the strategies employed across various industries to counteract the consequences of such global crises.

Supply chains are intricate networks [17] that encompass various interconnected processes with stock and forex [25], stakeholders [14], and dependencies, making them inherently complex systems. The complexity of supply chains arises from a multitude of factors, including global sourcing [27], diverse product portfolios [19], fluctuating demand (involving multiple suppliers, manufacturers, and uncertainties in customer demand), regulatory requirements [13], and sustainability considerations [16]. Understanding and managing this complexity is crucial for businesses aiming to optimize their operations, ensure customer satisfaction, and achieve sustainability goals.

The rest of the survey is organized as follows. In Sect. 2, we explore the concept of complexity within the supply chain and highlight the challenges, strategies, and opportunities that it presents. In Sect. 3, we propose a model of an open supply chain system, where we describe a simplified example of supply chain optimization (Sect. 3.1) and present the Monte Carlo simulation used to model a port system (Sect. 3.2). In Sect. 4, we provide general conclusions about the complexity of the supply chain and the challenges and strategies that must be addressed in future work.

2   Navigating Supply Chain Complexity, Challenges and Strategies

This section establishes the elements and variables of the complexity of the supply chain, influenced by industry 4.0, which is interconnected and influenced by technologies that benefit or have the capacity to enhance its operation and analysis, as well as decision making and that operate under environments of uncertainty and variability that affect the entire system as a whole, both in the data and its flow of information and transparency, as well as in costs and procedures. Challenges are identified such as bottlenecks, inefficiencies and vulnerabilities, coordination and collaboration; for risk mitigation and structuring of full contingents, within approaches of thinking systems, advanced technologies, and the optimization of their processes, for the resilience of the system as a whole in an integrated way in a circular economy.

Fig. 1. A supply chain Source: [9]

Supply chains are intricate networks involving numerous entities [8], such as suppliers, manufacturers, distributors, retailers, and customers, each with their own objectives, constraints, and interactions (see the Fig. 1). The actions of one entity can have ripple effects throughout the entire network, creating a complex web of dependencies. This interconnectedness within supply chains is a key factor in their complexity. These networks are further influenced by various actors in the Industry 4.0 era, which encompasses technologies for knowledge-sharing, suppliers, customers, and principles like the upstream flow of knowledge, strategic positioning, application-relatedness, and cyber-physical systems. Notably, technologies such as the Internet of Things, cloud computing, big data, and front-end technologies for smart working, manufacturing, and smart products play a pivotal role in synchronizing inter-organizational processes, managing this complexity effectively.

These networks often face various uncertainties and Variability [6], including unpredictable fluctuations in demand, unforeseen supplier disruptions, unexpected transportation delays, and regulatory changes that can send ripples through the entire system. This variability poses a significant challenge for businesses attempting to anticipate and plan for future scenarios effectively. In essence, the combination of uncertainty and variability within supply chains creates a formidable challenge that necessitates careful management and strategic approaches.

Costs, data, and procedures, as well as methodologies used by construction and engineering companies for their contingency factor components, are typically small, ranging from 2% to 5%. This indicates that these companies allocate a relatively modest portion of their resources to contingencies in most cases. However, the dynamics change when new technologies are introduced into the equation. In such scenarios, the contingent factors can significantly escalate, reaching as high as 50% to 100%. To manage these heightened contingencies effectively, construction and engineering companies turn to computer programs and advanced techniques for financial risk analysis and cost estimation, ensuring that the financial implications of these new technologies are thoroughly understood and accounted for.

Information flow within supply chains often faces fragmentation and incompleteness, resulting in information asymmetry among different stakeholders [20]. This fragmentation means that information is not consistently or comprehensively shared across the supply chain. As a consequence, stakeholders may experience varying levels of access to critical information, creating disparities in knowledge and understanding. The lack of transparency due to these challenges can act as a barrier, hindering effective decision-making, efficient coordination, and seamless collaboration. Enhancing transparency and information sharing becomes essential for mitigating these complexities and promoting effective communication and decision-making among all supply chain participants.

The nature of supply chains presents a challenge when it comes to achieving complete visibility and comprehensive understanding of the entire network [12]. This complexity can result in difficulties in pinpointing bottlenecks, inefficiencies, and vulnerabilities within the supply chain, all of which can impede effective decision-making and risk management. In recognition of these challenges, Wei and Wang [26] have proposed four main visibility processes that offer enterprises the means to reorganize their supply chains, aligning them with both internal requirements and external demands. By embracing these processes, companies can enhance their ability to navigate the intricacies of supply chains, optimize their operations, and make well-informed decisions to manage risks effectively.

Coordinating activities and fostering collaboration [18] among multiple stakeholders scattered across diverse geographies, cultures, and organizational structures within supply chains is a complex endeavor. Achieving alignment, synchronizing processes, and sharing information in a timely and efficient manner are pivotal for successful supply chain management. Robust communication channels and collaborative frameworks play a crucial role in addressing these challenges and ensuring that stakeholders can work in harmony. These mechanisms are essential for bridging the geographical, cultural, and structural gaps, enabling efficient communication and the synchronization of processes, ultimately enhancing the supply chain's performance and adaptability to the complexities of today's global landscape.

The complexity of supply chains introduces a spectrum of risks that span from potential supply disruptions to quality issues, regulatory non-compliance, and environmental impacts [3]. To safeguard the operational resilience and sustainability of supply chains, a proactive approach is essential. This approach entails the early identification of these risks, followed by comprehensive assessments to understand their potential impact. The subsequent step involves the development of contingency plans designed to effectively manage and mitigate these risks. By embracing this proactive risk management strategy, supply chain stakeholders can navigate the intricate challenges posed by complexity, ensuring that their operations remain resilient and sustainable, even in the face of multifaceted risks.

Embracing a systems thinking approach [24] is paramount for organizations seeking to gain a deeper understanding of the interconnections and dynamics within the supply chain. This approach involves viewing the entire network as a complex system, which in turn enables companies to identify critical leverage points. These points are strategic areas within the supply chain where making changes or interventions can yield substantial improvements in performance. Moreover, adopting a systems thinking perspective, allows organizations to uncover unintended consequences and feedback loops that can have a profound impact on the overall functioning of the supply chain. In essence, this approach promotes a holistic understanding of the supply chain's intricacies, facilitating more informed decision-making and strategic adjustments to optimize performance.

Advanced technologies, including artificial intelligence, big data analytics, and cloud computing, are instrumental in addressing the challenges of supply chain complexity [7]. These tools provide valuable opportunities to streamline and optimize supply chain operations. They excel in aggregating and analyzing vast amounts of data, facilitating real-time decision-making, and enhancing the overall efficiency of processes. Furthermore, these technologies foster collaboration among supply chain stakeholders, bridging geographical distances and organizational boundaries. In essence, they empower organizations to harness the full potential of data and technology, resulting in more agile and responsive supply chain management.

Integrating resilience into the supply chain is of paramount importance for effectively managing complexity [2]. This strategic approach involves adopting measures to ensure that the supply chain can withstand and recover from disruptions and challenges. Key strategies for enhancing resilience include diversifying sourcing, which entails having multiple suppliers or sources for critical materials, establishing backup plans to handle unforeseen disruptions, and fostering flexibility in manufacturing and distribution processes. By implementing these strategies, companies position themselves to better adapt to unexpected disruptions, maintain operational continuity, and navigate the complexities of the supply chain with greater agility and preparedness.

Recognizing the interconnectedness of social, economic, and environmental dimensions within the supply chain, integrating sustainability considerations into supply chain management becomes a vital strategy [21]. This approach acknowledges that actions in one dimension can have far-reaching effects on the entire system. By embracing sustainable practices, such as responsible sourcing, energy-efficient operations, and waste reduction, companies can effectively mitigate risks associated with supply chain complexity. Furthermore these sustainability initiatives have the potential to enhance the company's reputation, both among consumers and stakeholders, by demonstrating a commitment to responsible and ethical business practices. In the long run, the integration of sustainability practices creates enduring value, not only for the organization but also for the broader social and environmental context in which it operates.

In today's supply chain landscape, a significant transformation is underway. Products are no longer relegated to being discarded after their initial use; instead, forward-thinking companies have embraced a circular approach. For instance, they reintegrate used products into their supply chain, transforming what was once waste into a valuable resource. This reverse flow process (as depicted in Fig. 2) originates with the customers and seamlessly loops back to the production plants. Here the raw materials extracted from these returned products find a second life, serving as inputs for the creation of entirely new products. The result is twofold: companies reap the benefits of cost savings in their production processes while simultaneously reducing contamination and minimizing their environmental footprint [15].

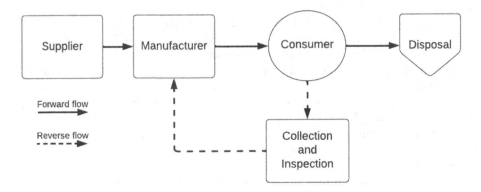

Fig. 2. An example of a Closed Loop Supply Chain. Source: Caramia, M., & Pizzari [5]

Supply chain complexity presents significant challenges, but it also offers opportunities for innovation, efficiency, and sustainability. Embracing complexity as an inherent aspect of modern supply chains allows organizations to adopt holistic approaches, leverage technology, foster collaboration, and build resilience. By understanding the interconnected nature of supply chains and implementing strategies that address complexity, businesses can navigate uncertainties, optimize performance.

The elements that cause changes in the system in a complex and global way involve both contingencies, such as covid, war and the interconnectivity of supply chains and climate change, but at the same time, elements of uncertainty, such as the lack of complete knowledge for decisions on the change in interest rates.

3   Modeling

A model represents the essential elements of a system to describe its specific functioning in relation to the elements that compose it. In this context, we propose a model of an open supply chain system that involves different products, components, suppliers, routes and customers. By identifying these elements, we proposed an algorithm approach to address the challenges of implementing them in the real world. Additionally, we present a pseudocode that demonstrates the feasibility of optimizing supply chain simulations with these variables. Furthermore, we have dedicated a section of the system to the processes of loading and unloading at a port using Monte Carlo simulation. This is facilitated through another pseudocode, enabling us to analyze port capacity and evaluate potential adaptation needs.

Modeling the complexity of a supply chain can be a difficult task due to the various factors and variables involved. Here is a simplified mathematical formula that represents the complexity of a supply chain:

$$\text{Complexity} = \frac{D \times V}{R \times C} \tag{1}$$

where:

D: Number of distinct products or components in the supply chain
V: Number of different suppliers or vendors involved in the supply chain
R: Number of different routes or paths through which the products flow in the supply chain
C: Number of different customers or end-users of the products

Equation 1 assumes that each distinct product/component follows a single route and is supplied by a single vendor. However, real-world supply chains can exhibit greater complexity, often involving multiple routes, vendors, and customers. This formula provides a simplified representation of this complexity by considering the number of distinct elements involved and the interactions between them, and its practical application may vary depending on specific supply chain characteristics and requirements. Each product also has to reach these points of sale with entry restrictions by suppliers, routes and customers.

3.1   Algorithm Approach and Real-World Challenges

Optimizing a supply chain is a complex task that demands a comprehensive understanding of the specific system and its constraints. In this subsection, we describes a simplified example of a supply chain optimization, a heuristic algorithm designed to determine transportation routes for a wide range of products, facilitating their journey from suppliers' facilities to their ultimate destinations.

The algorithm's primary task is to construct or identify a transportation route for each type of product, which may include items such as oil, electronics, perishable goods (such as food), automobiles, heavy machinery, clothing, and more. These routes facilitate the movement of products from supplier facilities to the customers' destinations.

A feasible solution must address a variety of constraints associated with both supply and demand. It must guarantee that the supply capacity of each supplier is not exceeded, that the quantity of products demanded by each customer is satisfied and that the capacity of the vehicles that transport the products is not exceeded. Additionally, the algorithm must take into account other critical factors, including sustainability, environmental contingencies, and efficient resource utilization.

The optimization algorithm's objective function is to find a feasible solution that minimizes the costs incurred during the transportation process. This encompasses expenses related to the use of various vehicles, such as trains, ships, planes, and trailers, as well as taxes applicable at each departure and entry port within different regions. It also must considers parameters like travel time, distance traveled, and mitigating potential losses associated with distribution.

Algorithm 1: $SUPPLY\_CHAIN\_OPTIMIZATION(P, S, C, I)$

   // INPUT: Sets of products P, suppliers S, customers C and itineraries I.

1 $h := 0$
2 $S_h :=$ CONSTRUCT_AN_INITIAL_FEASIBLE_SOLUTION(P, S, C, I)
3 **while** S_h *can be improved* **do**
4     $h := h + 1$
5     $S_h :=$ IMPROVE_SOLUTION(S_{h-1})
6 **return** S_h

Algorithm 1 takes as input the sets of products P, suppliers of the products S, customers who demand the products C, as well as the current maritime or railway route itineraries and other relevant details essential for cargo travel planning, cost and tracking I. In the initial iteration, when $h = 0$, the algorithm constructs the initial feasible solution S_0. At each subsequent iteration $h > 0$, the solution S_{h-1} is refined through a heuristic or metaheuristic algorithm. This iterative process continues until no further improvements are possible.

In practical settings, supply chain optimization encompasses a multitude of additional complexities, including logistical challenges, lead times, inventory management (including just-in-time concerns), geopolitical factors such as conflicts or wars, climate change impacts, human factors, uncertainties, variabilities, contingencies, and other complexities arising from a high number of elements involved.

Furthermore, successful supply chain optimization must also considers procedures, standardization, technological solutions, effective decision-making, information asymmetry, the need for collaboration and data sharing, risk management, resilience, flexibility, integration of various components, political and regulatory influences, and the necessity of utilizing advanced techniques and algorithms like big data analytics, machine learning, simulations, network analysis, predictive analysis using time series data, and real-time monitoring.

3.2 Monte Carlo Simulation of Port System

In this subsection, we describe the Monte Carlo simulation used to model a port system in the Algorithm 2, as proposed in [10]. This simulation primarily focuses on the arrival and unloading of ships within a port, taking into account various critical conditions. These conditions include restrictions such as the inability to unload more than one ship simultaneously, the arrival of 100 boats, and the generation of random arrival times between 15 and 145 min, as well as random unloading times between 35 and 75 min.

Let the following variables and functions, used in Algorithm 2, be described as follows:

- n: the number of ships considered
- $b_j \in B$: minutes between the arrival of the ship j and $j-1$
- $u_j \in U$: time required to unload the ship j (minutes)
- $a_j \in A$: time when the ship j arrives
- $s_j \in S$: time at which the unloading of the ship j begins
- $h_j \in H$: total time spent in the port of the ship j (minutes)
- $w_j \in W$: time the ship j waits, from the time it arrives at the port (minutes) until it starts unloading (minutes)
- $f_j \in F$: time in which the unloading of the ship j is finished
- $I_j \in I$: idle time between the ship j and $j-1$
- RANDOM(p, q): provides a value that falls between the range defined by p and q
- SUM($\overrightarrow{X}$): provides the sum of the values within vector $\overrightarrow{X}$
- max $\overrightarrow{X}$: provides the maximum value from vector $\overrightarrow{X}$

The Algorithm 2 initializes the vectors $\overrightarrow{B}$ and $\overrightarrow{U}$ with $n = 100$ random numbers that are not integers, drawn from a continuous uniform distribution. These numbers represent the minutes between the arrival of ship j and $j-1$, as well as the time required to unload ship j (in minutes), for $j = 1 \cdots, n$. The values in these vectors fall within the range of 10 to 120 for $\overrightarrow{B}$ and 35 to 75 for $\overrightarrow{U}$.

The time elapsed from time zero to the arrival of the first ship is equal to b_1, and time required to unload this ship is u_1.

Therefore, for the first ship:

- Arrival time, a_1, is b_1.
- Waiting time to be served, w_1, is 0.
- Port idle time, i_1, is a_1.
- Discharge start time, s_1, is b_1.
- Time at which the unloading ends, f_1, is $a_1 + u_1$.
- Total time spent at the port, h_1, is u_1.

Algorithm 2: $SIMULATION\_OF\_A\_PORT\_SYSTEM(n)$

---

1 $\vec{B} := (\ )$ // Between
2 $\vec{U} := (\ )$ // Unload
3 **for** $j = 1$ **to** n **do**
4 $\quad\vert\quad \vec{B} := \vec{B} \cup \mathrm{RANDOM}(10, 120)$
5 $\quad\lfloor\quad \vec{U} := \vec{U} \cup \mathrm{RANDOM}(35, 75)$

6 $\vec{A} := (b_1)$ // Arrive
7 $\vec{W} := (0)$ // Wait
8 $\vec{I} := (a_1)$ // Idle
9 $\vec{S} := (b_1)$ // Start
10 $\vec{F} := (a_1 + u_1)$ // Finish
11 $\vec{H} := (u_1)$ // Harbor
12 **for** $j = 2$ **to** n **do**
13 $\quad\vert\quad \vec{A} := \vec{A} \cup (a_{j-1} + b_j)$
14 $\quad\vert\quad t_j := a_j - f_{j-1}$
15 $\quad\vert\quad$ **if** $t_j \geq 0$ **then**
16 $\quad\vert\quad\vert\quad \vec{W} := \vec{W} \cup (0)$
17 $\quad\vert\quad\lfloor\quad \vec{I} := \vec{I} \cup (t_j)$
18 $\quad\vert\quad$ **else**
19 $\quad\vert\quad\vert\quad \vec{W} := \vec{W} \cup (-t_j)$
20 $\quad\vert\quad\lfloor\quad \vec{I} := \vec{I} \cup (0)$
21 $\quad\vert\quad \vec{S} := \vec{S} \cup (a_j + w_j)$
22 $\quad\vert\quad \vec{F} := \vec{F} \cup (s_j + u_j)$
23 $\quad\lfloor\quad \vec{H} := \vec{H} \cup (w_j + u_j)$
24 PRINT $\left(\text{“Average time in port} =", \frac{\mathrm{SUM}(\vec{H})}{n}\right)$
25 PRINT $\left(\text{“Maximum time in port} =", \max\{\vec{U} + \vec{W}\}\right)$
26 PRINT $\left(\text{“Average waiting time} =", \frac{\mathrm{SUM}(\vec{W})}{n}\right)$
27 PRINT $\left(\text{“Maximum waiting time} =", \max \vec{W}\right)$
28 PRINT $\left(\text{“Idle percentage} =", \frac{\mathrm{SUM}(\vec{I})}{f_n}\right)$

For the ships $j = 2$ to n:

- Arrival time of ship j, a_j, is $a_{j-1} + b_j$ (the arrival time of ship $j - 1$ plus the time between the arrivals of ships j and $j - 1$).
- Waiting time to be served, w_j, is 0 if $a_j - f_{j-1} \geq 0$, and $-a_j + f_{j-1}$ otherwise.
- Port idle time, i_j, is $a_j - f_{j-1}$ if $a_j - f_{j-1} \geq 0$, and 0 otherwise.
- Discharge start time, s_j, is $a_j + w_j$ (the arrival time of the ship j plus the time it took to be served).

- Time at which the unloading ends, f_j, is $s_1 + u_1$ (time at which ship j began to be unloaded plus the time of its unloading).
- Total time spent at the port, h_j, is $w_j + u_1$ (elapsed ship waiting time j plus unloading time).

After the n ships have been attended, the "Average time in port", "Maximum time in port", "Average waiting time", "Maximum waiting time" and "Idle percentage" are displayed.

Table 1. Results of a run of the program developed in Matlab.

Simulation	Average time port (from arrival to discharge)	Maximum time in port	Average waiting time (from arrival until download starts)	Maximum waiting time	% Time that port facilities are not being used
1	90.13	202.58	34.54	157.18	0.13
2	84.80	215.41	28.63	171.81	0.13
3	81.43	176.69	26.71	135.14	0.15
4	83.73	204.85	29.79	137.73	0.16
5	83.73	217.60	31.18	143.53	0.14
6	83.73	241.91	38.84	174.97	0.16

Table 1 shows the outcomes of six runs produced by the Algorithm 2 which was implemented by the authors in Matlab. It is essential to highlight that the data used for simulations is generated randomly, resulting in unique values each time the program is executed. The purpose of these simulations is to offer a straightforward approach for examining a segment of the supply chain, specifically the process involving the arrival and unloading of products at a port. This analysis can be particularly valuable to port management companies, aiding them in making informed decisions about the expansion of their infrastructure.

4   Conclusions and Future Work

For the model to be realistic, it is necessary to understand the complex dynamics between suppliers, manufacturers, distributors, retailers and costumers, each of whom intervenes with their objectives, time constraints and interactions. The number of elements linked to the complex system establishes restrictions that link the need to obtain more effective forms of product distribution to achieve optimal levels of resource sustainability, reduce scarcity to have a positive economic and social effect, through the use of information technology.

The system is complex and factors intervene that depend on the sensitivity to the conditions of the system and its interconnection; for example geopolitical events, wars, disruption in supply chains, and sustainability elements related to climate change, and government policies that affect the system as a whole. This number of elements is difficult to place in a mathematical model due to the number of variables that are dynamic and therefore could be considered as a complete non-polynomial, non-linear regression model.

Creating a comprehensive supply chain optimization solution demands a profound understanding of the specific system in question and often requires the development of advanced techniques and algorithms tailored to the unique challenges presented. These advanced solutions may become a focus in later stages of research and development.

In a more in-depth review, an attempt will be made to review elements to strengthen the heuristic model and analysis of the graphs will be carried out. For future research, specific examples of particular products will be carried out for a more qualitative analysis of the elements involved in the complexity of the supply chain as well as internal factors, the chain itself and external factors.

Funding Information. Supported by organization Faculty of Accounting, Administration & Informatics.

References

1. de Barros Martins, M.A., et al.: Evaluating the energy consumption and greenhouse gas emissions from managing municipal, construction, and demolition solid waste. Cleaner Waste Syst. **4**, 100070 (2023). https://doi.org/10.1016/j.clwas.2022.100070
2. Belhadi, A., Kamble, S.S., Venkatesh, M., Jabbour, C.J.C., Benkhati, I.: Building supply chain resilience and efficiency through additive manufacturing: an ambidextrous perspective on the dynamic capability view. Int. J. Prod. Econ. **249**, 108516 (2022). https://doi.org/10.1016/j.ijpe.2022.108516
3. Bø, E., Hovi, I.B., Pinchasik, D.R.: Covid-19 disruptions and Norwegian food and pharmaceutical supply chains: insights into supply chain risk management, resilience, and reliability. Sustain. Futur. **5**, 100102 (2023). https://doi.org/10.1016/j.sftr.2022.100102
4. Brusset, X., Teller, C.: Supply chain capabilities, risks, and resilience. Int. J. Prod. Econ. **184**, 59–68 (2017). https://doi.org/10.1016/j.ijpe.2016.09.008
5. Caramia, M., Pizzari, E.: A bi-objective cap-and-trade model for minimising environmental impact in closed-loop supply chains. Supply Chain Anal. **3**, 100020 (2023). https://doi.org/10.1016/j.sca.2023.100020
6. De Lima, F.A., Seuring, S.: A Delphi study examining risk and uncertainty management in circular supply chains. Int. J. Prod. Econ. **258**, 108810 (2023). https://doi.org/10.1016/j.ijpe.2023.108810
7. Dubey, R., Bryde, D.J., Dwivedi, Y.K., Graham, G., Foropon, C.: Impact of artificial intelligence-driven big data analytics culture on agility and resilience in humanitarian supply chain: a practice-based view. Int. J. Prod. Econ. **250**, 108618 (2022). https://doi.org/10.1016/j.ijpe.2022.108618
8. Eslami, M.H., Achtenhagen, L., Bertsch, C.T., Lehmann, A.: Knowledge-sharing across supply chain actors in adopting industry 4.0 technologies: an exploratory case study within the automotive industry. Technol. Forecast. Soc. Change **186**, 122118 (2023). https://doi.org/10.1016/j.techfore.2022.122118

9. Faena, L.: Cadena de suministro, 20 November 2020. https://www.trafimar.com. mx/blog/8-claves-para-mejorar-la-cadena-de-suministro-con-logistica. Accessed 7 Nov 2023

10. Giordano, F.R., Fox, W.P., Horton, S.B.: A First Course in Mathematical Modeling. Cengage Learning (2013)

11. Hosseini, S., Ivanov, D., Dolgui, A.: Review of quantitative methods for supply chain resilience analysis. Transp. Res. Part E Logist. Transp. Rev. **125**, 285–307 (2019). https://doi.org/10.1016/j.tre.2019.03.001

12. Javaid, M., Haleem, A.: Digital twin applications toward industry 4.0: a review. Cogn. Robot. **3**, 71–92 (2023). https://doi.org/10.1016/j.cogr.2023.04.003

13. Kannan, D., Solanki, R., Kaul, A., Jha, P.: Barrier analysis for carbon regulatory environmental policies implementation in manufacturing supply chains to achieve zero carbon. J. Clean. Prod. **358**, 131910 (2022). https://doi.org/10.1016/j.jclepro. 2022.131910

14. Kovalchuk, M., Gabrielsson, M., Rollins, M.: Industrial BRAND-personality formation in a B2B stakeholder network: a service-dominant logic approach. Ind. Mark. Manage. **114**, 313–330 (2023). https://doi.org/10.1016/j.indmarman.2023.05.006

15. Liu, W., et al.: Optimal pricing for a multi-echelon closed loop supply chain with different power structures and product dual differences. J. Clean. Prod. **257**, 120281 (2020). https://doi.org/10.1016/j.jclepro.2020.120281

16. Meena, P.L., Kumar, G., Ramkumar, M.: Supply chain sustainability in emerging economy: a negative relationship conditions' perspective. Int. J. Prod. Econ. **261**, 108865 (2023). https://doi.org/10.1016/j.ijpe.2023.108865

17. Mu, D., Ren, H., Wang, C., Yue, X., Du, J., Ghadimi, P.: Structural characteristics and disruption ripple effect in a meso-level electric vehicle lithium-ion battery supply chain network. Resour. Policy **80**, 103225 (2023). https://doi.org/10.1016/ j.resourpol.2022.103225

18. Nick, F.C., Sänger, N., van der Heijden, S., Sandholz, S.: Collaboration is key: exploring the 2021 flood response for critical infrastructures in Germany. Int. J. Disaster Risk Reduct. **91**, 103710 (2023). https://doi.org/10.1016/j.ijdrr.2023.103710

19. Saberi, S., Liu, Z., Besik, D.: Strategic decision for capacity portfolio in supply chain network considering emission permit price and demand uncertainty. J. Clean. Prod. **374**, 133797 (2022). https://doi.org/10.1016/j.jclepro.2022.133797

20. Sarkar, B., Guchhait, R.: Ramification of information asymmetry on a green supply chain management with the cap-trade, service, and vendor-managed inventory strategies. Electron. Commer. Res. Appl. **60**, 101274 (2023). https://doi.org/10. 1016/j.elerap.2023.101274

21. Schlüter, L., et al.: Sustainable business model innovation: design guidelines for integrating systems thinking principles in tools for early-stage sustainability assessment. J. Clean. Prod. **387**, 135776 (2023). https://doi.org/10.1016/j.jclepro.2022. 135776

22. Shen, Z.M., Sun, Y.: Strengthening supply chain resilience during COVID-19: a case study of JD.com. J. Oper. Manage. **69**(3), 359–383 (2023). https://doi.org/ 10.1002/joom.1161

23. Tiwari, S., Sharma, P., Choi, T.M., Lim, A.: Blockchain and third-party logistics for global supply chain operations: stakeholders' perspectives and decision roadmap. Transp. Res. Part E Logist. Transp. Rev. **170**, 103012 (2023). https://doi.org/10. 1016/j.tre.2022.103012

24. Tsolakis, N., Zissis, D., Tjahjono, B.: Scrutinising the interplay between governance and resilience in supply chain management: a systems thinking framework. Eur. Manag. J. **41**, 164–180 (2021). https://doi.org/10.1016/j.emj.2021.11.001

25. Wang, G.J., Wan, L., Feng, Y., Xie, C., Uddin, G.S., Zhu, Y.: Interconnected multilayer networks: quantifying connectedness among global stock and foreign exchange markets. Int. Rev. Financ. Anal. **86**, 102518 (2023). https://doi.org/10.1016/j.irfa.2023.102518

26. Wei, H.L., Wang, E.T.: The strategic value of supply chain visibility: increasing the ability to reconfigure. Eur. J. Inf. Syst. **19**(2), 238–249 (2010). https://doi.org/10.1057/ejis.2010.10

27. Wieland, A., Bals, L., Mol, M.J., Handfield, R.B.: Overcoming blind spots in global sourcing research: exploiting the cross-sections between supply chain management and international business. J. Int. Manag. **26**(1), 100709 (2020). https://doi.org/10.1016/j.intman.2019.100709

28. Williams, C., Sparks, J.L.D.: Fishery improvement projects: a voluntary, corporate "tool" not fit for the purpose of mitigating labour abuses and guaranteeing labour rights for workers. Mar. Policy **147**, 105340 (2023). https://doi.org/10.1016/j.marpol.2022.105340

Optimizing the Rework Area in an Automotive Parts Supplier Company by Digital Tools: A Foundation for Smart Industry Transformation

Jesús del Carmen Peralta-Abarca[1(✉)] , Pedro Moreno-Bernal[2] ,
Beatriz Martínez-Bahena[1] , Juana Enríquez-Urbano[1] ,
and Felipe Bonilla-Sánchez[2]

[1] Facultad de Ciencias Químicas e Ingeniería, Universidad Autónoma del Estado
de Morelos, Cuernavaca, Mexico
{carmen.peralta,bmartinezb,juana.enriquez}@uaem.mx
[2] Facultad de Contaduría, Administración e Informática, Universidad Autónoma
del Estado de Morelos, Cuernavaca, Mexico
{pmoreno,fbonilla}@uaem.mx

Abstract. This article introduces the Lean Principles methodology for optimizing a "rework" area in an automotive parts supplier company using digital tools. The main objective is to reduce work-in-process inventory and eliminate waste in production processes. Hence, the improvement process analysis is divided into two phases. The first phase includes a process analysis and waste elimination. The second phase includes developing and implementing a software system for reworked material tracking. The software system allows precise control of materials in rework and collects valuable data in real time. Results indicate that the implementation of the proposed improvements and the software has positively impacted the efficiency and productivity of the "rework" area. Work-in-process inventory has been reduced by 20%, and the number of defective parts has been reduced by 15%. The improvements proposed provide the basis for creating a smart industry, as they help to improve efficiency, productivity, and quality using emerging digital technologies.

Keywords: optimization · automotive industry · smart industry

1 Introduction

The growing demand for high-quality products and services open up many opportunities for businesses and organizations. This demand drives technology adoption as a catalyst for innovation and process optimization across all areas, from scheduling to onboarding new employees. Simultaneously, drives technology fosters the spread of disruptive ideas, potentially revolutionizing a company from

S. Nesmachnow and L. Hernández Callejo (Eds.): ICSC-Cities 2023, CCIS 1938, pp. 77–91, 2024.
https://doi.org/10.1007/978-3-031-52517-9_6

within. A prominent example is the digitization of processes and the incorporation of virtuality that now serve as reliable markers to distinguish between a conventional and a smart organization.

In the context of supply chain optimization in an automotive component's supplier, the proposal to introduce the concept of a "smart industry" emerges [7,13]. The concept involves critical steps towards improving operational efficiency, effectiveness, and waste reduction. The notion of a smart industry involves the strategic application of advanced technologies and the gradual adoption of innovative solutions that boost productivity and informed decision-making. However, the transition to a smart industry is not only based on technology but also emphasizes interdepartmental collaboration and the constant pursuit of improvement.

This work lays the groundwork for future technological implementations like the Internet of Things (IoT) [6,14]. Instead of a sudden transformation, the improvement analysis focuses on the initial steps toward modernizing current processes. The presented phase analysis considers the digitization of records to the integration of analytical tools to gain a more precise overview of workflow and product quality. The data collected in the phase becomes the cornerstone for future decisions on implementing IoT devices. The company can learn and adapt through progressive adoption as it moves towards more advanced automation and optimization.

In this line of work, this article proposes applying a Lean Principles methodology and developing and implementing a software system for optimizing a"rework" area (ReWA) in an automotive parts supplier company. The software system is essential in optimizing rework and workforce guided by the principles of Continuous Improvement and supported by Lean Manufacturing (LM). Results show an achievement of successful and sustainable processes, contributing to the generation of competitive products at the forefront of the industry.

The rest of the article is structured as follows. Section 2 describes related works on optimal management of production processes. Section 3 describes the ReWA optimization problem. The results and discussion of the proposed software system are described in Sect. 4. Finally, Sect. 5 presents the research conclusions and formulates the main lines for future work.

2   Problem Statement

This section describes the ReWA process in an automotive parts supplier company. Also, the section reviews the related works about Lean Principles applied for processes that require considerable time improvements and waste elimination.

2.1   ReWA Problem

Nowadays, industrial companies face the challenge of searching for and implementing new organizational and production techniques that allow them to compete in a global market. The LM model constitutes a consolidated alternative, which is a pillar philosophy in its strategy for the Factory.

Resource optimization by workload balancing in companies, particularly in the automotive industry, is crucial, specifically for the manufacturing of electronic components such as chassis control modules, transmission control modules, Antiblocker-System(ABS)/Electronic-Braking-System(EBS) control modules, among other products. Nearshoring is growing in Mexico, increasing demand for production and services.

Due to the increase in demand and the need to install new production lines for new Electronic Control for Suspension (CAirS) products, it is necessary to optimize labor and work area resources, in addition to reducing the Work in Process Inventory (WIPI), to eliminate waste in the processes. Also, reducing work area spaces helps optimize labor in the areas, helping to reduce WIPI covering the three work shifts for production. This way, it is necessary to analyze opportunity areas to optimize production processes to satisfy clients from Mexico, the United States, and Canada.

2.2 Related Works

Conventional manufacturing companies are facing several challenges today. These challenges include rapid technological evolution, inventory management difficulties, shortened innovation cycles, reduced product life span, demand volatility, price pressure, growing need for product customization, and the ability to maintain competitiveness in a globalized context [8]. As a result, the manufacturing industry is applying diverse LM strategies to improve the efficiency of its processes [2]. In addition, it is adopting smart initiatives and cutting-edge business models as part of its focus on digital transformation [1].

This way, smart industries are experiencing rapid growth and aspire to achieve digitization, automation, and integration of artificial intelligence into their operations. It is essential to consider that smart industries not only impact their development but also act as catalysts or incubators for the progress of other sectors [9].

Research in the smart industry uses Information and Communication Technologies (ICT) and emerging technologies based on Industry 4.0 to provide intelligent process systems that support digital applications for better process management in the industry. Current works propose different methodologies for better and more efficient processes in the context of the smart industry. A review of related works is presented next.

Paredes-Rodríguez et al. [11] evaluated LM tools in the operational risk management of Hass avocado supply chains in the Valle del Cauca, Colombia department. To identify the risks associated with the supply chain, they used the Value Stream Map (VSM). They proposed strategies based on Total Productive Maintenance (TPM), 5 s, Visual Management, and Standardization to mitigate these risks. The results showed that the implementation of these strategies had a positive impact on the results.

García-Alcaraz et al. [4] presented a structural equation modeling (SEM) model that integrated tools from Traditional Lean Manufacturing (LMT) such as Kaizen, Gemba, Andon, visual management, Poka-yoke, TPM, and Jidoka.

As dependent variables, these tools were related to sustainability in its social, economic, and environmental aspects. They applied these tools in the production lines of a maquiladora in Mexico, reducing waste, lowering energy consumption, improving labor relations, and economic and ecological benefits.

Cervantes-Zubirías et al. [16] implemented LM tools to continuously improve the Lean Six Sigma phases. Their focus was on reducing waste and variations in the cyclic counting of rolls of components in the Surface Mount Technology (SMT) production process. Analyzing rolls of different specifications improved economic performance and OEE equipment efficiency.

Bernardes and Legenvre [3] analyzed 11 case studies of the Internet of Things (IoT) in the smart industry, grouped into three categories: process, product, and technologies. All cases illustrate a variety of initiatives in the field of the smart industry.

Tang and Meng [15] presented an innovative data analysis and optimization structure in intelligent industrial engineering. This structure combines theoretical foundation with technological innovation to improve prediction and control in unknown areas, providing companies with a valuable tool.

The application of nanotechnology in the modern textile industry is a trend in the smart industry. Shah et al. [12] explored methods and techniques for functionalizing nanomaterials and integration into textiles, emphasizing aspects such as profitability, comfort, portability, energy efficiency, and environmental sustainability.

The Smart Factory approach proposed in research by the Universität Stuttgart [10] represents a context-sensitive and real-time manufacturing environment capable of managing production disruptions by using decentralized information and communication structures to achieve optimal management of production processes.

The related works identified several proposals showing a growing interest in LM tools. The optimization of the design of industrial processes is part of strategic management toward an optimal productive process. In this sense, the industry aims to improve its operations efficiently and productively by identifying waste in workflows to eliminate them. This work presents an LM methodology and develops and implements a software system for optimizing the ReWA in an automotive parts supplier company. The benefits of the proposed methodology include significant reductions in Work-in-process inventory and the number of defective parts. Next, the implementation of LM tools is described.

3   Lean Manufacturing for ReWA

This section describes the proposed LM methodology for ReWA optimization and the LM tools used.

3.1   ReWA

The smart industry concept is introduced as an integral part of the strategy to improve efficiency and reduce process waste. The smart industry is based on the integration of technologies to obtain a more complete and real-time view of operations to reduce WIPI and eliminate waste in processes. This way, this work focuses on improving the ReWA, which previously had certain deficiencies that affected production efficiency and inventory control.

The ReWA is responsible for repairing minor quality defects in raw materials or sub-assemblies as long as these defects do not affect the quality or functioning of the final product. The log that records the entry and exit of material in the area indicates that, at present, the rate of material that requires "rework" and is approved weekly is 41%. This quantity represents a high risk that the material will become waste due to the excessive time needed to be reworked. This can lead to products being declared "non-conforming" because the material could not be reworked in the required time and returned to the production line.

In the ReWA, seven workers initially rotate to cover the three work shifts. The space occupied by this area is $60\,\text{m}^2$. With the demand increase for CAirS products, it is essential to optimize resources. The aim is to reduce WIPI to eliminate process waste. This way, optimizing labor allocation and achieving a 20% decrease in WIPI is necessary, ensuring coverage of the three production shifts.

3.2 Current Situation

Process Mapping. LM tools are used to analyze the current situation to examine in detail the processes, activities, and flows of material and information. Through the evaluation, it was possible to identify processes that need to be optimized to achieve efficiency. The operators and specialists from the area were actively involved in the analysis, integrating them into Lean thinking and obtaining accurate information on current and actual situations of their daily activities. The purpose is to use knowledge as a resource to be more competitive and get the most out of the workers' experiences. In this sense, the analysis documents the process of continuous and systematic learning and how workers adapted to the constant changes. The interaction with the company's personnel workers allowed the study to obtain a valuable and well-founded perspective to identify opportunities for improvement. Figure 1 shows a flow diagram that summarizes the mapping, where the activities that add value to the process are marked with a dotted line.

Workload Analysis (Heijunka). Heijunka is based on eliminating disparities in the workload through uninterrupted and efficient production. The goal is to align the levels and sequences of products according to customer demand. This adaptation is essential to respond to changes in market demand and available resources, a crucial feature of a smart industry. Thus, based on the standard work sequence sheet of the seven operators, a detailed analysis was performed of the activities during the three shifts, including travel and unique reworks, considering the time required for each activity and its frequency during the shift. The analysis allows obtaining a percentage of occupation for each operator, improving the

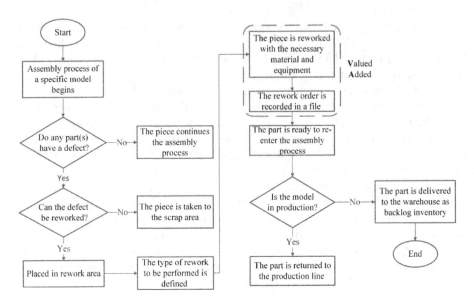

Fig. 1. Activities that generate value for the process

response to the customer with a leveled production. Figure 2 shows the workloads of the operators in the three shifts, showing a notable variation between the first shift and the other two shifts. The average occupation percentage of workers is 62.43%.

	First	Second	Third
Staff	3	2	2
Workload	46.82%	70.23%	70.24%
	Average of the three shifts	62.43%	

Fig. 2. Three-shift workloads

Spaghetti Diagram Analysis. The spaghetti diagram is an LM tool used to analyze and improve the flow of activities within a process, eliminating waste associated with transportation and movement [5]. Essentially, it involves tracing an unbroken line representing the path of people, materials, equipment, or information within a given space. The choice of the spaghetti diagram tool is based on the capacity to provide a detailed overview of the journeys and its contribution to identifying the underlying causes of these movements. Developing a spaghetti diagram creates a visual representation that can be shared and discussed between different teams. After examining the movements of personnel and materials between the production line and the ReWA, it has been identified that the journeys from their work area to the production lines they serve during their respective shifts are long and frequent. The analysis identifies the activities that do not add value (10.2%), those that do add value (62.43%), and those that, although they do not add value, are necessary for the process (29.5%). After examining these activities in detail, the critical problems in the area were identified, such as excessive travel, lack of order and cleanliness, and excess of work materials.

ReWA Workstation Analysis (5S and 5W). During the analysis process, a valuable opportunity was identified to improve efficiency and reduce waste in the area by redistributing work tables and optimizing available resources, including material, space, and activities. For this purpose, a detailed inventory of each work table in the area was carried out. This inventory includes crucial details such as the specific type of rework being performed at each station, the associated workload, the corresponding material inventory, and the number of square feet each table occupies. The 5S philosophy and the 5W method were applied. The main impact was reflected in the elimination of four work tables out of nine, which reduced the space needed from $8.15\,\text{m}^2$ to $3.01\,\text{m}^2$, and with this, the movements of operators were also reduced. The need to address the identified problems comprehensively underlines the need to redesign both the workstations and the overall layout of the area. A redesign approach aims to optimize workflows and maximize the utilization of available resources. The redesign helps reduce wasted time, minimize unnecessary movements, and create a more efficient and effective work environment.

Once the main problems that affect the ReWA production for WIPI and waste have been identified, an improvement analysis was applied through LM tools. LM tools help to develop ideas that can be implemented to increase the value flow through continuous improvement. The next section describes and discusses the results of the improvement analysis using LM for optimizing the ReWA.

4   Results and Discussion

This section describes the results of the LM implementation and the development and implementation of the software system for optimizing the ReWA production, and a specific case study is described.

4.1   Development and Execution Software System

The proposed software system was developed using ASP.NET and C# web forms. It was executed on an Internet Information Services (IIS) in a Windows Server operating system. The database (DB) was implemented on Oracle Server.

4.2 Studied Case

The automotive parts supplier company is located in Morelos, Mexico. The company operates in the automotive industry, specifically manufacturing electronic components such as chassis control modules, transmission control modules, and ABS/EBS control modules. The principal company clients are from Mexico, the United States, and Canada.

The factory has a staff of approximately two thousand workers. This factory is divided into two segments: Chassis and Safety (Tier 2) and Powertrain (Tier 1). The case study is focused on the Chassis and Safety segment. This segment has seven exclusive production lines for ABS/EBS control modules, in addition to support areas such as a Kitting room for electronic components, a dispatch area for mechanical components, a tooling room, a pick area, a ReWA of material in quarantine, "non-conforming" area, failure analysis, and calibration laboratory.

The focus of the study case was on the first of the following three support areas. First, the ReWA aims to repair any minor quality defect in the raw material or subassembly, as long as it does not affect the quality or operation of the product. According to the log of material entry and exit records to the area, the percentage of material reworked and released per week is 41%, representing a high risk of wasted material due to excess time. The time waits must be reworked; simultaneously, it can become "non-compliant". The ReWA has seven workers who rotate to cover the three work shifts, and the space occupied is 60m^2. Second, the "Non-compliant" area carried out personnel records and disposed of the "waste" during manufacturing. The area occupied for this process is 16.37 m^2. Finally, the "Peaks" Area is responsible for registering, controlling, and managing the "semi" or sub-assembly that, for some reason, had to leave its production process, and this remains stored until the production plan to which it belongs is executed again to continue its process. The space occupied by this support area is 15.18 m^2.

4.3 Flow Phase Analysis

After applying the VSM tools, an exhaustive analysis of the activities carried out. Movements, and workstations, opportunities for improvement were discovered in the area. In addition, specific needs and priorities were identified for each process. The analysis concludes that adopting digital solutions is crucial to address many identified opportunities.

The new management approach has been dubbed "Area R" (ArR), referring to the "rework" function. The team that already operates in interest areas continues to lead the space management, capitalizing on their knowledge and experience in the processes. However, the responsibilities and objectives remain the same. The essential proposals for eliminating waste in the implemented process are described next: i) A multidisciplinary team was created. The team comprises members of the ReWA to unite knowledge, experiences, and perspectives. It is important to use knowledge as a resource to make the organization more competitive and adapt better to constant changes. *ii*) a personalized software solution was developed. It permits identifying and reducing activities that do not add value to Non-Value-Added Activities (NVA) processes. The software system interacts with ArR and the production area, giving us a comprehensive value chain view. *iii*) optimization of the design of the ReWA using organization tools, i.e., the 5S tool, the 5W approach, and the application of the spaghetti diagram, were implemented. *iv*) Establishment of standards for activities to create coherence and efficiency. *v*) a balance in workloads was achieved, ensuring an equitable and efficient distribution.

The proposed approach involves creating relational DB to manage the area. The DB allows the elimination and reduction of the activities that do not generate value in the process. As an essential point, the existing databases, the production requirements, and the demands of the areas involved were considered to develop a integral database that uses formats and terminology familiar to the multidisciplinary team.

The integrated approach seeks to optimize operations from an informed and technological perspective, laying the groundwork for future implementations to turn the company into a smart industry. Close collaboration with other departments, especially the software development department, is crucial as it is responsible for the servers and software that host the vital information and traceability of the parts and production processes. Recognizing this importance, the development of the software began with the integration of three essential capture modules: *a*) Quarantine Material Record, *b*)Rework Record and *c*) Model in Line.

Detailed workflow diagrams were developed for the software modules. The diagram reflects the functionality of each module and its interaction with the ReWA and the production line. Figure 3 illustrates the process diagram of the ReWA. The flow diagram represents a defective piece being generated upon entry into the ReWA until it exits for reintegration into the production lines. The integration is contingent upon the condition that the model is in production on one of the lines. The collaboration, integration, and definition of workflows allow the analysis to leverage the potential of technology and interdepartmental collaboration to create a solid and efficient foundation to support an optimized supply chain and more ingenious production processes.

Once the new process flow for the "Future State" has been designed, which implies the integral digitization of this process, the implementation of capture stations is essential. These stations facilitate the interaction between the areas responsible for generating the material, either rework declared as "nonconforming" or delayed material, and the area responsible for its storage and management is the ArR.

4.4   Strategic Positioning of Capture Stations

A location analysis was carried out concerning the plant layout to optimize the efficiency and practicality of the capture stations. The main objective is to minimize travel and material transfers, making it more convenient for users. In

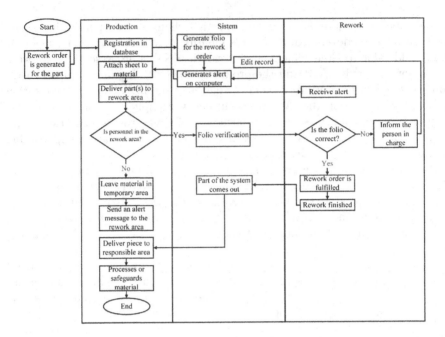

Fig. 3. ReWA process diagram

the end, it is proposed to locate the capture stations near the primary generation areas of the material to be stored. These strategic locations are represented in the Fig. 4, highlighted with the letter "S" inside a yellow circle. In addition, a dotted line is drawn to illustrate where the material route will take to reach the storage and ReWA.

4.5   Improvement Plan Implemented

The improvement plan is implemented, supervised, and validated in this stage. The capture station for production and rework users has been equipped with software system and a scanner to expedite and ensure the precise traceability of the parts that will enter the area. The capture stations have been located in the production area to assign workers the additional task of attending to rework orders issued through the software system.

Section 3.2 highlighted that operators had an uneven workload distribution. Employing the 5S and 5W approaches was possible to reduce and eliminate non-value-added activities. The balance of workloads resulted in savings of 55.6%. As a result, it was decided to assign two operators per shift, and the operator who was not incorporated into the new scheme was transferred to another line of work. Given that their workload is significantly below 85%, it is feasible for them to take on additional tasks administrated by software system.

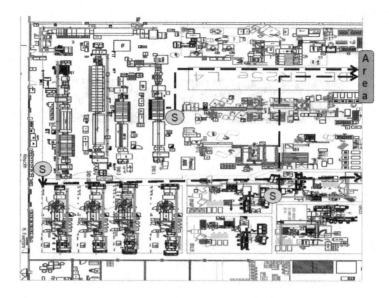

Fig. 4. Capture stations location

4.6 Software System Implementation

The software system implementation played a fundamental role in this project. The improvements in the process flow, the elimination of activities that lack value, the guarantee of material traceability, and the balance of workloads are direct results of this implementation. The software system was placed on the company's intranet, which interacts with the company's traceability system called MES. User guides were developed for capturing and tracking parts that can be downloaded from the software system. The software system was implemented through seven different modules, which allowed for the establishment of a reliable material registration process.

Additionally, a scanner has been implemented at each capture station to automate each part's data collection. The data recording interface for Rework has green highlighted fields automatically filled in when the part is scanned, while the red highlighted fields are mandatory and already contain preloaded information. This way, it has simplified and homogenized the data collection process. A section for remarks, identified by a blue box, has also been added. The interface provides general information (reports and graphs) to facilitate analysis and decision-making. Figure 5 shows the software system interface. Figure 5a presents the interface for the registration of "rework" data. Also, it shows that the fields highlighted with a green box are automatically completed when scanning the part. In contrast, the fields marked in red are mandatory and contain pre-loaded information, simplifying and homogenizing information collection. Likewise, an area was incorporated to add observations, presenting a blue box, which is optional. Figure 5b shows the visual notification issued by the ANDON system, which is intended to inform production staff about the availability of rework material for reintroduction into the production process.

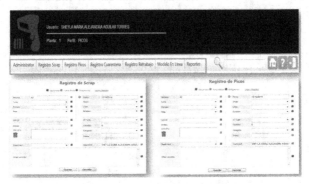

(a) Interface for capture "rework" data

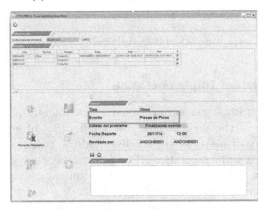

(b) ANDON visual notification

Fig. 5. Software system interfaces

The software system has been developed, tested, and implemented. The personnel responsible for the processes involved have been adequately trained, and the training of the set of plant employees who are users in charge of recording necessary reworks. This training plan aims to ensure that all staff interacting with the system are adequately informed and prepared to use it effectively. The training aims to provide users with the skills and knowledge necessary to carry out registration tasks accurately and in line with established standards. The ultimate goal of this training is to create a base of trained users who can effectively contribute to successfully using the software system, which will foster continuous process improvement, operational efficiency, and proper management of material and reworks in the plant.

4.7   Standardization

During the standardization process, a crucial concern that required immediate attention was the need to inform the production staff that the reworked parts, which matched the processed models, were ready to be integrated into the production line. This problem left the production team in a state of uncertainty, not knowing if the reworked parts could already be integrated into the production line. The incorporation of a notification (ANDON) function in the software system catalog was evaluated. The incorporation of visual aids proved to be a valuable resource in this process. Visual alerts were implemented to reinforce the proposed solution. The ANDON system, widely used for visual and audible notifications for machine breakdowns, scheduled maintenance, and inventory management, was successfully adapted to the software system. As a result, operators in the ReWA can trigger an ANDON notification in situations where reworked parts have not yet been removed from production. The visual notification issued by the ANDON system informs production personnel about the availability of the reworked materials for reintegration into the production process.

The system implementation was insufficient, as there was no mechanism to inform the production planner of the material availability in the reworked stock. It made it difficult to schedule and ship to the customer. Automatic alerts were established via email to expedite the release of accumulated material and contribute to inventory reduction. The alerts work as follows: once the parts are entered into the software, the system obtains the part's creation date from MES. From that point, 60 d are counted, the maximum period for the material to remain in wait. As the 40th day approaches, a yellow alert is sent to the production planner and the person responsible for generating the stored rework. The alert allows the part to be integrated into the production plan, and the process continues for shipment to the customer.

Suppose the material was not released from the software system during the remaining 20 d. In that case, a red alert is activated and sent directly to the material's responsible person and their immediate supervisor via email. This alert indicates that the material has exceeded its time limit and must be transferred to the "Non-compliant" state. The protocol is essential, as time management to avoid backlog and its transformation into "Non-compliant" is one of the crucial indicators and greatest attention in the plant. Implementing visual alerts prevents backlog material from ending in the "non-conforming" category. The process facilitates communication with the line supervisor and master production scheduler whenever parts are available for integration into the production line. In this way, a significant improvement is achieved in the coordination and workflow between both areas, reducing WIPI levels. The reduction in WIPI not only generates efficiency in the process. Also, it is converted into significant savings for the company.

After creating the future state, where the new processes use the software for several already integrated workflows, the workloads for the production team members were analyzed with the capture stations already operational in the production area. The supervisor and the Line Manager collaborate with the

Area of Guard and Administration of Rework Materials to manage the innovative process flow. For this purpose, the Standard Work Sheets corresponding to the Production Supervisor and the Production Line Manager were evaluated, presenting loads of 75.8% and 73.3%, less than 85%. Results concluded that the Production Supervisor and Line Manager could indeed absorb the capture activity and the transportation of the pieces to the ReWA.

5   Conclusions and Future Work

This article presented an LM methodology and the development and implementation of a software system for optimizing the ReWA in an automotive parts supplier company. The proposed Lean methodology combines Lean Manufacturing and Lean Office tools to identify WIPI delays and eliminate waste in production processes. LM methodology employed analysis tools, i.e., standardization mechanism, ANDON, 5S, 5W, spaghetti diagram, VSM, Workload analysis, and software development. The Lean tools helped to understand process failures to improve the ReWA production in an automotive parts supplier company.

The methodology validation focused on evaluating the time-saving of the optimization process in the ReWA. The computed results indicate that the proposed Lean methodology efficiently optimizes rework and workforce guided and supported by the principles of continuous improvement. Also, a dedicated rework materials tracking software was developed. The software system not only allowed more precise control of materials in rework but also provided the opportunity to collect valuable data in real-time. Data collected will be the basis for future informed decisions and continuous improvements in the supply chain and production processes.

Results show a WIPI reduction of 20%, and the number of defective parts has been reduced by 15%. The improvements proposed provide the basis for creating a smart industry.

The main lines for future work are oriented to extend the proposed Lean methodology to apply essential indicators, statistics, and Lean tools for improvement and optimization strategies in diverse value chain areas, e.g., production. Also, the integration of areas known as "Peaks' and "Non-conforming" into the software system must be extended to improve the management and control of surplus parts inventory from the process ("Peaks") and materials that become irrecoverable either due to severe quality defects or their lack of timely integration into the production line ("Non-conforming"). The new integration will effectively control work-in-progress inventory, eventually reducing the quantity of non-conforming materials.

Acknowledgements. This work acknowledges Ing. Sheila Maria Alejandra Aguilar Torres of the Facultad de Ciencias Químicas e Ingeniería of Universidad Autónoma del Estado de Morelos for his participation in the development of the work.

Funding. Facultad de Contaduría, Administración e Informática of the Universidad Autónoma del Estado de Morelos, funded this article.

References

1. Anthony, B., Jr.: Deployment of distributed ledger and decentralized technology for transition to smart industries. Environ. Syst. Decisions **43**(2), 298–319 (2023)
2. Benítez, F.R.F., Silva, G.B.N.: Aplicación del lean manufacturing a una pequeña empresa de fundición metálica. E-IDEA 4.0 Revista Multidisciplinar **4**(11), 18–30 (2022)
3. Bernardes, E., Legenvre, H.: Accessing and integrating distant capabilities in smart industry projects. In: Smart Industry-Better Management, pp. 125–149. Emerald Publishing Limited (2022)
4. García-Alcaraz, J.L., Morales García, A.S., Díaz-Reza, J.R., Jimenez Macias, E., Javierre Lardies, C., Blanco Fernández, J.: Effect of lean manufacturing tools on sustainability: the case of mexican maquiladoras. Environ. Sci. Pollut. Res. **29**(26), 39622–39637 (2022)
5. George, M.L., Maxey, J., Rowlands, D.T., Upton, M.: Lean six sigma pocket toolbook. McGraw-Hill Professional Publishing New York, NY, USA, New York (2004)
6. Grznar, M.G.S.M.P., Gregor, T.: Smart industry requires fast response from research to innovation. COMMUNICATIONS 19 (2017)
7. Gui, W., Zeng, Z., Chen, X., Xie, Y., Sun, Y.: Knowledge-driven process industry smart manufacturing. Sci. Sin. Inform. (2020)
8. Huang, Y., Fan, X., Chen, S.C., Zhao, N.: Emerging technologies of flexible pressure sensors: materials, modeling, devices, and manufacturing. Adv. Func. Mater. **29**(12), 1808509 (2019)
9. Jo, S.S., Han, H., Leem, Y., Lee, S.H.: Sustainable smart cities and industrial ecosystem: Structural and relational changes of the smart city industries in korea. Sustainability **13**(17), 9917 (2021)
10. Lucke, D., Constantinescu, C., Westkämper, E.: Smart factory-a step towards the next generation of manufacturing. In: Manufacturing Systems and Technologies for the New Frontier: The 41st CIRP Conference on Manufacturing Systems May 26–28, 2008, Tokyo, Japan. pp. 115–118. Springer (2008). https://doi.org/10.1007/978-1-84800-267-8_23
11. Paredes-Rodriguez, A.M., Chud-Pantoja, V.L., Peña-Montoya, C.C.: Gestión de riesgos operacionales en cadenas de suministro agroalimentarias bajo un enfoque de manufactura esbelta. Información tecnológica **33**(1), 245–258 (2022)
12. Shah, M.A., Pirzada, B.M., Price, G., Shibiru, A.L., Qurashi, A.: Applications of nanotechnology in smart textile industry: a critical review. J. Adv. Res. **38**, 55–75 (2022)
13. Silva, V.L., Kovaleski, J.L., Pagani, R.N., Corsi, A., Gomes, M.A.S.: Human factor in smart industry: a literature review. Future Stud. Res. J.: Trends Strategies **12**(1), 87–111 (2020)
14. Tabaa, M., Monteiro, F., Bensag, H., Dandache, A.: Green industrial internet of things from a smart industry perspectives. Energy Rep. **6**, 430–446 (2020)
15. Tang, L., Meng, Y.: Data analytics and optimization for smart industry. Front. Eng. Manage. **8**(2), 157–171 (2021)
16. Zubirías, G.C., Rodríguez, M.M., Rocha, L.A., Rodríguez, P.H., Guerrero, I.R.: Reducción de desperdicios a través de la implementación de herramientas de manufactura esbelta (mejora continua). 593 Digital Publisher CEIT **7**(3), 247–264 (2022)

An Allocation-Routing Problem in Waste Management Planning: Exact and Heuristic Resolution Approaches

Diego Rossit[1]([⊠])⬤, Begoña González Landín[2]([⊠])⬤, Mariano Frutos[3]⬤,
and Máximo Méndez Babey[2]⬤

[1] INMABB, Department of Engineering, Universidad Nacional del Sur-CONICET,
Bahía Blanca, Argentina
`diego.rossit@uns.edu.ar`
[2] Instituto Universitario SIANI, Universidad de Las Palmas de Gran Canaria, Las
Palmas de Gran Canaria, Spain
`bego.landin@uplgc.es, maximo.mendez@ulpgc.es`
[3] IIESS, Department of Engineering, Universidad Nacional del Sur-CONICET,
Bahía Blanca, Argentina
`mfrutos@uns.edu.ar`

Abstract. Efficient management of municipal solid waste systems is
vital for cities today, as it encompasses significant environmental, social,
and economic implications. To manage this intricate system, the integration of computational tools to support decision making process is
invaluable. This study presents a comprehensive model to simultaneously
address two distinct logistics problems, namely the sizing of collection
points and the design of collection routes, which are usually treated separately due to their individual complexity. In addition, the model is solved
with both a Mixed-Integer Linear Programming (MILP) model and a
Genetic Algorithm (GA). Regarding the GA, two chromosomes with two
different encoding schemes (binary and permutation) were considered to
define the representation and a 4×3^3 factorial design was performed to
tune four of the algorithm parameters: crossover and mutation operators,
and their respective rates. Initial results on small instances suggest the
potential of GA to address this problem in real-world instances when
exact mathematical model are not applicable, since it is able to improve
the results obtained with the MILP model.

Keywords: smart public services · waste management · allocation
routing problems · mixed linear integer programming · genetic
algorithms

1 Introduction

Inadequate Municipal Solid Waste (MSW) management can have far-reaching
implications, including not only environmental concerns but also economic and

S. Nesmachnow and L. Hernández Callejo (Eds.): ICSC-Cities 2023, CCIS 1938, pp. 92–107, 2024.
https://doi.org/10.1007/978-3-031-52517-9_7

social dimensions [22]. For example, in the case of the Argentinean city of Bahía Blanca, which serves as a case study in this work, the monthly collection of over 9,000 tons of MSW accounts for approximately 14% of the municipal government's budget. In this city, collection is carried out through a door-to-door pickup system, where the compactor vehicle responsible for collecting MSW must visit all households every day of the week, except Sundays. Although the choice between using a "door-to-door" or a "point-based" waste collection system depends on the specific location, recent studies demonstrate that the point-based system is more cost-efficient in terms of transportation costs, as it reduces the distances travelled by vehicles [21]. This can also lead to a lower environmental impact by reducing greenhouse gas emissions and other air pollution-related metrics. The savings in the overall MSW system that can be achieved through reduced transportation costs may be even more significant in countries with relatively high logistics costs, such as Argentina [1].

The issue of how waste accumulates in point-based systems is closely linked to another problem in the reverse logistics chain of MSW: collection. In Argentina, the design of MSW collection routes is based mainly on empirical knowledge of decision-makers [5]. While the valuable contributions of practical experience are acknowledged, the academic literature offers numerous contributions in terms of cost reduction and environmental impact through the use of decision support techniques. Considering these issues, a single integrated problem can be posed in which two decisions are made simultaneously.

The design of the point-based network involves defining the location and capacity of these points. On the other hand, waste collection involves the design and scheduling of routes in the planning horizon. The storage capacity of point-based sites or *collection points* will determine the visit frequency in order to avoid overflows. Moreover, the availability and type of vehicles affect the distribution and capacity of the collection points in an optimal (global) solution [17]. Therefore, there is a trade-off between the installation cost of the collection points and the cost of the collection plan, so solving both problems simultaneously can be beneficial from a cost perspective. However, solutions in the literature [9, 21] often address each problem separately. This is due to the complexity of addressing both problems together. In fact, solving just the route design is equivalent to solving a Vehicle Routing Problem (VRP) [24], a well-known NP-hard problem.

In this context, this paper contributes the following: a novel mathematical formulation to formalize the proposed problem which simultaneously considers the sizing of collection points and the design of a collection plan, and two resolution methodologies to solve this problem: an exact Mixed Integer Linear Programming (MILP) model and a Genetic Algorithm (GA) to address the resolution.

This work is structured as follows. Section 2 presents a description of the target problem, including the main related work and the mathematical formulation. Section 3 describes the resolution approaches along with the implementation details. Section 4 reports the analysis of the results obtained with both resolution approaches applied to a set of realistic instances for the exact approach. Finally, Sect. 5 discusses the main outcomes of this work and outlines the future research lines.

2 Bins Allocation and Collection Routing Problem in Waste Management

This Section presents the target problem including a description of the conceptual problem, the main related works and the mathematical formulation.

2.1 Conceptual Problem

This work considers a MSW system based on community bins in which citizens have to carry their waste from their households to nearby collection points where different waste bins are installed. Then, collection vehicles would visit these bins and empty the waste based on a defined visit schedule during the week. Thus, the target problem aims to simultaneously:

- solve a bin allocation problem: define the capacity of the collection points (i.e., number and types of bins to be installed).
- solve a collection routing problem: design and schedule collection routes in the planning horizon.

Both problems have to be solved considering some restrictions: the amount of waste accumulated in the collection points cannot exceed the capacity of the bins installed, the amount of waste collected on each route have to respect the capacity of the collection vehicles, and the travel times of the routes have to respect a time limit given according to the drivers' work shift.

2.2 Related Work

The problem of sizing the capacity of collection points and designing the collection routes have been addressed in a few previous works [21]. Among the main works in this topic is that of Hemmelmayr et al. [13] which developed the first exact model for simultaneously determining the number and required capacity of waste bins and the collection routes. They also presented a Large Neighborhood Search algorithm for addressing this problem. Then, Cubillos and Wøhlk [6] considered a simplified problem in which the collection phase is addressed by a Traveling Salesman Problem without considering the capacity of the vehicles as a constraint. Mahéo et al. [17,18] proposed integrated models to solve the allocation-routing problem and solved it by means of Benders decomposition.

2.3 Mathematical Formulation

The proposed mathematical model is based on the works of Mahéo et al. [17,18], with the difference that instead of considering a set of visit regimes to empty predefined point-based sites, any possible visit regime can be used as long as it does not allow the collection points sites to overflow (i.e., the accumulated waste does not exceed the capacity of the collection points). This is also a distinct feature from other relevant related works in the literature [13]. Additionally, the time to service each collection point depends on the number and type of bins that are installed and is not fixed as in previous works [17,18].

Therefore, the sets used in the mathematical formulation are as follows:

- $I = \{1, 2, ..., n_I\}$: Set of collection points.
- $L = \{1, 2, ..., n_L\}$: Set of collection vehicles.
- $T = \{1, 2, ..., n_T\}$: Set of days in the planning horizon.
- $U = \{1, 2, ..., n_U\}$: Set of bin combinations that can be installed.

A collection point site, denoted as $i \in I$, is a pre-defined location in an urban area where waste bins can be installed. Additionally, the super set: $I^0 = I \cup \{0\}$ is defined, where 0 represents the depot where vehicles start and end their daily routes, and where collected waste is deposited. Bin combinations are a set of bins that are feasible to install at a collection point, while respecting space limitations. Therefore, each element of set U can be determined by a single bin or a combination of bins. The methodology for selecting combinations of bins can be referenced in Mahéo et al. [18]. Finally, the subset $T' \subset T$ is also defined containing the days in which waste collection cannot be performed because they are associated with rest days for the crew, e.g., Sundays in Bahía Blanca.

Next, the following parameters are defined for the model:

- Q: Vehicle capacity.
- c_{ig}: Travel time between points $i \in I^0$ and $g \in I^0$.
- s_u: Service time of bin combination $u \in U$.
- h_i: Amount of waste generated daily at point-based site $i \in I$.
- cap_u: Capacity of bin combination $u \in U$.
- cin_u: Cost (adjusted over the planning horizon) of bin combination $u \in U$, considering both acquisition and installation costs.
- α: Cost per minute for collection vehicles.
- T_L: Duration of the working day.

It is worth noting that cin_u is an adjusted cost. This is because the model considers two different decision and cost levels: i) a strategic decision-making level involving the purchase and installation of bins that are expected to last several years; and ii) a tactical decision-making level involving transportation costs in the routing plan and maintenance of the bins. Therefore, the cost of purchasing and installing the bins needs to be amortized over the bin's lifespan.

Finally, the model defines the following variables:

- x_{iglt}: (binary) 1 if vehicle $l \in L$ travels between collection points $i \in I^0$ and $g \in I^0$ on day $t \in T$, and 0 otherwise.
- v_{iglt}: (continuous) load of vehicle $l \in L$ when going from collection point $i \in I$ to collection point $g \in I$ on day $t \in T$.
- w_{it}: (continuous) amount of waste accumulated on day $t \in T$ at collection point $i \in I$.
- w_i^{max}: (continuous) maximum amount of waste accumulated at collection point $i \in I$ in the planning horizon.

$-$ n_{ui}: (binary) 1 if bin combination $u \in U$ is selected for collection point $i \in I$, and 0 otherwise.

Taking into account these elements, the following mathematical model is proposed:
Minimize

$$\sum_{u \in U} \left(cin_u \sum_{i \in I} n_{ui} \right) + \alpha \sum_{t \in T} \sum_{l \in L} \sum_{i \in I^0} \sum_{g \in I^0} \left(x_{iglt} \left(c_{ig} + \left(\sum_{u \in U} s_u n_{ug} \right) \right) \right) \quad (1)$$

subject to

$$\sum_{u \in U} cap_u n_{ui} \geq w_i^{max}, \ \forall i \in I, \quad (1a)$$

$$\sum_{u \in U} n_{ui} = 1, \ \forall i \in I, \quad (1b)$$

$$\sum_{u \in U} n_{u0} = 0, \quad (1c)$$

$$\sum_{i \in I^0, \ i \neq g} x_{iglt} - \sum_{i \in I^0 \ i \neq g} x_{gilt} = 0, \ \forall g \in I^0, l \in L, t \in T \quad (1d)$$

$$\sum_{i \in I} x_{0ilt} \leq 1, \ \forall l \in L, t \in T - T' \quad (1e)$$

$$\sum_{i \in I} x_{0ilt} = 0, \ \forall l \in L, t \in T', \quad (1f)$$

$$\sum_{i,g \in I^0 \ i \neq g} x_{iglt} \left(c_{ig} + \left(\sum_{u \in U} s_u n_{ug} \right) \right) \leq T_L, \ \forall l \in L, t \in T - T' \quad (1g)$$

$$v_{iglt} \leq Q x_{iglt}, \ \forall i \in I^0, g \in I^0, l \in L, t \in T \quad (1h)$$

$$\sum_{i \in I^0 \ i \neq g} v_{iglt} + w_{gt} \leq \sum_{i \in I^0 \ i \neq g} v_{gilt} + Q \left(1 - \sum_{i \in I^0 \ i \neq g} x_{iglt} \right),$$
$$\forall g \in I, l \in L, t \in T \quad (1i)$$

$$w_{it} = h_i + w_{i(t-1)} \left(1 - \sum_{g \in I^0 \ i \neq g} \sum_{l \in L} x_{iglt} \right), \ \forall i \in I, t \in T - \{1\} \quad (1j)$$

$$w_{i1} = h_i + w_{in_T} \left(1 - \sum_{g \in I^0 \ i \neq g} \sum_{l \in L} x_{igl1} \right), \ \forall i \in I \quad (1k)$$

$$w_{it} \leq w_i^{max}, \ \forall i \in I, t \in T \quad (1l)$$

$$x, n \in \{0,1\}, v, w, w^{max} \geq 0 \quad (1m)$$

The provided mathematical model aims to address the MSW collection and container selection problem. The key components of the model are explained below. The objective function of Eq. (1) calculates the joint cost of the bins installment and maintenance and the waste collection derived from the travel time. Regarding the restrictions, Eq. (1a) sets that the installed capacity at a collection point is sufficient for storing the maximum amount of waste accumulated at each collection point in the planning horizon. Equation (1b) sets that one bin combination has to be installed in each collection point while Eq. (1c) prevents the model from selecting a bin combination for the depot. Equation (1d) sets each vehicle have to leave every collection point that is visited. Equation (1e) establishes that at most each vehicle can perform one route per day. Equation (1f) sets that no vehicle departs from the depot the rest days. Equation (1g) keeps the duration of every route within the working day. Equation (1h) forces the capacity of the vehicle to be respected during the collection routes. Equation (1i) is a subtour elimination constraint and also keeps a record of the load on the vehicles. Equations (1j) and (1k) keep a record of the waste accumulated at the end of each day, which depends on the waste generated within the day and whether the vehicle has visited the collection point the previous day. In particular, Eq. (1k) establishes the cyclical nature of the planning since the first day of the planning horizon has to consider the waste accumulated on the last day of the planning horizon in order to keep the solution feasible when it is implemented as a periodic Vehicle Routing Problem (pVRP) . Equation (1l) sets the maximum accumulated waste within the planning horizon for every collection point for the purpose of estimating the required capacity of the installed bin combination (linked to Eq. (1a)).

3 Resolution Approaches

This Section presents the resolution approaches that were used to address the allocation-routing problem, including an exact method based on MILP and a genetic algorithm.

3.1 Exact Method

The exact resolution was implemented using the model described in Sect. 2.3, in which there are three bi-linear terms, two in Eq. (1j) and Eq. (1k) and one in the objective function (1). For using a linear solver based on global optimization algorithms, which are usually more mature than their non-linear counterparts [20], the linearization technique proposed by Glover et al. [10] is applied. Then, for example, Eq (1j) is replaced by the following Eqs. (2a)- (2d) that comprehend non-negative continuous variable z_{iglt}.

$$w_{it} = h_i + w_{i(t-1)} - \sum_{g \in I^0} \sum_{i \neq g} \sum_{l \in L} z_{iglt}, \forall i \in I, t \in T - \{1\} \qquad (2a)$$

$$z_{iglt} \leq w_{it-1}, \forall i, g \in I, l \in L, T - \{1\} \qquad (2b)$$

$$z_{iglt} \leq x_{iglt}, \forall i, g \in I, l \in L, T - \{1\} \qquad (2c)$$

$$z_{iglt} \geq w_{it-1} - BigM(1 - x_{iglt}), \forall i, g \in I, l \in L, T - \{1\} \qquad (2d)$$

where $BigM$ is a sufficiently large value for the product of variables x_{iglt} and w_{it}. After some analysis, this parameter was set to $BigM = \max_{u \in U}\{cap_u\}$.

Similarly, Eq. (1k) is replaced by a set of equations considering variable z_{igl1} to represent the product of variables x_{igl1} and w_{in_T} and Eq. (1) is replaced by a set of equations considering variable y_{iuglt} to represent the product of variables x_{iglt} and n_{ug} in the objective function. For the sake of brevity, the linearizations of Eqs. (1k) and (1) are not presented in details but they follow a similar procedure to the aforementioned linearization of Eq (1j).

After the linearization of bilinear terms, the resulting MILP model was coded using pyomo [3] and solved with Gurobi v10.0.2 [12].

3.2   Genetic Algorithm

Genetic Algorithm (GA) was proposed by Holland in 1992 [14]. It is a population-based metaheuristic method inspired by the process of natural selection and designed to find the optimal or near-optimal solution in mono-objective optimization problems. GA belongs to the larger class of evolutionary algorithms (EAs). The evolution usually starts from a population of randomly generated candidate solutions, named chromosomes or individuals, and continues with an iterative process where biological-inspired operators: selection, crossover and mutation operators, are applied generation by generation until a stop criterion is verified. In order to avoid losing the best solution(s) found in a given generation, elitist strategies are often applied that may or may not copy these elitist solutions in the next generation.

The basic elements of GA are chromosome representation and biological-inspired operators. The selection is based on the fitness function value of the chromosomes and is therefore independent of the representation. However, the crossover and mutation operators are chosen according to the chosen chromosome representation.

To solve the problem proposed in Sect. 2, a mixed GA applied to a pVRP is proposed in which it is assumed that MSW collection in a given city is collected from Monday to Saturday with fixed daily routes, but collection points are not visited daily, i.e. MSW from one collection point may accumulate over several days.

The days on which waste is collected (set T) are numbered from 0 to 5 according to the 6 d of the week on which collection takes place (Monday to Saturday). As aforementioned, on Sundays there is no collection. In addition, matrix $B = [b_{it}]$ is defined where b_{it} indicates the type of bin combination (with smaller capacity) needed to contain the waste accumulated on day $t \in T$ at collection point $i \in I$. Finally, the bin combination chosen for each collection point $i \in I$ will be $b_i = \max_{t \in T} b_{it}$.

Two chromosomes were considered to encode the solutions: $Y = [y_{it}]$ and $mask = [m_{it}]$ with $i \in I$ and $t \in T$, where Y is a matrix whose rows correspond to the daily permutations of the order of collection of MSW from the $|I|$ collection points, assuming that all of they are visited every day, and $mask$ is a binary matrix whose terms m_{it} take the value 1, if on day t MSW is collected from collection point i, or 0 otherwise. Figure 1 shows a feasible solution (chromosome) in the case of considering only seven collection points.

Collection Points	MON		TUE		WED		THUR		FRI		SAT	
	y_{i0}	m_{i0}	y_{i1}	m_{i1}	y_{i2}	m_{i2}	y_{i3}	m_{i3}	y_{i4}	m_{i4}	y_{i5}	m_{i5}
1	3	0	4	1	1	0	5	0	4	0	0	1
2	5	0	5	0	4	1	3	0	1	0	3	1
3	1	0	6	1	5	0	4	0	5	1	6	0
4	2	1	3	0	6	0	6	1	3	0	2	0
5	4	1	1	0	2	0	0	1	0	0	4	0
6	0	1	0	0	3	0	2	1	6	0	5	0
7	6	1	2	0	0	1	1	0	2	1	1	0

● Chromosome I (permutation encoding) / ● Chromosome II (binary encoding)

MON	0 → 6 → 4 → 0 → 5 → 7 → 0
TUE	0 → 1 → 3 → 0
WED	0 → 7 → 2 → 0
THUR	0 → 5 → 6 → 4 → 0
FRI	0 → 7 → 3 → 0
SAT	0 → 1 → 2 → 0

Waste Collection Routes

Fig. 1. A feasible solution (chromosome) in the case of considering only seven collection points.

Taking into account that every day a collecting vehicle must visit some of the collection points (Eq. (3a)) , all waste bins should be emptied at least once a week (Eq. (3b)) and the waste accumulated in each collection point must not exceed the capacity of the combination of bins with the largest capacity (Eq. (3c)), the problem solved by the GA is as follows:

Minimize

$$\sum_{i \in I} cin_{b_i} + \alpha \sum_{t \in T} \sum_{l \in L_t} T_l^t \qquad (3)$$

subject to

$$\sum_{i \in I} m_{ti} > 0, \forall t \in T, \tag{3a}$$

$$\sum_{t \in T} m_{ti} > 0, \forall i \in I, \tag{3b}$$

$$w_{it} \leq \max_{u \in U} cap_u, \forall t \in T, \forall i \in I \tag{3c}$$

Here, α represents the cost per minute for collecting vehicles, L_t is the set of vehicles needed to make the scheduled waste collection on day t (assuming that each vehicle only goes out once per day) and T_l^t is the time taken by vehicle l to make its route on day t.

Let be $V_l^t = [v_z]_{1 \leq z \leq |V_l^t|}$ the sorted set (in order of collection) of the collection points whose waste is collected by vehicle l on day t, then

$$T_l^t = c_{0v_1} + \sum_{1 \leq z < |V_l^t|} c_{v_z v_{z+1}} + c_{|V_l^t|0} + \sum_{v_z \in V_l^t} s_{v_z} \tag{4}$$

where c_{0v_1} is the travel time between the depot and the collection point v_1 and $c_{|V_l^t|0}$ is the travel time between the last collection point, whose vehicle l collects on day t, and the depot.

The biological-inspired operators and the probabilities considered in this study were the following:

Selection. *Tournament selection* that randomly samples 2 individuals without replacement from the current population and selects the one with the best value of the objective function.

Crossover. According to the encoding of the chromosomes that are being crossed, the following crossover operators were considered:

– Binary encoding:
  • Two-point crossover. Two crossover points on the parent chromosomes are randomly selected and the gene/bit band between the two cutoff points is exchanged to obtain two children.
– Permutation encoding:
  • Partially Mapped Crossover (PMX) [11].
  • Order Crossover (OX) [7].
  • Cicle Crossover (CX) [19].
  • modified Cicle Crossover (CX2) [16].

Mutation. According to the encoding of the chromosomes that are being mutated, the following mutation operators were considered:

– Binary encoding:
  • Uniform mutation. Given a chromosome, the value of each gene/bit is altered with a mutation rate equal to 1/chromosome length.

– Permutation encoding:
  • Exchange mutation (EM). Two alleles are chosen randomly and exchanged with each other.
  • Insertion mutation (IM) Two alleles are chosen randomly and the second allele is placed just after the first one
  • Inversion mutation (INM). Two alleles are chosen at random and the order of the alleles between them is reversed.

4   Computational Experimentation

This Section presents the computational experimentation, including the description of instances, the parametrization of the GA and the numerical results of the comparison between the MILP model and the GA.

4.1   Description of Instances

In this article, a preliminary computational experimentation is performed over five small instances based on the city of Bahía Blanca, Argentina. The instances are named from i.1 to i.5. The instances are very similar to the ones used in Mahéo et al. [18] for a similar problem. Specifically, the largest instances used in Mahéo et al. [18] are used, which contained seven collection points. The instances can be retrieved from Github[1] which are based on information gathered on field studies in Bahía Blanca [5].

The waste collection company in Bahia Blanca currently utilizes a fleet of rear-loading trucks for their door-to-door collection system. In this study, we assess three distinct types of commercial side-loading waste bins available in Argentina. The specifications for these bins can be found in Mahéo et al.'s research [18], and these details were gathered through surveys conducted in collaboration with specialized companies in Argentina. The expected lifespan of these bins is estimated at ten years [2]. The maintenance cost for each bin is approximated at 5% of the purchase cost [8]. To calculate the estimated weekly cost, the purchase and maintenance expenses are added and divided by the total number of weeks of the expected lifespan.

Considering an available space of $5m^2$ at each collection point, the same eight bin combinations established through the preprocessing process detailed in Mahéo et al.'s work [18] are considered. However, in contrast to Mahéo et al.'s approach, where they assumed a uniform service time for all bin combinations, in this work the service time (s_u) is estimated by taking into account the specific type of bin combination used. This modification adds further complexity to the target problem since it explains the reason of the bi-linear terms in Eq. (1). Bins service times are estimated using the field work of Carlos et al. [4]. It is considered that the fleet of collection vehicles is homogeneous. The estimated cost per minute of vehicle operation (α) is estimated at US\$0.5764 per minute [8].

---

[1] https://github.com/diegorossit/ICSC_CITIES_2023.git.

As in Mahéo et al. [18], given that the instances are smaller than the actual collection zones in the city, the fleet's capacity and size and the duration of the working day are adjusted to ensure that the problem does not become trivial, where a single vehicle can collect all the waste in a single trip. Another different between this work and Mahéo et al. [18] is that here a larger planning horizon is considered using a whole week (seven days), with no waste collection scheduled on Sundays as it is a rest day.

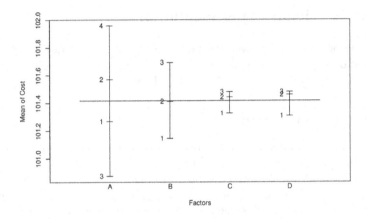

Fig. 2. Main effects in the factorial design considered.

4.2   GA Parametrization

First, a tuning of the mixed GA was performed, focusing on the crossover and mutation operators, as well as their respective probabilities, associated to the chromosome coded with permutations. The goal is to study the effect of these algorithm parameters on the value of the objective function defined by Eq. (3). For this purpose, a 4×3^3 factorial design on the instance i.1 was considered. The factors of the factorial design and their respective levels are:

A: Crossover operator: 1 (PMX), 2 (OC), 3 (CX) and 4 (CX2)
B: Crossover rate: 1 (0.8), 2 (0.85), 3 (0.9)
C: Mutation operator: 1 (EM), 2 (IM) and 3 (INM)
D: Mutation rate: 1 (0.05), 2 (0.10) and 3 (0.15)

The remaining GA parameters were set as follows: population size = 100, number of generations = 1000 and number of elite solutions considered = 2. For binary encoding, the crossover rate is the same as permutation encoding and the mutation rate is equal to 1/number of collection points.

Thirty independent runs of each treatment were carried out, with one treatment being understood as a combination of the factor levels. A total of 3240 runs of the mixed GA were performed.

Table 1. Kruskal-Wallis Rank Sum Test: p-values.

A: Crossover operator	B: Crossover rate	C: Mutation operator	D: Mutation rate
< 2.2e-16	4.023e-13	0.185	0.03067

Table 2. The multiple comparison test after Kruskal-Wallis: if TRUE, then statistically significant differences are found between the compared levels.

A: Crossover operator		B: Crossover rate	C: Mutation operator
1–2 TRUE	2–3 TRUE	1–2 TRUE	1–2 FALSE
1–3 TRUE	2–4 TRUE	1–3 TRUE	1–3 FALSE
1–4 TRUE	3–4 TRUE	2–3 TRUE	2–3 FALSE

Main effects are the changes in the mean of the response variable that are due to the individual action of each factor. From Fig. 2 it could be concluded that, on overage, the best combination of factors would be: (A = CX, B = 0.8, C = EM, D = 0.05). However, it is important to confirm this conclusion with the corresponding hypothesis tests.

A Kruskal-Wallis Rank Sum Test [15] has been performed to determine whether there are significant differences between the levels of each factor. When the value of a Kruskal-Wallis test is significant (p-value < 0.05), a multiple comparison test after Kruskal-Wallis [23] between treatments has been performed to determine which levels are different with pairwise comparisons adjusted appropriately for multiple comparisons. The test were performed using the available libraries in the programming language R^2. Table 1 shows the p-values obtained when the **kruskal.test()** function is run on the results obtained. It can be seen that no significant differences are found between the levels of factor C: Mutation operator. Table 2 shows the output of the multiple comparison test after Kruskal-Wallis when the **kruskalmc()** function of the R package *pgirmess*[3] is run on the results obtained. Consequently, hypothesis tests support that the treatment with the best performance with the problem defined in Sect. 3.2 has the following structure: (A = CX, B = 0.8, C = *, D = *) where "*" indicates that the level of that factor can be any of those considered. The best solution found in the factorial design has an overall cost, computed with Eq. (3), equals to 93.885 and was found with the combination: (A = CX, B = 0.8, C = EM, D = 0.1). Its chromosome is shown in Fig. 1.

4.3   Numerical Results

This section presents the numerical results of the comparison between the MILP model and the GA for the considered instances.

---

[2] https://www.R-project.org.

[3] https://www.R-project.org/package=pgirmess.

Table 3. Statistical summary of the results over 30 independent GA runs.

id	Best sol.			Worst sol.	Median	Mean	Standard deviation	Average runtime (sec.)	S-W p-value
	Overall Cost	Bins Cost	Routing Cost						
i.1	126.30	33.37	92.93	132.94	130.32	130.28	1.38	67.84	0.1004
i.2	126.97	32.26	94.71	132.68	129.99	129.85	1.20	69.99	0.2278
i.3	128.39	33.37	95.02	131.96	129.36	129.85	0.94	68.33	0.0054
i.4	134.93	30.04	104.89	141.93	138.38	138.24	1.61	66.28	0.7377
i.5	137.34	29.73	107.61	142.84	139.76	139.89	1.39	68.40	0.1978

Table 4. Results obtained with the MILP model and comparison with those obtained with the GA.

id	MILP				MILP vs GA			
	Overall Cost	Bins Cost	Routing Cost	Gurobi gap	Best sol			Mean/median
					% dif. overall cost	% dif. bin cost	% dif. routing cost	% dif. overall cost
i.1	160.97	21.82	139.16	53.62%	21.54%	-52.93%	33.22%	19.04%
i.2	153.26	22.96	130.30	49.58%	17.15%	-40.51%	27.31%	15.18%
i.3	150.75	20.32	130.43	52.34%	14.83%	-64.22%	27.15%	12.46%
i.4	163.65	20.37	143.28	48.44%	17.55%	-47.47%	26.79%	15.44%
i.5	164.02	22.49	141.53	47.82%	16.27%	-32.19%	23.97%	14.79%

Table 3 shows a statistical summary of the results over 30 independent GA runs for the five instances. The parameters considered were the same as those of the GA tuning, with treatment (A = CX, B = 0.8, C = EM, D = 0.05). From left to right, Table 3 reports: the overall cost, bins installment cost and the routing cost of the best solution; the overall cost of the worst solution; the median, mean and standard deviation of the overall cost; the average runtime and the p-value obtained in the Shapiro Wilk (S-W) test[4]. The bins installment and routing cost are post-processing disaggregations of the overall cost. Runs were performed on an Intel(R) Core(TM) i7-6700T CPU @ 2.80 GHz 2.81 GHz with 16 GB of RAM.

Table 4 shows, for each instance, the results obtained with the MILP model and their percentage difference with both the disaggregated costs of the best solution obtained with the GA and the mean or median value (depending on the result obtained with the S-W test) of the 30 overall costs of each sample obtained with the GA (see Table 3).

The results provide a basis for validating the performance of the GA when compared to the results obtained with the MILP model, which is an exact solver. On average, it is observed that the GA consistently yields solutions that have a statistically inferior cost to those obtained through the MILP model. This demonstrates the competitiveness of the usage of mataheuristics to address computationally complex problems, such as the target problem in this work.

When the overall cost is broken down into the installation cost of bins and the routing cost, it becomes evident that the GA excels in the routing component. It is capable of generating solutions that are up to 34.39% more cost-effective than the MILP formulation in this specific aspect. However, the MILP model

---

[4] https://www.rdocumentation.org/packages/stats/versions/3.6.2/topics/shapiro.
test.

demonstrates its capacity of optimizing the installation cost of bins. In fact, it can achieve solutions with up to 64.22% lower costs in this regard compared to the GA. Nevertheless, since the routing cost represents the largest portion of the overall cost, the GA maintains its overall superiority when this global cost is analyzed. Actually the GA computes solutions that are up to 29.54% more cost-efficient than the MILP.

5   Conclusions

The MSW systems are crucial for current cities as they provide vital support for the goal of enhancing the liveability and sustainability of smart cities. However, in order to achieve this goal they have to be carefully planned and operated. This work presented a Mixed-Integer Linear Programming (MILP) mathematical model and a Genetic Algorithm (GA) for addressing the integrated problem of waste bins allocation and design and schedule of waste collection routes. This NP-hard integrated problem is not commonly addressed in the related literature. Initial results over small instances suggest the potential of the GA for addressing this problem as it is able to improve the results obtained with the MILP model. Future work includes expanding the computational experimentation with larger realistic instances with the GA. Additionally, the MILP model can be enhanced using valid cuts to improve the performance. Finally, the problem can be addressed in a bi-objective fashion in which the installment and the routing costs are optimized separately.

Acknowledgements. The authors are grateful for the financial support granted by 319RT0574 - Red iberoamericana industria 4.0 of CYTED, to the "Consejería de Economía, Industria, Comercio y Conocimiento" of the Government of the Canary Islands through the direct grant awarded to the ULPGC called "Support for R+D+i activity. Campus of International Excellence CEI CANARIAS-ULPGC", and the research projects PICT-2021-I-INVI00217 of the Agencia I+D+i of Argentina and the PIBAA 0466CO of CONICET.

References

1. Asociación Latinoamericana de Logística: Indicadores costos logísticos países miembros de ALALOG (2023). https://www.alalog.org/es/studies Accessed Sept 2023
2. Brogaard, L., Christensen, T.: Quantifying capital goods for collection and transport of waste. Waste Manage. Res. **30**(12), 1243–1250 (2012)
3. Bynum, M., Hackebeil, G., Hart, W., Laird, C., Nicholson, B., Siirola, J., Watson, J., Woodruff, D.: Pyomo-optimization modeling in python, vol. 67. Springer (2021). https://doi.org/10.1007/978-3-319-58821-6
4. Carlos, M., Gallardo, A., Edo-Alcon, N., Abaso, J.R.: Influence of the municipal solid waste collection system on the time spent at a collection point: a case study. Sustainability **11**(22), 6481 (2019)

5. Cavallin, A., Rossit, D., Herrán, V., Rossit, D., Frutos, M.: Application of a methodology to design a municipal waste pre-collection network in real scenarios. Waste Management & Research **38**(1_suppl), 117–129 (2020)
6. Cubillos, M., Wøhlk, S.: Solution of the maximal covering tour problem for locating recycling drop-off stations. J. Oper. Res. Society **72**(8), 1898–1913 (2021)
7. Davis, L.: Applying adaptive algorithms to epistatic domains. In: International Joint Conferences on Artificial Intelligence (IJCAI), pp. 162–164 (1985)
8. D'Onza, G., Greco, G., Allegrini, M.: Full cost accounting in the analysis of separated waste collection efficiency: a methodological proposal. J. Environ. Manage. **167**, 59–65 (2016)
9. Ghiani, G., Laganà, D., Manni, E., Musmanno, R., Vigo, D.: Operations research in solid waste management: a survey of strategic and tactical issues. Comput. Oper. Res. **44**, 22–32 (2014)
10. Glover, F.: Improved linear integer programming formulations of nonlinear integer problems. Manage. Sci. **22**(4), 455–460 (1975)
11. Goldberg, D., Lingle, R.: Alleles, Loci and the traveling salesman problem. In: First International Conference on Genetic Algorithms and their applications, pp. 154–159. Psychology Press (2014)
12. Gurobi Optimization, LLC: Gurobi Optimizer Reference Manual (2023). https://www.gurobi.com
13. Hemmelmayr, V., Doerner, K., Hartl, R., Vigo, D.: Models and algorithms for the integrated planning of bin allocation and vehicle routing in solid waste management. Transp. Sci. **48**(1), 103–120 (2014)
14. Holland, J.: Adaptation in natural and artificial systems. MIT Press Cambridge (1992)
15. Hollander, M., Wolfe, D.: Nonparametric Statistical Methods. John Wiley & Sons (1973)
16. Hussain, A., Muhammad, Y., Nauman Sajid, M., Hussain, I., Mohamd Shoukry, A., Gani, S.: Genetic algorithm for traveling salesman problem with modified cycle crossover operator. Computational Intelligence and Neuroscience, pp. 1–7 (2017)
17. Mahéo, A., Rossit, D.G., Kilby, P.: A benders decomposition approach for an integrated bin allocation and vehicle routing problem in municipal waste management. In: Rossit, D.A., Tohmé, F., Mejía Delgadillo, G. (eds.) ICPR-Americas 2020. CCIS, vol. 1408, pp. 3–18. Springer, Cham (2021). https://doi.org/10.1007/978-3-030-76310-7_1
18. Mahéo, A., Rossit, D., Kilby, P.: Solving the integrated bin allocation and collection routing problem for municipal solid waste: a benders decomposition approach. Ann. Oper. Res. **322**(1), 441–465 (2023)
19. Oliver, I., Smith, D., Holland, J.: A study of permutation crossover operators on the traveling salesman problem. In: Second International Conference on Genetic Algorithms on Genetic Algorithms and their application, pp. 224–230. Psychology Press (1987)
20. Rodriguez, M., Vecchietti, A.: A comparative assessment of linearization methods for bilinear models. Comput. Chem. Eng. **48**, 218–233 (2013)
21. Rossit, D., Nesmachnow, S.: Waste bins location problem: a review of recent advances in the storage stage of the municipal solid waste reverse logistic chain. J. Clean. Prod. **342**, 130793 (2022)
22. Rossit, D., Toutouh, J., Nesmachnow, S.: Exact and heuristic approaches for multi-objective garbage accumulation points location in real scenarios. Waste Manage. **105**, 467–481 (2020)

23. Siegel, S.: Non parametric statistics for the behavioural sciences. MacGraw Hill Int (1988)
24. Toth, P., Vigo, D.: Vehicle routing: problems, methods, and applications. SIAM (2014)

Simulated Annealing Metaheuristic Approach for Municipal Solid Waste Collecting Route Problem in the Historical Center of a Mexican City

Ivonne Yazmín Arce-García[1], Pedro Moreno-Bernal[2]([⊠]),
Víctor Pacheco-Valencia[3], Maria del Carmen Torres-Salazar[1],
Sergio Nesmachnow[4], and Viridiana Aydee León-Hernández[1]

[1] Facultad de Ciencias Químicas e Ingeniería, Universidad Autónoma del Estado de Morelos (UAEM), Cuernavaca, Mexico
yazmin.arcegrc@uaem.edu.mx, {maria.torres,vleon}@uaem.mx
[2] Facultad de Contaduría, Administración e Informática, UAEM, Cuernavaca, Mexico
pmoreno@uaem.mx
[3] Centro de Investigación en Ciencias, UAEM, Cuernavaca, Mexico
[4] Universidad de la República, Montevideo, Uruguay
sergion@fing.edu.uy

Abstract. This article presents a metaheuristic approach applying simulated annealing for the Municipal Solid Waste collecting route problem in the Historical Center of Cuernavaca, Mexico. The solid waste collection route addressed requires finding an optimal collection route in the constrained polygonal area of the historical center of Cuernavaca. The experimental evaluation solves a realistic problem considering garbage truck information of the Cuernavaca municipality. The proposed approach finds an optimal tour that improves up to 29.3% of the solid waste collection distance over current municipal solid waste system tours.

Keywords: Simulated Annealing · Municipal Solid Waste · Optimization

1 Introduction

Nowadays, urban area expansion, technological advancement, and changes in consumption habits are essential elements in the development of modern cities. This way, population growth, and economic-social factors are closely linked to solid waste production. Treatment of solid wastes is a widespread problem for urban and rural areas in many countries. It is estimated that globally, 2,010 million tons of waste are generated annually [3].

Municipal Solid Waste (MSW) collection is a primary problem in urban environments today [11]. MSW management must consider legal, social, political,

© The Author(s), under exclusive license to Springer Nature Switzerland AG 2024
S. Nesmachnow and L. Hernández Callejo (Eds.): ICSC-Cities 2023, CCIS 1938, pp. 108–122, 2024.
https://doi.org/10.1007/978-3-031-52517-9_8

environmental, and economic factors, which make the collection and disposal process complex. Notably, the MSW collection problem requires proper scheduling for adequate collecting routes founded on technique specifications and good practices to choose the best scheduling according to the necessities of the population.

In 2020, the estimation of waste generation in Mexico was reported at 120,128 tons per day (TPD) [12]. Morelos, Mexico, contributes 1.6% of waste solids, equivalent to 1,878 TPD. Cuernavaca (state capital of Morelos) stands out as the region with the highest waste generation, reaching 500 TPD [7]. Since 2005, MSW management crises during municipal administrations have been evident through exposed garbage bags in the city streets, generating health and economic-social local problems. Also, tourism in Cuernavaca has been reduced because of the garbage problem, particularly in the Historic Center of the city (HC-CVA).

In this line of work, this article presents a Simulated Annealing (SA) metaheuristic approach for the collecting routes problem of MSW. The route exploration allows the computing and evaluation of different routes for a proper MSW collection route in the constrained polygonal area of the HC-CVA. A realistic problem instance considering garbage truck scheduling distances of the Cuernavaca municipality is solved in the experimental evaluation. Accurate results are reported: the proposed SA allows computing an optimal MSW collection tour that improves up to 29.3% of the MSW collection distance over current municipal solid waste system tours in the HC-CVA area.

The rest of the article is structured as follows. Section 2 describes the MSW collection route problem in Cuernavaca, related works about MSW optimization, and the optimization model of the MSW optimal collection tour. Section 3 describes the proposed SA metaheuristic approach for the MSW collection route problem in the constrained polygonal area of the historical center of Cuernavaca. Section 4 provides details of the experimental evaluation of the proposed approach, including the description of the real scenario of Cuernavaca and the discussion of the results. Finally, Sect. 5 presents the conclusions and formulates the main lines for future work.

2 The MSW Collection Route Problem

This section describes the MSW collection route problem in Cuernavaca (MSW-CVA), presents its mathematical formulation, and reviews related works about approaches to address the MSW problem.

2.1 Problem Description

In Mexico, the MSW system involves three levels of government: Federation, State, and Municipality. Article 115 of the Political Constitution of the United Mexican States confers attributions and responsibilities to the municipalities related to the intermediate phase of the waste management chain. Services included are cleaning, collection, transportation to final disposal, and treatment of generated waste. It is worth mentioning that waste collection represents between 70% and 85% of the budget assigned to solid waste management, making it a critical component in providing the service [1].

Cuernavaca local government is responsible for collecting MSW around the municipality. However, MSW collection and transportation is outsourced to a private company. The company transports solid waste from the municipal transfer station to the final disposal site after collecting solid waste from the city. This way, the private company determines the collection route itineraries across the city. Nevertheless, solid waste collection trucks travel up to four times through HC-CVA, generating an additional collection cost.

The waste-collect company has established two routes (eastern and western). Both routes connect the main avenues of Cuernavaca city. Two compacting trucks collect solid waste around the city during morning and night shifts [12]. The daily collection operates both during the day and at night, generating an average of 45.5 tons of MSW daily. This way, it is necessary to improve collection route itineraries to collect optimal waste.

In this context, an optimal schedule plan for a collection tour allows for traversing and covering all the streets of the HC-CVA within a suitable time to help the Economic Units deliver their waste directly to the collection system. This article focuses on optimizing the MSW collection tour in the HC-CVA. The goal is to generate an optimal tour to be analyzed in a posterior decision-making process to determine a proper route itinerary for MSW.

This addressed problem can be modeled as an optimization problem to minimize the distance costs of MSW collection. Today, the MSW itinerary route of Cuernavaca is designed by empirical methods based on each actual situation of the MSW system. Solving the MSW problem is of interest to municipalities as it improves sanitation conditions and positively impacts citizens' quality of life. It leads researchers to optimize collection tours in various cities worldwide, benefiting public administration and citizens' convenience.

2.2   Mathematical Formulation

The MSW-CVA is formulated as the NP-hard well-known Traveling Salesman Problem (TSP) [6] in a completed directed weighted graph $G = (V, E, d)$. Graph G represents the street intersection points used to discretize the area where the MSW collection route is to be optimized (Fig. 1). $V = \{v_1, v_2, ..., v_n\}$ is the set of graph nodes. Each node represents the point where two streets are intersected. $E = \{(v_{i1}, v_{j1}), (v_{i2}, v_{j2}), ..., (v_{im}, v_{jm}\}, v_{ik}, v_{jk} \in V$ is the set of edges; $n = |V|$ and $m = |E|$. An edge $(v_i, v_j) \in E$ connects nodes v_i, and v_j where two streets intersect in the corner. Function $d : E \to \mathbb{R}^+$ defined by Eq. 2, assigns a nonnegative cost based on the length in meters of the distance from two street corners, e.g., between v_i and v_j to each edge $(v_i, v_j) \in E$.

The problem proposes finding the minimum-cost tour from a source node v to the same destination node. The objective function to minimize (Eq. 1a) represents the total distance cost of edges chosen for the tour. In the proposed formulation, each edge (v_i, v_j) has associated a binary decision variable x_{ij} that is equal to 1 if the edge is included in the optimal tour and 0 otherwise.

$$\min f(x) \quad = \sum_{i=1}^{n} \sum_{j \neq i, j=1}^{n} d_{ij} \cdot x_{ij} \tag{1a}$$

subject to

$$\sum_{j=1, j \neq i}^{n} x_{ij} = 1 \qquad \text{for } i = 1, 2, \cdots, n \tag{1b}$$

$$\sum_{i=1, i \neq j}^{n} x_{ij} = 1 \qquad \text{for } j = 1, 2, \cdots, n \tag{1c}$$

Equation 1b expresses that each node $v \in V$ must be visited exactly once. Finally, Eq. 1c expresses that each node $v \in V$ must be left exactly once.

2.3 Related Work

The MSW system has been addressed from different perspectives, searching for a solution in particular cases. MSW stage solving depends on the strategy implemented for any case. Recent related works propose different methodologies, including optimization algorithms for efficient MSW collection. A brief review of related works is presented next.

Tirkolaee et al. [15] proposed a mathematical model for a robust periodic capacitated arc routing problem for urban waste collection considering driver's and crew's working time. The proposed model aims to minimize the total traversed distance and total usage cost of vehicles over a planning period. The model was solved by a hybrid algorithm that combined a simulated annealing (SA) and a constructive heuristic. The proposed metaheuristic approach was executed using CPLEX, and for all different deviation levels, SA has a significant difference in comparison with an exact method in terms of run time. SA is able to find the best solution with the objective value of 12,127.52 units and run time of 851.28 s for large-sized problems tested.

Toutouh et al. [16] proposed an optimization model for locating Garbage Accumulation Points in an urban area, aimed at maximizing the collected waste, minimizing the distance between users and bins, and minimizing the investment cost. Soft computing methods based on PageRank greedy algorithms and Multi-objective Evolutionary Algorithms were proposed to address the problem. Also, a multi-objective variant of PageRank was proposed following a linear aggregation approach. Experimental evaluation was performed on real Montevideo, Uruguay, and Bahía Blanca, Argentina scenarios. Three waste generation patterns were evaluated for each problem instance (normal, low, and high demand). Real scenarios represent the expected fluctuations of waste generation rate over a year. Results showed that the proposed MOEAs outperformed PageRank in all the studied scenarios regarding both distances walked to dispose of the waste.

Vazquez et al. [17] proposed a strategy to combine waste sorting from source to destination by analyzing the assessment and correlation of the amount and type of MSW considering the population's socioeconomic level in Bahía Blanca City, Argentina. The proposed methodology applies a socioeconomic analysis, a relationship between municipal solid waste and an ad hoc quality of life index selection of collection routes, and a sampling, sorting, and characterization of Municipal solid waste collection analysis. Results show a reduction of at least 80 wt% of the waste sent to landfills by the combination of sorting methodologies implemented in the city. Also, the valorization of different MSW streams could be reached by the proposed strategy consolidating an integrated MSW management that will create new jobs with competitive salaries and better job conditions. Finally, results present an efficient locating of disposal bins/containers for separation by restructuring MSW collection routes impacting the population's quality of life.

Cavallin et al. [2] proposed a study to determine the location of MSW-differentiated bins in two neighborhoods of Bahía Blanca, Argentina. A comprehensive methodology was proposed involving generation waste rate estimation to selecting bins' geographical distribution. Authors collected data through literature search and surveys, e.g., population density per block, the generation of MSW per inhabitant, and by type of shop and institution, as well as the characterization of MSW. The bins' location problem was addressed by a mixed-integer linear programming model for the location of facilities with capacity constraints, seeking the minimization of investment costs, given the maximum area available and the capacity of the bins. The analysis was applied for different scenarios considering diverse collection frequencies and the maximum distance to be traveled by users. Experimental results show that costs decrease the more significant the maximum distance to be traveled by the user by enabling fewer disposal points. Also, a higher frequency of collection requires less investment in bins.

Tirkolaee et al. [14] proposed a mixed-integer linear programming model to formulate the sustainable periodic capacitated arc routing problem for MSW management. The multi-objective model minimizes the total cost of environmental emissions, maximizes citizenship satisfaction, and minimizes workload deviation. The optimization was addressed by a hybrid multi-objective optimization algorithm based on a multi-objective simulated annealing algorithm and a multi-objective invasive weed optimization algorithm. Taguchi design technique is employed to set the parameters optimally to increase algorithm performance. Experimental validation was evaluated using several problem instances of the literature. Results reveal a high efficiency of the suggested model and algorithm to solve the addressed problem.

The related works allowed the identification of a growing interest in computational intelligence algorithms for MSW collection route problems in the context of smart cities. In this line of work, this article contributes to a metaheuristic approach for the MSW collection route problem in Cuernavaca, Mexico. The following section describes the implementation of the proposed metaheuristic approach based on a simulated annealing algorithm.

3   The Proposed SA for the MSW-CVA

This section describes the proposed SA metaheuristic approach to solve the MSW-CVA.

3.1   Simulated Annealing Method

SA is a stochastic search algorithm based on the solid annealing process. The annealing process modifies the structure of a solid, altering its properties [4]. The annealing process begins with a high initial temperature, and then the solid is gradually cooled to obtain a strong structure [13]. During the process, the atoms of the solid move randomly at high temperatures, and as the temperature cools, the atoms also rearrange themselves, producing a minimum energy state in the system. The cooling schedule allows a gradual decrease in temperature until it reaches an equilibrium state. This way, the analogy of solid annealing is applied to address optimization problems. The state of the system corresponds to the solution to the problem; the energy of the system is analogous to the cost of the objective function of the problem to be optimized; the slight changes of state (perturb the system state) are analogous to the local search for solutions in a neighborhood of solutions; the cooling schedule corresponds to the parameter control mechanism (initial temperature, equilibrium state, cooling function, stopping criteria or final temperature) of the algorithm; the final system state (frozen state) corresponds to the final solution of the algorithm (global optimum) [8].

In this context, SA is an iterative local search guided through a stochastic process, where a j state is accepted with a determined probability given by $\Pi(\Delta E, T) = exp^{-\Delta E/kT}$, where k is the Boltzmann constant. The Metropolis algorithm simulates the change of energy in the cooling process [5]. The iterated local search accepts lower-quality solutions than the current solution to escape from the local optimum. This way, SA explores and exploits the search space to find better solutions in a neighborhood [9].

3.2   SA for the MSW-CVA

The main features of the proposed SA algorithm for the MSW-CVA are described next.

Solution representation. A one-dimensional representation is used to encode candidate solutions in the proposed SA. One vector of integer numbers (x) is used to encode a tour path $p = \{v_0, v_1, \cdots, v_k\}$ between source and destination node v ($v_0 = v$, $v_k = v$). Value (x_i) in the representation correspond to the vertex number of the i-th node in the graph(G). Figure 1 presents a sample representation for a MSW-CVA solution.

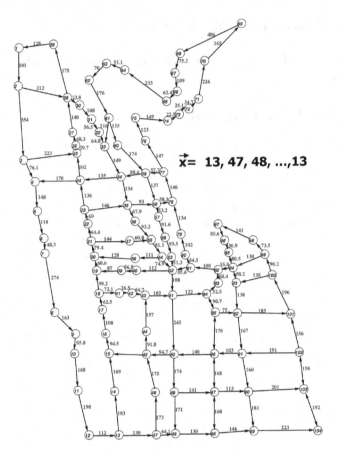

Fig. 1. Graph representation for a MSW-CVA solution

Objective function. The proposed SA for MSW-CVA minimizes the cost function defined in the mathematical formulation (Eq. 1a).

Initial solution. The initial cost matrix (M) is generated by estimating the length (*distance*) between two corners within the study area using Google Maps. Then, Dijkstra's algorithm completes M by finding the shortest distance (d') between two given non-adjacent nodes, v_i and v_j, creating a complete cost matrix (M'). Equation 2 expresses the distance calculated for d'_{v_i,v_j}. In addition, sub-tours are considered where the vehicular traffic flow goes in a unique direction, with more than two adjacent corners. Also, the sub-tour is generated considering a forced passing between a source node and a destination node. Finally, the initial SA solution for RSU-CVA is randomly generated.

$$d'_{v_i,v_j} = \begin{cases} d_{v_i,v_j} & \text{if } d_{v_i,v_j} \in M \\ DIJKSTRA(v_i,v_j,M) & \text{if } d_{v_i,v_j} \notin M \end{cases} \tag{2}$$

Figure 2 shows a sub-tour representation. Figure 2a represents a complete graph, and Fig. 2b represents sub-tours (red edges) where a unique direction of vehicular traffic flows in more than two adjacent corners. In Fig. 2b, vertex 11 represents a hard constraint S11 = (3,1,2), and vertex 12 represents mandatory sub-tour S12 = (6,8,9). This way, the G graph composed of 104 vertices representing the HC-CVA (Fig. 1) substitutes those sub-tours in the graph through auxiliary vertices labeled from 105 to 114, such as in Fig. 2b. In G graph, vertices 105 and 106 represent hard restrictions, while vertices 107 to 114 represent obligatory sub-tours. The sub-tours are S105 = (21, 37, 55), S106 = (23, 35), S107 = (29, 1, 2), S108 = (4, 5, 6, 7, 8, 9, 10, 11, 12, 13), S109 =(15, 16, 17, 18), S110 =(25, 26, 27), S111 =(30, 31, 32), S112 = (57, 56, 53), S113 =(76, 75, 74, 73, 72, 71, 70, 68, 68, 67, 66, 65, 64, 63, 62, 61), and S114 = (98,97,96,95). Additionally, vertices 21, 23, 35, 37, and 55, which belong to auxiliary vertices 105 and 106 are connected. Once M' is completed, a random initial solution is created.

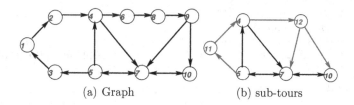

(a) Graph   (b) sub-tours

Fig. 2. Graph representation of sub-tours

Exploration. The exploration operator of SA applies two neighborhood procedures. Procedure SWAPS randomly selects two elements of the current solution (S) and exchanges their positions, generating a new solution (S'). Nevertheless, procedure INSERTION randomly selects one element in S. Then, it relocates the element between two adjacent elements in S, generating a new solution (S').

Annealing schedule. A geometric update scheme is applied for the temperature [13], i.e., $T^{k+1} = \alpha T^k$. The value of α is set by literature recommendations.

Stopping criterion. A fixed effort stopping criterion is applied. SA stops when the temperature reaches a fixed minimum value (determined empirically).

Algorithm 1 presents a pseudocode of the proposed SA for the MSW-CVA.

SA starts from the initial solution s^0 and proceeds to explore feasible solutions through the iterative local search in the neighborhood of size $N(s)$. A perturbed neighbor s^{k+1} is generated every iteration. Feasible perturbed solutions that improve the cost function (Eq. 1a) are accepted. Perturbed solutions that do not improve cost are accepted according to Boltzmann probability function $\Pi(\Delta f)$ and the current temperature T_k. A maximum number of iterations

---

Algorithm 1: Proposed SA for the MSW-CVA

---

1 k = 0
2 **initialize**(s^k)   ▷ generate initial solution
3 $T_k = T_{max}$ ▷ initialize temperature
4 **while** $T_k < T_f$ **do**
5      $i = 0$ ▷ Markov chain iterator
6   **while** $i < $ maxL **do**
7         $\gamma = $ random$\{0,1\}$
8   **if** $\gamma == 0$ **then**
9            $s^{k+1} = $ perturbationA(s^k) ▷ exploration by INSERTION
10   **else**
11           $s^{k+1} = $ perturbationB(s^k) ▷ exploration by SWAPS
12   **end**
13   **if** $f(s^{k+1}) < f(s^k)$ **then**
14           $s^k \leftarrow s^{k+1}$ ▷ acceptance criterion
15   **else**
16           $\Delta f = f(s^{k+1}) - f(s^k)$
17           $\Pi(\Delta f) = \exp^{-(\Delta f/T_0)}$
18           $\beta = $ random$(0,1)$
19   **if** $\beta \leq \Pi(\Delta f)$ **then**
20              $s^k \leftarrow s^{k+1}$ ▷ accept sub-optimal solution
21   **end**
22   **end**
23   **end**
24     $T_k \leftarrow \alpha T_k$ ▷ temperature decay
25     $i \leftarrow i + 1$
26 **end**
27 **return** s^k

($maxL$) are performed to analyze different perturbed solutions in a Markovian search with the same temperature parameter value. The value of $maxL$ is set by empirical analysis, evaluating the computational cost and the number of improved solutions in the Markovian search. The SA algorithm stops when the temperature reaches the final value T_f determined empirically.

This way, the proposed SA metaheuristic approach determines the optimal tour for MSW collection across the constrained polygonal area of the HC-CVA. The following section analyzes the experimental results of the proposed approach.

4   Experimental Results and Discussion

This section describes the experimental evaluation of the proposed SA for the MSW-CVA. Details about the platform used for development and execution are presented. Likewise, the studied area and the real-world problem instance are described. Finally, results are reported and discussed.

4.1   Development and Execution Platform

The proposed SA method was developed in Python3 and evaluated on a Quad-core Xeon E5430(2.66 GHz), 8 GB RAM, from National Supercomputing Center (Cluster-UY), Uruguay [10].

4.2   Studied Area and Problem Instance

The studied area is located in Morelos State in the south-central of Mexico. Cuernavaca is the state capital of Morelos. The municipality of Cuernavaca has a population of 378,476 inhabitants, according to the 2020 Population and Housing Census results from the National Institute of Statistics and Geography.

Two MSW collection routes (R1 and R2) transit the main streets of the buffer area, maintaining a significant presence in the HC-CVA. Figure 3a shows the buffer and study areas. The study area is covered in two shifts, morning and night, and in two segments covering the western and eastern zones of the HC-CVA. Morning Route One $(R1_m)$ covers 13.33 km of the HC-CVA in approximately 5:05 h. The total period of Route One is approximately 9 h from and to the Transfer Center, covering areas beyond the buffer area. Morning Route Two $(R2_m)$ covers 18.47 km in 7:45 h. The total duration of Route Two is approximately 9 h. In night shift routes, Route One $(R1_n)$ completes the RSW collection in an estimated 3:01 h of 8 h, covering a distance of 8.25 km. Night Route Two $(R2_n)$ covers a distance of 16.01 km in approximately 4:55 h of the route total duration of approximately 8:10 h. Figure 3b shows the collection routes in Cuernavaca. The map image was taken from Google Earth and used only for academic purposes, according to the "fair use" copyright. Table 1 reports the time and distance traveled by garbage trucks on collection routes in the buffer area, including HC-CVA. Local government provided geolocation information to calculate time and distances in Google Maps.

Table 1. Time and distances traveled by garbage trucks on collection routes

Route	Distance(km)		Time(h)	
	HC-CVA	Total	HC-CVA	Total
$R1_m$	13.33	30.70	5:05	9:00
$R2_m$	18.47	37.20	7:45	9:00
$R1_n$	8.25	33.01	3:01	8:00
$R2_n$	16.01	42.10	4:55	8:10
Total	56.06	143.01	20:46	34:10

This way, a problem instance was built using Geographical Position System (GPS) information of garbage trucks in the studied area. The tested instance includes intersections of all streets in the study area as the real-world MSW

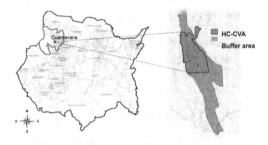

(a) Buffer and HC-CVA areas

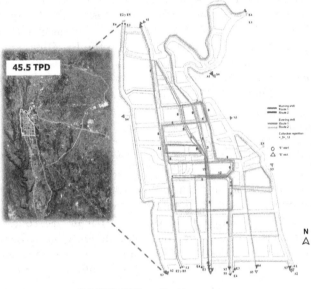

(b) HC-CVA collection routes

Fig. 3. Studied area and the MSW route itineraries in HC-CVA

collection route is doing it. The cost matrix considers the street flows, including sub-tours collection routes. The methodology to build the problem instance considers calculating distances and travel time of the length of streets where two corners streets are connected in the study area using Google Maps tools, real information, and Eq. 2.

4.3   Parameters Configuration

The SA parameters must be adjusted to determine the configuration that allows computing the best results. This way, the parameters tuning is made by an empirical sensitivity analysis performed over the problem instance following the next criteria. The criterion for initial temperature (T_0) was to achieve an acceptance

rate of approximately 95% for new solutions. The criterion for final temperature
(T_f) aimed for an acceptance rate of approximately 0.33% for new solutions, indicating that only solutions with lower cost than the current solution are accepted.
The literature recommendations of decay factors of the annealing schedule (α)
were considered. Finally, the length of the Markov chain used for exploration
$(maxL)$ was set by a fixed number to generate significant new solutions. Due
to the stochastic quality of the simulated annealing, 30 independent executions
of SA were performed. The parameter values that allowed computing the best
results on the tested instance are $T_0 = 7500$, $T_f = 1$, $\alpha = 0.99$, and $maxL =$
300. Figure 4 graphically shows the behavior of the cost solution $f(SA)$ for the
parameter setting instance.

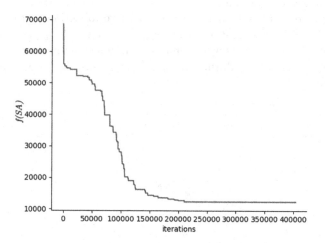

Fig. 4. Convergence of execution 22 of SA

4.4   Experimental Results

Experimental analysis performs 30 independent executions of SA in an average
execution time of 23 min. Table 2 reports best cost of $f(SA)$ found at each SA execution. The SA algorithm iteratively evaluates perturbed solutions at each local
search step, accepting feasible and better solutions than the current solution.

Results in Table 2 indicate that the proposed SA approach can significantly
improve the total collection route distance that the garbage truck tours in the
real world concerning the route distances reported by the Local government.
R1 and R2 in morning shift tours a distance of 31.8 km, and R1 and R2 in
night shift tours a distance of 24.26 km inside the HC-CVA area. Considering
the results computed by the SA proposed approach, improvements of up to 29%
were obtained for both shift routes in the problem instance tested. With the best
collection route by SA (marked in bold in Table 2), the morning shift route has a

Table 2. Best cost solutions at each SA execution

#	f(SA)	#	f(SA)	#	f(SA)	#	f(SA)	#	f(SA)	#	f(SA)
1	18527.0	6	18759.5	11	18245.0	16	18754.4	21	18357.0	26	17183.9
2	17361.7	7	18489.7	12	18357.0	17	18211.0	22	**17134.0**	27	17655.3
3	18155.8	8	17812.1	13	18416.1	18	17703.3	23	18160.8	28	17790.6
4	18686.0	9	17920.1	14	17262.3	19	18187.9	24	18868.0	29	17576.9
5	17253.3	10	17715.0	15	18855.9	20	17497.8	25	19731.7	30	18356.0

distance reduction of 46.11%, and the night shift tour has a distance reduction of 29.37%. SA approach computed significantly competitive collection tours in line with real-world problem instances. The competitive collection tour for the MSW-CVA is displayed in the HC-CVA map. Figure 5 shows the proposed collection route for MSW-CVA, reducing the number of times the garbage truck passes through a particular street during the shift tour, which, in the worst case, is 12 times (Fig. 3b).

Fig. 5. Optimal collection tour for MSW-CVA

5   Conclusion and Future Work

This article presented a metaheuristic approach to solve the MSW-CVA, a relevant problem related to the MSW collection routes in a Historical Center of a Mexican City.

The proposed exploration pattern applies two neighborhood procedures. Procedure SWAPS randomly selects two elements of the current solution and exchanges their positions, generating a new solution. Procedure INSERTION randomly selects one element in the current solution, then relocates the element between two adjacent elements in the current solution, generating a new solution.

The experimental evaluation focused on a realistic problem instance defined over real information from the Historical Center of Cuernavaca, Mexico. Parameter configuration was performed via an empirical sensitivity analysis. Using the best configuration from the previous analysis, the proposed SA allowed computing an MSW collection route that improves up to 29.3% of the results of real-world MSW collection routes in both shift tours, morning and night.

The main lines for future work are related to extending and improving the neighborhood search by applying hybrid approaches combining exact and metaheuristic methods to address real-world problem instances, including waste solid by kilograms and considering the garbage trucks' capacity. The experimental evaluation of the proposed approach should also be extended to consider a larger number of synthetic and real scenarios. Multiobjective versions of the problem and metaheuristics should be studied to compute and analyze distance and windows time simultaneously.

Acknowledgements. This work acknowledges Cuernavaca local government for the information facilitated in developing the work and Diego Rossit from the Universidad Nacional del Sur, Argentina, for his valuable comments regarding the MSW experience in Bahia Blanca, Argentina.

Funding. Facultad de Ciencias Químicas e Ingeniería of the Universidad Autónoma del Estado de Morelos, funded this article.

References

1. Betanzo, E., Torres-Gurrola, M., Romero Navarrete, J., Obregón-Biosca, S.: Evaluación de rutas de recolección de residuos sólidos urbanos con apoyo de dispositivos de rastreo satelital: Análisis e implicaciones. Revista Internacional de Contaminación Ambiental **32**, 323–337 (2016)
2. Cavallin, A., Rossit, D.G., Herrán Symonds, V., Rossit, D.A., Frutos, M.: Application of a methodology to design a municipal waste pre-collection network in real scenarios. Waste Manage. Res. **38**(1), 117–129 (2020)
3. Kaza, S., Yao, L.C., Bhada-Tata, P., Van Woerden, F.: What a Waste 2.0: A Global Snapshot of Solid Waste Management to 2050. Urban Development. World Bank (2018)

4. Kirkpatrick, S., Gelatt, C., Vecchi, M.: Optimization by simulated annealing. Science **220**(4598), 671–680 (1983)
5. Metropolis, N., Rosenbluth, A., Rosenbluth, M., Teller, A., Teller, E.: Equation of state calculations by fast computing machines. J. Chem. Phys. **21**(6), 1087–1092 (1953)
6. Miller, C.E., Tucker, A.W., Zemlin, R.A.: Integer programming formulation of traveling salesman problems. J. ACM **7**(4), 326–329 (1960)
7. Consejería Jurídica del Poder Ejecutivo del Estado de Morelos: Estrategia para la Gestión Integral de los Residuos del estado de Morelos, Morelos (2017)
8. Moreno-Bernal, P., Nesmachnow, S.: Simulated annealing metaheuristic approach for generating alternative corridor locations. In: Rossit, D.A., Tohmé, F., Mejía Delgadillo, G. (eds.) ICPR-Americas 2020. CCIS, vol. 1408, pp. 47–62. Springer, Cham (2021). https://doi.org/10.1007/978-3-030-76310-7_4
9. Nesmachnow, S.: An overview of metaheuristics: accurate and efficient methods for optimisation. Int. J. Metaheuristics **3**(4), 320–347 (2014)
10. Nesmachnow, S., Iturriaga, S.: Cluster-UY: collaborative scientific high performance computing in Uruguay. In: Torres, M., Klapp, J. (eds.) ISUM 2019. CCIS, vol. 1151, pp. 188–202. Springer, Cham (2019). https://doi.org/10.1007/978-3-030-38043-4_16
11. Rao, M., Sultana, R., Kota, S.H.: Solid and Hazardous Waste Management. Elsevier (2016)
12. Secretaría de Medio Ambiente y Recursos Naturales: Diagnóstico Básico para la Gestión Integral de los Residuos, Lucart (2020)
13. Talbi, E.G.: Metaheuristics: From Design to Implementation. Wiley, Hoboken (2009)
14. Tirkolaee, E.B., Goli, A., Gütmen, S., Weber, G.W., Szwedzka, K.: A novel model for sustainable waste collection arc routing problem: pareto-based algorithms. Ann. Oper. Res. **324**, 189–214 (2023)
15. Tirkolaee, E.B., Mahdavi, I., Mehdi Seyyed Esfahani, M.: A robust periodic capacitated arc routing problem for urban waste collection considering drivers and crew's working time. Waste Manage. **76**, 138–146 (2018)
16. Toutouh, J., Rossit, D., Nesmachnow, S.: Soft computing methods for multiobjective location of garbage accumulation points in smart cities. Ann. Math. Artif. Intell. **88**, 105–131 (2020)
17. Vazquez, Y.V., Barragán, F., Castillo, L.A., Barbosa, S.E.: Analysis of the relationship between the amount and type of MSW and population socioeconomic level: Bahía blanca case study, Argentina. Heliyon **6**(6), e04343 (2020)

Smart Industry Strategies for Shop-Floor Production Planning Problems to Support Mass Customization

Diego Rossit[1]([✉])[iD], Daniel Rossit[1][iD], and Sergio Nesmachnow[2][iD]

[1] INMABB, Dpto. Ing., Universidad Nacional del Sur-CONICET,
Bahía Blanca, Argentina
{diego.rossit,daniel.rossit}@uns.edu.ar
[2] Universidad de la República, Montevideo, Uruguay
sergion@fing.edu.uy

Abstract. The smart industry paradigm has revolutionized the landscape of production processes, ushering in new strategies to meet evolving demands. Among these strategies, mass customization stands out, for producing nearly tailored products based on customers preferences, while still using massive production techniques that allow keeping costs burdened. However, to embrace mass customization several operations at shop-floor level of the industry have to be adjusted, among them production planning strategies due to the emergence of missing operations. In this line, this article presents a suite of metaheuristic algorithms designed to tackle the multiobjective flowshop problem with missing operations while considering as optimization criteria the makespan, weighted total tardiness, and total completion time. Through extensive computational experiments on realistic instances, the performance of the applied metaheuristics is thoroughly evaluated. The results underscore the competitiveness of the proposed approaches in effectively addressing the intrinsic computational complexity of the addressed optimization problem, affirming their viability for real-world applications.

Keywords: Smart industry · Mass customization · Missing operations · Flowshop problem · Multiobjective evolutionary algorithms

1 Introduction

The concept of the smart industry, often referred to as Industry 4.0, encompasses a transformative paradigm shift in manufacturing and production processes, leveraging advanced technologies such as the Internet of Things, artificial intelligence, robotics, and data analytics [8]. It aims to create highly interconnected, data-driven, and adaptive manufacturing ecosystems, enabling real-time monitoring, optimization, and automation of production, supply chains, and services. Smart industry endeavors to enhance efficiency, flexibility, and innovation while fostering sustainable practices, ultimately reshaping traditional industrial practices into agile, intelligent, and interconnected systems.

© The Author(s), under exclusive license to Springer Nature Switzerland AG 2024
S. Nesmachnow and L. Hernández Callejo (Eds.): ICSC-Cities 2023, CCIS 1938, pp. 123–137, 2024.
https://doi.org/10.1007/978-3-031-52517-9_9

The smart industry also fosters an interconnected ecosystem where customers, suppliers, and producers collaborate harmoniously [10]. On the hand of customers, mass customization, a hallmark of this transformation, empowers customers to define their unique product preferences, shaping demand in real-time. On the other hand, through intelligent data-driven systems, suppliers seamlessly adjust their offerings, optimizing inventory and production processes to meet dynamic customization needs. This strategy enhanced interplay among smart industry's technological prowess, empowered customers, and agile suppliers has fundamentally reshaped conventional supply chains through comprehensive integration [24].

This new paradigm, paves the way to transform the classic production process into mass customization processes, where the client has an active role in the design of the final product. This situation of personalized products, has a significant impact in terms of production processes, since not all the finished product will be the same, then, their production processes must will not be the same. In production systems that are configured as flow shop, this personalization may impact in a missing operation fashion [25]. In missing operation flow shop scheduling problems, the operation route of each job may be different, where the differences are basically if a job may skip or not one of the operations. Then, the cardinality of the set of operations of jobs is not constant for all jobs. This modification represents a challenging scenario for production scheduling decision-making, because the orders to be planned are not all the same [20]. Furthermore, decision makers must fulfill many criteria for solving the scheduling of production efficiently nowadays, then, the complexity and difficulty of the problem enhances.

This article addresses a missing operation, multi-objective, flow shop scheduling problem using a metaheuristic approach [14]. Mainly, the problem considered is a regular flow shop system, where there is one machine or production resource per stage, and the jobs to be processed by that system may not require to be processed in every machine. Also, as mentioned before, to optimize this problem involves to consider simultaneously more than one criterion. In this case three different objective functions are analyzed, namely, makespan, total tardiness and total completion time. These goals treated as a multiobjective optimization problem, enable to optimize production system utilization, customer service level and production orders flow, respectively. As far as the authors know, this is the first time that a missing operation flow shop problem with three objectives is studied. The metaheuristics applied to solve the problem are NSGA-II, NSGA-III, MOEA/D and SPEA2.

The article is structured as follows. Section 2 formally presents the flowshop problem, describing its mathematical formulation and the main related works. Section 3 presents the metaheuristic algorithms used for the resolution of the multiobjective flowshop problem. Section 4 describes the computational experimentation, including the implementation details, the description of instances and the main results. Finally, Sect. 5 presents the conclusions of the research and formulates the main lines for future work.

2   Mass Customization and the Multiobjective Flowshop Problem with Missing Operations

This section presents a comprehensive presentation of mass customization in Smart Industry environments. Then, a detailed description of the problem addressed in this work is introduced, where the objectives function considered for the multi-objective approach are mathematically described. Finally, the related works found in literature are revised in order to highlight the main contributions of the reported research.

2.1   Mass Customization Impact on the Shop-Floor Operations

As aforementioned, an important aspect of smart industry is mass customization. Mass customization refers to the capacity of efficiently producing goods and services that are tailored to meet individual customer preferences and requirements, while still achieving economies of scale similar to mass production [1,18]. Several companies have successfully invested in enhancing their mass customization strategies to offer personalized products to their customers. One example is Nike, which allows customers to design their own sneakers through its Nike By You platform, where they can choose colors, materials, and customize various design elements [26]. Larger products also have entered to this wave of customization. For example in cars production, BMW enables customers to personalize their luxury vehicles with a wide range of custom features, including paint colors, interior materials, and technology options [27].

Smart industry enables manufacturers to gather insights from customer preferences, adapt production processes, optimize resource allocation, and dynamically reconfigure assembly lines, resulting in the cost-effective creation of highly customized products on a scale previously unattainable. Mass customization starts with an intelligent smart product design, in which the preferences of the user are translated into instructions for the shop-floor operations on how to plan the production phase. In this regard, mass customization has a huge impact in shop-floor operations [28]. Among the aspects that are involved in an efficient shop-floor management are: i) Workflow flexibility and Advanced manufacturing technologies: shop floors must be designed to accommodate varying product configurations and customization options based on advanced manufacturing assessts [11]. ii) Real-time data integration: shop-floor operations need to integrate data systems to ensure accurate and up-to-date information for decision-making [29]. iii) Inventory management: inventory management systems must be optimized to ensure that the right components are available for each customization option [6]; iv) Quality 4.0: robust quality assurance protocols and testing procedures are crucial to maintain customer satisfaction [30]; v) Skilled Workforce: training programs are essential to empower workers with the knowledge needed to execute customization tasks effectively [12]; vi) Smart production planning and control: aims to intelligently perform the activities of loading, scheduling, sequencing, monitoring, and controlling the use of resources and materials during production by means of data analytics, AI, and machine learning [17].

Figure 1 presents a summary of the main concepts involved in an Smart industry and the impact of mass customization to shop-floor operations management. This article focuses on smart production planning proposing new resolution methodologies to solve the flowshop problem that arises in the context of mass customization with missing operations.

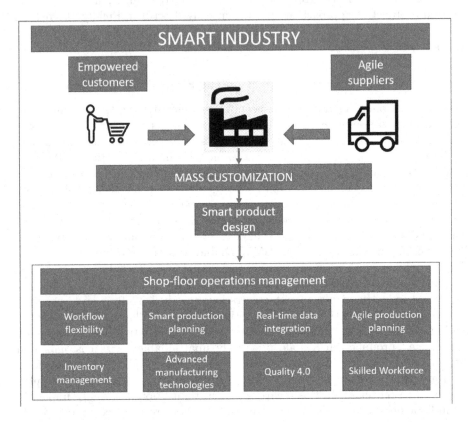

Fig. 1. Smart industry: the new paradigm and the impact on shop-floor operations management.

2.2   Mathematical Formulation

The mathematical formulation of the multiobjective flowshop problem with missing operations considers the following elements:

- A set of machines or operations M that can be performed.
- A set of jobs J that have to be delivered.
- A due date d_j in which each job has to be delivered.

- Given the matrix P_{JM} which contains the processing times p_{jm} for each job j on each machine m and the processing order of jobs on the machines Or, a completion time function $C(j) : P_{JM} \times Or \to \mathcal{R}_0^+$ that returns the completion time of job j, i.e., the time when the job has performed all the required operations in all the machines.
- A vector w_j that gives the relative importance of each job regarding the total completion time.

Then, the optimization problem addressed in this work is to define the processing order of jobs on the machines that simultaneously minimized the following three metrics: the makespan, the weighted total completion time and the total tardiness, which are computed as in Eqs. (1a)–(1c).

$$\min \quad \text{Makespan} = \max_{j \in J}\{C(j)\} \tag{1a}$$

$$\min \quad \text{Total Completion Time} = \sum_{j \in J} w_j \times C(j) \tag{1b}$$

$$\min \quad \text{Total Tardiness} = \sum_{j \in J} max(0; C(j) - d_j) \tag{1c}$$

The impact of missing operations affects the matrix of processing times P_{JM} since several parameters p_{jm} can be equal to 0. Regarding constraints, the problem at hand is bound by specific restrictions. First, there are non-overlapping constraints in place, which prohibit more than one job from being processed on the same machine simultaneously. Second, there are logical timely constraints, meaning that the start time for processing a job on a machine must occur after the finish time of the same job on the previous machine. These restrictions shape the flowshop problem which is known to be a computationally complex problem [4].

2.3   Related Work

The study of missing operation in regular flow shop problems (i.e., a single machine per stage) is not a new problem, it has been studied for more than two decades [5]. However, in the last years it has gained renewed attention in the scientific community since, as it was mentioned previously, there is a growing tendency in the transformation of traditional manufacturing processes towards personalized manufacturing processes. [3]. As for instance, the case of concrete personalized industry where the production process is configured as a flow shop with missing operation. In [25], the objective is to minimize the cycle time, and for this, the authors developed a comprehensive innovative approach that overcomes the particular restrictions the production process has, like lags between operations. Other type of problem is tackled at [19], where a non-permutation flow shop problem with missing operation is considered. Mathematical programming models are developed to optimize the makespan in this work. Also a non-permutation flow shop problem is analyzed at [20], but in this case total tardiness is considered as objective function and metaheuristics are used for optimization. More recently in [7] a missing operation flow shop problem arises at the semiconductor industry. At this case, a special feature of the studied problem is the presence of time waiting constraints, and the objective function is the minimization of total tardiness. For solving the problem heuristic algorithm are implemented. Regarding multi-objective optimization with missing operation in regular flow shop problems, the literature is more scarce. Basically, as far as the authors know, it can be found only [21,22], where in these works a bi-objective problem is approached by means of Evolutionary algorithms. In those studies makespan and total tardiness are minimized, and different levels of missing operations are considered.

Therefore, after revising the literature, it has not been detected a missing operation problem with three objectives, even less that analyzed makespan, total tardiness and total completion time simultaneously. These objectives involves different relevant interests for decision makers, whom must to cope with in their optimization processes. Makespan contribute to optimizing production resources usage, reducing the idle time of them. Meanwhile, total tardiness focus on service level to the client, trying to accomplish the due dates agreed with the client. And, total completion time, try to reduce the time a production order is on the system, that is, tries to reduce the time this order is considered as work-in-progress. The present article addresses these three objectives in a multi-objective manner.

3   Resolution Approach

This section describes the proposed resolution approach for solving the multiobjective flowshop problem.

3.1   Overall Description and Algorithms

Various strategies have been proposed to solve multi-objective optimization problems. Resolution approaches include exact methods rooted in mathematical programming [23], as well as heuristic and metaheuristic strategies [16]. For complex combinatorial challenges like the one described in this paper, metaheuristics offer an efficient resolution strategy to attain high-quality solutions in reasonable computing times and, thus, have been extensively used in similar problems [20,22].

Among metaheuristics, multi-objective evolutionary algorithm (MOEAs) are population-based methods inspired by the evolutionary process of species in nature. MOEAs have demonstrated to be successful methods with application in diverse complex optimization problems [14]. Particularly, this article proposes applying four state-of-the-art evolutionary metaheuristics to address the target problem: SPEA2, NSGA-II, NSGA-III and MOEA/D, which are described next.

Strength Pareto Evolutionary Algorithm 2 (SPEA2). is a MOEA that focuses on non-dominated sorting and density estimation to generate a diverse set of solutions, allowing for effective exploration of the Pareto front. In this line, a notable aspect of SPEA2 is its fitness calculation, which takes into account both Pareto dominance and diversity. The algorithm introduces the concept of strength to gauge how many candidate solutions are dominated by or dominate other solutions. Additionally, fitness assignment involves density estimation. Elitism is also incorporated through the use of a population that stores non-dominated individuals discovered during the search.

Non-dominated Sorting Genetic Algorithm II (NSGA-II). is a widely used evolutionary algorithm that employs non-dominated sorting, crowding distance, and elitism to evolve a diverse population of solutions, efficiently approximating the Pareto front. NSGA-II is characterized by an evolutionary search using a non-dominated elitist ordering that diminishes the complexity of the dominance check, a crowding technique for diversity preservation, and a fitness assignment method considering dominance ranks and crowding distance values. All these features are integrated to provide a robust and effective search, which has been successfully applied to solve multiobjective optimization problems in many application areas.

Non-dominated Sorting Genetic Algorithm III (NSGA-III). NSGA-III is an extension of NSGA-II that incorporates reference points to guide the optimization process, enhancing the spread of solutions along the Pareto front and supporting better convergence.

Multi-objective Evolutionary Algorithm based on Decomposition (MOEA/D). MOEA/D decomposes a multi-objective optimization problem into subproblems, each solved by a separate optimization process. It balances exploration and exploitation to efficiently approximate the Pareto front by iteratively updating solutions through collaboration among subproblems.

3.2   Description of the Proposed Metaheuristics

The proposed MOEAs operate using the following features:

Solution Representation. As it usual in similar works, solutions are denoted by permutations of integers within a vector. The index placement within the vector represents the processing sequence on the initial machine, with the associated integer values corresponding to individual jobs slated for scheduling. Thus, the length of the vector represents to the total job count.

Initialization. The population, comprising $\#P$ individuals, is initialized through a random procedure that generates permutations devoid of repeated integer values. Employing a uniform probability distribution, each value within a solution representation is chosen from the interval [1,n].

Evolutionary Operators. The well-known Partially Mapped Crossover (PMX) is employed as the recombination operator. This crossing mechanism pairs two chosen individuals with a probability of p_c, and it has been widely utilized in various studies tackling permutation-encoded scheduling issues. Subsequently, the mutation operator relies on Swap Mutation, involving the interchange of two elements within the permutation. Application of the mutation operator to an individual occurs with a probability of p_m. Notably, the proposed operators ensure the feasibility of the resultant solutions.

4   Computational Experimentation

This section presents the computational experimentation of the proposed approach, including the description of instances, the methodology used for the experimental evaluation, and the main numerical results.

4.1   Description of the Problem Instances

A set of realistic instances were constructed for the computational experimentation, following the procedure by Henneberg and Neufeld [9]. Processing times were generated as integer values within the range [0:100] following a pseudo-uniform distribution, with the probability of a processing time been zero with a relatively higher value compared to the other possible processing times. This approach ensured the existence of varied processing times including the possibility of missing operations. The sets of instances were constructed considering three different numbers of jobs (30, 40 and 50), two different numbers of machines or operations (10 and 20) and three different percentage probability of missing operations (0%, 10% and 20%). The instances were named using the following convention $n \times m - p\%$, where n is the number of jobs, m is the number of machines and $p\%$ for the percentage probability of missing operations.

4.2   Methodology for the Computational Experimentation

This subsection presents the description of how the computational experimentation of the proposed MOEAs is performed.

Implementation Details and Execcution Platform. The implementation of the proposed MOEAs was carried out in Java, using the JMetal framework version 6.1 [13]. The computational experimentation phase was executed on the National Supercomputing Center, Uruguay (Cluster-UY) [15].

Evaluation Metrics. The evaluation is performed considering two multiobjective optimization metrics: spread and relative hypervolume (RHV). Spread [2] is a metric of diversity that evaluates the distribution of the non-dominated solutions, assessing the capacity of correctly sampling the Pareto front. Unlike other typical distribution metrics such as spacing, the spread as formulated in Eq. (2)

takes into account the information about the extreme points of the true Pareto front to calculate a more accurate value of the dispersion.

$$Spread = \frac{\sum_{o \in \mathcal{O}} d_o^e + \sum_{i \in \mathcal{ND}} |\overline{d} - d_i|}{\sum_{o \in \mathcal{O}} d_o^e + |\mathcal{ND}|\overline{d}} \tag{2}$$

where $\mathcal{O}$ is the set of objectives, $\mathcal{ND}$ is the set of non-dominated solutions, d_o^e is the distance between the extreme point of the Pareto front regarding objective o and the closest non-dominated solution in the computed Pareto front, d_i is the distance between the non-dominated solution i in the computed Pareto front and the closest neighbor non-dominated solution, and $\overline{d}$ is the average value of all d_i. On the other hand, the RHV quantifies the ratio between the hypervolumes (in the search space of the objective functions) covered by the computed Pareto front and the true Pareto front of the problem. Thus, in an ideal situation the RHV value equals one. Consequently, RHV serves as a comprehensive metric that evaluates both numerical accuracy (proximity of the computed Pareto front to the real Pareto front) and the distribution of the non-dominated solutions. When the true Pareto front is unknown for a problem instance, as it is the case in this study, the true Pareto front is approximated using all the non-dominated solutions obtained from all the resolutions performed for that instance.

Parametrization. The determination of the optimal parametric configuration was guided by statistical analysis. This process was pivotal in establishing the values for the key parameters of the studied MOEAs: population size ($\#P$), crossover probability (p_c), and mutation probability (p_m). To determine these parameters different values were assessed: 50 and 100 for population size, 0.5, 0.7, and 0.9 crossover probabilities, and 0.01, 0.05, and 0.1 mutation probabilities. Consequently, a comprehensive evaluation encompassing sixteen parametric configurations ensued for each of the four MOEAs. The analysis for the parameter setting was based on the RHV, which as aforementioned is a robust summary metric. The stopping condition was set to 150,000 evaluations of the objective function. For the comparison three small instances different from the main computational study were used. As the RHV values did not follow a normal distribution according to the Shapiro-Wilk test, the Friedman rank test, a non-parametric method, was employed to assess the goodness of each configuration. Particularly, the neighborhood size of the MOEA/D was chosen in 3% of $\#P$ which showed a good performance in our previous work [21]. After the parameter setting, the following configurations were chosen for the studied MOEAs:

- MOEA/D: $\#P = 50$, $p_c = 0.5$, and $p_m = 0.1$
- NSGA-II: $\#P = 100$, $p_c = 0.7$, and $p_m = 0.1$
- NSGA-III: $\#P = 50$, $p_c = 0.7$, and $p_m = 0.1$
- SPEA2: $\#P = 100$, $p_c = 0.9$, and $p_m = 0.1$

4.3 Numerical Results

This subsection describes the result of the computational experimentation. For each instance and each MOEA, 30 independent runs were performed.

Multi-objective Optimization Metrics. Tables 1 and 2 present the summary of the results of the RHV and the spread respectively. The tables report the statistical test used to study if there are significant differences among the medians or averages, a central tendency and a dispersion measure for the studied MOEAs. In the instances in which results follow a normal distribution, the ANOVA test is applied as statistical test (expressed with "A" in the Tables 1 and 2) and the mean and standard deviation are used as central tendency and dispersion measures respectively. Conversely, in the case of non-parametric distributions, Kruskal-Wallis (expressed with "K-W" in the table) is applied as statistical test, and the median and interquartile range are used as central tendency and dispersion measures respectively. For each instance, the best result is marked with bold font. Results marked with gray background indicate the cases in which the test verified a significant statistical difference with respect to the other MOEAs. Regarding RHV, NSGA-II obtained the largest mean/median in 8 out of 18 instances. SPEA2 obtained the largest mean/median in 6 out of 18 instances. Finally, the NSGA-III obtained the largest mean/median in 4 instances out of 18 instances. The largest mean/median value was obtained by SPEA2 for instances 30J × 10M-0% (0.7822). In terms of spread, SPEA2 obtained the smallest value in 13 out of 18 instances. NSGA-II and NSGA-III obtained the smallest values in 3 out of 18 instances and in 2 out of 18 instances, respectively. The overall smallest value of spread was obtained by SPEA2 for instance 30J × 20M-0% (0.3895). Overall the SPEA2 and the NSGA-II had the best performance for the instances studied, been able to outperformed the other MOEAs in both analyzed metrics.

Table 1. Results of RHV metric for the studied MOEAs.

Instance	Test	MOEA/D		NSGA-II		NSGA-III		SPEA2	
		mean/ median	std/ iqr	mean/ median	std/ iqr	mean/ median	std/ iqr	mean/ median	std/ iqr
30J×10M-0%	A	0.4834	0.0911	0.7344	0.0518	0.7524	0.0590	**0.7822**	0.0411
30J×10M-10%	K-W	0.5928	0.1268	**0.7459**	0.1395	0.7402	0.1049	0.7242	0.1331
30J×10M-20%	A	0.4113	0.0598	0.7398	0.0845	0.6272	0.0885	**0.7485**	0.0933
30J×20M-0%	K-W	0.5013	0.0695	0.6984	0.0817	0.7126	0.0674	**0.7378**	0.0560
30J×20M-10%	A	0.5699	0.0623	**0.7748**	0.0518	0.7558	0.0575	0.7652	0.0425
30J×20M-20%	A	0.4467	0.0583	**0.7047**	0.0664	0.7037	0.0456	0.6746	0.0529
40J×10M-0%	A	0.4006	0.0940	0.6096	0.1067	0.6015	0.1227	**0.6584**	0.0750
40J×10M-10%	A	0.2673	0.1485	**0.5692**	0.1495	0.5126	0.1445	0.5341	0.1405
40J×10M-20%	A	0.4170	0.1131	0.5951	0.1074	0.5835	0.1231	**0.6331**	0.1178
40J×20M-0%	A	0.4858	0.0678	0.7385	0.0587	0.7399	0.0614	**0.7412**	0.0641
40J×20M-10%	A	0.3950	0.0825	0.6264	0.0875	**0.6289**	0.1242	0.5965	0.1136
40J×20M-20%	A	0.3477	0.0824	**0.5773**	0.1700	0.5427	0.0902	0.5396	0.1125
50J×10M-0%	A	0.3950	0.1255	**0.5622**	0.1170	0.5321	0.1107	0.5238	0.1147
50J×10M-10%	A	0.3238	0.1098	**0.5374**	0.1154	0.5689	0.0943	0.5204	0.0976
50J×10M-20%	K-W	0.4452	0.1381	**0.7027**	0.0682	0.5847	0.1650	0.6994	0.1385
50J×20M-0%	K-W	0.4351	0.1039	0.6146	0.0674	**0.6572**	0.1009	0.6379	0.1375
50J×20M-10%	A	0.3863	0.0978	0.6391	0.1111	**0.6595**	0.1260	0.6588	0.0909
50J×20M-20%	K-W	0.3891	0.1543	0.4894	0.1153	**0.6394**	0.1546	0.5096	0.1955

Table 2. Results of Spread metric for the studied MOEAs.

Instance	Test	MOEA/D		NSGA-II		NSGA-III		SPEA2	
		mean/ median	std/ iqr	mean/ median	std/ iqr	mean/ median	std/ iqr	mean/ median	std/ iqr
30J×10M-0%	A	0.6967	0.2133	0.6194	0.0791	0.6407	0.0930	**0.5875**	0.0734
30J×10M-10%	A	0.9320	0.2343	**0.5847**	0.0746	0.7396	0.1305	0.5855	0.0809
30J×10M-20%	A	0.6581	0.2059	0.5420	0.0500	0.5494	0.0725	**0.4328**	0.0559
30J×20M-0%	K-W	0.4926	0.3159	0.5277	0.0558	0.5673	0.0640	**0.3895**	0.0922
30J×20M-10%	K-W	0.5793	0.3295	0.5209	0.0775	0.4747	0.0760	**0.4289**	0.0550
30J×20M-20%	K-W	**0.4828**	0.1162	0.5819	0.0874	0.5589	0.0649	0.4928	0.0767
40J×10M-0%	K-W	1.0366	0.4067	0.8862	0.1077	0.9358	0.1001	**0.7415**	0.1895
40J×10M-10%	A	0.8685	0.2703	0.7688	0.0952	0.8219	0.1000	**0.7410**	0.1253
40J×10M-20%	A	0.8854	0.2373	0.6944	0.1232	0.7860	0.1174	**0.6862**	0.0972
40J×20M-0%	K-W	0.6562	0.4220	0.5989	0.1072	0.6249	0.1733	**0.5550**	0.0555
40J×20M-10%	A	0.8023	0.2096	**0.6358**	0.0833	0.6958	0.1037	0.6508	0.0944
40J×20M-20%	K-W	**0.4162**	0.3034	0.5463	0.0824	0.5882	0.0845	0.5103	0.0916
50J×10M-0%	K-W	1.0173	0.4402	0.7436	0.1380	0.8684	0.1498	**0.7416**	0.1084
50J×10M-10%	K-W	1.1669	0.3361	**0.8214**	0.1237	0.9201	0.1110	0.8666	0.1628
50J×10M-20%	A	0.9082	0.2717	0.8292	0.1095	0.9344	0.0620	**0.7920**	0.1228
50J×20M-0%	K-W	0.7270	0.3757	0.5938	0.1064	0.5604	0.1418	**0.5334**	0.0636
50J×20M-10%	A	0.7694	0.2483	0.6114	0.0690	0.6745	0.1350	**0.6059**	0.1003
50J×20M-20%	A	0.7759	0.2383	0.5840	0.0498	0.6184	0.0689	**0.5519**	0.0743

Consolidated Pareto Fronts. Table 3 reports the spread and RHV metrics for the consolidated Pareto fronts computed from all the nondominated solutions obtained by each MOEA for each instance in the 30 independent runs. Regarding RHV, the NSGA-II, SPEA2 and NSGA-III are able to outperformed the rest of the MOEAs in 6 instances, 6 instances, and 5 instances, respectively. Regarding spread, the NSGA-II, SPEA2, NSGA-III, and MOEA/D are able to outperformed the rest of the MOEAs in 10 instances, 6 instances, 1 instance, and 1 instance respectively. Similarly to the previous numerical results, the SPEA2 and NSGA-II are able to obtain the best results in more instances than the other two MOEAs.

Table 3. Consolidated Spread and RHV metrics for the studied MOEAs.

Instance	MOEA/D		NSGA-II		NSGA-III		SPEA2	
	RHV	Spread	RHV	Spread	RHV	Spread	RHV	Spread
30J × 10M-10%	0.8443	0.7738	**0.9735**	**0.5155**	0.9578	0.5232	0.9667	0.5931
30J × 10M-20%	0.6703	0.6574	0.9722	0.5058	0.9167	0.7268	**0.9805**	**0.4954**
30J × 10M-0%	0.7621	0.6836	0.9278	0.4737	0.9302	0.5108	**0.9710**	**0.4685**
30J × 20M-10%	0.8041	0.6126	**0.9712**	0.4558	0.9481	0.5927	0.9402	**0.4034**
30J × 20M-20%	0.6711	0.6427	0.9321	**0.3611**	**0.9592**	0.4497	0.8829	0.4754
30J × 20M-0%	0.7662	0.5835	**0.9506**	**0.4616**	0.9222	0.5188	0.9360	0.4655
40J × 10M-10%	0.6198	**0.6842**	**0.9855**	0.7670	0.8589	0.9604	0.8870	0.7849
40J × 10M-20%	0.7475	0.6930	0.8840	**0.5986**	0.9183	0.6737	**0.9617**	0.5987
40J × 10M-0%	0.6824	0.7807	0.9079	**0.5344**	0.9116	0.7246	**0.9540**	0.5988
40J × 10M-10%	0.6509	0.6051	**0.9346**	**0.4889**	0.9524	0.5193	0.9303	0.5545
40J × 10M-20%	0.5810	0.7644	0.9333	0.5719	0.8713	**0.4808**	0.9069	0.4997
40J × 20M-0%	0.7078	0.5367	0.9574	0.4930	**0.9619**	0.4996	0.9456	**0.4856**
50J × 10M-10%	0.6873	0.9384	0.8380	**0.5640**	**0.9383**	0.6974	0.8446	0.7364
50J × 10M-20%	0.8144	1.0288	0.9157	0.6397	0.8813	0.7216	**0.9815**	**0.7097**
50J × 10M-0%	0.7176	1.1333	0.8092	**0.7105**	**0.8943**	1.0291	0.8296	0.7702
50J × 10M-10%	0.6747	0.7259	**0.9508**	**0.4702**	0.9278	0.5466	0.9307	0.7395
50J × 10M-20%	0.7673	0.7998	0.8072	**0.5031**	0.9209	0.6806	**0.8914**	0.5758
50J × 10M-0%	0.7407	0.6757	0.8887	0.5255	**0.9480**	0.5379	0.8574	**0.4727**

Impact of Missing Operations Over Instances. For showing the relation between the values of the objectives, Fig. 2 presents the consolidated Pareto fronts of the instances according to the percentage of missing operations for instance 30J × 10M. Similar results were obtained for the rest of the instances. The Total Tardiness and the weighted Total Completion Time seem to be highly sensitive to the percentage of missing operation, i.e., the larger the percentage probability of missing operations, the smaller the values of Total Tardiness and the weighted Total Completion Ttime. On the other hand, the Makespan is less affected by the percentage probability of missing operation.

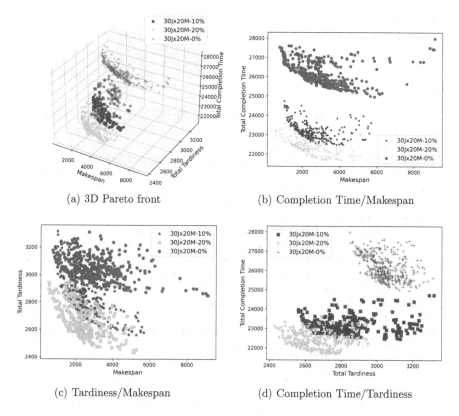

(a) 3D Pareto front

(b) Completion Time/Makespan

(c) Tardiness/Makespan

(d) Completion Time/Tardiness

Fig. 2. Pareto front of instance 30J × 20M with different levels of missing operations.

5   Conclusions and Future Work

Mass customization, as part of the Smart industry paradigm, seeks to combine the advantages of mass production with those of customization. This article studied the flow shop problem with missing operations that arises in shop-floor operations as a consequence of mass customization. Four state-of-the-art MOEAs were applied to simultaneously optimize three traditional metrics of flowshop problems: weighted Total Completion Time, total tardiness and makespan. In the computational analysis over realistic instances, SPEA2 and NSGA-II consistently computed the best results, regarding both convergence and diversity metrics. Moreover, another relevant result is the greater impact of the percentage of missing operations on total tardiness and weighted total completion time, whereas the makespan remained relatively unaffected.

Future work includes enlarging the computational experimentation, incorporating more instances and higher percentage probabilities of missing operations. Additionally, other MOEAs will be included in the analysis to assess their performance in this specific problem domain.

Acknowledgements. This work was partly supported by research projects Red Industria 4.0 (319RT0574, CYTED), PICT-2021-I-INVI-00217 of Agencia I+D+i (Argentina), and PIBAA 0466CO (CONICET).

References

1. Baranauskas, G., Raišienė, A., Korsakienė, R.: Mapping the scientific research on mass customization domain: a critical review and bibliometric analysis. J. Risk Financ. Manage. **13**(9), 220 (2020)
2. Deb, K.: Multiobjective optimization using evolutionary algorithms (2001)
3. Dios, M., Fernandez, V., Framinan, J.: Efficient heuristics for the hybrid flow shop scheduling problem with missing operations. Comput. Ind. Eng. **115**, 88–99 (2018)
4. Garey, M., Johnson, D., Sethi, R.: The complexity of flowshop and jobshop scheduling. Math. Oper. Res. **1**(2), 117–129 (1976)
5. Glass, C., Gupta, J., Potts, C.: Two-machine no-wait flow shop scheduling with missing operations. Math. Oper. Res. **24**(4), 911–924 (1999)
6. Guo, S., Choi, T., Shen, B., Jung, S.: Inventory management in mass customization operations: a review. IEEE Trans. Eng. Manage. **66**(3), 412–428 (2018)
7. Han, J., Lee, J.: Scheduling for a flow shop with waiting time constraints and missing operations in semiconductor manufacturing. Eng. Optim. **55**(10), 1742–1759 (2023)
8. Haverkort, B., Zimmermann, A.: Smart industry: how ICT will change the game! IEEE Internet Comput. **21**(1), 8–10 (2017)
9. Henneberg, M., Neufeld, J.: A constructive algorithm and a simulated annealing approach for solving flowshop problems with missing operations. Int. J. Prod. Res. **54**(12), 3534–3550 (2016)
10. Ibarra, D., Ganzarain, J., Igartua, J.: Business model innovation through industry 4.0: a review. Procedia Manuf. **22**, 4–10 (2018)
11. Keddis, N., Kainz, G., Zoitl, A., Knoll, A.: Modeling production workflows in a mass customization era. In: International Conference on Industrial Technology, pp. 1901–1906. IEEE (2015)
12. Liboni, L., Cezarino, L., Jabbour, C., Oliveira, B., Stefanelli, N.: Smart industry and the pathways to HRM 4.0: implications for SCM. Supply Chain Manage. Int. J. **24**(1), 124–146 (2019)
13. Nebro, A.J., Pérez-Abad, J., Aldana-Martin, J.F., García-Nieto, J.: Evolving a multi-objective optimization framework. In: Osaba, E., Yang, X.-S. (eds.) Applied Optimization and Swarm Intelligence. STNC, pp. 175–198. Springer, Singapore (2021). https://doi.org/10.1007/978-981-16-0662-5_9
14. Nesmachnow, S.: An overview of metaheuristics: accurate and efficient methods for optimisation. Int. J. Metaheuristics **3**(4), 320–347 (2014)
15. Nesmachnow, S., Iturriaga, S.: Cluster-UY: collaborative scientific high performance computing in Uruguay. In: Torres, M., Klapp, J. (eds.) ISUM 2019. CCIS, vol. 1151, pp. 188–202. Springer, Cham (2019). https://doi.org/10.1007/978-3-030-38043-4_16
16. Nesmachnow, S., Rossit, D., Toutouh, J.: Comparison of multiobjective evolutionary algorithms for prioritized urban waste collection in montevideo, Uruguay. Electron. Notes Discrete Math. **69**, 93–100 (2018)
17. Oluyisola, O., Bhalla, S., Sgarbossa, F., Strandhagen, J.: Designing and developing smart production planning and control systems in the industry 4.0 era: a methodology and case study. J. Intell. Manuf. **33**(1), 311–332 (2022)

18. Perez, A.T.E., Rossit, D.A., Tohme, F., Vasquez, O.C.: Mass customized/ personalized manufacturing in industry 4.0 and blockchain: research challenges, main problems, and the design of an information architecture. Inf. Fusion **79**, 44–57 (2022)
19. Ramezanian, R., Rahmani, D.: Milp formulation and genetic algorithm for flow shop scheduling problem with missing operations. Int. J. Oper. Res. **30**(3), 321–339 (2017)
20. Rossit, D., Toncovich, A., Rossit, D., Nesmachnow, S.: Solving a flow shop scheduling problem with missing operations in an industry 4.0 production environment. J. Project Manage. **6**(1), 33–44 (2021)
21. Rossit, D., Nesmachnow, S., Rossit, D.: A multi objective evolutionary algorithm based on decomposition for a flow shop scheduling problem in the context of industry 4.0. Int. J. Math. Eng. Manage. Sci. **7**(4), 433 (2022)
22. Rossit, D., Rossit, D., Nesmachnow, S.: Explicit multiobjective evolutionary algorithms for flow shop scheduling with missing operations. Program. Comput. Softw. **47**, 615–630 (2021)
23. Rossit, D., Toutouh, J., Nesmachnow, S.: Exact and heuristic approaches for multiobjective garbage accumulation points location in real scenarios. Waste Manage. **105**, 467–481 (2020)
24. Shen, B., Zhang, J., Cheng, M., Guo, S., He, R.: Supply chain integration in mass customization. Ann. Oper. Res. 1–22 (2023). https://doi.org/10.1007/s10479-023-05202-y
25. Smutnicki, C., Pempera, J., Bocewicz, G., Banaszak, Z.: Cyclic flow-shop scheduling with no-wait constraints and missing operations. Eur. J. Oper. Res. **302**(1), 39–49 (2022)
26. Supply Chain Resource Cooperative: Nike learns to mass customize shoes while near-shoring. https://scm.ncsu.edu/scm-articles/article/nike-learns-to-mass-customize-shoes-while-near-shoring, June 2016
27. Wintermaier, P: Customization vs. Scale - How BMW imagines the future of cars. https://d3.harvard.edu/platform-rctom/submission/customization-vs-scale-how-bmw-imagines-the-future-of-cars/, November 2018
28. Zawadzki, P., Żywicki, K.: Smart product design and production control for effective mass customization in the industry 4.0 concept. Manage. Prod. Eng. Rev. **7**(3), 105–112 (2016)
29. Zhong, R., Dai, Q., Qu, T., Hu, G., Huang, G.: RFID-enabled real-time manufacturing execution system for mass-customization production. Robot. Comput.-Integr. Manuf. **29**(2), 283–292 (2013)
30. Zonnenshain, A., Kenett, R.: Quality 4.0-the challenging future of quality engineering. Qual. Eng. **32**(4), 614–626 (2020)

Internet of Things

Aquality: A Scalable IoT-Enabled Drinking Water Quality Monitoring System

Víctor M. Ortega Pabón$^{(\boxtimes)}$ ⓘ and Eugenio Tamura ⓘ

Pontificia Universidad Javeriana – Cali, Calle 18 118-250, Santiago de, Cali, Colombia
{victor,tek}@javerianacali.edu.co

Abstract. To guarantee the quality of water for human consumption, it is necessary to have a monitoring system for drinking water treatment plants. For this purpose, an architecture is proposed for the development, deployment, and commissioning of a multi-node water quality monitoring system using MQTT and RS-485/Modbus protocols. For the solution to be scalable and customizable, the design employs standard notations and diagrams and considers the national and international regulations; besides, all the tools used are either Open or Freemium.

Keywords: Water Quality · Drinking Water Treatment Plants · Multi-Stage Filtration · IoT · MQTT · RS-485/Modbus · FreeRTOS

1 Introduction

Water is a basic human need, indispensable for human consumption and food preparation. For this very reason, water purification is one of the most critical public health challenges.

The 2030 Agenda for Sustainable Development, formulated 17 Sustainable Development Goals (SDGs). The report establishes that regarding Goal 6 –Ensure availability and sustainable management of water and sanitation for all–, for at least 3 billion people, the quality of the water they depend on is unknown due to a lack of monitoring. SDG Target 6.1 calls for "universal and equitable access to safe and affordable drinking water for all" [1].

The consequences of not dealing with this matter are severe. According to the World Health Organization (WHO), contaminated water is responsible for the transmission of diseases such as cholera, other diarrhea, dysentery, hepatitis A, typhoid fever, and polio; according to one estimate, contaminated drinking water causes 485,000 deaths from diarrhea each year. Improper use or treatment of water can put communities at risk for disease, infection, chemical poisoning, etc. Therefore, safe and readily available water is important for public health. The impact is worst for low-income countries; rural areas lie behind urban ones in terms of access to safe water and unsafe water sources account for 6% of deaths [2].

S. Nesmachnow and L. Hernández Callejo (Eds.): ICSC-Cities 2023, CCIS 1938, pp. 141–155, 2024.
https://doi.org/10.1007/978-3-031-52517-9_10

Access to safe water can boost countries' economic growth and contribute greatly to poverty reduction [3]. For The United Nations Educational, Scientific and Cultural Organization (UNESCO), safe drinking water is essential for eradicating poverty and for building prosperous, peaceful societies [4].

Regarding the costs of overcoming this situation, it has been estimated that achieving universal access to safe drinking water and sanitation (SDG Targets 6.1 and 6.2) in 140 low- and middle-income countries would cost approximately US$ 1.7 trillion from 2016 to 2030, or US$ 114 billion per year [5].

Drinking Water Treatment Plants (DWTPs) using Multi-Stage Filtration (MSF) technology are used worldwide in rural areas and small- to medium-sized municipalities in developing countries [6], as they are simple and low-cost sustainable technologies, in harmony with local conditions and the capacities of many communities [7]. These plants often rely on surface water (i.e. water drawn from rivers, streams, lakes, ponds, and springs).

2   Rationale

At the *Pontificia Universidad Javeriana - Cali* (PUJC), which is located in the south of Cali, the capital of Valle del Cauca, Colombia, water is made potable by means of a DWTP with MSF technology. The plant is fed by diversion number 4 of the Pance River, from which a concession was obtained in 1986, allowing it to take up to 3.72 L/s.

After approximately 37 years of use, a problem has become evident with the constant degradation of the Pance River water source upstream, in addition to the manual recording of water quality measurements required by government agencies. The main problem is that the filters become clogged when the water reaches the plant very turbid, as a result of rainfall, or also because of the cleaning of plants located before the University, where waste is dumped into the river due to the lack of drying beds.

Therefore, in order to supervise the quality and compliance with the standards of the inflow, the quality of the outflow water, and the plant's own capacity to supply water to the Javeriana Community, a monitoring system was proposed based on the variables of turbidity, flow, pH, and chlorine. Raw water should be monitored at the plant inlet and drinking water at the plant outlet (see Fig. 1).

This DWTP model is widely used throughout the region, and even in other parts of the world, so the aim is to have a standard approach that can be customized according to the particular requirements of the place where it is located.

Finally, this approach focuses on standardizing the design process by providing a design reference using architectural notation tools, which ultimately results in agile, highly customizable, and scalable solutions.

Therefore, this project could contribute to the development of monitoring for these plants, making a significant contribution to public health. It is expected

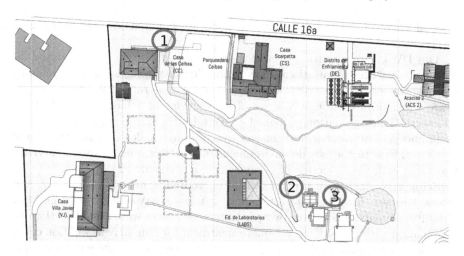

Fig. 1. Physical location of the monitoring points: ① sand trap at the river intake catchment, ② plant inlet, ③ plant outlet (Source: *Oficina de Recursos Físicos PUJC*)

that results should be transferable to various other DWTPs employed in rural or small communities such as those with Upflow Gravel Filter in Layers (UGFL) and Rapid Sand Filter (RSF) with downflow [8].

3 Background

Different metrics have been made available through WHO supervision for water quality monitoring [9]. In Colombia specifically, there is the Resolution 2115 of the National Ministries of Social Protection, and Environment, Housing and Territorial Development, which provides metrics for the evaluation and monitoring of the quality of water for human consumption, supervising DWTPs.

Water must meet three characteristics with different acceptable ranges for each of its components [10]:

- Physical characteristics (apparent color, turbidity, odor, and taste).
- Chemical characteristics (total carbon, fluorides, nitrites, nitrates, etc.).
- Microbiological characteristics (total coliforms and Escherichia coli).

Each service provider organization has the responsibility to establish a monitoring and control plan in relation to its DWTP water quality according to Decree 1575 of 2007 [11].

3.1 Drinking Water Treatment Plant

DWTPs with MSF technology were created as a joint research project by the Cinara Institute and the Universidad del Valle with the support of the International Water and Sanitation Center (IRC) in search for improving public health in small rural communities, at low cost and easy maintenance and monitoring for operators.

This DWTP works with a combination of coarse filtration and slow sand filtration. Each with its limitations, Slow Sand Filtration (SSF) is a simple, reliable, and efficient technology. SSF works with a water flow rate of 0.1 to 0.3 m^3/h, where water passes through a series of mechanisms of a biological and physical nature. Thus, predation of algae by invertebrates and bacteria by protozoa, consumption of detritus or dead matter by saprophytes, death or inactivation of microorganisms in the hostile environment of the filter, and metabolic activity associated with the reduction of organic carbon is generated [12].

Being very efficient in the removal of microorganisms, organic matter, and others, however, for its good performance it is necessary a slow speed and low turbidity effluents. Therefore, two pre-treatment stages were added so that, in combination with the SSF, an adequate treatment for human consumption could be achieved. After the evaluation of alternatives, these stages were the Dynamic Coarse Filter (DCF) and the Ascending Coarse Filter (ACF). Finally, the combination of these three technologies is what is known as Multi-Stage Filtration (MSF) [12].

The general scheme of an MSF plant can be seen in Fig. 2. It works by first removing the larger suspended solids and then the fine matter down to the microorganisms as seen in the treatment process schematic in Fig. 3.

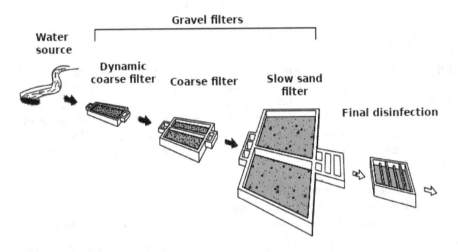

Fig. 2. A Multi-Stage Filtration (MSF) treatment system. It is composed of coarse filtration and slow sand filtration stages, followed by a disinfection stage [12,13].

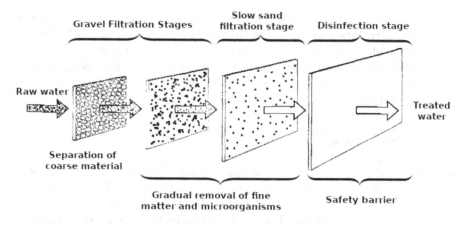

Fig. 3. An MSF process works by first removing the larger suspended solids and then the fine matter down to the microorganisms [12,13].

According to the various policies involved, the following are the variables of interest for measuring water quality:

Flow Rate. The flow rate is important for the treatment plant in the first place to comply with the surface water concession, and also because the plant is designed to operate at a flow rate of approximately 3 L/s; for this reason it is important to have a measurement of this to ensure the proper operation of the plant according to its design.

Turbidity. Turbidity is caused by suspended solids within the liquid which may be due to the presence of clay, silt, chemical particles, plant decomposition residues, and organisms. As turbidity increases, the color of the liquid becomes darker. High turbidity can indicate heavy rainfall, spills, and contamination; and because of the technology used for treatment, it reduces the efficiency of the DWTP [14]. If it exceeds 50 NTU of turbidity at the plant inlet, the plant filters may quickly become clogged. For this reason, it is important to use it as an indicator; together with pH and chlorine, it guarantees to a great extent the quality of the water for human consumption if they are maintained in the appropriate ranges [12].

pH. pH refers to the concentration of hydrogen ions within the water. A scale of 0–14 is used where 7 is neutral; lower values tend to be more base and higher ones tend to be more acidic. pH affects most chemical and biological processes in water; according to the U.S. Environmental Protection Agency (EPA) and the Ministry of Social Protection, it should be in the range of 6.5 to 9.0 and monitored daily [9,10]. In addition, it is an indicator to evaluate the possible chemical or biological change within the tributary [15].

Chlorine. Chlorine is the most widely used disinfectant barrier because of its characteristics of elimination of unpleasant odors and tastes, low cost, ease of transport and storage, as well as being a great agent against microorganisms [16]. In the distribution network, the objective is to maintain free chlorine at a concentration of a maximum of 2 ppm and a minimum of 0.3 ppm at the farthest point of the network in order to maintain disinfectant protection along its route to the points of consumption; this must be monitored daily according to the number of current users at the University [10].

4   Related Works

Water monitoring is of utmost importance to determine, for example, the presence of different plant populations or water pollution, as evidenced in *"Water Quality Analysis of Remote Sensing Images Based on Inversion Model"* where remote analysis of images based on a model is used to estimate the amount of dissolved oxygen and permanganate; these image-based approaches are generally used for large bodies of water [17].

In the article *"Water Quality Monitoring Using Wireless Sensor Networks: Current Trends and Future Research Directions"* the current and future trends in water quality monitoring systems are explored. They list the recommended variables with their acceptable ranges, as well as the main projects deployed around the topic giving an overview of water quality monitoring applications.

In *"Paper-Sensors for Point-of-Care Monitoring of Drinking Water Quality"* propose a low-cost solution for water quality monitoring by means of paper sensors that detect the presence of contaminants within the liquid; the sensing method and implementation of the same are developed [18].

The article *"Connected Sensors, Innovative Sensor Deployment, and Intelligent Data Analysis for Online Water Quality Monitoring"* comments on the disconnection, lack of standardization, and challenges for proper sampling with the connection of the monitoring system in its different components from the data collection stage to the time of analysis for the end user [19].

The *"WQMS: A Water Quality Monitoring System using IoT"* project has a single node connected to pH, turbidity, and temperature sensors. They offer a prediction of future data from the sensors, MQTT communication, mobile and desktop visualization via a web server, and data storage in a MongoDB database [20].

In [21] an implementation is presented that uses Wemos D1 as a means to monitor pH and turbidity; using WiFi it is uploaded to the Ubidots platform where there is a dashboard that allows observing changes in the process, measuring only those variables of interest. Another study monitors pH, turbidity, conductivity, and temperature to monitor water quality for an agricultural system by taking a large amount of data to develop a machine-learning model.

In *"Fault Diagnosis of Water Quality Monitoring Devices Based on Multiclass Support Vector Machines and Rule-Based Decision Trees"*, the architecture by nodes of a monitoring system, its components, and a fault detection system for these systems focused on the proper functioning of the sensors is proposed [22]. A monitoring system is also proposed for large-area water bodies using solar panels and the GSM network to send text messages with data from each monitoring node [23].

Then, H2O is a project that seeks to measure the quality of the water where they measure the parameters of pH, *Oxidation-Reduction Potential (ORP)* and temperature; using them to create a time series that is analyzed with a neural network showing these values on a dashboard and their predictions [24].

Most of these projects propose and implement the measurement of certain variables at a single point, while those that propose measurement at several points show their results from simulations. In this project, the monitoring of variables in at least three points was proposed, with a standardized protocol, real-time visualization, and standardization of the sampling nodes.

5   Design Process

The idea is to develop a standard architecture, yet adaptable and scalable in different contexts, for the monitoring of DWTPs. Therefore, it is important to examine the design requirements and constraints. From Fig. 1 it is clear that the solution must be a distributed one.

Data must be gathered on a central computer from distant, outdoor endpoints; this requires an industrial physical communication protocol such as RS-485 (TIA/EIA 485 Standard), which uses differential signaling over twisted pair cabling and provides point-to-point, multi-dropped connectivity. On top of it, Modbus, a de facto client-server communication protocol standard is used.

To transform plant operation data into information for traceability purposes and further analysis, a connection to the University servers is needed. For this reason, Wi-Fi is the choice since the central server has access to it. Besides, the Message Queue Telemetry Transport (MQTT), an OASIS Open standard messaging protocol, is used because it is designed as a lightweight publish/subscribe reliable messaging transport protocol ideal for connecting remote devices with a small code footprint and minimal network bandwidth [25].

Chlorine, pH, and water color measurements must be read by an operator at probe points along the campus by using handheld instruments. To register these values, an app was developed using Flutter, a development kit used to generate cross-platform applications from a single codebase. Data must be preserved; for this, PostgreSQL was chosen. For visualization purposes, Streamsheets, a powerful and flexible platform to process event streams, was selected.

Figure 4 shows the Context Diagram for the proposed solution; that is, the different subsystems, inputs, and outputs required to fulfill the system requirements. The monitoring system consists of three parts: the Central Computer, the Sampling Nodes with their different sensors, and the Mobile Client, which is used as a Manual Sampling Node.

Abstract system functionality is described by using the Specification and Description Language (SDL, International Telecommunication Union Recommendation Z.100 [26]). In it, the system architecture shows the structure of the

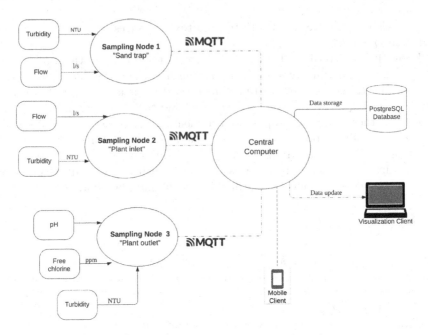

Fig. 4. Context Diagram for the proposed solution. A context diagram shows how the system is broken into subsystems, as well as the system inputs and outputs.

system: its abstract components, represented by processes; how processes are interconnected; and the means used for interaction between processes (see Fig. 5).

MQTT needs a broker, that is, a server that receives all messages from the MQTT clients and then forwards them to the appropriate subscribing clients by using topics. Mosquitto was selected for this purpose. To assist in processing data, Node-RED, a low-code programming platform for event-driven applications, was also incorporated into the solution.

A high-level perspective of the system behavior can be described by using Message Sequence Charts (MSC) description diagrams (International Telecommunication Union Recommendation Z.120 [27]).

Figure 6 shows the behavioral diagram for the operation of the Central Computer, illustrating how its different processes interact and evolve over time with other processes in the system by reacting to exchanging messages using the MQTT communication protocol.

SDL allows describing not just the architecture, but also, its detailed behavior using Process Diagrams, which are Extended Finite State Machines (EFSMs); that is Finite State Machines (FSMs) that can process data.

Figure 7 shows the Process Diagram for an MQTT publisher: states are represented in pink, inputs in gray, and transitions in green. Following the semantics

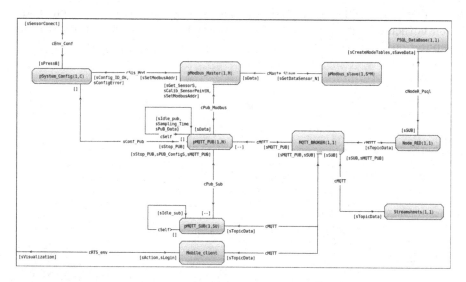

Fig. 5. The System Architecture shows the structure of the system: its abstract components (represented by processes, denoted by rectangles with chamfered corners), how they are interconnected (via channels), and the means used for interaction between processes (messages, which represent events of any type, i.e., physical or logical).

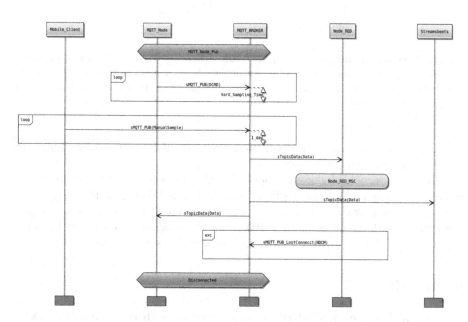

Fig. 6. Message Sequence Chart (*MSC*) for normal operation of the Central Computer. An MSC shows how processes in the system evolve over time by exchanging messages in a given scenario.

of an FSM, the EFSM is blocked until an event arrives; the subsequent transition is then executed, involving the generation of another event(s) and some computation if the need arises.

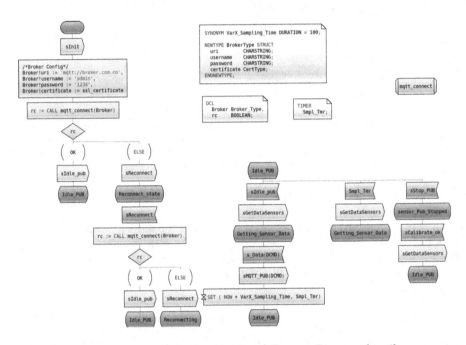

Fig. 7. Process Diagram for process pMQTT_PUB. A Process Diagram describes a process behavior by means of an extended finite state machine, which reacts to inputs (events conveyed as messages). It then executes the corresponding transition according to its inputs and current state.

Figure 8 shows a Logical Deployment diagram: how software modules are distributed on hardware components.

The design process followed a model-based approach: An iterative process of modeling and debugging was carried out using PragmaDev Studio, a suite that comprises system specification, description, and verification tools. By modeling the system at different levels of abstraction, the functionality in each instance of the system can be verified by means of executable specifications.

6   Results

Figure 9 depicts the Physical Deployment diagram with the 3 sampling nodes conceived in the design. These nodes measure water quality at the intake, water

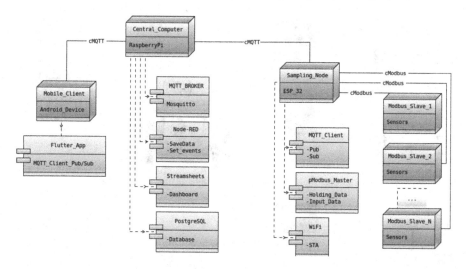

Fig. 8. Logical Deployment diagram. A logical deployment diagram shows how software modules (in blue) are distributed over hardware components (in gray). (Color figure online)

quality at the plant inlet after pretreatment with a sand trap, and finally water quality for human consumption employing sensors (pH, turbidity, and free chlorine). The Central Computer, the visualization client, and the mobile application, which is used for general operations (visualization, manual sampling, and sensor calibration), can also be observed.

The Central Computer, as its name indicates, is the center of the system where the services with the heaviest system load are executed. Because of this, a Raspberry Pi 4 Model B was selected. For the Sampling Nodes boards, a 32-bit ESP32-WROOM-32UE, generic Wi-Fi + Bluetooth + BLE microcontroller module was chosen. The selected sensors comply with the measurement ranges required by regulatory bodies.

Since the model is verified, the software implementation is correct-by-design. For translating processes into the firmware of the sampling nodes, the task model of FreeRTOS, a real-time operating system where each defined task temporarily consumes processor cycles and is executed concurrently employing a real-time scheduler, is used. The kernel variant of FreeRTOS for ESP-32 has been modified by Espressif to take advantage of the dual-core present in the ESP-32 family [28].

The system was tested and validated in indoor laboratory conditions for more than 3 weeks, without any interruption, thus allowing us to obtain a stable system, capable of recovering from external events and being a customizable platform for different monitoring and event notification requirements.

Figure 10 shows the final prototype of the Sampling Node board, and Fig. 11 shows the different components of the system.

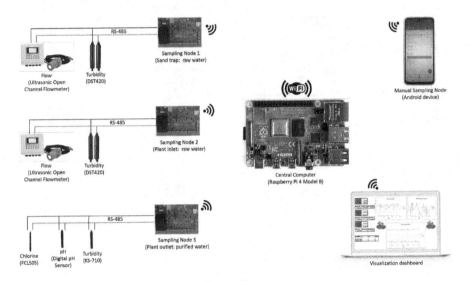

Fig. 9. Physical Deployment diagram: devices, communication channels, and protocols. Processing elements communicate via WiFi/MQTT while data from sensors are sent via RS-485/Modbus.

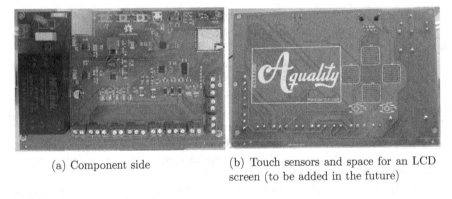

(a) Component side

(b) Touch sensors and space for an LCD screen (to be added in the future)

Fig. 10. Printed Circuit Board for the designed Sampling Node Board

In addition to providing real-time data based on the configured sampling time, the Sampling Node allows sensor configuration and calibration. It is also capable of notifying in real-time events such as variables out of range, disconnection, or failure of the sensor reading. With this, the status and traceability of the variables in question are permanently monitored, enabling quick response times according to the decision of the operator or plant manager.

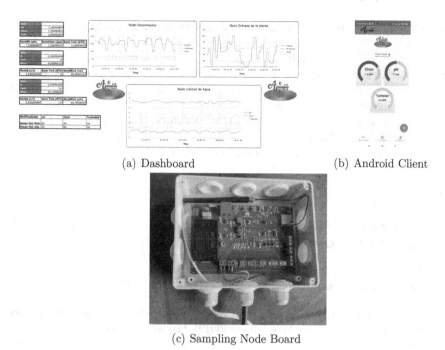

(a) Dashboard   (b) Android Client

(c) Sampling Node Board

Fig. 11. Resources resulting from the project

7 Conclusions

The resulting system satisfies international (US EPA, ISO) and national (Ministries of Social Protection, and Environment, Housing and Territorial Development) regulations for monitoring drinking water; the proposed instrumentation was intended to be suitable for application in water treatment plants for human consumption. Hence, it can be used in other places where drinking water treatment plants with multi-stage filtration are used.

The system was designed in a hierarchical manner, which allows it to scale in several ways. At the edge side, each of the developed sampling node boards can be scaled up to connect other sensors, nodes, and platforms that employ RS-485. Since the connection between sampling node boards and the central computer is done via Wi-Fi, it is possible to connect several sampling boards to the Raspberry Pi 4. This, in turn, can also connect to other platforms using its on-board Gigabit Ethernet port. The central computer uses MQTT, but it may also provide connectivity to other messaging protocols by incorporating them via Node-RED. The resulting system also provides an app and a visualization dashboard that were developed utilizing widely used tools.

By modeling the system using standard notations and an appropriate tool for specification, description, and verification, it was possible to describe the hierarchical, distributed system comprising heterogeneous processing platforms in such a manner that it is quite easy to modify, scale, and adapt the solution. Besides, using a model facilitates the work division of tasks within the system and its ulterior implementation using a real-time operating system. Message sequence charts and the specification and description language proved to be very useful for this purpose: using processes and messages have played a key role in the model since it is possible to describe clearly and concisely the desired behavior in the different scenarios expected for the behavior of the system.

Finally, it is possible to say that the design process allowed the building of a modular sensing platform for IoT-enabled solutions.

References

1. United Nations, Department of Economic and Social Affairs: Goal 6 (2015). https://sdgs.un.org/goals/goal6
2. Ritchie, H., Roser, M.: Our World in Data. Clean Water and Sanitation (2021). https://ourworldindata.org/clean-water-sanitation
3. World Health Organization: Drinking-water (2022). https://www.who.int/en/news-room/fact-sheets/detail/drinking-water
4. UNESCO World Water Assessment Programme: UN World Water Development Report 2019 - Leaving No One Behind (2019). https://www.unesco.org/en/wwap/wwdr/2019
5. UNESCO World Water Assessment Programme: The United Nations World Water Development Report 2021: Valuing Water (2021). https://www.unesco.org/reports/wwdr/2021/en/download-report
6. Mushila, C., Ochieng, G., Otieno, F., Shitote, S., Sitters, C.: Hydraulic design to optimize the treatment capacity of Multi-Stage Filtration units. Phys. Chem. Earth Parts A/B/C **92**, 85–91 (2016). https://doi.org/10.1016/j.pce.2015.10.015
7. Visscher, J.T., Latorre Montero, J., Galvis Castaño, G.: Multi-stage filtration: an innovative water treatment technology. Stichting IRC International Water and Sanitation Centre (1998)
8. Castro-Jiménez, C.C., Grueso-Domínguez, M.C., Correa-Ochoa, M.A., Saldarriaga-Molina, J.C., García, E.F.: A coagulation process combined with a multi-stage filtration system for drinking water treatment: an alternative for small communities. Water (2022). https://doi.org/10.3390/w14203256
9. World Health Organization: Guidelines for drinking-water quality, 4th edition, incorporating the 1st addendum (2017). http://www.who.int/water_sanitation_health/publications/drinking-water-quality-guidelines-4-including-1st-addendum/en/
10. Ministerio de Ambiente, V., Territorial, D., de la Protección Social, M.: Resolución 2115 del 2007 (2007). https://www.minvivienda.gov.co/sites/default/files/normativa/2115%20-%202007.pdf
11. Ministerio de la Protección Social: Decreto 1575 de 2007 (2007). https://www.ins.gov.co/TyS/Documents/Decreto%201575%20de%202007,MPS-MAVDT.pdf
12. Galvis Castaño, G., Latorre Montero, J., Visscher Teun, J.: Filtración en Múltiples Etapas: Tecnología innovativa para el tratamiento de agua, vol. 34. Artes Gráficas de Univalle, Cali (1999)
13. Sánchez, L.D., Sánchez, A., Galvis, G., Latorre, J.: Filtración en Múltiples etapas. IRC Centro Internacional en Agua y Saneamiento (2007)

14. World Health Organization: Water Quality and Health - Review of Turbidity: Information for regulators and water suppliers. Technical report, World Health Organization (2017). https://apps.who.int/iris/handle/10665/254631

15. United States Environmental Protection Agency: pH (2022). https://www.epa.gov/caddis-vol2/ph

16. Fisher, I., Kastl, G., Sathasivan, A.: A suitable model of combined effects of temperature and initial condition on chlorine bulk decay in water distribution systems. Water Res. **46**(10), 3293–3303 (2012). https://doi.org/10.1016/J.WATRES.2012.03.017

17. Wang, J., Zhang, J., Li, T., Wang, X.: Water quality analysis of remote sensing images based on inversion model. In: IGARSS 2018–2018 IEEE International Geoscience and Remote Sensing Symposium, pp. 4861–4864 (2018). https://doi.org/10.1109/IGARSS.2018.8519442

18. Mandal, N., Mitra, S., Bandyopadhyay, D.: Paper-sensors for point-of-care monitoring of drinking water quality. IEEE Sens. J. **19**(18), 7936–7941 (2019). https://doi.org/10.1109/JSEN.2019.2919269

19. Manjakkal, L., et al.: Connected sensors, innovative sensor deployment, and intelligent data analysis for online water quality monitoring. IEEE Internet Things J. **8**(18), 13805–13824 (2021). https://doi.org/10.1109/JIOT.2021.3081772

20. Subramaniam, S., Chew, L.J., Haw, S.C., Ziauddin, M.T.B.: WQMS: a water quality monitoring system using IoT. In: ACM International Conference Proceeding Series, pp. 177–182 (2019). https://doi.org/10.1145/3372422.3372429

21. Samsudin, S.I., Salim, S.I.M., Osman, K., Sulaiman, S.F., Sabri, M.I.: A smart monitoring of a water quality detector system. Indonesian J. Electr. Eng. Comput. Sci. **10**(3), 951–958 (2018). https://doi.org/10.11591/IJEECS.V10.I3.PP951-958

22. Sukor, A.S.A., Muhamad, M.N., Ab Wahab, M.N.: Development of in-situ sensing system and classification of water quality using machine learning approach. In: 2022 IEEE 18th International Colloquium on Signal Processing and Applications, CSPA 2022 - Proceedings pp. 382–385 (2022). https://doi.org/10.1109/CSPA55076.2022.9781984

23. Demetillo, A.T., Japitana, M.V., Taboada, E.B.: A system for monitoring water quality in a large aquatic area using wireless sensor network technology. Sustain. Environ. Res. **1**(1) (2019). https://doi.org/10.1186/S42834-019-0009-4

24. Quinn, J., et al.: H2O: smart drinking water quality monitoring system. In: 2022 IEEE International Conference on Imaging Systems and Techniques (IST), pp. 1–2 (2022). https://doi.org/10.1109/IST55454.2022.9845799

25. OASIS Open: OASIS Message Queuing Telemetry Transport (MQTT) TC (2020), https://www.oasis-open.org/committees/tc_home.php?wg_abbrev=mqtt

26. ITU Telecommunication Standardization Sector (ITU-T): Rec. Z.100: Specification and Description Language. https://www.itu.int/rec/T-REC-Z.100

27. ITU Telecommunication Standardization Sector (ITU-T): Rec. Z.120: Message Sequence Chart (MSC). https://www.itu.int/rec/T-REC-Z.120

28. Espressif Systems: FreeRTOS (Overview) - ESP32 – ESP-IDF Programming Guide latest documentation (2023). https://docs.espressif.com/projects/esp-idf/en/latest/esp32/api-reference/system/freertos.html

Computational Intelligence and Urban Informatics for Smart Cities

Enhancing Solar Cell Classification Using Mamdani Fuzzy Logic Over Electroluminescence Images: A Comparative Analysis with Machine Learning Methods

Hector Felipe Mateo-Romero[1]([⊠]) [iD], Mario Eduardo Carbonó dela Rosa[2] [iD],
Luis Hernández-Callejo[1]([⊠]) [iD], Miguel Ángel González-Rebollo[1] [iD],
Valentín Cardeñoso-Payo[1] [iD], Victor Alonso-Gómez[1] [iD],
and Sara Gallardo-Saavedra[1] [iD]

[1] Universidad de Valladolid, Valladolid, Spain
{hectorfelipe.mateo,luis.hernandez.callejo,valentin.cardenoso,
victor.alonso.gomez,sara.gallardo}@uva.es, mrebollo@eii.uva.es
[2] Universidad Nacional Autónoma de México, Mexico City, Mexico
mecr@ier.unam.mx

Abstract. This work presents a Mamdani Fuzzy Logic model capable of classifying solar cells according to their energetic performance. The model has 3 different inputs: The proportion of black pixels, gray pixels, and white pixels. One additional output for informing of possible bad inputs is also provided. The three values are obtained from an Electroluminescence image of the cell. The model has been developed using cells whose performance has been obtained by measuring the Intensity-Voltage Curves of the cells. The performance of the model has been shown by testing it with a validation set, obtaining a 99.0% of accuracy, when other methods such as Ensemble Classifiers and Decision Trees obtain a 97.7%. This shows that the presented model is capable of solving the problem better than traditional Machine Learning methods.

Keywords: Fuzzy Logic · Photovoltaic · Electroluminescence · Machine Learning

1 Introduction

A number of different issues (energy crisis, climate change, wars, etc.) are reducing the use of traditional energies in favor of more clean and accessible sources such as renewable energies [1]. This change is also important in Smart Cities since

© The Author(s), under exclusive license to Springer Nature Switzerland AG 2024
S. Nesmachnow and L. Hernández Callejo (Eds.): ICSC-Cities 2023, CCIS 1938, pp. 159–173, 2024.
https://doi.org/10.1007/978-3-031-52517-9_11

it provides cheaper and cleaner energy. Among the different types of renewable energy, solar energy is one of the most important ones for its facility to be installed in the urban area.

Photovoltaic (PV) modules are composed of a high amount PV cells. These small units can suffer from diffehm,rent problems (mechanical, thermal, or artificial) which can reduce their performance, the amount of energy provided. It is extremely important to verify the conditions of the solar cells in order to optimize production and avoid possible security threats.

Traditionally, the maintenance of PV installations was made by human labor but this is not the best alternative in urban areas or in big installations. To solve this issue, Artificial Intelligence (AI) techniques are being used, helping to optimize the production and to monitor the conditions of the modules [2,3].

Checking the production of the PV modules is one of the most frequently addressed problems. Different works [4,5] propose systems to detect defects in the surface of the PV modules. The majority of these methods use a technique known as Electroluminescence (EL) [6] to capture the light emitted by the PV cells/modules when they are injected with electric current, this technique makes visible more kinds of defects than direct visual inspection. These images are used in different AI methods, being Convolutional Neural Networks (CNNs) [7] the method that produces the best results. However, CNN-based methods have some limitations: they need a large amount of data to find patterns, they are highly computer-demanding and their training can be slow.

Other articles have tackled the idea of using fuzzy logic-based models to classify PV cells. The work presented in [8] is applied to detect microcracks in Electroluminescence images, obtaining an efficient system. Another proposal [9] combines fuzzy logic with mathematical morphology to classify the defects from PV cells using photography of the PV. Another work presented in [10] tackles this issue at plant level, comparing the performance of Neural Networks with the performance of Fuzzy Logic Models. Fuzzy logic has been also used in other PV problems such as Max Power Point Tracking [11] or Modelling of PV systems [12]. More works can be found in reviews about the topic [13,14] but any of them tackles the issue of classifying the PV cells using their EL image in terms of their performance.

This paper presents a new way of analyzing the state of photovoltaic cells, using not only the information about the surface of the cell with the EL images but also the information about the energetic production of the cell, obtained by measuring the Intensity-Voltage (IV) Curve. Another innovation of this paper is that it proposes a Fuzzy Logic (FL) [15] algorithm for solving this problem by analyzing the histogram of the EL images. The advantages that FL provides are that is a not computer-demanding algorithm and it can produce knowledge comprehensible to humans, which is extremely important to understand the effects of the defects in the performance of the cell.

The rest of the paper is organized as follows: Sect. 2 explains the basis of fuzzy logic, Sect. 3 explains the methodology used, Sect. 4 shows the results and findings that can be observed from them, finally Sect. 5 presents the conclusions of the paper.

2   Introduction to Fuzzy Logic

The term fuzzy represents values that are not clear. Fuzzy Logic [16] is an extension of the traditional logic [17] where the truth value of a variable is a real number between 0 and 1, instead of the traditional values of true or false. It can be applied to models that use imprecise information and for dealing with uncertainty in decision-making.

The most important concept of Fuzzy Logic is the membership function, which defines the degree of membership of the variable to a certain set or category. The membership is a function that can provide any value between 0 and 1, being 0 non-membership and 1 full-membership. FL systems are tolerable to errors or noise in the input data.

Among the different kinds of fuzzy logic systems, the Mandami systems are the most used FL Inference Systems [18], their most important features are to following:

- They are more intuitive and have easier-to-understand rules.
- Each Output has a corresponding membership function
- The surface of the output is discontinuous
- High Expressive Power and Interpretable
- Less Flexibility in the system design

3   Methodology

This section will explain the different processes followed in the creation of the models which include the gathering, preprocessing, and labeling of the data, the creation of the rules of the fuzzy model, and its optimization.

3.1   Data Gathering

Image acquisition was not a trivial process, since it was necessary to obtain two different things: The Electroluminescence (EL) image of each cell using a EL camera and the Intensity-Voltage Curve (IV) using an IV-tracer [19] which will provide the information about the energetic performance of the cells; more details about the processes of gathering can be found in [20].

The dataset is composed of the original measurements presented in [20] with some additional data that was obtained exclusively for this work, resulting in 666 different images and their IV curve.

3.2   Image Preprocessing

The preprocessing of the images was performed using the same procedure as in other works: Removal of dead pixels and luminous noise, fixing the scale of lighting of the images, removing the black surrounding contours of the images, and fixing the perspective. Figure 1 shows an example of an image after each of the processes. More information can be found in [20] and was performed using Python.

(a) Original Image. This image needs to be preprocessed.

(b) Image after the preprocessing

Fig. 1. A sample image before and after preprocessing.

3.3   Maximum Power Normalization

As explained before, the IV curve of each PV cell provides information about the energetic production of the cell, but it is necessary to perform certain steps to make the data useful for a model. Two different techniques (Z-score normalization and Min-Max normalization) are used together to obtain a normalized variable with values between 0 and 1. The following process is used:

1. Computation of the Power-Voltage curve of each cell using the information about the IV curve.
2. Calculation of the maximum value of power (Maximum Power Point) for each of the curves.
3. The cells are divided into six different groups, depending on the irradiance that was used to obtain the measures. For each group:
   (a) The mean value and the standard deviation of maximum power are computed.
   (b) A Z-score normalization is performed, using the computed values of mean and standard deviation, this results in a variable with a mean of 0 and std of 1, with values between -2 and 2.
   (c) The maximum value and minimum value of the obtained variable are computed for each group.

    (d) A Min-max normalization is performed on each group, using the computed values of the maximum and the minimum. This results in a variable with values between 0 and 1, a mean of 0.5, and std of 0.2.

4. This value measures the relative performance of a cell, high values correspond with cells that have high energy production, and low values with cells that are not producing as much as they should.

5. After that, the data was divided into 3 groups, according to their value:

    (a) Class 0 ($0.81 <= X$) represents the cells that are in good condition since their performance is near the expected value.

    (b) Class 1 ($0.572 <= X < 0.81$) represents the cells whose performance is enough but not as high as it should be.

    (c) Class 2 ($X < 0.572$) represents the cells that do not have enough performance, due to their defects or other problems.

3.4 Feature Extraction

Traditional AI methods can not deal directly with images, so it is necessary to obtain manageable characteristics from the images for these methods.

    Figure 2 presents an image and its intensity histogram. It can be seen how the histogram has three different regions: The area of the first peak corresponds with pixels with low-intensity values (Black or dark), and these pixels correspond with zones where the cell is not emitting light in response to the electric current. The second peak corresponds with the zones where the cell is active since it is producing light in response to the electric current. The area after the second peak corresponds with areas where energy production is extremely high.

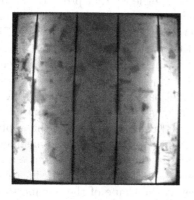 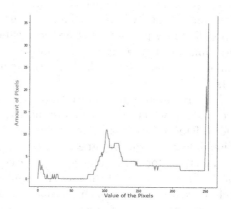

Fig. 2. Sample of Image and its histogram

    After analyzing all the images, it can be seen that these aspects appear in most of the images of the dataset, the number of dark areas is directly connected with the performance of the cells (more dark areas imply less production).

Taking these facts into consideration, the final features selected were the proportion of dark pixels, the proportion of gray pixels, and the proportion of white pixels. The following process was used:

- The data is divided into two different sets: Training (80%, 532 samples) and Validation (20%, 134 samples). The training set is composed of 92 images of Class 0, 228 of Class 1, and 212 of Class 2. The validation set is composed of 22 images of Class 0, 53 of Class 1, and 58 of Class 2. The following steps are repeated for each set.
- For each image, the intensity histogram is computed and all the histograms are accumulated into a summary histogram, normalized between 0 and 1.
- The separation intensity value between the black and the gray zone is calculated using the intensity at the minimum between the two first peaks. The resulting value after rounding was 0.35.
- The point to divide the gray area and the white area is calculated using the minimum point between the two peaks. The resulting value after rounding was 0.70.
- For each image, the amount of pixels for each group is computed and divided by the number of total pixels of the image to get the ratio of black, gray, and white pixels which provide the features to characterize the image.

3.5 Model

As it has been discussed before, the main objective of this article is to create a mode capable of classifying PV cells in terms of their performance. Fuzzy Logic models have some great benefits, that are extremely interesting for this problem: FL is a symbolic method, which means that the knowledge that provides can be easily understood by humans. This is an extremely important quality since it can help to find new patterns that are not visible to the human mind. Moreover, FL algorithms are not computer-demanding and they can be run on almost every kind of device nowadays, which makes them extremely useful in a lot of different areas.

The presented model is a Fuzzy Logic Model based on the Mandami Inference System, which provides more intuitive and easier-to-understand rules and other Inference Systems, it has been implemented using Matlab with the application of Fuzzy Logic Designer. The design parameters of the proposed membership functions for each input were set according to the expert's experience and based on the behavior of the model's input variables at each actual classification level. Moreover, other design parameters such as the shape of the membership functions, the degree of membership, and the range of the output membership functions were set based on the statistical error between true and predicted classification.

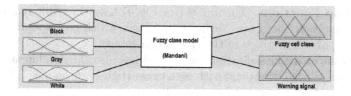

Fig. 3. Structure of the FL model: 3 inputs and 2 outputs

The model (see Fig. 3) has been designed with 3 different inputs: The proportion of dark pixels, the proportion of gray pixels, and the proportion of white pixels in the image. It also has two different outputs: The condition of the cell and a warning that indicates inputs that should be checked due to a possible problem in the image (proportions not summing up 100% or extreme values such as black 100%).

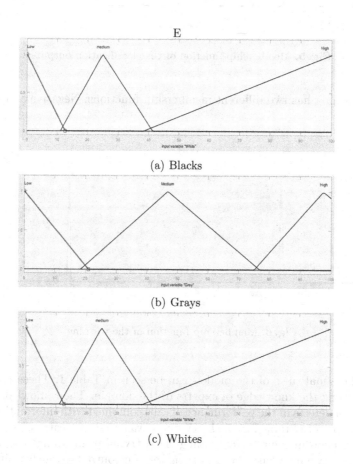

(a) Blacks

(b) Grays

(c) Whites

Fig. 4. Membership functions of the inputs

Membership Functions. The inputs (see Fig. 4) have three different membership functions each one: Low, Medium, and High which corresponded directly with the proportion of pixels of that particular input.

The output of the classification (see Fig. 5) has also three different membership functions which correspond with each class: High Performance (0), Medium Performance (1), and Low Performance (2).

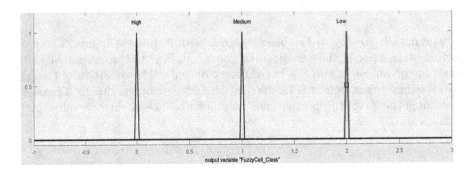

Fig. 5. Membership function of the classification output

The warning has two different membership functions: Negative and Positive (Fig. 6).

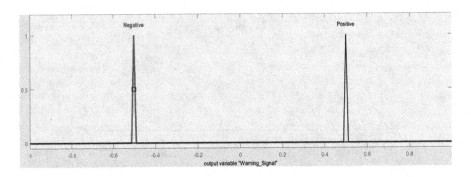

Fig. 6. Membership function of the warning

Rules. The final rules of the models can be seen in Table 1. These rules were obtained using the knowledge of experts of the domain. Their knowledge about the effects of defects in the performance of cells combined with information about the output power obtained from the IV curve was used to create rules that classified the images in their corresponding class, trying to maximize the accuracy of the classification output in the training set. The output of the warning is not taken into account, as it is only used to detect when the inputs are not valid in order to warn the users that they should check that input. This process of parameter fitting is completely manual, in contrast with the training phase of Machine Learning algorithms. The validation test has not been considered in this modeling process. 27 rules were obtained by combining all of the possible states of the three inputs ($3^3 = 27$).

Table 1. Fuzzy Rules of the model

Rule	Black	Gray	White	Classification Output	Warning Signal
1	Low	Low	Low	High	Positive
2	Low	Low	Medium	Low	Negative
3	Low	Low	High	Low	Negative
4	Low	Medium	Low	Low	Negative
5	Low	Medium	Medium	Low	Negative
6	Low	Medium	High	Low	Negative
7	Low	High	Low	Medium	Negative
8	Low	High	Medium	Low	Negative
9	Low	High	High	Low	Positive
10	Medium	Low	Low	High	Positive
11	Medium	Low	Medium	Medium	Negative
12	Medium	Low	High	Medium	Negative
13	Medium	Medium	Low	Medium	Negative
14	Medium	Medium	Medium	Medium	Negative
15	Medium	Medium	High	Medium	Positive
16	Medium	High	Low	High	Negative
17	Medium	High	Medium	High	Positive
18	Medium	High	High	High	Positive
19	High	Low	Low	High	Negative
20	High	Low	Medium	High	Negative
21	High	Low	High	High	Negative
22	High	Medium	Low	High	Negative
23	High	Medium	Medium	High	Negative
24	High	Medium	High	High	Negative
25	High	High	Low	High	Positive
26	High	High	Medium	High	Negative
27	High	High	High	High	Positive

Figure 7 presents the surface 3D diagram of the classification output. The diagram represents the knowledge of the model, and how the inputs blacks and

grays modify the output depending on their values. It can be seen how low values
of black implies an output of 0. Class 1 only appears when black is around 20%–
30% and grays are less than 60%. Class 2 is selected in the other cases.

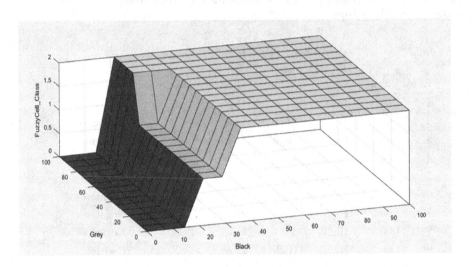

Fig. 7. 3D diagram for the classification output for two inputs: Blacks and Grays

4   Results

This section assesses the quality of the model by showing its performance in
the validation set and compares the performance with other methods. The other
methods have been implemented using the application Classification Learner
from Matlab.

As explained before, the dataset was composed of 666, divided into two sets:
Training (80%, 532 samples) and Validation (20%, 133 samples).

Figures 8 and 9 present the distribution of the validation dataset, which can
be seen in Fig. 8a how the mean of all of the images of Class 0 represents a cell in
good condition, Fig. 8a also show this fact, with the stacking of all of the images
of this class. Similar reasoning can be used with the images of class 1 (Figs. 8b
and 9b), since they present minor defects that do not cover a high amount of
the surface of the cell. Finally, Figs. 8c and 9c show how the images in class 2
have shadows that cover a high amount of the surface of the cell.

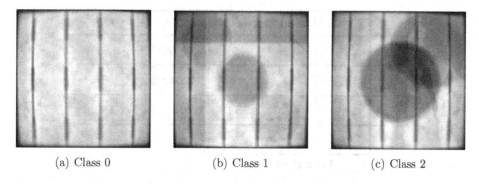

(a) Class 0   (b) Class 1   (c) Class 2

Fig. 8. Image obtained after making the mean of all of the images of each class from the validation set.

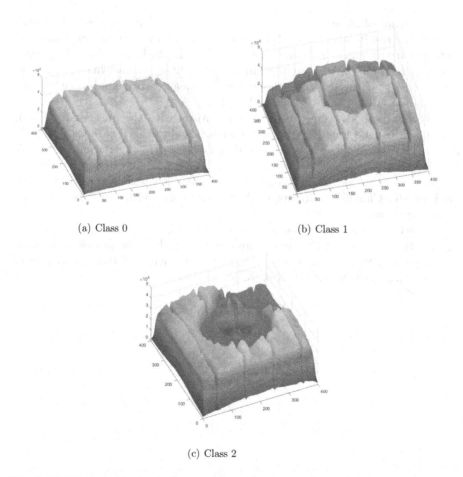

(a) Class 0   (b) Class 1

(c) Class 2

Fig. 9. 3D Diagram obtained after stacking the images of the same class of the validation set.

		Confusion Matrix			TPR	FNR
True Class	0	21	1	0	99,09%	0,91%
	1	1	52	2	98,12%	1,88%
	2	0	2	53	99,31%	0,69%
		0	1	2		

Predicted Class

Fig. 10. Results of the classification of the proposed fuzzy model on the Validation Set. TPR: True Positive Rate, FNR: False Negative Rate.

The model obtained a 99% of accuracy in the Validation set. Figure 10 presents the results of the classification of this set, with information about the confusion matrix and the accuracy for each class. It can be seen how the performance in the three classes is quite similar, with a slight decrease in class 1. It can also be seen that the incorrect classification appears between adjacent classes, there are not any mistakes between class 0 and class 2.

Different methods were chosen for comparison with the presented method, all of them can be found in the application Classification Learner of Matlab. The selection of methods was composed of Decision Trees, Discriminant Analysis, Logistic Regressions Classifiers, Naive Bayes classifiers, Support Vector Machines, Nearest Neighbor Classifiers, and Ensemble Classifiers. Decision Trees and Ensemble Classifiers obtained the best performance with a 97.7% of accuracy in both of them.

Figure 11 presents the classification matrix for both methods, they provide a good classification but the results are a bit lower than the proposed method, as can be seen in their accuracy. This is clear evidence of the importance of applying fuzzy logic to solve this problem.

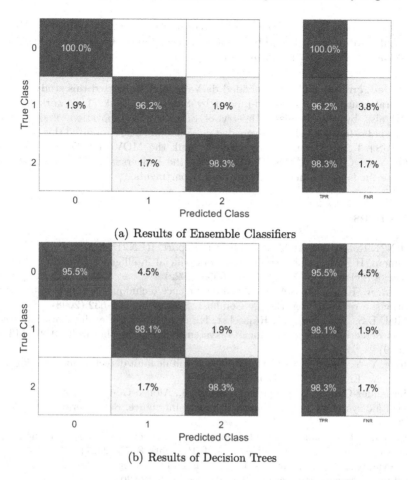

(a) Results of Ensemble Classifiers

(b) Results of Decision Trees

Fig. 11. Results of the classification of other models on the Validation Set. TPR: True Positive Rate, FNR: False Negative Rate

5   Conclusions and Future Work

The detection of the conditions of the solar cells is a really important problem since it provides information that is vital in the optimization of photovoltaic production. The introduction of fuzzy logic to solve this problem is innovative since few works have tried this approach. The presented model has been tested with a 99% of accuracy as opposed to the 97.5% that obtains other models such as Ensemble Classifiers and Decision Trees.

The method has some flaws that need to be addressed to improve it. First of all, the creation of the rules has been made manually which can produce a certain bias, even if the knowledge of experts has been used to ensure the quality of the rules. To solve this different measures would be necessary: The inclusion of a new dataset of images, completely different from the images of training of validation, to verify the performance of the model in completely foreign conditions. Another important improvement would be the automatization of the creation of the rules, using Machine Learning to optimize this process.

Acknowledgements. The Universidad de Valladolid supported this study with the predoctoral contracts of 2020, co-funded by Santander Bank. This work has been financed also by the Spanish Ministry of Science and Innovation, under project PID2020-113533RB-C33. The Universidad de Valladolid also supported this study with ERASMUS+ KA-107. Finally, we have to thank the MOVILIDAD DE DOCTOR-ANDOS Y DOCTORANDAS UVa 2023 from the University of Valladolid. We also appreciate the help of other members of our departments.

References

1. REN21. Renewables 2022 Global Status Report. REN21 (2022)
2. Romero, H.F.M., et al.: Applications of artificial intelligence to photovoltaic systems: a review. Appl. Sci. **12**(19), 10056 (2022)
3. Mellit, A., Kalogirou, S.A.: Artificial intelligence techniques for photovoltaic applications: a review. Prog. Energy Combust. Sci. **34**(5), 574–632 (2008)
4. Pillai, D.S., Blaabjerg, F., Rajasekar, N.: A comparative evaluation of advanced fault detection approaches for PV systems. IEEE J. Photovolt. **9**(2), 513–527 (2019)
5. Hong, Y.-Y., Pula, R.A.: Methods of photovoltaic fault detection and classification: a review. Energy Rep. **8**, 5898–5929 (2022)
6. Hernández-Callejo, L., Gallardo-Saavedra, S., Alonso-Gómez, V.: A review of photovoltaic systems: design, operation and maintenance. Sol. Energy **188**, 426–440 (2019)
7. Alzubaidi, L., et al.: Review of deep learning: concepts, CNN architectures, challenges, applications, future directions. J. Big Data **8**, 53 (2021)
8. Chawla, R., Singal, P., Garg, A.K.: A Mamdani fuzzy logic system to enhance solar cell micro-cracks image processing. 3D Res. **9**, 1–12 (2018)
9. Wei, J., Zaibin, C.: Defect detection on solar cells using mathematical morphology and fuzzy logic techniques **1**, 3 (2023)
10. Dhimish, M., Holmes, V., Mehrdadi, B., Dales, M.: Comparing Mamdani Sugeno fuzzy logic and RBF ANN network for PV fault detection. Renew. Energy **117**, 257–274 (2018)
11. Chekired, F., Larbes, C., Rekioua, D., Haddad, F.: Implementation of a MPPT fuzzy controller for photovoltaic systems on FPGA circuit. Energy Procedia **6**, 541–549 (2011). Impact of Integrated Clean Energy on the Future of the Mediterranean Environment?
12. Garud, K.S., Jayaraj, S., Lee, M.-Y.: A review on modeling of solar photovoltaic systems using artificial neural networks, fuzzy logic, genetic algorithm and hybrid models. Int. J. Energy Res. **45**(1), 6–35 (2021)
13. Sridharan, M.: Short review on various applications of fuzzy logic-based expert systems in the field of solar energy. Int. J. Ambient Energy **43**(1), 5112–5128 (2022)
14. Kedir, N., Nguyen, P.H.D., Pérez, C., Ponce, P., Fayek, A.R.: Systematic literature review on fuzzy hybrid methods in photovoltaic solar energy: opportunities, challenges, and guidance for implementation. Energies **16**(9) (2023)

15. Chen, G., Pham, T.T., Boustany, N.M.: Introduction to fuzzy sets, fuzzy logic, and fuzzy control systems. Appl. Mech. Rev. **54**, B102–B103 (2001)
16. Novak, V., Perfiljeva, I., Mockor, J.: Mathematical Principles of Fuzzy Logic. Springer, New York (1999). https://doi.org/10.1007/978-1-4615-5217-8
17. Shapiro, S., Kissel, T.K.: Classical logic. In: Zalta, E.N. (ed.) The Stanford Encyclopedia of Philosophy, Spring 2021 edition. Metaphysics Research Lab, Stanford University (2021)
18. Mamdani, E.H.: Applications of fuzzy algorithms for control of a simple dynamic plant. Proc. IEEE **121**, 1585–1588 (1974)
19. Morales-Aragonés, J.I., et al.: Low-cost three-quadrant single solar cell I–V tracer. Appl. Sci. **12**(13), 6623 (2022)
20. Mateo-Romero, H.F., et al.: Synthetic dataset of electroluminescence images of photovoltaic cells by deep convolutional generative adversarial networks. Sustainability **15**(9), 7175 (2023)

Estimation of the Performance of Photovoltaic Cells by Means of an Adaptative Neural Fuzzy Inference Model

Hector Felipe Mateo-Romero[1]([⊠])[ID], Mario Eduardo Carbonó dela Rosa[2][ID],
Luis Hernández-Callejo[1]([⊠])[ID], Miguel Ángel González-Rebollo[1][ID],
Valentín Cardeñoso-Payo[1][ID], Victor Alonso-Gómez[1][ID],
Óscar Martínez-Sacristán[1][ID], and Sara Gallardo-Saavedra[1][ID]

[1] Universidad de Valladolid, Valladolid, Spain
{hectorfelipe.mateo,luis.hernandez.callejo,victor.alonso.gomez,
oscar.martinez,sara.gallardo}@uva.es, mrebollo@eii.uva.es,
valen@infor.uva.es
[2] Universidad Nacional Autónoma de México, Mexico City, Mexico
mecr@ier.unam.mx

Abstract. This paper presents an Adaptive Neuro-fuzzy Inference System capable of predicting the output power of photovoltaic cells using their electroluminescence image and their IV curve. The input consists of 3 different features: the number of black pixels, grey pixels and white pixels. ANFIS combines the learning capabilities of Artificial Neural Networks with the comprehensible rules of Fuzzy Logic, being optimal for this problem, as demonstrated by the metrics of MAE of 0.064 and MSE of 0.009, which are better than the performance of other tested methods such as Support Vector Machines or Linear Regressor.

Keywords: Fuzzy Logic · Photovoltaic · Electroluminescence · Machine Learning · ANFIS

1 Introduction

Energy is the motor of every sector, being fossil fuels the most important source of energy, with an 80.2% in 2019 [16]. This trend is changing in recent years with the inclusion of renewable energies. Different problems such as wars, and climate change are provoking a shift in favor of these kinds of energies. Of the different kinds of renewable energies, solar energy is one of the most important ones for smart cities since solar panels can be easily installed in buildings.

Photovoltaic (PV) energy is produced by PV panels using the energy from the sun. These modules are composed of a big amount of small units known as PV cells. They can suffer from different conditions [1] that can affect their performance and security. Constant monitoring of their condition is vital when the optimization of their production is needed.

© The Author(s), under exclusive license to Springer Nature Switzerland AG 2024
S. Nesmachnow and L. Hernández Callejo (Eds.): ICSC-Cities 2023, CCIS 1938, pp. 174–188, 2024.
https://doi.org/10.1007/978-3-031-52517-9_12

The monitoring and maintenance of PV installations have been traditionally a manual process but this is not feasible when the size of the facilities reaches high dimensions or when they are included at places of difficult access. Artificial Intelligence (AI) takes an important place in this field since AI techniques can be used to improve the production and control the conditions of the modules [10,12].

The technique known as Electroluminescence (EL) [4] is the most used technique to capture the surface of PV modules and cells, consisting in capturing the light emitted by the PV units when they are being injected with electric current. Different works have used these images to detect the defects in the surface of PV cells [15]. Of the different AI techniques, Convolutional Neural Networks [2] are usually the best performing, but they have some limitations since it is a non-symbolic method, meaning that no knowledge can be extracted from the reasoning of the method.

This paper presents a new approach to analyzing the state of PV cells. The data is not only obtained with the EL techniques but also with the information about the energy produced by the PV cell by measuring their Intensity-Voltage IV curve. Another important feature of this paper is that it applies a combination of two different methods (Fuzzy Logic and Neural Networks) known as Adaptative Neuro-fuzzy Inference System (ANFIS) [7]. This combination is capable not only of obtaining a good performance in the problems, using the capacities of Neural Networks but also to obtain understandable knowledge thanks to the symbolic aspect of the fuzzy logic.

Other PV problems have been tackled in other problems using Fuzzy logic or ANFIS systems for detecting microcracks [3], modeling the PV systems [13] or finding the Max Power Point [8]. ANFIS has been also applied to forecasting problems [5]. However, no work has dealt with our exact issue, of finding the performance of a PV cell based on the IV curve using the EL images.

The rest of the paper is organized as follows: Sect. 2 explains the basics of ANFIS, Sect. 3 explains the methodology used, Sect. 4 shows the results and the conclusions that can be drawn from them, finally Sect. 5 presents the conclusions of the paper.

2 ANFIS

The Adaptative Neuro Fuzzy Inference System [6] links Artificial Neural Networks (ANN) [2] with Fuzzy Logic (FL). Its inference system is based on the Takagi-Sugeno fuzzy logic [17] with IF-THEN rules. The combination of ANN and FL creates a model that is capable of updating under new situations thanks to the training function of the ANN. The basic architecture of the network (See Fig. 1) is composed of 5 different layers:

- Fuzzification layer: In this layer, the parameters of the input membership functions are determined, for example: number, range, and the type of each membership function (triangle, trapezoid, generalized bell, and Gaussian), among others. Moreover, each node (information processing points) is adaptive.

- RRules layer: In this layer, the knowledge rules that relate the inputs and outputs established in the system are created. It is composed of fixed nodes that represent the firing power of each rule.
- Normalization Layer: The function of this layer is to normalize the firing strength of each rule by dividing it by the sum of the firing strength of all rules.
- Defuzzification Layer: This layer produces a weighted output of each rule using the normalized values.
- Output Layer: The output of this layer is the sum of all its inputs and provides the overall output of the network.

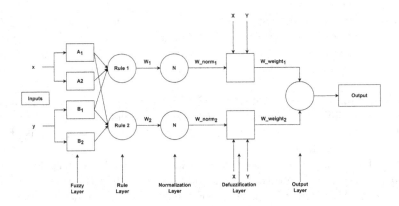

Fig. 1. Structure of a generic ANFIS model.

3   Methodology

This section explains the different procedures that were performed to prepare the model. This includes the collection, labeling, and preprocessing of the data, as well as the creation and optimization of the ANFIS model.

3.1   Data Gathering

The retrieval of the data was divided into two different processes, a more detailed explanation can be found [11]:

- Electroluminescence images: These images were captured using an "InGaAs C12741-0" silicon detector camera with an 8 mm focal length lens and an f-number of 1.4 in the same temperature conditions. The images were taken in total solar shielding to reduce light noise. Different irradiance levels were used to obtain more images.

– IV Curve: They were obtained using a 3-quadrants IV-tracer [14], obtaining only the information of the active zone for the experiments. Figure 2 presents different IV curves for the same cell.

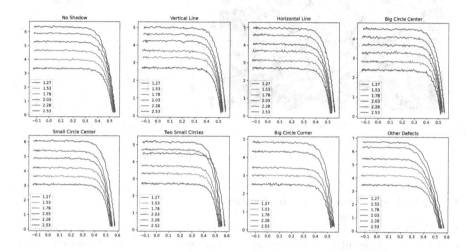

Fig. 2. Different IV curves for the same cell. Each diagram represents a different defect, and each line a IV curve measured a certain irradiance. The label indicates the current used

The obtained dataset is composed of 666 EL images with their corresponding IV curve.

3.2   Image Preprocessing

The images presented some problems related to the noise of the lights, the scale of the lights in the images, the black contours presented in the images, and their perspective. These problems are harmful for visual inspection and also for Artificial Intelligence algorithms since it is more difficult for them to find patterns in the images. For this reason, a preprocessing has been performed on the images removing the luminous noise, standardizing the histogram, and finally cropping the image to the cell surface. (See Fig. 3), more information can be seen in [11].

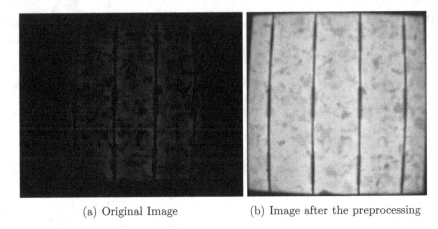

(a) Original Image   (b) Image after the preprocessing

Fig. 3. A sample image before and after preprocessing.

3.3   Maximum Power Normalization

The IV curve provides information about the amount of energy produced by each PV cell. This information cannot be obtained directly: First, the IV curves are separated according to the irradiance used to take the measurement, and then according to the Max Power Point of the curve.

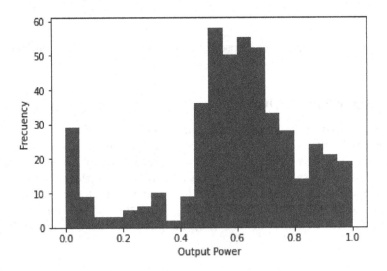

Fig. 4. Architecture of the model

Finally, two different normalizations are performed: A z-score normalization using the mean and standard deviation, and a min-max normalization using the maximum and minimum values. The objective of this normalization is to obtain an output that is independent of the level of irradiance used for taking the measure.

The variable obtained after the multi-normalization has a range of $[0, 1]$, with low values corresponding to cells with poor performance and high values to cells with good performance. The histogram of the distribution of the power values can be seen in Fig. 4, which shows the values over the whole domain. This variable will be considered as the output of the system.

3.4   Feature Extraction

The ANFIS architecture is built using ANNs, which are not suitable for dealing with images directly [9]. The most common solution to this problem is to extract features from the images. These features describe the most important details of the images.

The data set is divided into 3 different sets: Training (70%), Validation (15%), and Testing (15%). Three different features (Blacks, Grays, and Whites), which will be the inputs of the model, are extracted from the images using their color histogram, previously normalized between 0 and 1. These features are obtained by dividing the histogram into different subgroups and obtaining the number of pixels in each group. The boundaries between the different subgroups are computed using the following steps:

- The color histogram of each image is obtained and accumulated in order to general histogram of all images
- The minimum point between the first and second peaks is used to separate the black area from the gray area.
- The minimum point between the second and third peaks is used to separate the gray area from the white area.
- The mean between all of the values of each minimum point is computed. These values are rounded an used for the limit of each group (0.35 and 0.7). Figure 5 presents a cell and its histogram where 3 different peaks can be seen, the divisions between the three groups are also presented.
- The amount of pixels of each group is divided by the total amount of pixels of each image.

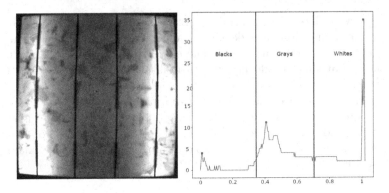

Fig. 5. A PV cell and its histogram. Red dots represent the peaks. The green lines represent the division between the groups for calculating the features (Color figure online)

3.5 Model and Architecture

As explained before, the method chosen to solve this problem is ANFIS, since it combines the powerful learning capabilities of ANN with the comprehensible rules of FL. The ANFIS model was implemented with the Neuro-Fuzzy Designer application of Matlab. The diagrams and graphics were also obtained with that application.

The design of the model architecture was chosen based on the best performance of the mean absolute error (MAE), mean square error (MSE) and root mean square error (RMSE) in the training, testing and validation stages. For this it was necessary to run multiple tests varying the training epochs, the number and type of input membership functions. Taking care not to overfitting the model to obtain an acceptable number of rules that would not generate additional computational expense.

The optimization of the membership functions for the inputs has consisted of a combination of a manual process (The selection of the shape of the functions and the number of membership functions for each input) and an automatic process during the training of the network (The size of the intervals and the intersections between them). Different shapes for the membership functions such as Triangular Functions, Trapezoidal Functions, Phi-Shaped, Simple Gaussian Functions, and Double Gaussian Functions) were tested, being the Double Gaussian function the one that produced the best performance in the model. In a similar way, a different number of membership functions were tested for the three inputs, obtaining that two for the black input, four for the gray input, and five for the white input were the optimal values

The final model contains 40 if-then rules due to the combination of all different input membership functions ($2 * 4 * 5 = 40$). Figure 6 shows the architecture of the model.

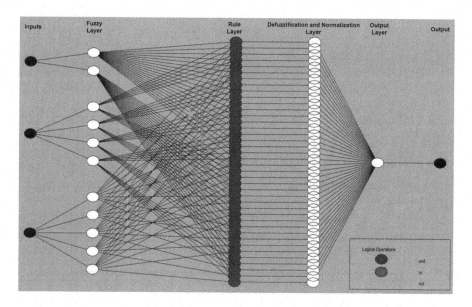

Fig. 6. Architecture of the model

3.6 Training

The developed model must be trained using the data from the training and validation sets. Each sample has 3 inputs and 1 output. As mentioned before, there are 666 samples, divided into 70%, 15%, and 15%. The optimization is done with a combination of backpropagation for the input membership functions and least squares for the outputs, trying to minimize the Mean Squared Error for the output. Figure 7 shows the evolution of the training and validation errors over 1000 epochs.

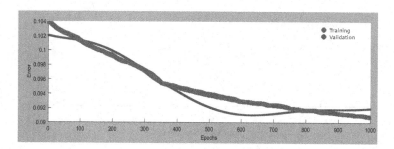

Fig. 7. Evolution of the training error and Validation error during the training process

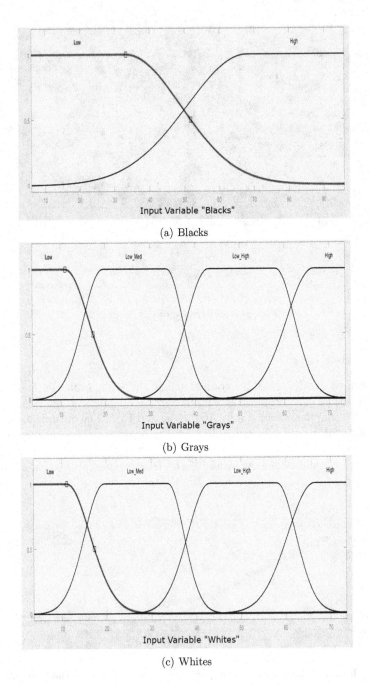

(a) Blacks

(b) Grays

(c) Whites

Fig. 8. Membership functions of the three different inputs. These functions have been obtained by the combination of manual optimization and the automatic training of the ANFIS method.

It can be seen that around epoch 600 the validation error is minimized (0.0911), since after this epoch the error increases steadily, a clear indication of an overfitting problem when training continues for more than 600 epochs.

Figure 8 shows the membership functions of the inputs after their optimization in the training process.

3.7   Rules

As explained before, the rules are obtained automatically during the training process, Fig. 9 shows the 40 rules of the system, for every possible combination of inputs.

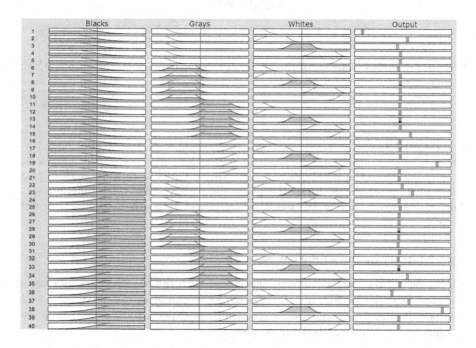

Fig. 9. Fuzzy Rules

In ANFIS and Fuzzy Logic systems, it is typical to present 3D graphics that show the relationship between the variables and as a graphical representation of the rules, showing the effects of the rules in the output. Figure 10 shows the effects of the variables black and gray in the output. It can be how the different values of both variables change notably the output.

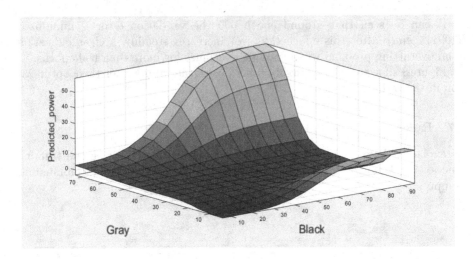

Fig. 10. 3D surface diagram of the effects of Gray and Black on the output (Color figure online)

4   Results

This section tests the capabilities of the created model to show its performance and find its weaknesses. First, the performance is checked with different sets. Then the performance of the model is compared with other machine learning models.

4.1   Metrics in the Different Sets

Table 1 shows the performance of the model with different metrics. it can be observed how the performance of the model is stable in the three sets, with a minor decrement in the testing set, which is expected since that data was completely unrelated to the training process.

Table 1. Results according to the model of the model in the different sets. MAE: Mean Absolute Error, MSE: Mean Squared Error, RSME: Root Square Mean Error

Metric	Training	Validation	Testing
MAE	0.05878	0.06416	0.06474
MSE	0.00871	0.00830	0.00940
RSME	0.09297	0.09112	0.09695

Figure 11 presents the diagram of the outputs for the training and validation sets. It shows how in most cases the actual value and the predicted value are extremely close, this is a shred of clear evidence that the model's performance is good. Moreover, the number of outliers that have a high distance from their label is considerably low, and even most of them continue to maintain the essence of the actual value.

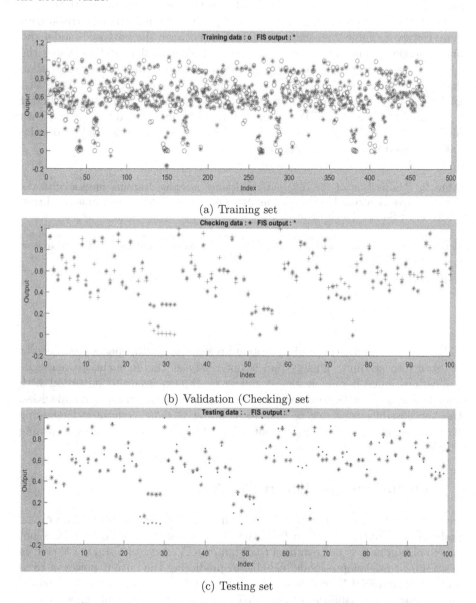

(a) Training set

(b) Validation (Checking) set

(c) Testing set

Fig. 11. Distribution of the predictions of the model and the original values over the three sets. Blue dots original data. Red stars: Model output (Color figure online)

4.2   Comparison with Other Methods

Although the results show that the method is capable of performing the task with low error, it is necessary to compare its performance with other methods. There are no other previous works that address the issue of predicting the output power of a cell using EL images, so it is not possible to make a comparison with them. However, Table 2 presents a comparison between the proposed model and some traditional machine learning methods implemented in Python using the Sklearn library. It can be seen that ANFIS has a significantly lower error than Linear Regression and Support Vector Machine. In the case of Gradient Boosting, both methods have similar performance, with Gradient Boosting slightly better in terms of MAE and ANFIS better in terms of MSE and RMSE. Even with similar results, ANFIS provides more robust results as it provides the set of rules that were used to make the inference.

Table 2. Comparison of the different traditional machine learning models with the proposed ANFIS method. MAE: Mean Absolute Error, MSE: Mean Squared Error, RSME: Root Square Mean Error

Metric	ANFIS	Linear Regressor	Support Vector Regressor	Gradient Boosting Regressor
MAE	0.0647	0.09169	0.06830	0.05933
MSE	0.00940	0.02153	0.01291	0.01058
RSME	0.09695	0.14673	0.11362	0.10285

Despite its results, the ANFIS system presents some drawbacks that need to be taken into account. This system is not ready at this moment for real-time applications since it only works at cell level. It also needs to be tested with other kinds of PV cells to determine and improve its generalization capacities. Another possible drawback is that its training is more computer-demanding than traditional Machine-learning but it is still much faster than Deep Learning methods.

5   Conclusions and Future Work

Predicting the power generated by PV cells is a complex problem. The model needs to be trained with data from the IV curve of the cell. This data is not easy to obtain as it is not common to obtain the IV curve of a single PV cell. In an attempt to develop a model capable of predicting the output power, a combination of Artificial Neural Networks and Fuzzy Logic is presented. This model has the learning capabilities of the ANN and the human-readable knowledge of Fuzzy Logic.

The resulting model is shown to be able to solve the problem more effectively than other traditional machine learning models, with an RSME of 0.09695. The model also produces 40 human-understandable rules that can be used to analyze the behavior of the model or to find new patterns unknown to domain experts. However, the model is not without shortcomings, as it has only been trained on one type of PV cell (polycrystalline). Another improvement should be the further optimization of the membership functions, using methods such as genetic algorithms or other metaheuristics to optimize not only the number of functions for each input but also their shapes.

Finally, it would be extremely interesting to adapt the algorithm to be able to work in Real-Time applications but it would need a method to take the EL of the panels without harming the production of the PV installations and an optimized segmenting algorithm to divide the panels into cells.

Acknowledgements. The Universidad de Valladolid supported this study with the predoctoral contracts of 2020, co-funded by Santander Bank. This work has been financed also by the Spanish Ministry of Science and Innovation, under project PID2020-113533RB-C33. The Universidad de Valladolid also supported this study with ERASMUS+ KA-107. Finally, we have to thank the MOVILIDAD DE DOCTORAN-DOS Y DOCTORANDAS UVa 2023 from the University of Valladolid.

References

1. Acciani, G., Falcone, O., Vergura, S.: Typical defects of PV-cells. In: 2010 IEEE International Symposium on Industrial Electronics, pp. 2745–2749 (2010). https://doi.org/10.1109/ISIE.2010.5636901
2. Alzubaidi, L., et al.: Review of deep learning: concepts, CNN architectures, challenges, applications, future directions. J. Big Data **8**, 53 (2021). https://doi.org/10.1186/s40537-021-00444-8
3. Chawla, R., Singal, P., Garg, A.K.: A Mamdani fuzzy logic system to enhance solar cell micro-cracks image processing. 3D Res. **9**, 1–12 (2018). https://doi.org/10.1007/S13319-018-0186-7/METRICS. https://link.springer.com/article/10.1007/s13319-018-0186-7
4. Hernández-Callejo, L., Gallardo-Saavedra, S., Alonso-Gómez, V.: A review of photovoltaic systems: design, operation and maintenance. Solar Energy **188**, 426–440 (2019). https://doi.org/10.1016/j.solener.2019.06.017. https://linkinghub.elsevier.com/retrieve/pii/S0038092X19305912
5. Jahic, A., Konjic, T., Pihler, J., Jahic, A.: Photovoltaic power output forecasting with ANFIS. In: Mediterranean Conference on Power Generation, Transmission, Distribution and Energy Conversion (MedPower 2016), pp. 1–8 (2016). https://doi.org/10.1049/cp.2016.1056
6. Jang, J.S.: ANFIS: adaptive-network-based fuzzy inference system. IEEE Trans. Syst. Man Cybern. **23**(3), 665–685 (1993). https://doi.org/10.1109/21.256541
7. Karaboga, D., Kaya, E.: Adaptive network based fuzzy inference system (ANFIS) training approaches: a comprehensive survey. Artif. Intell. Rev. **52**(4), 2263–2293 (2019). https://doi.org/10.1007/s10462-017-9610-2
8. Khosrojerdi, F., Taheri, S., Cretu, A.M.: An adaptive neuro-fuzzy inference system-based MPPT controller for photovoltaic arrays. In: 2016 IEEE Electrical Power and Energy Conference (EPEC), pp. 1–6 (2016). https://doi.org/10.1109/EPEC.2016.7771794
9. Òscar Lorente, Riera, I., Rana, A.: Image classification with classic and deep learning techniques (2021)

10. Mateo Romero, H.F., et al.: Applications of artificial intelligence to photovoltaic systems: a review. Appl. Sci. **12**(19) (2022). https://doi.org/10.3390/app121910056
11. Mateo-Romero, H.F., et al.: Synthetic dataset of electroluminescence images of photovoltaic cells by deep convolutional generative adversarial networks. Sustainability **15**(9), 7175 (2023). https://doi.org/10.3390/su15097175
12. Mellit, A., Kalogirou, S.A.: Artificial intelligence techniques for photovoltaic applications: a review. Prog. Energy Combust. Sci. **34**(5), 574–632 (2008). https://doi.org/10.1016/j.pecs.2008.01.001. https://www.sciencedirect.com/science/article/pii/S0360128508000026
13. Mellit, A., Kalogirou, S.A.: ANFIS-based modelling for photovoltaic power supply system: a case study. Renew. Energy **36**(1), 250–258 (2011). https://doi.org/10.1016/j.renene.2010.06.028. https://www.sciencedirect.com/science/article/pii/S0960148110002843
14. Morales-Aragonés, J.I., et al.: Low-cost three-quadrant single solar cell I–V tracer. Appl. Sci. **12**(13) (2022). https://doi.org/10.3390/app12136623
15. Pillai, D.S., Blaabjerg, F., Rajasekar, N.: A comparative evaluation of advanced fault detection approaches for PV systems. IEEE J. Photovolt. **9**(2), 513–527 (2019). https://doi.org/10.1109/JPHOTOV.2019.2892189
16. REN21: Renewables 2022 Global Status Report. REN21 (2022). https://www.ren21.net/
17. Takagi, T., Sugeno, M.: Fuzzy identification of systems and its applications to modeling and control. IEEE Trans. Syst. Man Cybernet. SMC-**15**(1), 116–132 (1985). https://doi.org/10.1109/TSMC.1985.6313399

Framework for Upscaling Missing Data in Electricity Consumption Datasets Using Generative Adversarial Networks

Diana Romero[1] , R. Alcaraz-Fraga[2],
and Ponciano J. Escamilla-Ambrosio[2]([⊠])

[1] University of California, Irvine, CA 92617, USA
[2] Centro de Investigación en Computación, Instituto Politécnico Nacional,
Ciudad de México, 07738 Mexico City, Mexico
pescamilla@cic.ipn.mx

Abstract. One of the leading issues in adopting electricity load prediction today is the lack of high-quality and high-resolution real-world datasets. This poses a major problem especially in the context of electricity load prediction where high quality data are essential. To address this issue, this paper presents a framework that transforms datasets with missing values into high quality and high-resolution datasets using Generative Adversarial Networks (GANs). The capability of this framework was exhibited through a case study, the CIC-IPN electricity consumption dataset. Results show that the framework was able to successfully impute the missing values in the dataset while capturing the general patterns in the data. This framework can then be used to upscale other electricity datasets that contain missing values which can then be further used for electricity load prediction for smart cities and smart buildings.

Keywords: Electricity consumption dataset · Generative Adversarial Networks · Upscaling · Missing Data

1 Introduction

Electricity load and forecast management is one of the foundations of smart cities. This importance arises from the core principle that smart cities are being developed in order to urge society towards a more sustainable future. Furthermore, a core infrastructure of a smart city is assured electricity supply, since one of the core sustainable challenges of smart cities is to improve energy and utility infrastructure [2]. Thus, electricity load and forecast management plays an important role in smart cities to ensure a reliable and robust grid that can satisfy the electricity demand all the time in a sustainable manner.

One of the foundations of a reliable and robust electricity forecast model is a sufficient amount of data that can be used to adequately train a prediction model. However, in real world scenarios, dataset resolution can be lacking or could have missing values for a multitude of reasons: one such reason is the

S. Nesmachnow and L. Hernández Callejo (Eds.): ICSC-Cities 2023, CCIS 1938, pp. 189–202, 2024.
https://doi.org/10.1007/978-3-031-52517-9_13

irregular sampling collection of data, another possible reason is the temporary malfunction of data collection apparatus, or the loss of data that could have been caused by network issues where the data was not transmitted properly due to network failure. To address this issue of real world datasets being incomplete or having missing values, this paper presents a framework that is capable of increasing the fidelity of an electricity consumption dataset using generative adversarial networks (GANs).

This paper is organized in the following manner, Sect. 2 presents related works in using GANs in relation to electricity data, Sect. 3 presents the framework for upscaling an electricity consumption dataset with missing values, and lastly, Sect. 4 presents the conclusion and possible future directions of this study.

2   Related Works

There have been numerous works exploring the use of GANs in relation to electricity consumption data. One such study is the one by Bendaoud, et. al., where they compared different types of conditional GANs for short-term load forecasting using the data from the Algerian National Electricy and Gas for their experiments [3]. Additionally, a study by Yilmaz and Korn compared the performance of different GANs in creating a synthetic electricity demand data by comparing the generated demand data to the empirical data. It was found that the Conditonal Wasserstein GAN (CWGAN) model developed the synthetic demand data that had the most similar characteristics to the empirical data, while the TimeGAN model performed the worst [9].

GANs have also been used for solar photovoltaic (SPV) data. A study by Liu, et. al., proposed a dual-dimensional time series adversarial neural network based on gated recurrent neural network which aimed to capture the temporal patterns in an SPV dataset and augmenting the data in time and feature dimension [6].

GANs are known for their ability to generate a good quality image dataset and a lot of researchers have tried to exploit this capability of GANs to inform electricity and SPV data augmentation. An example of such a study is SolarGAN where the researchers used a GAN to generate synthetic fisheye images of vertical buildings along with corresponding irradiance which can then be used for urban planning of vertical PV panels to buildings [11]. Another study used deep convolutional GANs to generate synthetic Electroluminescence Images which can be used to maintain photovoltaic systems [8].

There is a growing interest in building load prediction as it has been made apparent that variability in different regions, i.e. weather, location, etc., introduces inconsistencies in energy demand, especially when a renewable energy generator is connected locally [7]. However, a paper reviewing the application of machine learning in building load prediction identified that one of the main impediment in fully utilizing the capabilities of machine learning for building load prediction is the lack of high-resolution real world collected datasets [10].

In this work the usage of GANs to create a framework that transforms low to mediocre quality electricity consumption dataset to a high-resolution dataset is proposed, that will address the current limitations of building load prediction. It is to the best of our knowledge that while GANs have been used extensively in conjunction to electricity and SPV data, there doesn't exist a framework with general guidelines on how to utilize GANs to transform real-world electricity dataset with missing values to a high-quality and high resolution dataset.

2.1 CIC-IPN Electricity Consumption

In order to demonstrate the capabilities of the designed framework, in this research the electricity consumption dataset of the CIC-IPN building is used. The building is located at Av. Juan de Dios Bátiz s/n esq. Miguel Othón de Mendizábal, Col. Nueva Industrial Vallejo, Gustavo A. Madero, C.P. 07738, Mexico City, Mexico. The CIC-IPN building has two main usages which are teaching and research activities. The dataset of this building provides a good opportunity to showcase the capability of the framework for data upscaling because the dataset itself contains missing values brought about by the monitoring sensor malfunctioning. See Fig. 1a, which shows the collected daily electricity consumption of the building for the year of 2019 and it exhibits that there is a period with missing values.

3   Electricity Consumption Data Upscaling Framework

This section presents the necessary steps in order to successfully upscale an electricity consumption dataset with missing values. The steps involved in this framework are as follows: (1) pre-process the dataset, (2) identify the general patterns in the dataset, (3) design the GAN architecture, (4) train the necessary GAN models and impute the missing values using the trained models. In order to illustrate the process of each step this paper conducts a case study by applying the methodology to the CIC-IPN Electricity Consumption dataset.

3.1 Data Pre-processing

In order to use the available electricity consumption data, it is necessary to apply data pre-processing. The data contains information from years 2017 to 2022 and electricity consumption is measured each 10 min. This time period is not regular in all measures and more than one measure per time period can also be found in some cases. Although it is important to notice that data from 2017 and 2018 follows a different wrong-formatted style, and so it is left outside of the pre-processing.

The proposed framework to deal with this scenario is the following:

1. Set seconds to zero: the data is intended to be measured each 10 min, meaning seconds should be always zero.
2. Floor minutes: take the nearest multiple of 10 min values, as the data is meant to be measured each 10 min there should be no values different other than 0, 10, 20, 30, 40 and 50.

3. In cases in which there is more than one measure for a time value the mean value of the measures is imputed, using an interquartile range (IQR) approach in order to detect outliers and keep them out of the mean value.

Following this approach the resulting data is now pre-processed, for example, going from 01/03/2019 01:23:02 to 01/03/2019 01:23:00.

3.2   Identifying General Patterns in the Dataset

In order to design the right architecture for the general adversarial network, a crucial step is to identify what are the general patterns that are present in the dataset. These identified patterns will become a motivation when designing the GAN model that will learn these patterns. The following subsections will contain an in depth analysis and observation of the daily electricity consumption at CIC-IPN in order to recognize the general patterns. It should be noted that the observations made below are unique to the CIC-IPN electricity consumption dataset, therefore different patterns and observations may arise when applying this methodology to a different dataset.

A) Daily Electricity Consumption for the Year 2019. Starting with the year 2019, it can be observed in Fig. 1a that there is a long contiguous section where data does not exist, specifically between 4/20/2019 22:20 and 5/27/2019 13:10. It should be especially noted that another characteristic of the CIC-IPN dataset is that for long contiguous sections of missing data, such as the mentioned section above, the total electricity consumption for this period was added to the next available date and time. For example, for the period mentioned above the total electricity consumption was approximately 74,000 kWh and this value was added to the next available data entry which was on 5/27/2019 13:20. This is important to note because this will be a condition that needs to be satisfied when values are generated for this period.

Looking at a more granular level, the behavior of daily consumption throughout a week can be seen in Fig. 2a. It can be observed that the daily consumption during Monday to Friday is similar while there is a lot less electricity consumption during the weekend. This observation will need to be incorporated in the development of the GAN architecture later on because these are two separate behaviors that need to be accounted for.

B) Daily Electricity Consumption for the Year 2020. For the year of 2020 most of the data for the month of January for this year is missing as can be seen in Fig. 1b. It can also be observed that for the first quarter of 2020 the daily consumption behavior is similar to 2019. This implies that the GAN trained using the 2019 data can also be used to impute the missing values for the month of January 2020.

Another observation is that for most of the year the daily consumption is very low with a small range. This is caused by the quarantine protocols enforced

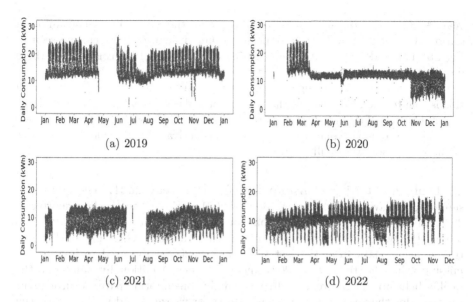

Fig. 1. Scatter plot of the daily electricity consumption at CIC-IPN for the years of 2019–2022.

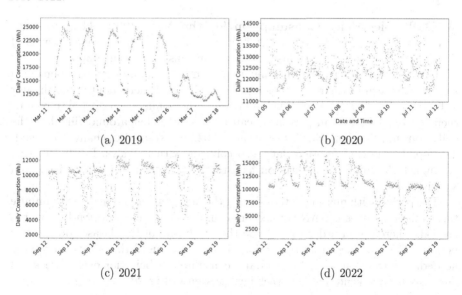

Fig. 2. Scatter plot of the daily electricity consumption for a random week at CIC-IPN for the years of 2019–2022.

by the government due to the COVID-19 outbreak wherein the institution was conducting it's activities remotely. Because of this drastic change in the pattern, a different GAN model would need to be trained for this period of the year. Additionally, during this period of the year, the daily pattern consumption during the weekend and weekday do not differ dramatically as can be seen in Fig. 2b. This indicates that when training a GAN model for this period, there does not need to be a distinction between the weekend and weekdays.

Lastly, the pattern changes again during the last quarter of the year and this is due to the activation of the solar photovoltaic (SPV) plant at CIC-IPN. Again, because of the different scenario, a different GAN is needed to capture the consumption behavior once the SPV plant was activated and while the activities of the institution were still remote.

C) Daily Electricity Consumption for the Year 2021. The daily consumption behavior for the whole year of 2021 is similar to the last quarter of 2020, this is due to the situation that for the whole year of 2021 the activities of CIC-IPN was fully remote. This means that the same GAN model that was trained using data from the last quarter of 2020 can be used to impute the missing values for the year of 2021 and vice versa. Additionally, similar to the weekly behavior for the year of 2019, the daily consumption pattern throughout the week for the year of 2020 does not differ for weekend and weekdays as seen in Fig. 2c.

D) Daily Electricity Consumption for the Year 2022. The daily consumption pattern for the year of 2022 at CIC-IPN is more diverse because of the changing activities at the institution during this year. Some important notes to date are that starting from January 4, 2022, the administrative personnel started to return to their on-site activities at CIC and then about a month later at February 14, 2022, the teaching and research personnel have started to resume their activities at CIC in person. It can be observed that around this date the daily consumption behavior for the year of 2022 has started to change. The sudden dips in the consumption data also coincide with holidays. Lastly, starting in August 15, 2022, the institution has started to return to it's fully in-person activities.

The period with missing data is during the last quarter and in order to impute these missing values a GAN trained on a similar daily consumption behavior is needed. Therefore in order to increase the resolution of the dataset during this period a GAN trained from the period of August 15 until the end of the year is needed. For the year of 2022, the daily consumption behavior over a week did differ for the weekend and the weekdays as seen in Fig. 2d.

3.3 Designing the GAN Architecture

In the previous section, we have identified the general patterns and the different GANs needed to fill in the missing values. To summarize, a GAN that captures the weekend and weekday behavior is required for the year of 2019 and 2022 because of the different electricity consumption pattern during the weekends. There is a total of 4 different GANs needed to impute the missing values for the dataset, namely, (1) a GAN for the missing values of 2019 and the first quarter of 2020, (2) a GAN during the year of 2021 where the institution was undergoing remote activities and the SPV plant wasn't activated yet, (3) a GAN for the year of 2021 where the activities of the institution were remote and the SPV plant was active, and (4) a GAN for when CIC has resumed to in-person activities with the SPV plant active.

GANs were first proposed by Ian Goodfellow where the framework is to simultaneously train two models, namely a generative model and a discriminative model, where the generative model aims to capture the data distribution and the discriminative model estimates the probability that the generated data came from the training data [4]. Because GANs are at least two models being trained simultaneously, they are notoriously known to be difficult to train and to have a lot of instability. Because of this, obtaining the correct GAN architecture for a specific dataset requires a lot of experimentation. This section will demonstrate the evolution of the GAN architecture for the CIC-IPN electricity consumption dataset and the reasoning behind the progressive changes applied to the architecture.

To begin with, we start with a simple GAN where the generator and the discriminator are both neural networks with 3 dense layers and a small number of neurons for each layer (less than 50). The chosen activation function for the output layer of the generator was linear as this is a common choice when generating continuous data such as electricity consumption. The key is to begin with a simple architecture and to progress to a more complex model as needed. The results of training this simple GAN model extensively on the 2019 data can be seen in Fig. 3. It is obvious that this simple GAN was not able to capture the pattern present in the dataset and that the generated values were concentrated on a small range. This is known as mode collapse which happens when the GAN fails to produce a diverse and representative set of outputs and only focuses on a small range of outputs.

A popular GAN architecture that addresses the problem of mode collapse is the Wasserstein-GAN (WGAN) where an Earth Mover (EM) distance, the Wasserstein distance, is used instead of using probability distances and divergences as a measure of how likely the generated data is part of the training data [1]. A proven stable way of training GANs that use Wasserstein distance as a loss metric is by penalizing the norm of the gradient of the critic with respect to its input in order to enforce the Lipschitz constraint [5]. Moving forward with this work, GANs that use the Wasserstein loss and gradient penalty for training the critic will be referred to as WGAN-GP. Because of the aforementioned characteristics of a WGAN-GP, and it's benefits of stable training and diverse outputs, it was opted to implement a WGAN-GP architecture. The results of training a model with these modifications to the architecture can be seen in Fig. 4. It can be seen in the figure that the model is now able to produce a much more diverse output but it still fails to capture the desired pattern of the dataset.

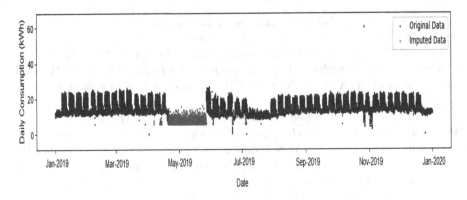

Fig. 3. Results of imputing 2019 data with a simple GAN.

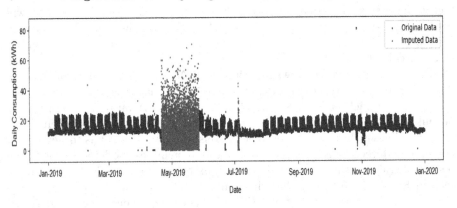

Fig. 4. Results of imputing 2019 data with a WGAN-GP architecture.

A possible point of improvement at this stage is to use a different activation function for the output layer of the generator because the linear function might not be able to capture the complex data distributions. A chosen alternative activation function is the sigmoid function where the output is [0,1]. This was chosen because the dataset only yields positive values. If the dataset used for training contained negative values, a better alternative function would have been the tanh function because it's output are of the range [-1,1]. It is very important to note that when using non-linear activation functions, like sigmoid or tanh, it is necessary to normalize the dataset before using it to train the model. This ensures that the model satisfies the generated output ranges. Similarly, it is then necessary to denormalize the generated values of the generator when imputing the missing values of the dataset.

In Sect. 3.2, it was observed that the daily consumption patterns during the weekend and during the weekday was different and in order to capture this difference in behavior, a conditional label indicating whether the sample belongs to weekend or weekday was introduced to the WGAN-GP architecture, thus transforming it into a conditional WGAN-GP (CWGAN-GP). This class label, indicating if the sample from the training set belongs to weekend or weekday, conditions the network to learn the different distributions present within these two categories. Results of implementing the conditional labels and changing the activation function of the output layer can be seen in Fig. 5. The model at this stage produces different patterns for the weekend and weekday as can be seen by the intermittent dips in the imputed data section but it is still unable to capture the trend of electricity consumption throughout a day.

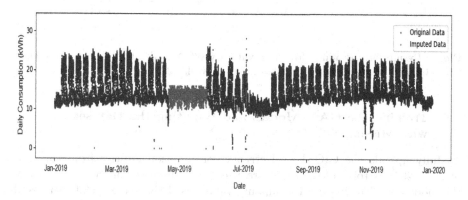

Fig. 5. Results of imputing 2019 data with a CWGAN-GP architecture where class labels indicate if the sample is from weekday or weekend.

The results shown in Fig. 5 suggest that the network might need to be conditioned at a more granular level (i.e. hourly) than just weekend and weekday. Therefore, to examine the daily consumption pattern further we can refer again to Fig. 2a. It can be seen that the electricity consumption for each day has a fairly symmetrical pattern where the electricity consumption peaks at around 12 noon. This implies that if the network were to learn the data distribution of the dataset for 1am-2am, it would have also learned the data distribution for 10pm-11pm. This indicates that we can use 12 class labels to condition the network to learn the data distribution at an hourly level (considering a symmetric behavior pattern). However, as we've observed, the weekend and weekday behavior differs, thus the class labels also need to account for this resulting to a total of 24 class labels (12 for weekdays and 12 for weekend days). The results of imputing the 2019 dataset using a model trained with 24 conditional labels can be seen in Fig. 6. It is apparent that the model is now able to exhibit the general pattern present in the dataset which yield to a successfully upscaled dataset.

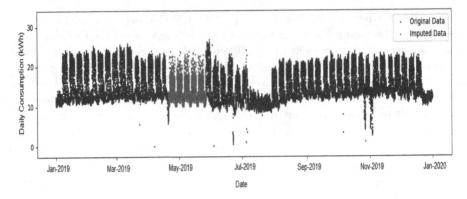

Fig. 6. Results of upscaling 2019 data with a CWGAN-GP architecture where class labels indicate if the sample is from weekday or weekend.

3.4   Training the GAN Models and Imputing the Dataset with Missing Values

To fully upscale the CIC-IPN electricity consumption dataset from the year of 2019–2020 a total of 4 GANs are needed as discussed in Sect. 3.2. All of the models used to impute the missing values used the same architecture and training parameters, the only difference was the subset of training data used for each model and the conditional labels because the conditional labels depended on the representative pattern. It should be noted that when imputing the missing values the condition that the sum of daily consumption for these missing values is equal to the difference of consumption between the date-time prior to the missing period and the date-time after the missing period. This condition was implemented outside of the GAN model training by simply scaling the generated values within the missing period to satisfy the required sum.

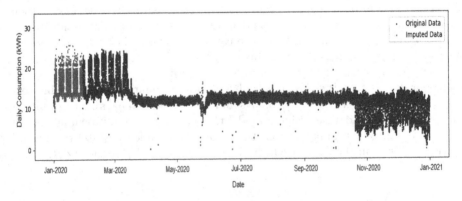

Fig. 7. Results of imputing first quarter of 2020 data with a CWGAN-GP architecture where class labels indicate if the sample is from weekday or weekend.

a) GAN Model for 2019 and First Quarter of 2020 . This model was discussed at length in Sect. 3.3 as this was used as a working example in the designing and choosing of the GAN architecture. Since the first quarter of 2021 exhibit the same pattern as the year of 2019 the same trained model was used to impute the missing values for the month of January in 2020. The results of using the same model for upscaling the missing values of the year of 2020 can be seen in Fig. 7.

b) GAN Model for Data During the Remote Activities Period of 2020 and No Active SPV Plant. As discussed in Sect. 3.2 this period of the dataset had no drastic difference in the daily consumption pattern during the weekend and during the weekday. Because of this the class labels used to train this model was only 12 because there was no need for a distinction between the data distribution of the weekend and weekday. The results of upscaling the 2020 data during the remote activities period can be seen in Fig. 8. This period does not have a long section with missing values as can be seen by the sparse red points in Fig. 8 and it seems that the generated values are between the maximum and minimum values of the period.

c) GAN Model for Data During Remote Activities and Activation of SPV Plant. The data for this period also did not show a great difference in the daily consumption behavior for weekend and weekday and thus similarly only used 12 class labels for training. The results of the upscaled data can be seen in Fig. 9. The general pattern of the dataset was captured by the GAN however there is not a lot of variation in the maximum daily values as can be seen in the figure.

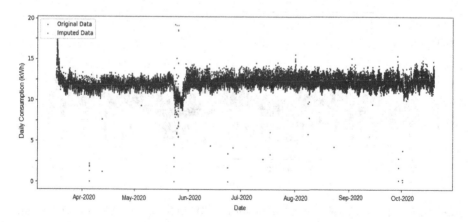

Fig. 8. Results of upscaling 2020 data with a CWGAN-GP architecture where class labels indicate only hours of the day.

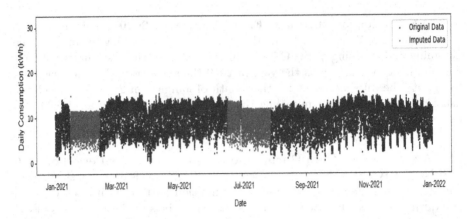

Fig. 9. Results of upscaling 2021 data with a CWGAN-GP architecture where class labels indicate only hours of the day.

d) GAN for When CIC Has Resumed to In-Person Activities with the SPV Plant Active . During this period the weekend and weekday behaviors have started to shown diversity again and thus, similar to the first GAN model, 24 class labels were used to train the model. The results of the upscaled 2022 data can be seen in Fig. 10. Results show that the GAN was able to capture the general patter of the data for the period that CIC has resumed to in-person activities. However, it was not completely able to capture the range of the consumption as the lower values of the generated data does not typically reach the minimum values possible. The generated data was still of good fidelity as it was able to capture the general pattern.

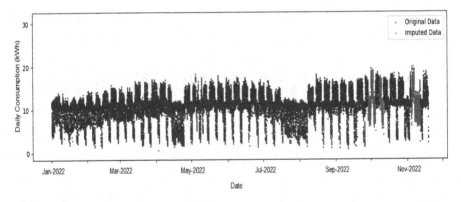

Fig. 10. Results of upscaling 2022 data with a CWGAN-GP architecture where class labels indicate if the sample is from weekday or weekend.

4   Conclusions and Future Work

From the results shown before, it can be concluded that the framework presented in this paper is successful in fully upscaling the CIC-IPN electricity consumption dataset from the years of 2019 to 2022. The framework presented advises it's adopters to do the following steps: (1) pre-process the dataset, (2) identify the general patterns in the dataset, (3) design the GAN architecture, (4) train the necessary GAN models and impute the missing values using the trained models. The capability of the framework to upscale datasets with missing values was shown as it was able to successfully impute the missing values in the CIC-IPN electricity consumption dataset thus transforming an originally incomplete dataset into a high quality and high resolution dataset. Future work includes exploring the design of a dynamic GAN architecture that detects the changes in the patterns of a dataset to mitigate the current solution of having multiple GANs for a single dataset. Similarly, designing a GAN that can create and cluster the conditional classes automatically is also an avenue that would be worth exploring.

Acknowledgements. The first author acknowledges the support of the Mexican Graduate Research and Education Program. This work was supported by Instituto Politecnico Nacional under grants SIP-20230990 and SIP-20232782.

References

1. Arjovsky, M., Chintala, S., Bottou, L.: Wasserstein GAN, December 2017
2. Bagoury, S.M.E., Yousef, P.H.A.: Sustainable development goals and smart settlements, Linkages, April 2018. https://doi.org/10.2139/ssrn.3163514
3. Bendaoud, N.M.M., Farah, N., Ben Ahmed, S.: Comparing generative adversarial networks architectures for electricity demand forecasting. Energy Build. **247**, 111152 (2021). https://doi.org/10.1016/j.enbuild.2021.111152
4. Goodfellow, I.J., et al.: Generative adversarial networks, June 2014
5. Gulrajani, I., Ahmed, F., Arjovsky, M., Dumoulin, V., Courville, A.: Improved training of Wasserstein GANs, December 2017
6. Liu, L.M., Ren, X.Y., Zhang, F., Gao, L., Hao, B.: Dual-dimension Time-GGAN data augmentation method for improving the performance of deep learning models for PV power forecasting. Energy Rep. **9**, 6419–6433 (2023). https://doi.org/10.1016/j.egyr.2023.05.226
7. Potter, C.W., Archambault, A., Westrick, K.: Building a smarter smart grid through better renewable energy information. In: 2009 IEEE/PES Power Systems Conference and Exposition, pp. 1–5, March 2009. https://doi.org/10.1109/PSCE.2009.4840110
8. Romero, H.F.M., et al.: Synthetic dataset of electroluminescence images of photovoltaic cells by deep convolutional generative adversarial networks. In: Nesmachnow, S., Hernández Callejo, L. (eds.) Smart Cities, pp. 3–16. Communications in Computer and Information Science, Springer, Switzerland (2023). https://doi.org/10.1007/978-3-031-28454-0_1

9. Yilmaz, B., Korn, R.: Synthetic demand data generation for individual electricity consumers?: generative adversarial networks (GANs). Energy AI **9**, 100161 (2022). https://doi.org/10.1016/j.egyai.2022.100161
10. Zhang, L., Wen, J., Li, Y., Chen, J., Ye, Y., Fu, Y., Livingood, W.: A review of machine learning in building load prediction. Appl. Energy **285**, 116452 (2021). https://doi.org/10.1016/j.apenergy.2021.116452
11. Zhang, Y., Schlueter, A., Waibel, C.: SolarGAN: synthetic annual solar irradiance time series on urban building facades via deep generative networks. Energy AI **12**, 100223 (2023). https://doi.org/10.1016/j.egyai.2022.100223

Detection of Personal Protection Elements in a Recycling Plant Using Convolutional Neural Networks

Diego Alberto Godoy[1]([⊠]) [iD], Cesar Gallardo[1] [iD], Ricardo Selva[1] [iD], Nicolas Ibarra[1] [iD], Carlos Kornuta[1] [iD], and Enrique Marcelo Albornoz[2] [iD]

[1] Centro de Investigación en Tecnologías de la Información y Comunicaciones (CITIC), Universidad Gastón Dachary, Avenue López y Planes 6519, 3300 Posadas, Argentina
diegodoy@citic.ugd.edu.ar
[2] Instituto de Investigación en Señales, Sistemas e Inteligencia Artificial - Sinc(I), CONICET-UNL, Santa Fe, Argentina
emalbornoz@sinc.unl.edu.ar

Abstract. The use of personal protective equipment (PPE) in industries is mandatory, since current regulations dictate the use of various types of PPE depending on the activity carried out. The correct use of these elements can be the difference between an incident and an accident with serious consequences for the people involved. In different industries, supervisors spend a large portion of their time ensuring that workers use their PPE correctly at all times. In order to help monitor worker safety, this work addresses the development of a prototype that allows the use of PPE to be detected automatically and send relevant notifications to supervisors. The prototype is developed in Python, and the detection of PPE is carried out through a deep neural network (YOLOv5). Preliminary inferences show that it can be adapted in a wide variety of scenarios with promising results.

Keywords: Convolutional Neural Networks · PPE · PPE Identification

1 Introduction

For an organization, people are its most valuable asset, since they are the ones who carry out productive activities such as manual operational tasks or the operation of certain machines. These employees are exposed to the dangers of the work environment on a daily basis, where an accident can result in wounds, injuries, disabilities, and even death [1]. Furthermore, in some work environments certain risk agents are present that, in the long term, can cause various occupational diseases [2]. The goal of using PPE (Personal Protective Equipment) is to avoid or mitigate the consequences of accidents and risk agents, increasing worker safety. Not using or incorrectly using this equipment represents a great risk for both employees and employers; the latter can even be sanctioned by the regulatory body even in the absence of an accident. The use of PPE is mandatory for the operations in any industry. In Argentina, there are regulations in force in Law 19587 of the Superintendence of Occupational Risks (SRT) [3], which require employers to

© The Author(s), under exclusive license to Springer Nature Switzerland AG 2024
S. Nesmachnow and L. Hernández Callejo (Eds.): ICSC-Cities 2023, CCIS 1938, pp. 203–215, 2024.
https://doi.org/10.1007/978-3-031-52517-9_14

provide employees with appropriate PPE for the tasks they perform, as well as to control that employees use this PPE correctly throughout the working day. Some PPE that may be required are hard helmet, face protector, eye protector, gloves, refractory vest and appropriate shoes. Each PPE can be specific for certain types of tasks. For example, latex gloves are designed to be used in laboratories, where it is necessary to protect the hands from pathogenic elements or other substances. There are also cut-resistant gloves for handling sharp elements, thermal gloves for handling very hot or very cold elements, and work gloves that improve the adhesion of elements on the hand and protect against abrasive elements.

In recent years, advances have been made in the automatic detection of PPE. For example, in [5], the authors discuss the misuse of PPE by workers and visitors at sites where construction projects are carried out. This is also supported by European and North American studies and reports, which indicate that the majority of work-related injuries caused by impact to the head are due to the lack of use of a safety helmet. The objective proposed is designing and testing a methodology for detecting the correct use of PPE in videos without a fixed camera, through computer vision (CV) and machine learning techniques, to prevent workplace accidents. As regards the methodology used in their work, they propose using an algorithm and the OpenPose network to detect the anthropometric points of an individual and, based on these, determine to which part of the body they correspond. The main goal of this approach is to determine the anthropometric points first and then verify if, given the points obtained, the corresponding PPE is present in that part of the body. For example, by obtaining the points that link to the individua's head, the algorithm then detects whether the person is wearing a hard helmet. Also, when detecting anthropometric points on the individua's trunk, the presence or absence of a refractory vest is checked. A disadvantage of this research is that, when detecting PPE based on anthropometric points, the partial classifications caused by the different positions a person might adopt while working are not taken into account, since it is likely that, due to the dynamic nature of work-related activities, sometimes the shots cannot capture the entire body of the individual. There is also another, not very positive aspect, and that is the amount of resources that must be used to carry out the experiment, both in terms of computation for processing the anthropometric points, as well as in relation to network implementation and the resources necessary to capture samples of people working.

The work concludes that it is a powerful tool because it is able to recognize objects with a 0.99 accuracy for the detection of PPE in different environments. As future work, the authors propose working on the detection of more protection elements.

Another related work [6] mentions how workers in dangerous and toxic environments often prefer not to use the corresponding PPE when performing their tasks. This may be so because the PPE is uncomfortable or it might affect the accuracy of the actions involved. It has been shown that one way to obtain accurate results in the identification of people and personal protection elements is the use of a detector and a classifier. The prototype is responsible for recognizing the person and after that, PPE identification is carried out. Following this last model, in this article a new approach is proposed to improve the detection of personal protection equipment using three components: a person detector, pose estimation, and one or several PPE classifiers (one for each type of PPE to be detected). The person detector is based on the YOLOv3 object detector, which is pre-trained with the MS COCO dataset. This detector offers good performance and speed when performing classifications. For each entry, it returns the boxes of the objects it recognized with their corresponding labels. In this case, the objects belonged to the "people" category. Pose estimation is used to capture the pose of each identified person and is based on [7]. For each input, the image is processed to recover body orientation, which is then represented by means of a graphical skeleton. This skeleton is made up of nodes and links that represent the different segments of the body. With this information, maps can be created representing the parts of the person that are of interest. The classifier is a CNN whose architecture is based on the MobileNetV2 neural network, which is equivalent to the AlexNet network in terms of accuracy but better in terms of speed. This network is trained with the ImageNet dataset. The training process starts with person detection models, pre-trained pose estimation models, and one or more PPE classifiers. The number of classifiers will depend on the number of personal protection elements to be identified. Three datasets were used, each of them on a specific piece of PPE. In this case, the work focused on identifying hard helmets, masks and boots. Each image is entered into the person detector, which outputs the image with boxes that enclose each detected person. These boxes set processing limits for the following steps. Then, the pose estimation model is used, which outputs a "skeleton" of the body that indicates its position and the location of the different parts of the body. From this output, the regions of the body that could contain PPE are automatically cut out and sent to the corresponding classifier (the head is sent to the helmet classifier, the hands to the glove classifier, etc.). Each input image is processed by a series of convolutional blocks to then perform the classification. The person detector is used in test images to obtain the limits to be classified. The pose estimation model is not used in this case, but rather relevant cropped sub-areas are sent to the corresponding classifier (the upper area is sent to the helmet classifier, the lower area is sent to the boot classifier, etc.). Each classifier provides a binary prediction for each received sub-area, indicating whether the analyzed body part is using the corresponding personal protection equipment. In conclusion, the work offers a new approach for the detection of PPE which turned out to be effective and efficient, with promising results.

Part of the Urban Solid Waste Management (GIRSU) [4] program is carried out at a recycling plant located in the Municipal Green Center that contributes to sustainable development, is responsible for the reduction of waste sent to final deposit centers, and promotes reutilization and recycling (Fig. 1). This plant is presented as an industrial environment with many machines, which presents various health risks. Operators must use personal protective equipment at all times, such as hard helmets, gloves, appropriate shoes, and vests, among others.

In this context, this work addresses the automatic identification of PPE in a recyclable waste plant through computer vision in order to mitigate the negative effects of workplace accidents in an industry.

Fig. 1. Workers at the recycling plant [4]

2 Methodology

This section starts with a detailed analysis of the data model used, the development of a solution prototype for the problem at hand, and its assessment using the CRISP-DM methodology, which was selected due to its flexible and adaptable nature. Then, a detailed description is made of the images that are used by the neural network model to identify whether workers are wearing their PPE correctly.

3 Understanding the Data Model

The activities are described below, taking into account the state of the art on images of workers using PPE in operational environments. First, the collection and preparation of the image dataset is detailed, and then labels are added for prototype modeling.

3.1 Image Dataset Collection and Preparation

First, Hard Hat Workers dataset images are selected [8]. Only 1280 images of this dataset could be used due to limitations of the Roboflow pricing plan at the time of import. Then, 136 photos were taken of the workers performing their duties at the Green Center recycling plant (Fig. 2) to assess model behavior with images of the target scenario. In these images, workers can be seen carrying out their habitual tasks on the conveyor belt. Some of them were asked to pose for front images showing their complete equipment and some images where they had removed part of their equipment in order to carry out different tests.

Additionally, a set of images were captured for prototype validation tasks. The dataset created includes a wide variety of examples and elements that are used for prototype training, validation and testing, as shown in Fig. 3. In some cases, images with augmentation are observed (with inverted heads to improve neural network performance).

Fig. 2. Some of the images captured at the Municipal Green Center

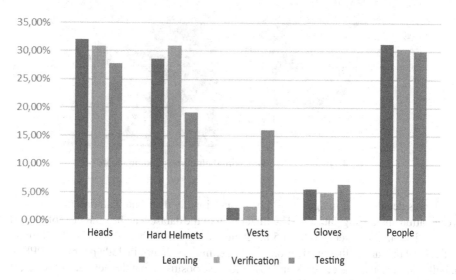

Fig. 3. Percentage of images used for training, validation and testing processes.

3.2 Data Labeling

For the hard helmet class labeling process, the helmet was enclosed as accurately as possible within the label, trying to minimize the area of the workers' heads in the labels. Then, the heads class was labeled, which includes heads that are not wearing a helmet as well as heads that are wearing it. These labels included both the head and the helmet if it was present. The purpose of this label is enabling the prototype to determine if the person is in a position where the helmet is visible, since if the head can be seen, the helmet should be visible too.

To determine the subjects for the verification tasks, the entire body of the people who appear in the images is labeled. An attempt is made to enclose the entire body in the label, avoiding as much as possible including other people who may be superimposed.

As with the previously mentioned PPE, images of workers using protective gloves of various types were selected. Additionally, it was determined that labeling the bare hands of people not wearing gloves would be useful in determining the lack of gloves, in a similar strategy to that used for helmets and heads.

Once the classes and guidelines for labeling them were defined, each image was put through the process, carefully defining the boundaries of each label. For each person, up to 6 labels could be generated; that is, a maximum of one helmet, one head, one vest, two gloves or hands and the whole person were labeled. Figure 4 presents examples of images with their final labeling.

Fig. 4. Images of workers with their corresponding labels

It was decided that images would be proportionally distributed among the learning, verification and testing datasets. The final result of the dataset can be seen in Table 1, and Fig. 5. The final dataset also has 65 unlabeled images—46 that are part of the training set and 19 that are in the verification set. These images do not include people or PPE to label—they are used as controls and to avoid false positives that the network may detect during the training phase (and then make the necessary corrections).

Table 1. Dataset description

Label	Learning	Percentage	Verification	Percentage	Testing	Percentage
Heads	8054	32.08%	806	30.94%	90	27.86%
Hard helmets	7201	28.68%	808	31.02%	62	19.20%
Vests	597	2.38%	67	2.57%	52	16.10%
Gloves	1404	5.59%	129	4.95%	21	6.50%
Individuals	7852	31.27%	795	30.52%	97	30.03%
Total	25699	100%	2650	100%	323	100%
Percentage	90%	-	9%	-	1%	-

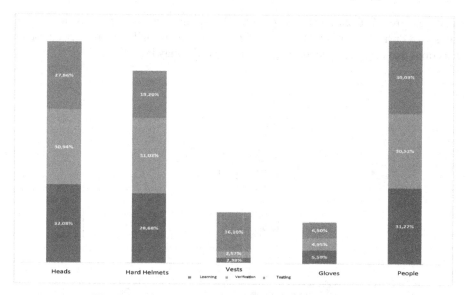

Fig. 5. Graphical representation of each class in the datasets

4 Prototype Modeling

This phase consists of analyzing and designing a solution prototype that is capable of identifying PPE. In one of the reference articles, a very good confidence percentage (0.99) is obtained for PPE identification in the construction industry, but with a significant investment in computational power. The authors used high-quality video processing and capture images from it to identify the anthropometric points and then check if the relevant PPE is present. To reduce costs, in this work the problem is solved in a simpler way, using a convolutional neural network for detecting objects in an image. For this implementation, the YOLOv5 network was used due to its high precision, low computational cost and thorough documentation [9]. Network output is processed by a small algorithm that decides whether a person is wearing their PPE.

The architectural diagram of the prototype (Fig. 6) illustrates the training and operating processes, their inputs, and the respective outputs for each. The goal is to provide the reader with a general, abstract structure of the parameters necessary for the prototype to run effectively. For the network training stage, a set of images labeled with their respective classes is required in order to produce a set of weights that can be used later. The weights obtained during the learning phase and the images captured by a device are used as network input. They are processed and, based on the weights introduced to the network and the photograph used as input image, it will be determined if a person is wearing the regulatory PPE.

Detections serve as input to the algorithm that evaluates whether people are using their PPE. Figure 7 shows a UML activity diagram that summarizes the operation of the algorithm. The algorithm takes each detected person and, based on their coordinates, identifies any PPE they are wearing. Then, stores its findings as a list for later review. The decision criterion is given if at least one of the coordinates of the segment is contained within the area that represents the person. This design was chosen so as not to rule out gloves or hands that may be a little far from the body, and in turn filter out other detections that may correspond to another person who may be nearby.

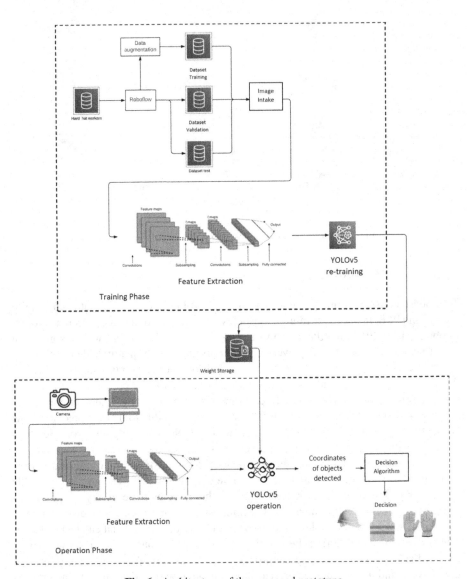

Fig. 6. Architecture of the proposed prototype

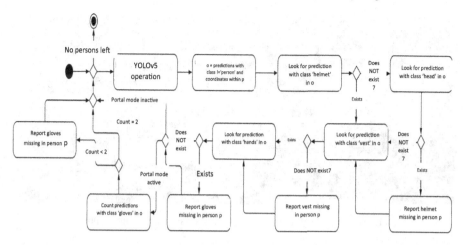

Fig. 7. Decision activities diagram

5   Experiments and Results

The next section focuses on the description of the tests carried out and on the interpretation of their results to evaluate the performance of the designed prototype in different environments that largely cover the scenarios where the trained convolutional neural network could be used. The prototype is also evaluated to find the weaknesses of the model and identify potential future work of interest to be carried out. To obtain more understandable results in this report, the output format of the decision algorithm was slightly modified. In addition to text alerts, when the algorithm ends, each person analyzed is marked with a box on the original image. When no PPE non-compliances are detected, the box is green and has the legend "OK"; otherwise, it is red. In this case, the legend details what the missing equipment is using two-letter codes. Possible options are: CA (hard helmets), CH (vests), and GU (gloves).

5.1   Tests in Portal Mode

Figure 8 shows the output of the prototype with portal mode activated. On the left, a correct detection is shown: the person (*persona* in Spanish) is wearing gloves (*guantes* in Spanish) but not a helmet (*casco* in Spanish) or vest (*chaleco* in Spanish), and the legend correctly indicates "OK". The image on the right depicts another correct detection – despite the position of the worker, the prototype is able to identify that there are no missing PPE.

Figure 9 presents network detections on the left and the final result of the prototype on the right. In this case, the result obtained was incorrect – as it can be seen in the images, the person is wearing all equipment pieces correctly; however, the image on the right indicates that the prototype detected that the gloves are missing. This may be due to brightness and contrast in the image: the areas that are under sunlight caused the rest of the image to appear darker and with a little noise, which could have caused the

Fig. 8. Correct results in portal mode. Decision algorithm output

detection of both gloves to fail. Another factor that could have caused the error is the position of the person with respect to the camera, since the worker is somewhat leaning to one side, but this should not be a reason for failure.

Fig. 9. Wrong and correct results in portal mode

5.2   Testing on the Conveyor Belt

Figure 10 presents a simple test, where a single operator is seen up close with acceptable contrast and clearly visible hands. On the left, the network graphical output is shown; it is of note that none of the objects on the conveyor belt interfered with the network and all detections were correct with good confidence values. On the right, the graphic output of the prototype is shown. Here, it can be seen that it was able to detect that the worker's vest and gloves were missing. In this test, where helmet color is different from that of normally used helmets, the prototype was still capable of identifying it on the image, indicating that slight changes to PPE do not require retraining the network.

Fig. 10. Correct result on conveyor belt operator

The prototype was then tested under more difficult conditions. Figures 11 and 12 present a detection scenario of an operator with her back turned to the camera and people who are partially visible. In the case of the operator not facing the camera, although the use of gloves could not be determined, helmet and vest were correctly detected. The correct detection of the operator on the right is also highlighted despite only being able to see half of his body, demonstrating that the prototype is capable of working in scenarios where an object partially hides workers. The people on the left triggered some flaws in the prototype. It is acceptable that the person with his back turned to the camera is not detected, since less than half his body is visible. It is expected that the network will detect at least the hand; however, based on the legend, the hand was not detected since only the lack of a helmet and vest were marked. Even though the hands of the marked person cannot be seen, the decision algorithm should have detected the missing gloves. The detections seen in the image on the left are completely correct and with good confidence values, with the exception of the hand of the person on the left that was not detected, and the glove of the person on the right, although this detection failed because the photo came out blurry. Even though the graphic output does not correctly display the confidence values of the person on the right, the text output indicates values of 0.24

for the helmet and 0.47 for the vest, which are very good considering that the workers are only partially visible.

Fig. 11. Results on conveyor belt operator

Fig. 12. Mixed results with overlapping workers. Decision algorithm output

6   Conclusions

A prototype of a computer vision system has been developed for the identification of PPE in industrial scenarios. In particular, it has been tested at the Municipal Green Center of the city of Posadas (Argentina). Based on the results presented, it can be concluded that its implementation is feasible; the characteristics that should be taken into account for future research and development are highlighted.

It is notable that with the training parameters and the dataset used, great results were achieved in a first iteration of a project of these characteristics aimed at optimizing controls for the occupational safety of workers in an industry. The network performs very well in a standard hardware, which also indicates that the project is highly feasible and that in the future a similar model could be implemented in a scenario such as the Municipal Green Center (MGC). As lines of future work, continuing with this research, the following activities are proposed: Different sets of tests in other environments such as factories or industries, where the increase in traffic is considered, prototypes of the application on cell phones with Android and iPhone systems, increase the level of precision, include other types of camera technologies, among others.

References

1. Ray Asfahl, C.: *Seguridad industrial y administración de la salud.* Pearson Education (2010)
2. Soto-Chávez, L.E., Ugalde-Vicuña, J.W., Chang-Camacho, L.: *Evaluación de la Exposición a agentes de riesgo físico en centros de salud* (2020)
3. Gobierno de la Republica Argentina (Jul. 20, 2020) *Equipos y elementos de protección personal.* Accessed Jan 12 (2022). https://www.argentina.gob.ar/sites/default/files/04_guia_equipos_y_elementos_de_proteccion_personal_ok.pdf
4. Municipalidad de Posadas, (Mar. 20, 2020). *Centro Verde Municipal.* Accessed Dic 05, 2023 https://posadas.gov.ar/sustentable/centro-verde-municpal/
5. fernández, M.M., Fernández, J.Á., Bajo, J.M., & Delrieux, C.: Sistema automatizado para monitorear el uso de equipos de protección personal en la industria de la construcción. *Revista Iberoamericana de Automática e Informática industrial* (2020)
6. Sandru, A.R., Duta, G., Georgescu, M., Ionescu, R.T.: SuPEr - SAM: using the supervision signal from a pose estimator to train a spatial attention module for personal protective equipment recognition. In: 2021 IEEE Winter Conference on Applications of Computer Vision (WACV), pp. 2816–2825 (2020)
7. Cao, Z., Simon, T., Wei, S., Sheikh, Y.: Realtime Multi-person 2D pose estimation using part affinity fields. In: 2017 IEEE Conference on Computer Vision and Pattern Recognition (CVPR), pp. 1302–1310 (2016)
8. Northeastern University-China, (Mar. 31, 2022.) *Hard Hat Workers Object Detection Dataset.* last access: Dic 05, 2023 https://public.roboflow.com/object-detection/hard-hat-workers
9. Open Source Project (Mar. 20, 2015). *Yolo V5 Documentation.* GitHub. last access: Dic 05, 2023 https://github.com/ultralytics/yolov5

A New Sentiment Analysis Methodology for Football Game Matches Utilizing Social Networks and Artificial Intelligence Techniques

José Alberto Hernández-Aguilar[1]([⊠]) [iD], Yessica Calderón-Segura[1] [iD],
Gustavo Medina-Angel[2] [iD], Pedro Moreno-Bernal[1] [iD], Felipe Bonilla-Sánchez[1] [iD],
Jesús del Carmen Peralta-Abarca[3] [iD], and Gennadiy Burlak[2] [iD]

[1] Facultad de Contaduría, Administración e Informática,
Universidad Autónoma del Estado de Morelos (UAEM), Cuernavaca, Mexico
{jose_hernandez,ycalderons,pmoreno,fbonilla}@uaem.mx
[2] Centro de Investigación en Ingeniería y Ciencias Aplicadas, UAEM, Cuernavaca,
Mexico
gustavo.medina@uaem.edu.mx, gburlak@uaem.mx
[3] Facultad de Ciencias Químicas e Ingeniería, UAEM, Cuernavaca, Mexico
carmen.peralta@uaem.mx

Abstract. This article presents a sentiment analysis using data from X
social media platform (Twitter) using artificial intelligence techniques.
Two artificial intelligence techniques perform sentiment analysis: *i*) bag
of words and *ii*) computer vision. The first is used for Natural Language Processing (NLP) and sentiment identification, while the second
is for computer-based emotion identification in photographs or frames.
The proposed methodology is applied to the soccer match between the
Querétaro White Roosters and the Atlas Football Club in Guadalajara,
Mexico. The study case involves 2,000 tweets from the March 5, 2022,
soccer match, collected from Twitter, and 200 photographs/images taken
on the game day. The experimental analysis examined data by NLP in R
language and computer vision using DeepFace. Results indicate negative
sentiment perceptions with similar percentages of 74% for NLP and 81%
for DeepFace, with an average negative perception of 77.5%.

Keywords: sentiment analysis · Artificial Intelligence techniques ·
social networks · case study · football soccer game

1 Introduction

Sentiment analysis identifies and classifies the emotions expressed in users' messages, comments, posts, or publications on social networks. The main objective
is determining whether the sentiment expressed is positive, negative, or neutral
[4,20].

© The Author(s), under exclusive license to Springer Nature Switzerland AG 2024
S. Nesmachnow and L. Hernández Callejo (Eds.): ICSC-Cities 2023, CCIS 1938, pp. 216–230, 2024.
https://doi.org/10.1007/978-3-031-52517-9_15

Sentiment analysis is a hot topic of discussion and an emerging trend to understand people's sentiments that can be applied to different types of content on social media, such as Twitter posts, Facebook comments, or product reviews [7,20]. According to [28], many networking platforms have been used, including blogs, microblogs, and forums where thousands of new topics are posted daily, and millions of net surfers view and comment on them.

Sentiment analysis in social networks is a technique that allows us to understand and classify the emotions expressed by users in messages and comments on social networks. It provides a deeper insight into user perception and attitude, which can be used to make informed decisions in various fields, from brand management to market research and customer service. Some of the most common applications of social media sentiment analysis include Brand monitoring, market research, competence analysis, customer service, and analysis of marketing campaigns [20].

In this sense, many of the activities with numerous attendees that have been carried out after the COVID-19 pandemic, including concerts, soccer games, basketball, and car races, among others, are documented and posted by the attendees on their social networks, using text and audio messages, emoticons and short videos. In this research, we will focus on soccer games.

According to [9,27], Football soccer is classified as one of the most popular sports globally; the colossal crowds of attendees in the stadiums sometimes exceed the police's control. Because of this lack of control, unfortunate events have occurred throughout history, marking a regrettable milestone for such a sport. Occasionally, the fans present at the event get out of control and become the main protagonists of the event, as happened in the match of the year 2022 on March 5, between the teams Atlas versus Querétaro, Mexico, in which the soccer fans actions (that set the scene for the event) from opposing sides intensified, ending with each other attacking each other.

The background to this unfortunate event occurred on March 5, 2022, when the friendly match between the soccer teams was held, Atlas versus Querétaro. Everything was going well until halftime when, in an instant, the fans of both teams began to attack each other, entering the playing field and breaking into the game. The tension was such that the security of the place was not enough to control the brawl. That occurred at the scene, resulting in several seriously injured men and women.

The match on March 5, 2022, at the Corregidora stadium, was considered a high-risk match by the fans of both teams. The first half of the game usually passed until halftime. Atlas had the advantage on the scoreboard after Julio Wolff's goal in minute 29. The brawl began at the start of the second half when a Querétaro fan invaded the field; the White Roosters goalkeeper asked him not to cause problems. After separating, an intense discussion broke out in the stands.

The fight began when a security member opened the gate, and the Querétaro bar reached where dozens of Atlas fans were. Entire families tried to escape the Querétaro mob by entering the field in the middle of rooster players calling for calm. In seconds, the stands emptied, people were left on the side of the crowd, and every Atlas fan was attacked until some were naked, beaten, and even unconscious. The danger was wearing the shirt; the Corregidora stadium officially closed its doors at 10:34 at night day. The events were recorded on the media and social networks.

In this line of work, this article presents a new sentiment analysis methodology for football game matches that analyses information obtained from social networks using Artificial Intelligence (AI) techniques: NLP for analyzing texts and computer vision for images. We analyze a study case involving 2,000 tweets from the March 5, 2022, soccer match collected from Twitter and 200 photographs/images taken on the game day. The rTweet library of R Language was used to download the Tweets issued by considering a keyword [8]. The messages of the Tweets were analyzed using a variation of the methodology proposed by [2] in which texts are classified into positive, negative [unfavorable], or neutral comments using NLP. Images or frames were analyzed using DeepFace to identify dominant emotions. Then, positive and negative feelings were compared with both AI techniques; the average of positive and negative comments is performed, and if negative comments are superior to 60%, an alert is emitted.

1.1 Problem Statement

The research question addressed in this study is: How can artificial intelligence techniques be used to analyze the information available (texts and videos) on social networks (Twitter) to identify the emotional state of football soccer team fans?

1.2 Scope and Limitations

The scope of this research will be a study case from a soccer match between the Querétaro White Roosters and the Atlas Football Club in Guadalajara, Mexico. The study case involves 2,000 tweets from the March 5, 2022, soccer match, collected from Twitter, and 200 photographs/images taken on the game day. The experimental analysis examines the data using NLP in R language and computer vision using the DeepFace Python Library.

1.3 Structure of the Document

The rest of the article is structured as follows. Section 2 describes the sentiment analysis in social networks using IA and related works. Section 3 discusses and applies the proposed methodology for the sentiment analysis using IA techniques. Section 4 compares the results obtained by the DeepFace and Sentiment Analysis in R, then calculates the average positive and negative sentiment, and shows in which cases an alert is emitted. Finally, Sect. 5 presents the conclusions and formulates the main lines for future work.

2 Related Work

The sentiment analysis has been addressed from different perspectives, searching for a solution in particular cases. Recent related works propose different methodologies. A brief review of related works is presented next.

AI has gained significant attention recently due to its potential to revolutionize various fields [15]. One of these areas is the application of AI techniques to social media, which has emerged as a promising field of research. The literature review provides an overview of existing studies on the use of AI in computer social networks, highlighting its applications, challenges, and future directions.

INEGI [2] proposed a methodology that uses Machine Learning (ML) to determine the mood of Mexican tweeters; the data source is based on the recovery of information from Twitter, which is taken as a significant data source. Subsequently, the messages are pre-processed by human annotators who classify the tweets into three categories according to [23]: positive, negative, and neutral; in this process, a cross-classification process is carried out. Later, these messages are cleaned by eliminating contradictions and repetitions. Once cleaned, the tweets are used to train an ensemble of classification models, which are used to classify new tweets. This proposal was implemented on the INEGI site and allows us to see the evolution of the mood of tweeters in Mexico over time.

Hung et al. [12] proposed ML methods of AI to analyze data collected from Twitter. The study examined illness-related discussions using tweets originating exclusively in the United States and written in English during the first and second waves of COVID-19. Social network and sentiment analyses were also conducted to determine the social network of dominant topics and whether the tweets expressed positive, neutral, or negative sentiments. Out of 902,138 tweets analyzed, sentiment analysis techniques classified 48.2% of tweets as having a positive feeling, 20.7% as neutral, and 31.1% as unfavorable[negative].

Babu and Kanaga [7] present a literature review; they discuss how social media is utilized to analyze and classify text data, emoticons, and emojis using machine learning and deep learning techniques. They describe four steps for sentiment analyses: Data collection, Data pre-processing, Feature extraction, and Sentiment classification. They found many studies using binary and ternary classification perform well. However, Multi-class classification provides a more precise classification. Support Vector Machine 85% and Random Forest %84.6 are the ML Algorithms that report better accuracy. Deep Learning shows a higher accuracy value during sentiment analysis, by using CNN + LSTM (Long Short Term Memory) network obtains 92.06%. Data sets were obtained from Twitter, Facebook, and Reddit.

Alsaeedi and Khan [4] present a study on sentiment analysis (also called opinion mining) of Twitter data, whose purpose is discovering the sentiments behind the opinions on subjects like movies, commercial products, and daily societal issues. They mention that opinion mining is closely related to natural language processing (NLP), text mining, and computational linguistics. They identified three analysis approaches for sentence-level sentiment: 1) Using Machine learning, 2) Using Ensemble approaches, and 3) Using Lexicon-based. According to these authors, the main classification techniques of machine learning used for sentiment analysis are Naïve Bayes (NB) and Support Vector Machine (SVM). Ensemble methods combine multiple classifiers (i.e. NB, MaxEnt, and SVM) to get accurate predictions. Lexicon-based approaches depend on understanding the polarity of a text sample. Because the complexity of natural languages could be inadequate since many aspects of the language are not considered.

Kumar and Garg [14] propose a multi-modal approach to analyze text and images from a tweet that can be used to determine the sentiment and its score. For Image sentiment scoring, authors used SentiBank and SentiStrength scoring using a CNN. For scoring Text sentiment, they use a hybrid (lexicon + Gradient Boosting) technique. For a text only tweet a lexicon based approach is used, which captures contextual semantics and determines the sentiment polarity and strength of the tweet, the polarity from ML and Lexicon stages is combined to score the sentiment in a range from [-3, 3]. When images contain text, they separate text from images using an OCR (optical character recognizer) and calculate independently processed scores for further analysis. The multi-modal approach obtains a high-performance accuracy of 91.32.

Some application areas of Sentiment Analysis to social networks using AI are:

Opinion Mining. AI techniques, particularly NLP and ML, have been applied extensively to analyze user sentiments and opinions on computer social networks. According to [14], sentiment analysis models have been developed to automatically classify posts, comments, and reviews as positive, negative, or neutral, allowing companies and organizations to assess public sentiment and make decisions. NLP and ML algorithms analyze sentiment in this order of ideas. The algorithms examine the text and apply data mining techniques to identify keywords, phrases, or patterns that indicate the emotional polarity of a message [4].

Recommendation Systems. AI-powered recommender systems play a vital role in computer social networking by suggesting personalized content, products, or connections to users [11]. These systems use collaborative filtering, content-based filtering, and hybrid approaches to analyze user preferences, behaviors, and relationships on the social network. By leveraging AI algorithms, social media can improve user engagement, increase user satisfaction, and increase platform usage [13].

Social network analysis and graph mining. AI techniques have been instrumental in analyzing and extracting information from social networks on a large scale. Graph-based algorithms such as community detection, centrality analysis, and influence maximization have been used to uncover hidden patterns, identify key influencers, and understand the structure and dynamics of social networks [22]. The insights help social media platforms optimize content distribution, detect fake accounts or malicious activity, and improve user experience.

Modeling and Prediction of User Behavior. AI has been used to model and predict user behavior on computer social networks. ML algorithms, including decision trees, support vector machines, and deep learning models, are applied to analyze user interactions, such as clicks, likes, and shares, to anticipate future actions [10]. By understanding user behavior patterns, social networks can personalize content delivery, optimize advertising strategies, and increase user engagement [6].

Fake News Detection and Misinformation Mitigation. AI is crucial in combating fake news and misinformation on computer social networks [3]. Then, NLP techniques are used to identify misleading content, detect suspicious accounts, and flag potential misinformation. AI-powered fact-checking systems are being developed to verify the credibility of information shared on social media, helping to promote trustworthy and reliable content [25].

The related works identified a growing interest in AI algorithms for sentiment analysis in the context of smart cities. In this line of work, this article contributes to a sentiment analysis methodology that uses two AI techniques (Natural Language Processing and Computer Vision) to process Twitter social network data. The following section describes the proposed methodology based on these AI techniques.

3 Artificial Intelligence Methodology

This section describes the proposed AI methodology for sentiment analysis using football game data (texts) and (videos) from the Twitter social network.

3.1 AI for Sentiment Analysis

This article analyzes the behavior of the fans involved in the confrontation between the fans of both opposing teams. The analysis uses artificial intelligence techniques such as face emotion recognition and analysis of text tweets on the social network Twitter to analyze the sentiments experienced. This article contributes with relevant sentiment analysis in the context of smart cities, as it discusses applications that can be implemented, thanks to the Internet, social networks, and advances in AI, in what has been called intelligent buildings and, more specifically, smart stadiums to improve the safety of attendees in recreational spaces. Figure 1 shows the proposed sentiment analysis methodology using social network data.

The upper part of Fig. 1, shows how the proposed methodology investigated and collected all those images of the unfortunate event, where attendees and media captured digital videos and images, which were later uploaded to the Internet through social networks and electronic newspapers.

The emotions in images are analyzed using computer vision; for this purpose, the DeepFace Convolutional Neural Network [1] was utilized, allowing us to explore a wide range of characteristics, as well as the ethnic percentages of

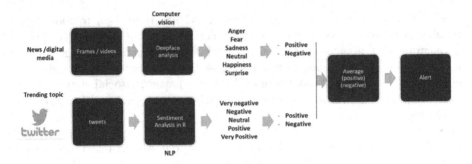

Fig. 1. Proposed methodology, source [Own]

people, age, and gender, and what interests for our case study is to perceive the emotion in which a person is. Fear, anger, sadness, happiness, neutrality, and surprise include such emotions. Sentiments are binary grouped: fear, anger, and sadness as negative; happiness and surprise as positive.

The lower part of Fig. 1 shows the pipeline to analyze sentiments in the Twitter social network; for this purpose, we use R language, rTweet was used to download the Tweets issued considering a keyword [8]. The texts of the Tweets are analyzed using a variation of the methodology proposed by [2] in which texts are classified into positive, negative, or neutral comments using NLP. The text's sentences are automatically classified into very positive, positive, neutral, negative, and very negative. Sentiments are binary grouped: Very positive and positive as positive; negative and very negative as negative.

Once the above pipelines are finished, the average of positive and negative comments is calculated. If negative comments exceed 60%, an alert is emitted.

DeepFace Analysis. DeepFace is a Lightweight Face Recognition and Facial Attribute Analysis Framework that allows for identifying Age, Gender, Ethnicity, and Emotion, with specific percentages for each variable or attribute of the person. It is a project in Python [1]. This library has a precision of 97.53 or superior. According to [30] [24], Face recognition consists of five stages: detection, aligning, normalization, representation, and verification. DeepFace manages all these specific stages in the background, and a single line of code calls its verification, finding, or analysis function [23]. Figure 2 shows the stages used for DeepFace analysis.

As shown in Fig. 2, the first step was to collect all the images that could be used to analyze emotions using the DeepFace library, which was reliable (from the event and the date of origin). This information was validated as coming from newspapers and electronic media of high credibility and reliability. The sources from which the images and data were collected were reliable media and newspapers and can be consulted in the following references [5,16,19,21,26]. The images are not shown for copyright and reader sensitivity reasons but can be consulted in the above references. In the first stage, a file bank of 200 images was created. Images were cleaned in the second stage. In the third stage, using

Fig. 2. DeepFace analysis, source [Own].

DeepFace, 74 images were successfully recognized. In stage four, emotions were identified, and in stage five, these emotions were grouped binary into positive and negative feelings. Anger, fear, and sadness were grouped as unfavorable. Happiness and surprise were grouped as positive. Neutral remains as neutral.

Sentiment Analysis on Twitter. The proposed pipeline for this section is based on [2] and [20]. Figure 3 shows the stages considered.

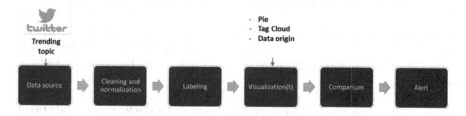

Fig. 3. Proposed pipeline for social network analysis in R, based on [2] and [20]

In the first stage, the data source is obtained from a trending topic on Twitter, and texts from posts are cleaned and normalized; then, tweets are automatically labeled using a dictionary and classified as very positive, positive, neutral, negative, and very negative. Later, the information is visualized, binary classified, and compared with the results of DeepFace analysis. Finally, an alert is emitted if a threshold is reached (for instance, average negative sentiments > 60%).

This way, the proposed methodology determines positive and negative feelings for sentiment analysis using data from social networks. The following section analyzes the experimental results of the proposed approach.

4   Experimental Results and Discussion

This section describes the experimental evaluation of the proposed methodology for sentiment analysis using data from social networks. Details about the platform used for development and execution are presented. Likewise, the studied case is described. Finally, results are reported and discussed.

4.1 Development and Execution Platform

The proposed AI techniques were implemented in Python3 (computer vision) and R Language (sentiment analysis using NLP) and evaluated on an Intel Xeon E5430(2.66GHz) with 32GB RAM and the Debian 11 Bullseye Operating System. Analyzing emotions in images was done using the DeepFace library, and tweets were downloaded using rTweet, an R language library.

4.2 Data Sources and Cleaning Process

Data source. Twitter is a micro-blogging and social network platform where users post and interact with messages called "tweets." According to [29], Twitter is a valuable data source for social media discussion at national and international levels, with more than 166 million daily users. This social network Manages short messages of 140 characters that are publicly visible and georeferenced; each message includes text, hyperlinks, memes, emoticons, photographs, and videos [20]. This study collected data from the Twitter website by applying machine learning (ML) methods in artificial intelligence. For this research, we used an R script with the rTweet library [8] to connect to Twitter. Two thousand tweets were downloaded and analyzed considering the keywords "Querétaro atlas."

Cleaning and Normalization. In this stage, empty tweets (no words, only videos or memes) were deleted, and contradictions and repetitions in the same tweet were eliminated. An inconsistent tweet has a positive and negative charge in the same message. Duplication refers to the use of repeated and consecutive words in the same statement, for example: LOL LOL LOL equals LOL. Figure 4 shows how cleaning and normalization were implemented. In the first step, 2000 tweets are considered entries; in the second step, tweets are cleaned and normalized; and in the third step, 1810 tweets were successfully processed.

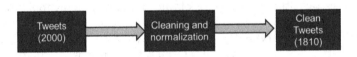

Fig. 4. Cleaning and normalizing Tweets based on [2]

Labeling. In this process, the emotional charge of each tweet is rated; the aim is to identify the emotion of the tweeter when they wrote the tweet. The classification is automatic (positive or negative), based on a dictionary. Each tweet is broken down into tokens that are compared to the words within the dictionary, and when a match is found, a numerical value is assigned to the tweet. Only complete terms were considered. The labeling process was carried out automatically, using the Afinn lexicon from [17] using a script in R language. The tweets were classified as very positive (if score > 2), positive (if score > 0 and score < 3), negative (if score < 0 and score > -3), and very negative (if score < -2), neutral equals zero. Figure 5 shows the bilingual dictionary used to label tweets [18]. The first column has the in word in Spanish, the second column the rating, and the third column the word in English.

```
Palabra,Puntuacion,Word
a bordo,1,aboard
abandona,-2,abandons
abandonado,-2,abandoned
abandonar,-2,abandon
abatido,-2,dejected
abatido,-3,despondent
aborrece,-3,abhors
aborrecer,-3,abhor
aborrecible,-3,abhorrent
aborrecido,-3,abhorred
adoptar,1,embrace
abrazo,2,hug
abrazos,2,hugs
abriga,2,cherishes
absolver,2,absolve
absolver,2,acquit
absolviendo,2,absolving
absolviendo,2,acquitting
absorbido,1,absorbed
absorto,1,engrossed
absueltos,2,absolved
absuelve,2,absolves
absuelve,2,acquits
aburrido,-2,bored
aburrido,-3,boring
```

Fig. 5. Bilingual dictionary to label tweets

Visualization. This module lets us visualize the relationship between the number of very positive, positive, neutral, negative, and very negative tweets per event. This module was designed considering what was described by [20] for the analysis and visualization of Tweets. With the labeled tweets, the percentages of Tweets by category are calculated and displayed in a pie chart (see Fig. 6). Subsequently, a tag cloud graph shows the frequency of the words that make up each analyzed Tweet (see Fig. 7). It should be noted that the display of tweets regarding a particular topic varies over time (t). Given Twitter restrictions, information is only available for two weeks on the platform. If historical data is required, the services of third parties must be hired to access historical information on the platform.

Comparison. The graphs obtained can be compared with previous charts over time and can be used to analyze the evolution of a particular topic (see Fig. 8). Average Negative sentiment and average Positive sentiment are calculated.

Alert. An alert is issued if the Average Negative Sentiment analysis returns a high percentage (> 60%) at a time (t) or during a particular period.

4.3   Experimental Results

For the Querétaro White Rooster's soccer match case study against Atlas Club from Guadalajara, the results of NLP indicate a Negative-Very negative sentiment (74%) and a positive-very positive feeling (26%). Figure 6 shows the sentiment analysis for the football match.

Sentiment Analysis % 2022

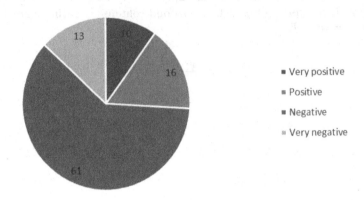

Fig. 6. Sentiment analysis in R using NLP for the football match

Although the sentiment of tweeters in Mexico about this encounter has changed over time, words that indicate very negative - negative environments, such as strange, crazy, terror, and evil, continue to appear. Figure 7 shows the tag cloud of sentiments. Several words indicate negative emotions, e.g., terror, bad and crazy.

Fig. 7. Tag Cloud of sentiments

Figure 8 compares the sentiments in the year 2022 and in April 2023; it is observed that the sentiment continues to be negative over time. Although the very negative sentiments dropped four percentage points, these were absorbed by the negative sentiments. The above results indicate that an alarm must be raised for the club directors, and the necessary measures must be taken to change the perception. In the case of shorter periods of evaluation of social networks, in something close to real-time, early alarms may be issued to avoid confrontations in the soccer stadium where the match takes place.

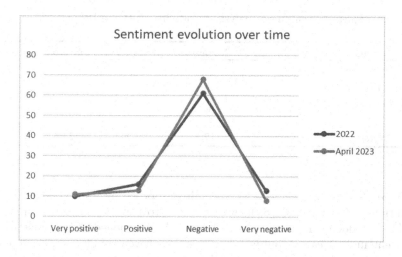

Fig. 8. Comparison over time of the sentiments of Twitter users.

Table 1 shows the summarized results of sentiment analysis using the proposed methodology. The first row shows the results obtained for the sentiment Analysis in R using NLP, the second row shows the results obtained using Computer Vision (DeepFace), and the third row shows the average Negative or Positive sentiment. The first column shows the technique, the second column is the negative perception, and the third column is the positive perception.

The last row calculates the average sentiment perception using the next formula.

$$Average(Sentiment \quad Analysis \quad in \quad R(Ci) + DeepFace(Ci)),$$
$$Ci = \%positive, \%negative \quad for \quad 1 < i <= 3$$

Table 1 shows that Sentiment Analysis in R using NLP obtained 74% and DeepFace 81% of Negative Sentiments and 26% and 19% for positive comments, respectively. Both results are similar, and when averages in columns are calculated, the Average Negative Sentiment obtained is 77.5 %, and the Average Positive Sentiment is 22.5 %. Considering the previously configured threshold and average results, an alarm must be emitted due to a high percentage of average negative sentiments.

Table 1. Sentiment analysis considering NLP and Deepface.

Technique	Negative	Positive
Sentiment Analysis in R	74	26
Deep face	81	19
Average	**77.5**	**22.5**

Table 1 shows that we use the basic idea proposed by [4] to detect polarity in sentiment investigation. Still, we extend it to consider images from videos besides text documents and short messages. As mentioned in [14], most of the sentiment analysis carried out last decade is text-driven, and few studies reported visual analysis of images; the proposed methodology uses a state-of-the-art convolutional network to identify dominant sentiment in videos and images posted on the Twitter social network, combining visual sentiment analysis with a text-driven approach, providing a robust multi-modal approach that outperforms separate models.

5   Conclusions and Future Work

This article presented a methodology for sentiment analysis in social networks combining two AI techniques, a relevant problem related to the perception of feelings on the Internet. Using natural language processing in R and computer vision (DeepFace). The proposed methodology allows us to identify fans' sentiments in a football match.

The literature review highlights the critical contributions of AI to social media analysis, spanning sentiment analysis, recommendation systems, social network analysis, user behavior modeling, and fake news detection.

The study case involves 2,000 tweets from the March 5, 2022, soccer match, collected from Twitter, and 200 images taken on the game day. Results indicate negative perceptions with similar percentages of 74% for NLP and 81% for DeepFace, with an average negative perception of 77.5%.

While AI has shown immense potential in computer social networking, several challenges still exist. These include privacy concerns, ethical implications, algorithmic biases, and the need for robust AI models that can adapt to evolving user behaviors.

The main lines for future work are extending and improving AI techniques, such as deep reinforcement learning for network identification and AI-based social influence analysis. The experimental evaluation of the proposed approach should also be extended to improve the proposed methodology to emit alarms in time close to real-time. Finally, the proposed methodology could be tested in music concerts and crowd events.

References

1. Deepface. a lightweight face recognition and facial attribute analysis framework (age, gender, emotion, race) for python. https://pypi.org/project/deepface/ Accessed 27 Sept 27 2023
2. Instituto nacional de estadística y geografía. inegi, estado de ánimo de los tuiteros en méxico. (2020). https://www.inegi.org.mx/app/animotuitero/#/app/multiline Accessed 27 Sept 2023
3. Aïmeur, E., Amri, S., Brassard, G.: Fake news, disinformation and misinformation in social media: a review. Soc. Netw. Anal. Min. **13**(1), 30 (2023)
4. Alsaeedi, A., Khan, M.Z.: A study on sentiment analysis techniques of twitter data. Int. J. Adv. Comput. Sci. Appl. **10**(2), 361–374 (2019)
5. Alvarado, A.: Querétarovs.atlastragedia:¿quépasóenelpartidodelaligamxqueterminó con muertos y suspendido? https://elpopular.pe/deportes/2022/03/06/mexico-queretaro-vs-atlas-tragedia-paso-partido-liga-mx-termino-muertos-suspendido-futbol-mexicano-video-114847 (2022) Accessed 28 Sept 2023
6. Anshari, M., Almunawar, M.N., Lim, S.A., Al-Mudimigh, A.: Customer relationship management and big data enabled: Personalization and customization of services. Appl. Comput. Inform. **15**(2), 94–101 (2019)
7. Babu, N.V., Kanaga, E.G.M.: Sentiment analysis in social media data for depression detection using artificial intelligence: a review. SN Comput. Sci. **3**, 1–20 (2022)
8. documentation, R.: rtweet. https://www.rdocumentation.org/packages/rtweet/versions/1.1.0 (2023) Accessed 28 Sept 2023
9. Douglas, R.: 13 most popular sports in the world for 2023. https://theathleticbuild.com/most-popular-sports/ (2023) Accessed 11 Oct 2023
10. G. Martín, A., Fernández-Isabel, A., Martín de Diego, I., Beltrán, M.: A survey for user behavior analysis based on machine learning techniques: current models and applications. Applied Intell. **51**(8), 6029–6055 (2021)
11. Habil, S., El-Deeb, S., El-Bassiouny, N.: AI-based recommendation systems: the ultimate solution for market prediction and targeting. In: The Palgrave Handbook of Interactive Marketing, pp. 683–704. Springer (2023). https://doi.org/10.1007/978-3-031-14961-0_30
12. Hung, M., et al.: Social network analysis of Covid-19 sentiments: Application of artificial intelligence. J. Med. Internet Res. **22**(8), e22590 (2020)
13. Josimovski, S., Dodevski, D., et al.: Advantages of implementing artificial intelligence in e-business for consumers (2023)
14. Kumar, A., Garg, G.: Sentiment analysis of multimodal twitter data. Multimed. Tools Appl. **78**, 24103–24119 (2019)
15. Lu, Y.: Artificial intelligence: a survey on evolution, models, applications and future trends. J. Manage. Anal. **6**(1), 1–29 (2019)
16. Mancera, D.: 26 heridos, tres de gravedad y ningún detenido horas después de la batalla campal de querétaro. el país. https://elpais.com/mexico/2022-03-06/26-heridos-3-de-gravedad-y-ningun-detenido-horas-despues-de-la-batalla-campal-de-queretaro.html (2022). Accessed 28 Sept 2023
17. Mendoza-Vega, J.: Análisis de sentimientos con r - léxico afinn. https://rpubs.com/jboscomendoza/analisis_sentimientos_lexico_afinn (2018). Accessed Sept 27 2023
18. Mendoza-Vega, J.: Léxico afinn. https://raw.githubusercontent.com/jboscomendoza/rpubs/master/sentimientos_afinn/lexico_afinn.en.es.csv (2018) Accessed 27 Sept 2023

19. Murillo, M.: Gobernadordequerétaro, mauriciokuri, confirma26heridosyquenohubo muertos, tras lo ocurrido en el querétaro vs atlas. uno tv. https://www. unotv.com/deportes/gobierno-de-queretaro-confirma-26-heridos-y-que-no-hubo-muertos-tras-lo-ocurrido-en-el-queretaro-vs-atlas/ (2022) Accessed 28 Sept 2023

20. Najera-Salmeron, J.: Fundamentos del análisis de redes sociales en r: Introducción teórica y práctica al análisis de redes sociales para mercadólogos e investigadores sociales, spanish Tech. rep, México (2022)

21. Navarro, J.: Atlas: 26 heridos | resumen y últimas noticias, as méxico-diario as. https://mexico.as.com/mexico/2022/03/06/futbol/1646527770_037496. html (2022) Accessed 28 Sept 2023

22. Peng, S., Wang, G., Xie, D.: Social influence analysis in social networking big data: opportunities and challenges. IEEE Netw. **31**(1), 11–17 (2017). https://doi.org/10. 1109/MNET.2016.1500104NM

23. Rustam, F., Ashraf, I., Mehmood, A., Ullah, S., Choi, G.S.: Tweets classification on the base of sentiments for us airline companies. Entropy **21**(11) (2019). https:// doi.org/10.3390/e21111078

24. Serengil, S.I., Ozpinar, A.: Lightface: A hybrid deep face recognition framework. In: 2020 Innovations in Intelligent Systems and Applications Conference (ASYU), pp. 1–5 (2020)

25. Sharma, K., Qian, F., Jiang, H., Ruchansky, N., Zhang, M., Liu, Y.: Combating fake news: a survey on identification and mitigation techniques. ACM Trans. Intell. Syst. Technol. (TIST) **10**(3), 1–42 (2019)

26. SNStaff: Querétaro-atlas,   incidentes,   horrorysus-pensión:lasúltimasnovedadesdelhecho que conmueve a méxico. the sporting news. https://www.sportingnews.com/mx/liga-mx/news/invasion-cancha-atlas-queretaro-liga-mx-suspension/pdvc7cfahc5ywjkwqiiqqscp (2022) Accessed 28 Sept 2023

27. SportyTell, E.: Top-10 most popular sports in the world 2023. https://sportytell. com/sports/most-popular-sports-world/ (2023) Accessed 23 Nov 2023

28. Wang, C., Xiao, Z., Liu, Y., Xu, Y., Zhou, A., Zhang, K.: Sentiview: sentiment analysis and visualization for internet popular topics. IEEE Trans. Human-Mach. Syst. **43**(6), 620–630 (2013)

29. Wong, Q., Skillings, J.: Twitter'susergrowthsoarsamidcoronavirus, butuncertain-tyremains. cnet. 2020 apr 30. https://www.cnet.com/tech/mobile/twitters-user-growth-soars-amid-coronavirus-but-uncertainty-remains/ (2022) Accessed 28 Sept 2023

30. Zhao, K., Xu, J., Cheng, M.M.: Regularface: deep face recognition via exclusive regularization. In: 2019 IEEE/CVF Conference on Computer Vision and Pattern Recognition (CVPR), pp. 1136–1144 (2019). https://doi.org/10.1109/CVPR.2019. 00123

Intelligent Urban Cycling Assistance Based on Simplified Machine Learning

Alejandro Hernández-Herrera[1]([✉]) [iD], Elsa Rubio-Espino[1] [iD],
Rogelio Álvarez-Vargas[2] [iD], and Victor H. Ponce-Ponce[1] [iD]

[1] Centro de Investigación en Computación (CIC), Av. Juan de Dios Bátiz, esq.
Miguel Othón de Mendizábal, Col. Nueva Industrial Vallejo, C.P. 07738 Alcaldía
Gustavo A. Madero, CDMX, Mexico
{ahernandezh2020,erubio,vponce}@cic.ipn.mx
[2] ProfTech Servicios S. A. de C. V., Semilla 2, Col. Arquitos, C.P. 76048 Querétaro,
QRO, Mexico
rogelio.alvarez@pts.mx
https://www.cic.ipn.mx, https://www.prof-tech.com.mx

Abstract. Urban cycling is a sustainable mode of transportation in
large cities, and it offers many advantages. It is an eco-friendly means of
transport that is accessible to the population and easy to use. Additionally, it is more economical than other means of transportation. Urban
cycling is beneficial for physical health and mental well-being. Achieving
sustainable mobility and the evolution towards smart cities demands a
comprehensive analysis of all the essential aspects that enable their inclusion. Road safety is particularly important, which must be prioritized to
ensure safe transportation and reduce the incidence of road accidents.
In order to help reduce the number of accidents that urban cyclists are
involved in, this work proposes an alternative solution in the form of an
intelligent computational assistant that utilizes simplified machine learning to detect potential risks of unexpected collisions. This technological
approach serves as a helpful alternative to the current problem. Through
our methodology, we were able to identify the problem involved in the
research, design and development of the solution proposal, collect and
analyze data, and obtain preliminary results. These results experimentally demonstrate how the proposed model outperforms most state-of-the-art Siamese network models that use a similarity layer based on the
Euclidean or Mahanthan distances for small sets of images.

Keywords: Simplified Machine Learning · One-Shot Learning ·
Intelligent cycling assistance · Urban cycling

Supported by Project 20220268, Programa Institucional de Formación de Investigadores (PIFI), Instituto Politécnico Nacional (IPN), México.

S. Nesmachnow and L. Hernández Callejo (Eds.): ICSC-Cities 2023, CCIS 1938, pp. 231–245, 2024.
https://doi.org/10.1007/978-3-031-52517-9_16

1   Introduction

1.1   Urban Mobility

There is no doubt that population growth is consistent and in Mexico during the last 25 to 30 years, this growth combined with very poor urban planning has caused a problem of vehicle congestion in the nation's large cities. This situation causes the daily transfer from one point to another and on the outskirts of these large urban cities to take between one and three hours on an average trip, when these trips could normally be made with a duration of between thirty minutes and one hour.

Faced with these circumstances, sustainable mobility became a highly relevant issue for planning urban mobility systems, since it is a model that promotes the use of different means of transport that are friendly to the environment, inclusive and accessible [17]. In this research we are mainly considering three means of mobility that, due to their nature and hierarchy in mobility [10], are considered sustainable: walking, urban cycling and public transport, including this last hierarchy are considered common public transport in Mexico such as the metro, metrobus, light rail, commuter train, trolleybus and cable car. There are multiple benefits that this type of mobility contributes to the environment by not having large amounts of gas emissions, by not having energy waste and even contributing to reducing the carbon dioxide footprint in the atmosphere. With respect to social benefits, since these are collective and individual means of transportation, they significantly promote inclusion and are viable options for making long-distance journeys at a reduced cost.

Within these three means of mobility mentioned above, it is worth highlighting urban cycling, since it is a transportation choice that lightens the load on vehicles in road congestion. It is an ecological option because it promotes the significant reduction of harmful gases such as CO^2, it is an accessible means of transportation, easy to use and that, at the same time, contributes to improving both emotional and physical health. However, this alternative requires more attention from the authorities in charge of planning mobility in large cities, since the exclusive lanes are insufficient, the public access systems are limited and high cost for a sector of the population there are not enough spaces to park bicycles or store them, there is also an inequality of spaces to travel and urban cyclists are not given priority in terms of road safety.

1.2   Road Safety for Cyclists

Pedestrians and cyclists head the mobility hierarchy (see Fig. 1), which classifies modes of transportation according to the vulnerability they present, as well as both negative and positive peculiarities that they cause as a means of transportation. It is worth mentioning that the negative peculiarities include the possible risks that a certain modality represents for users in other hierarchies.

To promote the use of bicycles, it is necessary to guarantee safety conditions through a focus on preventing road events that cause deaths and injuries. According to the philosophy of the Vision Zero road safety concept [23], which is based

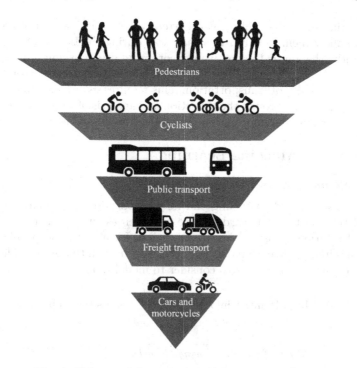

Fig. 1. Urban mobility hierarchy (adapted from [10]).

on the simple fact that we are all human beings and therefore make mistakes. This is why there is a need to generate systems that support the cyclist during their road trajectory, thereby reducing the possibility that these errors end in injuries and deaths. Institutions such as the World Health Organization (WHO) point out that in the event of a transport accident, the population of cyclists and pedestrians is more vulnerable and their safety is strategic in a global culture that needs to intensify sustainable travel [24].

In Mexico as in other countries we face a great public health challenge as a result of injuries generated by poor road safety. Statistically, it has been reported that traffic injuries are the leading cause of death among children between the ages of 4 and 14 years. Among the highest percentage of deaths are young people between 15 and 30 years old (32.2%), followed by the group between 30 and 44 years old (25.5%) [9], which has a strong impact on the economy and emotional stability of families, as well as society as a whole.

1.3   Intelligent Urban Cycling

Although it is true that the bicycle is in the subconscious of citizens as a pleasant element, associated with a livable city, a majority of citizens would use it when traveling if there were a safe and coherent infrastructure and pleasant environments. In this sense, technology can currently be used as a cyclist's assistant, which will allow them to travel in a safer way during the trip.

Currently, the aim is to effectively incorporate urban cycling into the transportation networks within the so-called smart cities and promote more modern, clean and safe modes of transportation. This requires establishing an individual mobility model that, through the collection and analysis of various types of data, generate as a result the information that integrates smart mobility [8,18,20].

2   Simplified Machine Learning

2.1   The Challenge of Machine Learning

Increasing safety in urban cycling and its incorporation as a smarter and safer means of transportation towards future smart cities suggests a technologically supported solution to assist the urban cyclist. Intuitively, the problem shows that there is information available and other information that is not. The Table 1 summarizes these two aspects to consider to model a possible solution.

Table 1. Intuitive information that presents the problem.

Available	Not Available
Position	Types of possible moving obstacles
Orientation	Number of moving obstacles
Velocity	Position of moving obstacles
Acceleration Image/Video	Known data set according to the problem for analysis and testing

Also intuitively, Fig. 2 presents in a general way, the characteristics that a suggested machine learning model should have to be applied to the problem of this research.

The information and intuitive characteristics of the problem to be solved suggest that the proposed solution can be oriented towards the area of artificial intelligence and specifically within the field of machine learning, because to assist the cyclist in identifying the risk of a collision, it must have an accelerated learning process also using previously learned information. Recently, machine learning has been very successful in various tasks, specifically in image and speech classification, pattern recognition or improved searches for information on the web. However, it is also known that these models usually require a large amount of data and training time to have a reliable learning process.

Therefore, the purpose of this research is that based on the approach and description of the problem, a technological solution is proposed that supports the urban cyclist in reducing the risk of collision by focusing on automatic detection within a dynamic environment, so the Research question is defined as follows: *Can a machine learning model be used, based on some examples, to learn the concept of unexpected collision risk and detect it in real time?*

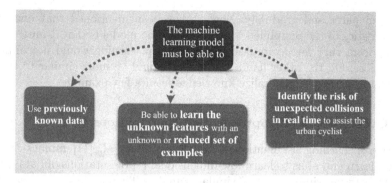

Fig. 2. Intuitive features that the proposed machine learning model should be able to handle.

2.2   Related Work

Reviewing possible technological proposals for solutions to this problem, there are preventive approaches that rely on unsupervised machine learning to explore the circumstances associated with urban cycling safety, such as those exposed by Zhao, H. et al. [25], in where large amounts of publicly available data, such as satellite images, neighborhood and city maps, are used to collect information from the environment of cyclist accidents and use machine learning methods, such as Generative Adversarial Networks (GAN) to learn from these data sets and explore the factors associated with cyclist crashes. In this same sense, it is known that work has been carried out in this regard in Spain, such as the one presented by Galán R. et al. [5], where the variables that are causes of accidents in bicycle users are studied, with the aim of reducing the number of accidents and thus increase the number of people who use it as a means of transportation with greater safety.

However, in the time in which this research has been carried out, no evidence has been found that a technological proposal that involves a means of transport such as the bicycle and supports the reduction of accidents in this sense has been contemplated. Nor has specific evidence been found of a geospatial analysis of accidents in urban cycling to be able to make a comparison of methodology and results.

It is known that recently machine learning has been very successful in various tasks, such as pattern classification and searching for massive information on the web, as well as image and speech recognition. However, these machine learning models often require, as training input, a large amount of example data to learn. Likewise, the technology known as deep learning [1,4] is booming and has been playing an important role in the advancement of machine learning. However, it also requires large amounts of data.

In addition to this, the large size of the data tends to lead to slow learning, this is mainly due to the parametric aspect of the deep learning algorithm, in which, due to the operating characteristics, the training examples must be learned in parts and gradually. Now, it has been mentioned that one of the characteristics of the Simplified Machine Learning model is that it must be able to learn from very few examples, therefore deep learning would not apply for this purpose. On the other hand, the model should be more similar to the way humans learn, that is, generalize knowledge from a few examples.

2.3   Overview of the Approach and Contributions

Contrastive learning as mentioned in Khosla, P. et al. [11] mimics the way humans learn and aims to learn low-dimensional representations of data by contrasting between similar and dissimilar samples. Therefore, humans can learn new things with a small set of examples. When a person is presented with new examples, they are able to understand new concepts quickly and will then recognize variations of those concepts in the future. Just like that, a child can learn to recognize a cat from a single image. However, currently a machine learning system needs many examples to learn the characteristics of a cat and recognize them in the future or in other examples.

We can observe that in standard associative learning, i.e., an animal must repeatedly experience a series of associations between a stimulus and a consequence before it completely learns a particular stimulus. Therefore, learning is inevitably incremental. However, animals sometimes conclude or infer results that they have never even observed before and from which they need to learn quickly to survive. In such cases, animals can learn from a single exposure to the stimulus, in this situation but making an analogy towards machine learning, this is what we have defined as *Simplified Machine Learning* [7] and that generally It is known in the literature as one-time learning [14].

Compared to computers, it is a hallmark of human intelligence to be able to learn quickly, whether it is recognizing objects from a few examples or quickly learning new skills after a few minutes of experience. Today it is claimed that artificial intelligence systems should be able to do the same, learn and adapt quickly from a few examples and continue to adapt as these systems are exposed to more and more available data. This type of learning with characteristics of speed and flexibility is a challenge, since the system must integrate its prior knowledge with a small amount of new information, efficiently avoiding overfitting to new data. Likewise, this previous experience and the new data will depend on the task at all times (see Fig. 3).

Our solution proposal in terms of being able to support an urban cyclist to ride safely in urban environments is to specify and design the model that can perceive and perform machine learning with few training examples, which assists in risk detection of collision and thus be able to alert the cyclist of the possible danger.

The main justification behind this Simplified Machine Learning will then be to able to train a cognitive model with one or very few examples, as well as being able to generalize unknown categories without extensive retraining and thus being able to better adapt as a solution to the problem posed in this research.

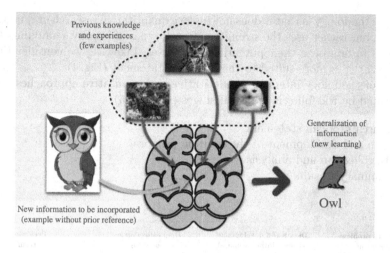

Fig. 3. Learn new information based on some prior knowledge.

So far, no concrete evidence of specific work related to the problem has been found, so it is considered that this research is the first attempt to define a machine learning model that allows detecting and evaluating the risk of unexpected collisions in urban cycling.

Some of the work done during our research and presented in this article was inspired by what was developed in [19], which showed how similarity using Euclidean distance ($L1$) was superior to similarity using cosine distance presented in [22]. Therefore, it was assumed that adding a combined affinity layer will improve the classification accuracy. With this approach, we proposed to implement this combined affinity layer in our Siamese artificial neural network for One-Shot learning. This is a major contribution to what we have called Simplified Machine Learning, by developing a new type of affinity layer (bi-layer) for deep affinity neural networks, which is the basis of our Siamese Artificial Neural Network.

3 Materials and Methods

Below in this section, a brief general description of the methodology used is presented, the substantial description of the proposed solution that includes the explanation of the architecture of the proposed cognitive model as well as its essential parts such as the Affinity Layers and the Layer Combined Affinity.

3.1 Methodolgy

For the development of this research, the mixed methodology or mixed research route, proposed by Hernández-Sampieri and Mendoza [3] was used as a basis with some variations required for the present work. The main reason for using this mixed methodology is that it does not replace quantitative research or qualitative research, but rather uses the strengths of both types of inquiry, combining them and tries to minimize their potential weaknesses. Likewise, we consider that it harmonizes or is more suited to the problem statement (Fig. 4).

Our methodology integrates quantitative and qualitative approaches, and is constituted by the following general stages (see Fig. 5):

1. Research problem statement
2. Design and development of the solution proposal
3. Data collection and analysis
4. Preliminary Results

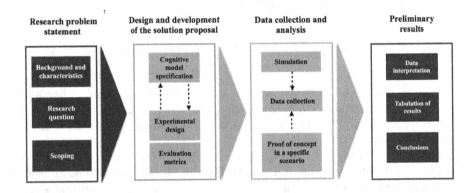

Fig. 4. General methodology and research development.

3.2   Cognitive Model Architecture

The general description of the architecture of the Siamese cognitive model is presented in Fig. 5. We established as a basis for our Siamese network model an approach similar to the one shown in [12], but adjusting the CNNs to generate 1024 features instead of 4096, they will also share the same parameters since they are copies of the same CNN. The neural network architecture that learns image embeddings and attribute vectors in the same vector space (embedding space) was used in the implementation of the feature extractor, in this way the distances between affinity features can be calculated. The two input images (x_i, x_j) feed the CNNs, where the two fixed-length feature vectors, $f(x_i)$ and $f(x_j)$ are obtained. Since both feature extraction networks are the same, $f(x_i) \simeq f(x_j)$ if the two images are affine and $f(x_i) \neq f(x_j)$ otherwise.

As main feature extractors, the standard CNNs in the state of the art (ResNet-18 [6] and EfficientNet-B0 [21]) were used, which helped to accelerate the training time of the proposed model when generating fewer parameters on the network. Subsequently, these results will feed the affinity layers as detailed in the following section.

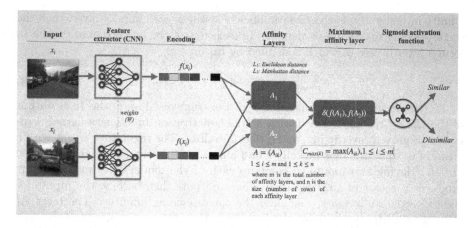

Fig. 5. The architecture of the Siamese Cognitive Model. The model feeds, through the input images, the extraction of features using CNNs. The outputs are two feature vectors that are passed to the affinity layers $A1$ and $A2$. They are then integrated into the combined affinity layer (bi-layer), where the maximum affinity is calculated. The output of the combined affinity layer is passed through the activation function to determine the similarity or dissimilarity between the inputs.

3.3 Affinity Layer Overview

In the design and specification of the affinity layer, these are calculated using for A_1 the Euclidean distance, shown in Eq. 1 and for A_2 the Mahanthan distance, as seen in Eq. 2, where u and v are the feature vectors. We adapt for the proposed model, a perspective shown in [12, 15] to integrate as the layers in an artificial learning neural network. In this way, a one-to-one operation is performed on each element of the feature vectors and to finally generate a new one.

$$\delta_e(u, v) = \sqrt{\sum_{i=1}^{n} (u_i - v_i)^2} \tag{1}$$

$$\delta_m(u, v) = \sum_{i=1}^{n} |u_i - v_i| \tag{2}$$

3.4 Combined Affinity Layer Overview

The basis of our Siamese artificial neural network is the so-called combined affinity layer C that unifies the feature vectors of the Euclidean (A_1) and Mahanthan (A_2) layers to form a single one that will evaluate similarity or dissimilarity of the input images.

The combined affinity layer C works as follows, we take the element-wise maxima of the two affinity layers (A_1 and A_2). Assuming that $A = (A_{ik})$ is the affinity layer, for $1 \leq i \leq m$ and $1 \leq k \leq n$, where m is the total number of affinity layers, and n is the size (number of rows) of each affinity layer, then the corresponding maximum of elements in each row of the two layers are taken to form a layer of size n, which is defined by Eq. 3.

$$C_{max(k)} = \max(A_{ik}), 1 \leq i \leq m \tag{3}$$

In the design and implementation of the combined layers, the 1024 output of the CNNs was conditioned with a RELU activation function, a kernel regularizer to prevent overfitting, and a bias initializer. The regularizer works with a mean of 0, while the bias initializer had a mean of 0.5 and a standard deviation of 0.01. Having two inputs to compare each of the model's feature extractors produces a vector of 1024 features. Those outputs then become the inputs for the two separate layers to calculate the corresponding affinities. The layer A_1 (Euclidean distance, $L1$) and the layer A_2 (Mahanthan distance, $L2$). In each of these affinity layers an output of 1024 features is produced. Subsequently, it is passed through the Maximum Affinity Layer $C_{max(k)}$, which finds the maximum number of elements of the two layers and generates a maximum vector of 1024 features. As a last step, a sigmoid activation function is applied on a layer with a filter, which will produce a value between 0 and 1, which establishes the probability of affinity between the input images.

4   Experiments with the Proposed Model

4.1   Dataset Overview

In the area of One-Shot learning, much of the research evaluating models for image categorization commonly uses the MiniImageNet [13] and CIFAR-100 [13] datasets. For this reason, we used both data sets in the experimental phase, which allowed us to compare them with other state-of-the-art methods that have also used them. Furthermore, we add the DroNet dataset [16] to establish a comparison with a proposed autonomous drone driving approach for obstacle avoidance and make our evaluation and comparison more comprehensive.

As a common practice in the area of machine learning, each dataset was divided into three subsets for One-Shot learning: the training set (T_s), the validation set (V_s) and the search/query set (Q_s). T_s is a disjoint set of the sets Q_s and V_s, but V_s and Q_s belong to the same category or class. Suppose there are a number i of categories in the training set, a number j of categories in the validation set, and a number k of categories in the search set. The set of category labels in T_s, V_s, and Q_s would then be $C_i;C_j$ and C_k, respectively.

Therefore, the label pairs for the images in the training set would be set by Eq. 4.

$$T_s = \{(x_i, x_j), \alpha(x_i, x_j)\} \forall i, j = 1..n \tag{4}$$

For which (x_i, x_j) are the image pairs in the training set and $\alpha(x_i, x_j)$ will be the affinity score of the image pair. Therefore, if x_i and x_j are equal, then the score will have a value of 1 and otherwise it will have a value of 0. It is set to n as the number of training samples or examples.

Continuing with the label specification, Eq. 5 names the image label pairs in the validation set.

$$V_s = \{(x_k, x_l), \alpha(x_k, x_l)\} \, \forall k, l = 1..m \tag{5}$$

For which (x_k, x_l) are the image pairs in the validation set and $\alpha(x_k, x_l)$ is the affinity score of the image pair. Therefore, if x_k and x_l are equal, then the score will take a value of 1 and otherwise it will have a value of 0. m is the number of samples or examples for training.

Finally, the images that form the query set are specified in Eq. 6:

$$Q_s = \{x_k\} \, \forall k = 1..n \tag{6}$$

For which x_k are image samples from categories in the validation set. The final objective sought in this learning is to classify samples in the search/query set given some examples in the validation set meeting the following restrictions: $C_i \notin C_j$; $T_s \cap V_s = \emptyset$; $T_s \cap Q_s = \emptyset$ and $Q_s \in V_s$. Therefore, the categories in the training versus validation set are disjoint, but those classes in the validation and query set are intersecting sets.

4.2   Experimental Setup

In our experimental phase, two CNN networks were used: EfficientNet-B0 and ResNet-18. These two networks were chosen mainly for their characteristics as feature extractors, generalized use in other One-Shot learning models and to be able to compare our results against those in the state of the art. For our model, the ResNet-18 implementation was similar to the one shown in [6], except that the input image size was set to 100×100. On the other hand, the EfficientNet-B0 network implementation is similar to the one presented by [21], except also that the input image size was also set to 100×100. The outputs are then passed through the proposed combined affinity layer with a sigmoid activation to determine similarity or dissimilarity.

In the experimental design, the number of epochs was established as 200, as well as the size of the processing block was defined as 18. For the training part of the Siamese network, the binary cross-entropy loss function was used as an objective function. Likewise, an Adam Optimiser was also used with an initial learning rate set to 0.0005.

A comparison was made with the current reference models in the literature, which are based on the cosine, Manhattan and Euclidean similarity layers, with the combined affinity layers proposed for the three datasets miniImageNet, CIFAR -100 and DroNET detailed in previous Sect. 4.1. The evaluation was specifically performed on the accuracy of five random example images in 1-Shot mode and five random example images in 5-Shot mode. In the Discussion section, the comparison of these results is shown in tabular form.

5 Discussion

As shown in this section, in the experiments carried out with the described data sets and the CNN networks, the proposed Siamese network model was able to perform better in the One-Shot and Five-Shot learning methods. Because the ResNet-18 CNN learns from residuals and as shown in [2], it is a practical feature extractor for one-shot learning tasks. It could also be seen that its demonstrated classification accuracy was very close to EfficientNet-B0 and was consistent with the CNNs that have been used for comparison.

Table 2. The table presents the average accuracy with 95% confidence in performing data classification using the three datasets CIFAR-100, MiniImageNet and DroNet; using the proposed Siamese artificial neural network model trained with the miniImageNet dataset and the ResNet-18 and EfficientNet-B0 CNNs as feature extractors.

Feature extractor	Dataset	A_1		A_2		Proposed model	
		1-Shot	5-Shot	1-Shot	5-Shot	1-Shot	5-Shot
ResNet-18	CIFAR-100	62.83	68.50	64.30	67.99	**67.14**	**74.17**
	MiniImageNet	62.93	69.66	62.86	67.66	**67.05**	**75.40**
	DroNet	59.93	66.56	59.28	63.07	**64.51**	**74.85**
EfficientNet-B0	CIFAR-100	68.72	73.59	66.95	68.99	**71.17**	**79.12**
	MiniImageNet	64.14	70.47	61.65	76.90	**66.90**	**79.71**
	DroNet	61.99	69.14	60.08	64.28	**64.35**	**78.85**

It can also be observed that when classifying new data with the experimental models, the accuracy within the classification decreases and this is due to the change in the distribution of the data present in the dataset. Although the data used in One-Shot learning comes from disjoint classes, they all present and come from the same data distribution. Likewise, based on the work presented in [15], we present that the accuracy demonstrated in the classification of our model using the CNNs ResNet-18 CNN and EfficientNet-B0, which have been trained with the MiniImagenet dataset and validated with the CIFAR-100 and DroNet data sets, and the classification accuracy is presented in Table 2 with 95% confidence.

5.1 Proposed Model Performance and Generalization

Our experimental phase with the datasets and CNNs networks resulted in our proposed model performing better in classification accuracy than One-Shot learning methods that use the cosine function as a similarity layer. As shown in particular, our Siamese network when using the ResNet-18 feature extractor had better performance than when using EfficientNet-B0 for the MiniImageNet dataset. Architectures with fewer parameters were used, similar to those used in [2] and [22]. It should be noted that the performance of our model is due to the fused affinity layer (bi-layer) that was developed, and it is also emphasized that the careful combination of the affinity layers allowed us to have a significant improvement in the classification accuracy in 1-Shot and 5-Shot learning tasks.

When classifying new data with existing models, the accuracy decreases due to the change in the data distribution as demonstrated in [15], where all the data have the same statistical distribution although they come from different classified groups. Our Siamese network, using the ResNet-18 feature extractor was trained with the MiniImagenet dataset and validated with the CIFAR-100 and DroNet datasets. Very similar CNN networks and datasets were used and the results were evaluated using their classification accuracies with the two ranges, 1-Shot and 5-Shot, with 95% confidence. Below in Table 3 we present what we have described.

Table 3. A comparison of the classification accuracy between the state-of-the-art methods and the proposed model is presented using the three data sets described. By columns, the name of the network used, the feature extractor and the average classification accuracy with 95% confidence are presented. The best results of our Siamese artificial neural network are highlighted.

Method	CNN	CIFAR-100		DroNET		MiniImageNet	
		1-Shot	5-Shot	1-Shot	5-Shot	1-Shot	5-Shot
MAML	ResNet-12	49.28	58.30	45.59	54.61	48.70	63.11
MatchNet	ResNet-12	50.53	60.30	48.09	57.45	63.08	75.99
Meta-SGD	ResNet-50	53.83	70.40	48.65	64.74	50.47	64.66
DELM+Meta-SGD	ResNet-50	61.62	77.94	62.25	79.52	58.49	71.28
Dual Trinet	ResNet-18	63.41	78.43	63.77	80.53	58.12	76.92
Proposed model	ResNet-18	**67.14**	**74.17**	**64.51**	**74.85**	**67.05**	**75.40**
Proposed model	EfficientNet-B0	**71.17**	**79.12**	**64.35**	**78.85**	**66.90**	**79.71**

6   Conclusion

The Siamese artificial neural network model that is proposed as a solution to automatically recognize a possible collision risk for a cyclist within the urban environment is basically based on two layers of affinity, resembling human contrastive learning, to perform the One-Shot learning task. The results generated experimentally demonstrate that the proposed model performs better and above the baseline set by almost all Siamese network models in the state of the art using the aforementioned data sets.

It was also observed that our Siamese artificial neural network model produces results whose consistency is compared to other feature extraction networks, but using a smaller size in the example data set for training. Likewise, it was possible to verify that our model trained with the MiniImagenet data set can generalize what has been learned, even surpassing its performance when compared with other models in the state of the art using unlearned random data. Finally we can mention that this is a work in progress whose usefulness can be extended to various fields of application and whose components can be improved as the research advances, such as feature extractors with better performance, faster and greater precision.

Acknowledgements. The authors are thankful for the financial support of the projects to the Secretería de Investigación y Posgrado del Instituto Politécnico Nacional with grant numbers: 20220268, 20232264, 20221089 and 20232570, as well as the support from Comisión de Operación y Fomento de Actividades Académicas, BEIFI Program and Consejo Nacional de Humanidades Ciencia y Tecnología (CONAHCYT).

References

1. Caterini, A.L., Chang, D.E.: Deep Neural Networks in a Mathematical Framework, 1st edn. Springer, New York (2018). https://doi.org/10.1007/978-3-319-75304-1

2. Chen, Z., Fu, Y., Zhang, Y., Jiang, Y.G., Xue, X., Sigal, L.: Multi-level semantic feature augmentation for one-shot learning. IEEE Trans. Image Process. **28**(9), 4594–4605 (2019). https://doi.org/10.1109/TIP.2019.2910052

3. y Christian Paulina Mendoza Torres, R.H.S.: Metodología de la Investigación: Las rutas cuantitativa, cualitativa y mixta. McGraw-Hill Interamericana (2018)

4. Cuomo, S., Di Cola, V.S., Giampaolo, F., Rozza, G., Raissi, M., Piccialli, F.: Scientific machine learning through physics–informed neural networks: where we are and what's next. J. Sci. Comput. **92**(3), 88 (2022). https://doi.org/10.1007/s10915-022-01939-z

5. Galán, R., Calle, M., García, J.M.: Análisis de variables que influencian la accidentalidad ciclista: desarrollo de modelos y diseño de una herramienta de ayuda. In: XIII Congreso de Ingeniería de Organización Barcelona-Terrassa, 2-4 September 2009, pp. 696–703. Asociación para el Desarrollo de la Ingeniería de Organización - ADINGOR (2009)

6. He, K., Zhang, X., Ren, S., Sun, J.: Deep residual learning for image recognition. In: Proceedings of the IEEE Conference on Computer Vision and Pattern Recognition, pp. 770–778 (2016)

7. Hernández-Herrera, A., Espino, E.R., Álvarez Vargas, R., Ponce, V.H.P.: Una exploración sobre el aprendizaje automático simplificado: Generalización a partir de algunos ejemplos. Komputer Sapiens **3**, 36–41(13) (2021)

8. Hilmkil, A., Ivarsson, O., Johansson, M., Kuylenstierna, D., van Erp, T.: Towards machine learning on data from professional cyclists (2018)

9. INEGI: Estadísticas a propósito del Día de Muertos, DATOS NACIONALES. Technical report, Instituto Nacional de Estadística y Geografía, México (2019)

10. ITDP: Manual Ciclociudades I. la movilidad en bicicleta como política pública. In: Manual Ciclociudades, vol. 1, p. 62. Instituto de Políticas para el Transporte y el Desarrollo, México D.F. (2011)

11. Khosla, P., et al.: Supervised contrastive learning (2021)

12. Koch, G.R.: Siamese neural networks for one-shot image recognition. In: Proceedings of the 32nd International Conference on Machine Learning (2015)

13. Krizhevsky, A., Hinton, G.: Learning multiple layers of features from tiny images. Technical report 0, University of Toronto, Toronto, Ontario (2009). https://www.cs.toronto.edu/kriz/learning-features-2009-TR.pdf

14. Lee, S.W., O'Doherty, J.P., Shimojo, S.: Neural computations mediating one-shot learning in the human brain. PLOS Biol. **13**, 1–36 (2015). https://doi.org/10.1371/journal.pbio.1002137

15. Li, X., Yu, L., Fu, C.W., Fang, M., Heng, P.A.: Revisiting metric learning for few-shot image classification. Neurocomputing **406**, 49–58 (2020). https://doi.org/10.1016/j.neucom.2020.04.040, https://www.sciencedirect.com/science/article/pii/S092523122030607X

16. Loquercio, A., Maqueda, A.I., del Blanco, C.R., Scaramuzza, D.: DroNet: learning to fly by driving. IEEE Robot. Autom. Lett. **3**(2), 1088–1095 (2018). https://doi.org/10.1109/LRA.2018.2795643

17. López Gómez, L.: La bicicleta como medio de transporte en la movilidad sustentable. Technical report, Dirección General de Análisis Legislativo, Senado de la República, México (2018)

18. Ngiam, J., Khosla, A., Kim, M., Nam, J., Lee, H., Ng, A.Y.: Multimodal deep learning. In: Getoor, L., Scheffer, T. (eds.) Proceedings of the 28th International Conference on Machine Learning, ICML 2011, Bellevue, Washington, USA, 28 June–2 July 2011, pp. 689–696. Omnipress (2011)

19. Snell, J., Swersky, K., Zemel, R.: Prototypical networks for few-shot learning. In: Guyon, I., et al. (eds.) Advances in Neural Information Processing Systems, vol. 30. Curran Associates, Inc. (2017). https://proceedings.neurips.cc/paper/2017/file/cb8da6767461f2812ae4290eac7cbc42-Paper.pdf

20. Srivastava, N., Salakhutdinov, R.: Multimodal learning with deep Boltzmann machines. J. Mach. Learn. Res. **15**(1), 2949–2980 (2014)

21. Tan, M., Le, Q.: EfficientNet: rethinking model scaling for convolutional neural networks. In: International Conference on Machine Learning, pp. 6105–6114. PMLR (2019)

22. Vinyals, O., Blundell, C., Lillicrap, T., Kavukcuoglu, K., Wierstra, D.: Matching networks for one shot learning. In: Lee, D., Sugiyama, M., Luxburg, U., Guyon, I., Garnett, R. (eds.) Advances in Neural Information Processing Systems, vol. 29. Curran Associates, Inc. (2016). https://proceedings.neurips.cc/paper/2016/file/90e1357833654983612fb05e3ec9148c-Paper.pdf

23. Vision Zero Network: What is vision zero? (2022). https://visionzeronetwork.org/about/what-is-vision-zero/

24. WHO: Global status report on road safety 2018. Technical report, World Health Organization, Geneva (2018)

25. Zhao, H., et al.: Unsupervised deep learning to explore streetscape factors associated with urban cyclist safety. In: Qu, X., Zhen, L., Howlett, R.J., Jain, L.C. (eds.) Smart Transportation Systems 2019, pp. 155–164. Springer, Singapore (2019). https://doi.org/10.1007/978-981-13-8683-1_16

Linear Predictive Coding vs. Kalman Filter for Urban Finance Prediction in Smart Cities with S&P/BMV IPC

Luis Enrique Andrade-Gorjoux[1]([✉]) [iD], César Castrejón-Peralta[1] [iD],
Jordi Fabián González-Contreras[1] [iD], Jesús Yaljá Montiel-Pérez[1] [iD],
and José Luis López-Bonilla[2] [iD]

[1] Centro de Investigación en Computación, Instituto Politécnico Nacional,
Ciudad de México, Mexico
{landradeg2022,ccastrejonp2021,jgonzalezc2023,jyalja}@cic.ipn.mx
[2] Escuela Superior de Ingeniería Mecánica y Eléctrica, Instituto Politécnico Nacional,
Ciudad de México, Mexico
https://proyectosrym.cic.ipn.mx/

Abstract. This paper presents a comparison between two prediction methods, Linear Predictive Coding (LPC) and Kalman Filter (KF), in the context of Smart Cities. The research uses historical data from one of the financial index in Mexico: the S&P/BMV IPC Index, a crucial indicator that reflects the performance of the Mexican stock market. The main objective of this study is to evaluate the effectiveness of these prediction methods to improve financial management and decision-making in smart urban environments. To carry out this comparison, some factors are taken into consideration, such as the accuracy of the predictions, their error, and the ability to adapt to changes in the market. The results show that both methods have advantages and disadvantages but can be highly useful in different academic and financial contexts, as in both cases relative errors below 4% were achieved; however, the KF method exhibited even lower mean squared errors than the LPC method. This contributes to the field of urban finance, providing decision-makers and investors with a deeper understanding of these two tools available for prediction. In addition, the results can be considered for efficient and sustainable economic management in a world increasingly focused on digital transformation and resource optimization in smart cities.

Keywords: Financial Prediction · Kalman Filter (KF) · Linear Predictive Coding (LPC) · S&P/BMV IPC · Urban Finance

1 Introduction

Digital transformation and technological revolution have redefined the way cities manage their resources, interact with their inhabitants, and seek sustainability through the efficiency of all their resources for their operation. This is why smart

S. Nesmachnow and L. Hernández Callejo (Eds.): ICSC-Cities 2023, CCIS 1938, pp. 246–260, 2024.
https://doi.org/10.1007/978-3-031-52517-9_17

cities have emerged as a paradigm that promises more efficient urban management, reflected in a higher quality of life for citizens and a more sustainable use of resources.

One of the most relevant aspects for the success of this urbanization approach is effective financial management, as in an environment where resource optimization is essential, the ability to accurately predict key economic indicators becomes a factor that allows evaluating the financial performance of a city, such as considering the S&P/BMV IPC Index of the Mexican Stock Exchange.

In addition, this work is aligned with the Sustainable Development Goals (SDGs) [1] established by the United Nations to achieve a sustainable future for all, with the following goals being the most aligned with the present work:

- **SDG 9 - Industry, Innovation and Infrastructure:** since this work focuses on the analysis and forecasting of the S&P/BMV IPC for a Smart City, which implies the use of technology and innovation to improve its financial management.
- **SDG 11 - Sustainable Cities and Communities:** the results of the work help to improve the economic planning and sustainable development of a smart city by highlighting the relevance of predictive tools in this emerging context.
- **SDG 12 - Responsible Production and Consumption:** using prediction methods to improve financial management in Smart Cities, we seek to optimize resources and promote responsible practices

On the other hand, predicting the S&P/BMV IPC is a complex challenge due to the dynamic and volatile nature of financial markets, such as the Mexican market and the 35 companies that make up this index. This is why this article focuses on the comparison of two parametric prediction methods: LPC and the KF.

The choice of these prediction methods is based on the fact that they have proven to be effective in different fields, from engineering to economics, due to their proven effectiveness in predicting time series, their applicability in financial environments, and their ability to adapt to changing market conditions.

Mentioning the methods to be compared, on the one hand, the LPC method is based on predicting a signal at a given time as a linear combination of samples in previous instants, minimizing the error between the starting signal and the predicted one [2]. On the other hand, the KF is one important estimation algorithms. This produces estimates of hidden variables based on inaccurate and uncertain measurements. In addition, this filter provides a prediction of the future state of the system, based on past estimates [3].

These methods not only have the potential to improve financial decision-making, but they can also be crucial for attracting investment, planning infrastructure, and promoting sustainable economic development in the context of smart cities in the 21st century.

It is possible to carry out a technical analysis of the movements of quotations through the prices of assets, using econometric indicators, which allow experts to see the behavior over time. The evolution of market quotations only reflects the balances between asset demanders and suppliers. Therefore, by analyzing the price of an asset in a specific market, all factors related to that asset are implicitly analyzed [4].

Through the analysis of historical data and its application in an urban environment, this study contributes to improving the economic planning and sustainable development of Smart Cities [5]. In addition, the importance of prediction tools and their potential to optimize financial management in this type of cities is highlighted.

2 Problem Definition and Literature Review

2.1 Problem

Derived of the necessity from the need to improve financial management in Smart Cities, using prediction tools to assume the future behavior of the Mexican financial market, LPC and KF are methods used in signal processing and data analysis to perform tasks such as predicting and filtering information.

This is how the evaluation of the effectiveness of these two prediction methods in the analysis and forecasting of the S&P/BMV IPC is addressed, whose main objective is to evaluate the ability of these methods to predict market trends and provide valuable information for decision-making in intelligent urban environments.

Stock market indices are indicators that allow us to assess the financial situation of a set of assets, such as the case of the S&P/BMV IPC, which reflects the financial health of Mexico based on the analysis of the 35 companies with the highest liquidity, allowing us to guide the decisions that are considered necessary for a group with investment capital. However, their behavior is complex due to the number of factors that influence their behavior [6], which makes it difficult to make an accurate prediction and it becomes necessary to use various prediction methods, intended to reduce the error of the calculated values since this can lead to less optimal financial decisions, affect the attraction of investments and limit the economic development of a certain region, such as Mexico considering the S&P/BMV IPC.

2.2 Related Work

New technologies integrated into smart city models, as mentioned by [7], include cloud computing, AI, big data, and rapidly evolving fintech tools. These technologies prioritize risk prevention and control in financial entities through prediction and assessment. Blockchain technology, explained by [8], bolsters financial security. Internet of Things (IoT), as discussed by [9], manages big data via mobile devices in finance, enhancing the advantage of technology in this sector. Artificial Intelligence (AI), as per [10], advises on investments and handles tasks like money laundering detection, fraud prevention, chatbot financial advising, and customer recommendations.

Furthermore, [11] notes that AI, paired with cloud computing, forecasts smart city finances to grow banking infrastructure. This technological revolution, if driving smart city growth, has implications for zero-emission economies, online commerce, aging populations, urban expansion, and public finance pressures, as mentioned by [12]. Accurate financial forecasting becomes crucial under these circumstances, enabling better planning and resource allocation for smart city initiatives.

Additionally, [13] extended that economic systems of smart cities rely on productivity and the growth of new industries, directly impacting financial indices. An intelligent financial system facilitates efficiency measurement and the financing of technological innovations.

In their work, [14,15] emphasize the significance of financial forecasting, involving modeling, data analysis, scenarios, and risk assessment. This process ensures the fiscal sustainability of smart city projects, including infrastructure and services. Also, it aids in assessing project feasibility, identifying financing sources, and constructing decision-support financial models.

Nevertheless, as pointed out by [16], securing financing remains a notable hurdle for smart city projects. Addressing this challenge, [17] suggests that one initial approach, at least in the Indian context, is to increase taxes as a means of funding these projects. The establishment of a robust intelligent financial system holds promise for predicting funding for regional development programs.

Financial data analysis offers insights into business and industry performance and the overall economic well-being of the smart city, is explained by [6]. The ability to predict and classify data allows for the identification of trends and patterns, informing decision-making and fostering effective strategies for growth and economic development.

To achieve this, it is possible to use some statistical algorithms for market modeling and prediction. These procedures are subject to the assumptions of stationarity of time series and linearity between variables with normal distribution. In other words, it is assumed that the data are linear and follow a normal distribution [18].

Some of those that have been implemented are Monte Carlo [19], Autoregressive Integrated Moving Average (ARIMA) [20], Principal Component Analysis (PCA) [21], Decision trees [22], Support Vector Regression (SVR) [23], Artificial Neural Networks (ANN) [24,25].

However, for this research, it was decided to compare two methods: linear predictor coding (LPC) and KF to complement existing information and explore its use in the financial sector. This will allow for the development of research and application in various environments such as smart cities in the field of intelligent urban finance.

On the one hand, linear predictor coding (LPC) has poor information when used for financial forecasting purposes. In the reference [26], this predictive method is mentioned as a basis for comparison with other artificial intelligence-based prediction algorithms such as neural networks, mentioning that it was the least favorable. Likewise, in the work [27], LPC prediction is used in financial topics; however, presented for the estimation of stock volatility, showing favorable results compared to the Generalized AutoRegressive Conditional Heteroskedasticity (GARCH) method.

On the other hand, the KF has demonstrated good option for financial forecasting, taking into account the specific context and amount of the data, in addition to being able to take advantage of its variants [28]. Likewise, in [29], the results of prediction tests using this filter are presented, concluding an increase in the performance of stock market prediction.

3 Prediction Methods

3.1 Linear Prediction Coding (LPC)

LPC analysis is constructed with any kind of time series from the linear combination of its samples at previous times [2].

Thus, the predicted signal can be expressed as:

$$\hat{s}(n) = -\sum_{k=1}^{p} a_k s(n-k) \,, \tag{3.1}$$

and the error between the original signal and the prediction is:

$$e(n) = s(n) - \hat{s}(n) \,, \tag{3.2}$$

where $s(n)$ is the original signal, $\hat{s}(n)$ is the calculated signal, a_k are the prediction coefficients, p the order of the prediction filter, and $e(n)$ is the prediction error.

Using substituting Eq. (3.1) in (3.2), the error can be redefined as:

$$e(n) = s(n) + \sum_{k=1}^{p} a_k s(n-k) \,. \tag{3.3}$$

Calculating the Z-transform, we obtain:

$$E(z) = S(z) \left[1 + \sum_{k=1}^{p} a_k z^{-1} \right] \,, \tag{3.4}$$

and defining the term $A(z)$ as:

$$A(z) = \frac{E(z)}{S(z)} = 1 + \sum_{k=1}^{p} a_k z^{-1} \,. \tag{3.5}$$

Exciting the prediction error with the transfer function $1/A(z)$, the desired signal is obtained as output. In this prediction model, it is assumed that $H(z)$ follows a pole-all model with q poles:

$$H(z) = \frac{S(z)}{U(z)} = \frac{G}{1 + \sum_{k=1}^{p} a_k z^{-1}} \,. \tag{3.6}$$

Identifying $H(z)$ with the linear prediction filter $1/A(z)$ and assuming that the number of poles is equal to the linear prediction order, $p = q$, we have that:

$$H(z) = \frac{G}{A(z)} , \qquad (3.7)$$

where G is the aging and $E(z) = GU(z)$.

From this analysis, it is possible to obtain the transfer function $H(z)$ by calculating the coefficientes a_k. Since this $H(z)$, which is defined the signal parameters, is modeled as $1/A(z)$, the prediction error represents the excitation.

Therefore, the objective of the method is to find the set of coefficients a_k that minimize the mean squared error in each analysis window.

3.2 KF Method

KF is an algorithm to update by each observation the linear projection of a system of variables on the set of information available, as new information becomes available.

In [30,31], a proposal for the prediction of problems is developed. The basic sequence of steps is to find the predicted mean $M_{\overline{k}}$ using the Eq. (3.8):

$$M_{\overline{k}} = A_{k-1}M_{k-1} + B_kU_k , \qquad (3.8)$$

where A_{k-1} is the state transition matrix, M_{k-1} is the estimate of the mean of the system state at time $k - 1$, B_k is the system control matrix, and U_k is the system control input at time k.

The predicted covariance $C_{\overline{k}}$ can be estimated with the use of:

$$C_{\overline{k}} = A_{k-1}C_{k-1}A_{k-1}^T + Q_{k-1} , \qquad (3.9)$$

where Q_{k-1} is the system process noise covariance matrix.

The predicted values are previously calculated using the estimated mean M_k, which is defined as:

$$M_k = M_{\overline{k}} + K_kV_k , \qquad (3.10)$$

and the estimated covariance C_k after the measurement at k time.

$$C_k = C_{\overline{k}} + K_kS_kK_k^T . \qquad (3.11)$$

In addition to performing an update at time k of the residual measurement parameters V_k with Eq. (3.12), the prediction of the covariance S_k with Eq. (3.13), and the Kalman gain K_k with Eq. (3.14).

$$V_k = Y_k - H_kM_{\overline{k}} , \qquad (3.12)$$

$$S_k = H_kC_{\overline{k}}H_k^T + R_k , \qquad (3.13)$$

$$K_k = C_{\bar{k}} H_k^T + S_k^{-1} \, , \tag{3.14}$$

where Y_k is the measured mean at time k, R_k is the measurement noise covariance matrix, and H_k is the load matrix at time k, respectively.

4   Metodology and Results

4.1   Database

The database used to test the proposal in this work consists of 3456 tuples, were taken the value of the *closing price* as the main time series of a day and published. Additionally, this data is free of charge for anyone interested, in media such as **Yahoo! Finance**[1] or **Investing.com**[2].

4.2   Tests with LPC Method

Using MATLAB software, prediction tests were carried out by applying the filter generated from the different configurations of the LPC to the time series.

To have a broad overview of the experimentation, a test was prepared in which 3 amounts of coefficients to be used in the LPC (5, 20, 40) were defined, as well as different percentages of the database (2%, 10% and 20%) to be used to determine the value of the coefficients to be used in the filter for LPC.

According to the methodology presented, the graphs of the original data, compared with the estimated prediction from different numbers of coefficients for LPC are shown in Fig. 1. The X-axis shows the index of the data point in the data set generated within the aforementioned time window, while the Y-axis shows the closing price value of the stock index.

It is emphasized that the part of the original signal plus the predicted signal is presented, this union can be observed in the various valleys in the time series that reaches the value of 0 and resume values close to the original signal, that is, the valleys represent the beginning of the prediction. In all configurations, a lag in the predicted signal can be observed due to the nature of the modeling according to its linear combination of previous samples, which could be solved by modifying the indices of the generated *arrays*. For this work, the lag was maintained in all the graphs.

To visualize the mentioned lag and a better observation of the comparison between the two series, Fig. 2 shows the last 30 samples of each of the previous graphs. In this plot, the prediction has the same tendency of the original time series and presents near values between the two time series, could be confirm with the Fig. 3.

---

[1] Yahoo! Finance (2023). *IPC MEXICO (^MXX)*. Retrieved September 28, 2023, from https://finance.yahoo.com/quote/%5EMXX/history?p=%5EMXX.

[2] Investing.com (2023). *S&P/BMV IPC (MXX)*. Retrieved September 28, 2023, from https://www.investing.com/indices/ipc-historical-data.

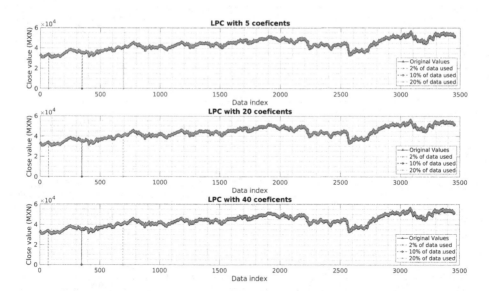

Fig. 1. Prediction of the S&P/BMV IPC using a filter based on LPC with 5, 20 and 40 coefficients for 2%, 10% and 20% of the database.

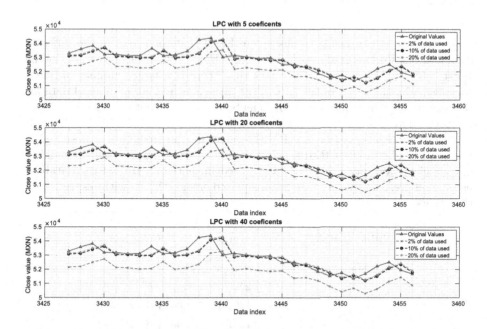

Fig. 2. Prediction of the S&P/BMV IPC of the last 30 samples of the time series, using a filter based on LPC with 5, 20 and 40 coefficients for 2%, 10% and 20% of the database.

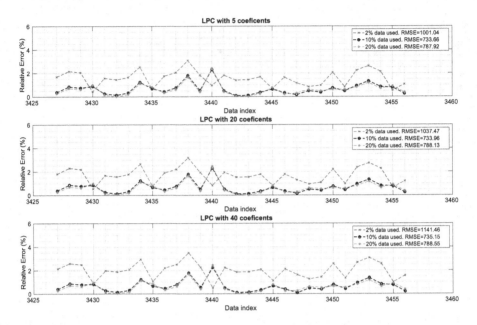

Fig. 3. The relative errors with 5, 20 and 40 coefficients for 2%, 10% and 20% of the database. In addition, the respective root mean square errors (RMSE) for each one are mentioned.

In general, it is possible to observe in Fig. 3 that the errors in the different combinations for the prediction of the S&P/BMV IPC are close to 2% (in the worst case 4%). Furthermore, the fact that there is a larger number of linear coefficients in the design of the LPC filter, as well as a larger number of data for the definition of the values these coefficients, no indicate that the results improve the prediction.

The root mean square errors (RMSE) values for the prediction is presented in the Table 1. The smallest RMSE is in the middle of the proposals of the number of coefficients and percentage of data (10 coefficients and 10% of the database used), and presents the smallest mean squared error (RMSE) with respect to all the others.

Table 1. RMSE of the predictions with LPC method

Number of coefficients	Percentages of data used		
	2%	10%	20%
5	1001.04	733.66	787.92
10	1037.47	733.96	788.13
20	1141.46	735.15	788.5

4.3   Test with KF Method

Using MATLAB software, prediction tests were carried out by applying the simulated designed to the time series generated from definitions of the state matrices, as well as the recursive execution of the equations that describe this filter.

To have a broad overview of the experimentation, a test bench was carried out in which 3 amounts of values were defined for the state transition matrix, which is used to predict the next state of the system. This matrix A has a dimension of 2×2, whose main diagonal varies with values of 0, 1 and 10. Likewise, a noise or uncertainty factor is added by varying the value of the element $(0,1)$ with values between 1, 10 and 20.

Figure 4 shows graphs of the original data against the prediction made from the different combinations between the elements of the state transition matrix. It is worth mentioning that in each iteration, the filter updates its coefficients to predict the next one. In this case, there is no lag because it starts from an initial condition that can be considered as the first prediction and that coincides with the value of the original time series.

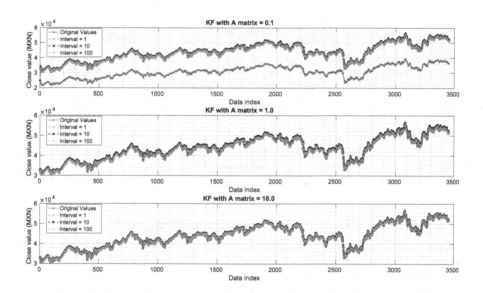

Fig. 4. Prediction of the S&P/BMV IPC using a KF with variation in the state transition matrix whose diagonal can take values between 0.1, 1 and 10, as well as a noise value between 0, 1 and 10.

In Fig. 4, it can be observed that, in general, the predictions follow the trend of the original data. It is noticeable that in the upper left graph there is a drastic separation between the two time series (with a root mean square errors, RMSE = 13,087.88). An RMSE value higher than the rest can be appreciated in Table 2. To visualize the mentioned lag and a better observation of the comparison between the two series, Fig. 5 shows the last 30 samples of each of the previous graphs.

To validate the error of the prediction with respect to the original data, the calculation of relative errors and root mean square errors (RMSE) was performed for each of the combinations shown, similar to the case of the prediction with the LPC method of absolute errors. Figure 6 shows each of the previously mentioned errors for the last 30 samples of each time series, as well as the value of the RMSE for each of the predictions made.

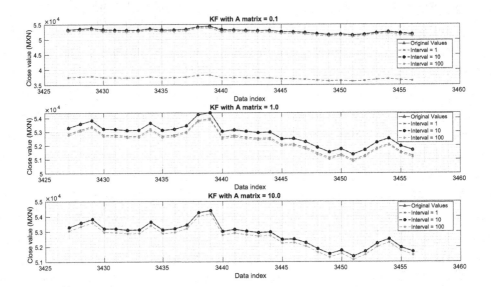

Fig. 5. Prediction of the S&P/BMV IPC of the last 30 samples of the time series, using a KF with variation in the state transition matrix whose diagonal can take values between 0.1, 1 and 10, as well as a noise value between 0, 1 and 10.

In Fig. 6, the errors calculated for this method are shown. It can be observed that, unlike LPC, the errors in the different combinations for the prediction of the S&P/BMV IPC are larger, reaching values close to 30% error, meanwhile in other cases the relative error was near to the 0%.

Likewise, this can be confirmed with the values of the RMSE calculated for each of the combination for the test with KF and shown in Table 2, showing that noise does not define the quality of the prediction, but the elements that make up the main diagonal in the state transition matrix, at least with the proposed filter.

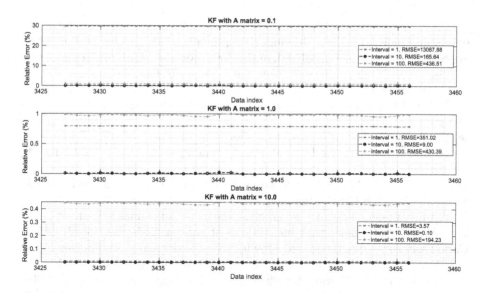

Fig. 6. The relative errors with variation in the state transition matrix whose diagonal can take values between 0.1, 1 and 10, as well as a noise value between 0, 1 and 10. In addition, the respective root mean square errors (RMSE) for each one are mentioned.

Table 2. Comparison of the root mean square errors (RMSE) of the predictions with KF.

Value on diagonal A	dt interval in A		
	1	10	100
0.1	13087.88	165.64	436.51
1	351.02	9.00	430.39
10	3.57	0.10	194.23

5 Conclusions and Future Works

Financial management in Smart Cities is a matter of great importance for the sustainable development of intelligent cities. In this paper, the effectiveness of two prediction methods, LPC and the KF methods, in the analysis and forecasting of the S&P/BMV IPC Price and Quotations Index was evaluated. The results indicate that both methods are effective in predicting the trends of the analysed dataset of the Mexican financial market, each with certain peculiarities in the development of the desired prediction. In this regard, it is the KF, with certain configurations in the transition matrix and noise values, that allows to achieve a low RMSE compared to LPC. These findings are relevant for making informed decisions in smart urban environments and can contribute to improving economic planning and sustainable development in Smart Cities.

Based on the data shown in Fig. 1, it can be said that the LPC method allows obtaining predictions that, although they present errors, can be used as a first approximation. On the other hand, in the data shown in Fig. 4, better prediction results can be observed derived from situations using more accurate models in the design of this filter.

Unlike the use of machine learning techniques, where large amounts of information are required to train the algorithms, the two methods analyzed in this work only require a small amount of prior information (from 2% of data used, approximately 65 data, for LPC, and the beginning of the time series for KF) to generate an output or an iterative process based on the dimension of the time series, so they can be used, with the necessary considerations, in environments where there are no large databases.

Another possibility, which would allow the inclusion of finance in smart cities, is to propose workflows that include one of the methods mentioned (Monte Carlo, Autoregressive Integrated Moving Average, Principal Component Analysis, Decision trees, Support Vector Regression), presented (LPC and KF), and machine learning algorithms (artificial neural networks), as is the case of [31]. This would allow for the inclusion of information from various sources, in addition to the information obtained from stock portals, such as social networks, government portals, among others.

In this way, this work demonstrates that financial prediction, under a vision of smart urban finance, is possible from the use of prediction models such as LPC and KF in the analysis and forecasting of the S&P/BMV IPC stock index. It also highlights the importance of prediction tools in promoting responsible and sustainable practices in smart cities.

Acknowledgements. I would like to thank the *VI Iberoamerican Congress of Smart Cities (ICSC-CITIES 2023)* for the valuable opportunity to contribute to this article in this valuable event, promoting the exchange of knowledge in the field of Smart Cities.

Data Availability. The database used is available at https://github.com/LuisGorj oux1/Pred_IPC_LEAG/blob/main/Datos_SP_BMV_IPC10a22/Datos_SP_BMV_IPC_1 00101a230922.csv.

References

1. United Nations. Sustainable Development Goals. https://www.un.org/sustainable development/sustainable-development-goals/. Retrieved 29 Sept 2023
2. Galve, Y., Miguel, A.: Diseño de herramientas de asistencia a la logopedia en una plataforma distribuida. Universidad de Zaragoza (2012). https://core.ac.uk/download/pdf/289972235.pdf. Retrieved 29 Sept 2023
3. Becker, A.: Introducción al Filtro de Kalman (2022). https://www.kalmanfilter.net/ES/background_es.html. Retrieved 29 Sept 2023
4. Rodríguez, F.: Análisis técnico de los mercados financieros. Universidad de Valladolid (2021). https://uvadoc.uva.es/bitstream/handle/10324/46903/TFG-E-1202.pdf. Retrieved 29 Sept 2023

5. Balicka, H.: An influence of deep learning and the internet of things on directions of development of integrated financial systems supporting smart cities for green economy. Przestrzeń, Ekonomia, Społeczeństwo (17/I), 77–102 (2020)
6. Fu, X.: Research on artificial intelligence classification and statistical methods of financial data in smart cities. Comput. Intell. Neurosci. **2022**, 9965427 (2022)
7. Wang, K., Yan, F., Zhang, Y., Xiao, Y., Gu, L.: Supply chain financial risk evaluation of small-and medium-sized enterprises under smart city. J. Adv. Transp. **2020**, 1–14 (2020)
8. Choo, K.K.R., Ozcan, S., Dehghantanha, A., Parizi, R.M.: Blockchain ecosystem-technological and management opportunities and challenges. IEEE Trans. Eng. Manage. **67**(4), 982–987 (2020)
9. Hsiao, Y.C., Wu, M.H., Li, S.C.: Elevated performance of the smart city-a case study of the IoT by innovation mode. IEEE Trans. Eng. Manage. **68**(5), 1461–1475 (2019)
10. Liu, X., Yuan, X., Zhang, R., Ye, N.: Risk assessment and regulation algorithm for financial technology platforms in smart city. Comput. Intell. Neurosci. **2022**, 9903364 (2022)
11. Javed, A.R., Ahmed, W., Pandya, S., Maddikunta, P.K.R., Alazab, M., Gadekallu, T.R.: A survey of explainable artificial intelligence for smart cities. Electronics **12**(4), 1020 (2023)
12. Lai, C.S., Strasser, T.I., Lai, L.L.: Editorial to the special issue on smart cities based on the efforts of the systems, man, and cybernetics society. IEEE Trans. Syst. Man Cybern. Syst. **52**(1), 2–6 (2021)
13. Dobos, P., Takács-György, K.: Possible smart city solutions in the fight against black economy. Interdisc. Description Complex Syst. INDECS **17**(3-A), 468–475 (2019)
14. Blanck, M., Ribeiro, J.L.D.: Smart cities financing system: an empirical modelling from the European context. Cities **116**, 103268 (2021)
15. Papa, C., Rossi, N.: Smart cities and sustainable finance. Eur. J. Islamic Finance **9**(2), 18–26 (2022)
16. Robinson, C.: The smart money. Am. City County **132**(3), 1 (2017)
17. Malhotra, A., Mishra, A.K., Vyas, I.: Financing urban infrastructure in India through tax increment financing instruments: a case for smart cities mission. J. Public Aff. **22**(3), e2554 (2022)
18. Nikouei, M.A., Darvazeh, S.S., Amiri, M.: Artificial intelligence and financial markets in smart cities. In: Mining, D.-D. (ed.) Learning and Analytics for Secured Smart Cities: Trends and Advances, pp. 313–332. Springer, Cham (2021). https://doi.org/10.1007/978-3-030-72139-8_15
19. An, D., Linden, N., Liu, J., Montanaro, A., Shao, C., Wang, J.: Quantum-accelerated multilevel Monte Carlo methods for stochastic differential equations in mathematical finance (2021). https://doi.org/10.22331/q-2021-06-24-481
20. Tang, X., Xu, S., Ye, H.: The way to invest: trading strategies based on ARIMA and investor personality. Symmetry **14**(11), 2292 (2022)
21. Zhong, X., Enke, D.: Predicting the daily return direction of the stock market using hybrid machine learning algorithms (2019). https://doi.org/10.1186/s40854-019-0138-0
22. Salas, M.B., Alaminos, D., Fernández, M.A., López-Valverde, F.: A global prediction model for sudden stops of capital flows using decision trees. PLoS ONE **15**(2), e0228387 (2020)

23. Khan, W., Malik, U., Ghazanfar, M.A., Azam, M.A., Alyoubi, K.H., Alfakeeh, A.S.: Predicting stock market trends using machine learning algorithms via public sentiment and political situation analysis. Soft. Comput. **24**, 11019–11043 (2020)

24. Chen, S.Y.C., Yoo, S., Fang, Y.L.L.: Quantum long short-term memory. In: ICASSP 2022–2022 IEEE International Conference on Acoustics, Speech and Signal Processing (ICASSP), pp. 8622–8626. IEEE, May 2022

25. Verdon, G., et al.: Learning to learn with quantum neural networks via classical neural networks. arXiv preprint arXiv:1907.05415 (2019)

26. Reid, D., Hussain, A.J., Tawfik, H.: Financial time series prediction using spiking neural networks. PLoS ONE **9**(8), e103656 (2014)

27. Mello, L.: Linear predictive coding as an estimator of volatility. arXiv preprint cs/0607107 (2006)

28. Li, X., et al.: Applications of Kalman filtering in time series prediction. In: Liu, H., et al. (eds.) International Conference on Intelligent Robotics and Applications, vol. 13457, pp. 520–531. Springer, Cham (2022). https://doi.org/10.1007/978-3-031-13835-5_47

29. Deepika, N., Nirupama Bhat, M.: An efficient stock market prediction method based on Kalman Filter. J. Inst. Eng. (India) Ser. B **102**, 629–644 (2021)

30. Kalman, R.E.: A new approach to linear filtering and prediction problems. J. Basic Eng. **82**(1), 35–45 (1960). https://doi.org/10.1115/1.3662552

31. Bhooshan, A., Hari, V.S.: Recurrent neural network estimator for stock price. In: 2021 International Conference on Electrical, Communication, and Computer Engineering (ICECCE), pp. 1–6. IEEE, June 2021

Innovative Informatic Approaches
for Smart Cities

3D Printing as an Enabler of Innovation in Universities. Tellus UPM Ecosystem Case

Juan Antonio Rodríguez Rama$^{(\boxtimes)}$ [ID], Alfredo Marín Lázaro,
Domingo A. Martín Sánchez[ID], Javier Maroto Lorenzo, Fernando Barrio-Parra[ID],
and Luis J. Fernández Gutiérrez del Álamo[ID]

Universidad Politécnica de Madrid, Madrid, Spain
jrodriguez@alumnos.upm.es, {alfredo.marin,domingoalfonso.martin,
javier.maroto,fernando.barrio,luis.fdezgda}@upm.es

Abstract. In the current academic landscape, innovation emerges as a fundamental pillar, driving the transformation towards a more integrated and practical education. This study highlights how the implementation of 3D printing technologies, centered on projects developed under the framework of the Tellus ecosystem at the Universidad Politécnica de Madrid (UPM), is fostering a renaissance of innovation within the university sphere. By exploring the convergence of technology, education and sustainability, it is revealed that FabLabs, specifically FabLab ETSIME-UPM, act as catalysts for this change, providing the necessary tools and resources to transform theoretical ideas into tangible prototypes and viable solutions. Furthermore, this study demonstrates how 3D printing aligns with the Sustainable Development Goals, facilitating the creation of projects that are not only innovative but also sustainable. Through the analysis of specific methods and materials employed in the 3D printing process, it illustrates that this technology is a driving force in enhancing adaptability and efficiency in project development. Therefore, this study postulates that the incorporation of 3D printing in academia, especially in the context of the Tellus UPM Ecosystem.

Keywords: 3D printing · innovation · university · ODS · digitalization

1 Introduction

1.1 Relevance of Innovation at the University Level and the Role of Technology

The university, traditionally conceived as a space for learning and knowledge acquisition, has evolved in recent decades to become an epicenter of innovation and development [1–3]. In this context, innovation refers not only to the creation of new ideas, but also to the ability to translate them into practical and applicable solutions that generate a positive impact on society [4–6].

© The Author(s), under exclusive license to Springer Nature Switzerland AG 2024
S. Nesmachnow and L. Hernández Callejo (Eds.): ICSC-Cities 2023, CCIS 1938, pp. 263–276, 2024.
https://doi.org/10.1007/978-3-031-52517-9_18

1.2 The FabLab Concept

FabLabs, or Digital Fabrication Laboratories, represent one of the most significant advances in the confluence of technology and creativity in the field of manufacturing. These spaces emerge as specialized workshops that transcend the traditional barrier between the digital and physical worlds, facilitating the transition from ideas and concepts to tangible realities. In this context, they have established themselves as epicenters of innovation and production, particularly in the university environment [7, 8].

It has its roots in the Center for Bits and Atoms (CBA) at the Massachusetts Institute of Technology (MIT). Under the direction of Neil Gershenfeld in 2001, the CBA received funding from the National Science Foundation (NSF). This initiative was born with the vision of turning ideas generated at MIT into working prototypes. By 2002, the first FabLabs were up and running in places as diverse as India, Costa Rica, Norway, Boston and Ghana, positioning themselves as local production units [9, 10].

At the university level, FabLabs emerge as digital fabrication spaces that catalyze innovation and hands-on learning, taking advantage of advanced technologies, in particular 3D printing, supporting from undergraduate work [11, 12] to research [13], FabLabs provide the tools and environment necessary for members of the university community to experiment, research and innovate [14].

1.3 The Tellus UPM Ecosystem: Confluence of Technology, Education and Sustainability

At the confluence of modern education, advanced technology and sustainability is the Tellus UPM Ecosystem [15], an initiative of the Unidad de Emprendimiento Social, Ética y Valores en la Ingeniería (UESEVI) of the Escuela de Ingenieros de Minas y Energía of the Universidad Politécnica de Madrid (ETSIME-UPM). This ecosystem represents not only a physical space, but also a mindset [16] and an approach to training and innovation that positions the university as an environment for testing and developing educational and technological change [17].

In which no it is not just about learning about digitization or sustainability in the classroom, but about experimenting, designing and developing real solutions in these areas [18], where ideas do not remain on paper, but are transformed into real, operational prototypes and it situates the university as a microcosm of society in which the campus acts as a testing ground, simulating the challenges of urban areas [19], and provides a scalable model for addressing complex real-life problems.

To achieve this, they collaborate in the same system that involves teachers, researchers, technical staff and students, through laboratories and platforms, represented in Fig. 1, such as the Living Lab "La Pecera" the design of the projects, the machining of their electronic components and their testing in different test conditions to ensure that the environmental data monitored by the sensors are reliable, The ETSIME-UPM FabLab, which provides customized parts and solutions printed in the most suitable materials to meet the requirements of each prototype, Tellus IoT, is the proprietary IoT platform that, as shown in Fig. 2, provides the prototypes with communications systems, storage of collected data, This facilitates the adoption of a data-driven culture underlining the importance of informed decisions [20], the ETSIME-UPM ODS Nodes focus on

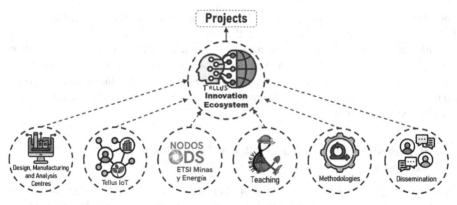

Fig. 1. Conceptual scheme of the Tellus-UPM Ecosystem.

sustainability [21, 22], incorporating it in the objectives and goals of each project, with actions such as the reuse of components, approaches to electronic designs and scalable or interchangeable parts between prototypes to reduce waste, selective re-cycling of waste, reduction of the use of paper and single-use plastics, designs that minimize the materials needed in their manufacture, prototypes with low energy consumption or the use of environmentally certified electronic components. In turn, UESEVI provides a teaching space and facilitates student engagement through collaboration in its credit-bearing activities, such as "Entrepreneurship and Social Innovation: Interethics and Values". In this course, students learn how to utilize low-cost technologies like Arduino or Raspberry Pi, as well as web content management systems like WordPress, to support their projects. Additionally, it serves as a platform for the completion of undergraduate and postgraduate final projects [23–25] allowing the transfer of the knowledge acquired, in an adapted manner, to the students. The central methodologies of the system that set the guidelines for action are mainly those known as "Learning by Doing", in which students learn by doing and developing their ideas, and ApS or Service-Learning, which combines learning and community service processes in a single project in which participants are trained to work on real needs of the environment with the aim of improving it. Finally,

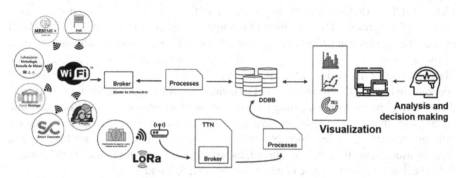

Fig. 2. Conceptual diagram of the Tellus IoT platform.

one of the objectives of this proposal is to achieve a communication adapted to the different actors in society, so scientific contributions are made through articles and papers at conferences, dissemination in seminars and technical conferences and dissemination through the use of social networks such as Twitter and TikTok, as well as face-to-face activities, such as the workshop "Make your first mini environmental station" proposed on the occasion of the Science and Innovation Week 2023, organized by the Foundation for Knowledge (Madrid + d).

1.4 Hypothesis: 3D Printing as a Pillar of Innovation in the Tellus UPM Ecosystem

In academia and research, the potential of 3D printing is immense [26–28], this reality highlighted the need to integrate digital printing technologies in the ETSIME-UPM, putting them at the service of the university community. As of 2020, this recognition began to materialize with the creation of the ETSIME-UPM FabLab, equipped with specialized 3D printing equipment, a process that gained significant momentum during the pandemic and played a crucial role in supporting projects such as CanarIoT [29], whose primary objective was to strengthen environmental security measures on the university campus, thus contributing to transforming the university into a safer space.

FabLabs are integral to engineering education, promoting hands-on learning that is intimately connected with digitalization and the advancement of new technologies. These labs allow for the practical application of theoretical knowledge, offering a holistic education that ranges from ideation to prototype production. Utilizing modern tools and techniques as if 3D printing not only deepens understanding and problem-solving abilities but also equips future engineers with the skills to navigate a dynamic professional landscape. This educational strategy, merging theoretical learning with practical experience, is essential for cultivating critical digital-era skills such as analytical thinking, inventiveness, and innovation [30, 31]. Tellus UPM, as seen in the previous points, has recognized the value of 3D printing by incorporating it thanks to the collaboration with the FabLab ETSIME-UPM. Within the challenges that the ecosystem addresses such as the monitoring of environmental variables in cities and subway spaces, as exemplified by the project "Applicability of low-cost sensors for environmental monitoring of particle immission levels" (MANIP) and "Monitoring of Underground Spaces of the ETSIME-UPM" (MESEME), the improvement of the management of green spaces as is the case of the project "Digitalization of urban green spaces in a world 4.0" (DEVUM) [32] or the digitization of tests performed on concrete specimens in laboratories such as the one carried out in collaboration with the Laboratorio Oficial para Ensayos de Materiales de Construcción (LOEMCO) [33], 3D printing emerges as an effective and economical tool for the advancement of innovative solutions. This technology improves the quality of prototypes, including the fabrication of suitable containers for electronic components that must be resistant, adaptable to heritage environments and scalable for different projects, allowing microcontrollers and sensors to have a longer lifetime and their measurements to remain unaltered, as well as the creation of customized parts to hold specific components, as can be seen in Figs. 4, 5, 6 and 7.

Thanks to this laboratory, students and professionals have access to digital fabrication tools with which to transform a theoretical concept into a physical model in a matter of hours, thus accelerating the iteration process, This accelerates the process of iteration, refinement and validation of solutions and enhances their training as shown by teaching activities developed in the framework of the Educational Innovation Projects of the UPM as is the case of the project "Implementation of FabLabs in the Engineering Studies of ETSIME-UPM" that trains students in a practical way in design and 3D printing in various subjects, including challenges from different areas of knowledge, not only improving the training but also the motivation and active participation of students [34].

2 Materials and Methods

These equipment and materials allow FabLab ETSIME-UPM to offer customized solutions to a wide range of projects, from rapid prototyping to the manufacture of high quality final parts. The variety and adaptability of these tools make the 3D printing process an essential component in Tellus UPM's innovation ecosystem.

2.1 3D Printing Equipment and Technologies at FabLab UPM

Currently, the main core of the laboratory is made up of printers based on Fused Deposition Modeling (FDM) or Fused Filament Fabrication (FFF) technology, chosen for

Table 1. Main characteristics of the 3D printers of the FabLab ETSIME-UPM.

Feature/Model	XYZ Da Vinci Pro 3 in 1	Creality CR-10 PRO	Tumaker NX Pro	Abax Titan 500	CoLiDo D1315 Plus	Creality Ender 3 PRO
Printing Volume (L × W × H)	200 × 200 × 200 mm	300 × 300 × 400 mm	295 × 185 × 200 mm	310 × 310 × 500 mm	DIA - 130 × 150 mm	220 × 220 × 250 mm
Layer Resolution	0.02–0.4 mm	0.01 mm	Variant according to nozzle	Up to 50 micros	0.05 mm	0.1–0.35 mm
Filament Material	PLA, ABS, PETG, HIPS, etc	TPU, PA	Various (TPU, PLA, ABS, etc.)	PLA, ASA, PETG, Nylon, etc	PLA	PLA, ABS, PETG, Flexible
Maximum Extrusor Temperature (°C)	240	300	300	265	–	255
Maximum Bed Temperature (°C)	40–90	100	100	120	–	110
Extrusion Type	FDM/FFF	FDM/FFF	FDM/FFF	FDM/FFF	FDM/FFF	FDM/FFF
Connectivity	USB 2.0, Wi-Fi	SD, USB	Wifi, Micro SD, Ethernet	SD, USB	USB	SD card, USB cable
Printer dimensions (L × W × H)	468 × 558 × 510 mm	550 × 490 × 650 mm	550 × 440 × 410 mm	582 × 555 × 885 mm	281 × 254 × 466 mm	440 × 410 × 465 mm
Printer Weight (kg)	23 kg	14 kg	30 kg	40–50 kg	3.6 kg	10 kg
Nozzle	0.4 mm	0.4–1.0 mm	0.4–0.8 mm	0.2–1.2 mm (upon request)	0.4 mm	0.4–0.8 mm

being one of the most prominent pillars in the world of 3D printing. As a detail, we can see the particular specifications of our configuration in Table 1.

Table 2. Main software available at FabLab ETSIME-UPM.

Software	Stage of Use	Committed
Ultimaker Cura	Laminated	Preparation of models for printing, generating the necessary G-code for FDM machines
Autodesk Fusion 360	CAD Design	3D modeling and simulation for part, tool and assembly design
AutoCAD	CAD Design	Architectural and engineering oriented 2D and 3D design
SketchUp	CAD Design	Graphic design and 3D modeling that allows users to create visualize and modify models in a three-dimensional environment user-friendly interface and high integration capabilities, with other tools and services. In addition, it has an extensive library of models called "3D Warehouse"
Proprietary Software	Laminating/CAD Design	Specific software provided by manufacturers of 3D printers to optimize printing on your machines

The starting point for any 3D printed part is a digital model, conceived using 3D modeling software. Throughout this process, various software applications play a fundamental role in the design and preparation phases for printing. Table 2 presents the main applications and features of the software available at FabLab ETSIME-UPM.

2.2 Materials Used in the 3D Printing Process

The quality and efficiency of a 3D print depends on both the technology used and the material selected. It is essential to choose a material that supports the desired durability, strength and functionality of the printed object.

Several materials stand out in FDM/FFF 3D printing due to their unique characteristics and versatile applications, here are some of the most commonly used:

ABS, a tough, flexible thermoplastic, is widely used in the production of automotive components and appliance housings. It is capable of withstanding extreme temperatures and is recyclable and amenable to chemical welding. It is therefore the material with which to scale parts that have already been tested and are to be subjected to increased wear and tear.

PLA, on the other hand, is appreciated for its ease of printing, does not emit harmful gases during printing and has minimal shrinkage once printed. This makes it ideal for prototypes, allowing the creation of a larger number of versions with which to incorporate improvements quickly at reduced costs.

ASA and PET are similar materials to ABS, but differ in key aspects: ASA has a higher resistance to ultraviolet radiation, so when project parts must be exposed to the elements for long periods, its resistance is essential to ensure its durability, and PET is suitable for applications involving contact with food.

2.3 Integration of 3D Printing in Tellus UPM Ecosystem Projects

It aims to optimize the use of this technology in academic and research contexts. Initially, a phase of identification of the needs and goals of the project is carried out, determining in which phases 3D printing can be beneficial.

The stages of 3D printing applied in the development of Tellus UPM projects in the FabLab ETSIME-UPM are described in Fig. 3.

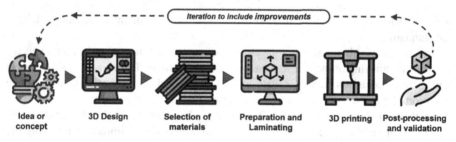

Fig. 3. Stages of the component 3D printing process.

Idea or Concept: Before the modeling phase, a conceptual design process is carried out to define the form, function and characteristics of the object to be printed.

3D Design: Using 3D modeling software, a digital model of the object is created. If you want to replicate an existing object, 3D scanners can be used to obtain an accurate digital model.

Material Selection: Depending on the application and the printer, a suitable material is chosen (PLA, ABS, specials, etc.). Each material has different properties in terms of strength, flexibility and melting temperature.

Preparation and Lamination: Once you have the 3D model, you need to export it to a format that the 3D printer can interpret, usually in STL or OBJ format. After that, the 3D model is divided into horizontal layers and printing parameters such as layer thickness, fill type, printing speed, material temperature and support structure if necessary are set.

Printing: Depositing or fusing material layer by layer to build the object.

Post-processing and Validation: Improving the appearance or properties of the object and pre-testing to ensure proper performance.

3   Results and Discussion

In the following section, we will apply the methodology outlined in the previous section to several of the projects we have developed, in order to illustrate their effectiveness and applicability in practical contexts. This discussion will allow us to closely examine the results obtained and ponder their significance in the advancement of this area of study.

3.1   Smart Heritage Project ETSIME-UPM

The ETSIME-UPM, founded in Almadén in 1777 and moved to Madrid in 1893, has a valuable collection of approximately 10,000 documents dating from the sixteenth century to the first half of the twentieth century, stored in the Historical Library of the ETSIME-UPM. Due to the deterioration of part of this collection due to the passage of time and inappropriate storage, the company Titanio Estudio was commissioned to evaluate the condition of the collection and its facilities, which led to the development of a Preventive Conservation Plan between 2019 and 2020 [35], which establishes guidelines, protocols and actions for its preservation, in accordance with national and international guidelines and standards.

In support of this plan, it has developed a line of work to respond to the need for real-time monitoring of the storage spaces of the collections. The objective is to support management decisions based on data and alerts, as well as to have a history of the evolution of the spaces for the analysis of future improvement actions.

To this end, a system based on IoT technology has been developed that enables this dialogue with the infrastructures without causing any aesthetic impact or affecting the performance of the Library's normal activities. This system makes heritage spaces, technology and environmental management compatible, minimizing their impact as shown in Fig. 4(4).

At this point, 3D printing brings its greatest value to the project. Thanks to the use of special PLA filament, made from wood fibers (40%) and the binding polymer [36], a wood-like surface finish and texture is recreated (Fig. 4(2)). This effect can be enhanced with temperature modifications during printing to generate a grain effect. In this way, the full integration of the prototypes in heritage spaces is achieved.

In addition, the flexibility in the design, thanks to the different 3D modeling software available, allows the electronic components to be distributed in such a way that they occupy the smallest possible size, are adequately cooled and minimize the alteration of

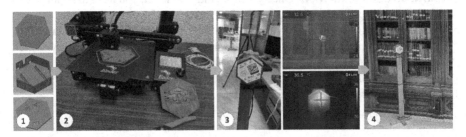

Fig. 4. Integration of 3D printing in the Smart Heritage ETSIME-UPM project.

the measurements taken (Fig. 4(1)) and, based on various iterations of improvement, the result of the tests performed on the prototypes, among which their thermal behavior is analyzed thanks to the use of thermographs and data sampling that are then compared with reference instruments (Fig. 4(3)).

3.2 CanarIoT Project

The CanarIoT project has been designed with the essential purpose of optimizing safety and health in university spaces. Inspired by the preventive utility of canaries in old mines, this "Canary 4.0" focuses its innovation on real-time monitoring of CO_2 levels and thermal comfort, contributing significantly, in time, to the prevention of COVID-19 infections and to the general improvement of air quality.

Based on reports from the Spanish Ministry of Health [37] and Science [38], together with numerous scientific studies, CanarIoT recognizes the transmission of the virus through aerosols in poorly ventilated spaces. These collective reports emphasize the need to monitor CO_2 concentrations to ensure adequate ventilation [39–44], preserve thermal comfort, maintain users' cognitive abilities and optimize energy efficiency.

It is essential to underline the contribution of 3D printing technology through the use of the FabLab ETSIME-UPM as a design and manufacturing center (Fig. 5(1)) of customized protective housings for these devices, were manufactured using mainly standard PLA filament, customized with the representative colors of ETSIME- UPM (Fig. 5(2)). Through successive tests with prototypes (Fig. 5(4)), significant improvements have been incorporated in areas such as resistance, ventilation and monitoring optimization. This iterative process has facilitated rapid adaptation, essential given the health emergency caused by the COVID-19 pandemic, something that would not have been possible without 3D printing technology (Fig. 5(3)).

Fig. 5. Integration of 3D printing in the CanarIoT-UPM project.

In addition to allowing modularity and adaptability to also protect the historical interior spaces of great use and importance in a university, such as the Cloister and the Student Library, developing a specific solution that dialogued with these heritage spaces by mimicking part of the existing architecture (Sects. 1 and 2 of Fig. 6) and also adapting its appearance in a very realistic way to the materials present, being the choice for the marble type PLA filament for the Library [45]. And in the case of the choice of filament for the Cloister, the same filament was chosen as in the case of the Smart Heritage ETSIME- UPM project, as the requirements were similar (Sects. 3 and 4 of Fig. 6).

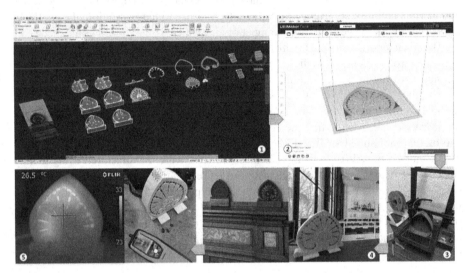

Fig. 6. Integration of 3D printing in the CanarIoT-UPM project in heritage spaces.

3.3 Digitalization of Urban Green Spaces Project (DEVUM)

It addresses the imperative need for adaptation and transformation in the context of the digital industrial revolution and the growing concern for the environment. Situated at the confluence of Social Responsibility, the Sustainable Development Goals (SDGs) and contemporary ethical demands, this project focuses on the synergy between universities, industry and society, promoting research and experimentation on university campuses to address the challenges of the future.

The initiative recognizes the importance of understanding the complexities of the urban environment, particularly the environmental dynamics that are strongly influenced by human interventions. Growing environmental concerns, such as the "heat island" effect in metropolises, underscore the relevance of technological solutions in the management and conservation of urban green spaces. Through the adoption of IoT technology, for which it incorporates as main control electronics an Arduino 1300 MKR [46], environmental sensors such as the BME680 (temperature, humidity, barometric pressure and volatile organic compound (VOC) content sensor) [47] and the LTR390 (real light sensor in the UV spectrum) [48] and long distance communication systems such as LoRa [49, 50]. The project aims to establish a modular monitoring network to support conventional networks. This technological integration aims to enable an agile dialogue between technology, humanity and the environment, marking a milestone in the sustainable management and conservation of urban green heritage.

The starting point was a conceptualization of the sensors that this system might need to be able to mount (Fig. 7(1)). Next, a design was made of the parts that would be necessary to carry these sensors and connectors to give consistency to the device (Fig. 7(2)), a standard PLA was selected for the prototype that would allow rapid prototyping at a low cost (Fig. 7(3)), which once validated would be replaced by a material resistant to weathering and UV rays of the ASA type [51]. After which, it was post-processed and assembled (Fig. 7(4)) and the necessary tests were carried out to validate it under real conditions through periodic analyses that included thermography and comparative data sampling against reference instrumentation (Fig. 7(5)).

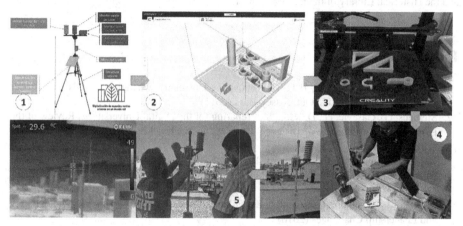

Fig. 7. Integration of 3D printing in the DEVUM project.

4   Conclusions

The implementation of 3D printing in the university environment has proven to be an essential tool, endowed with a wide range of applications and advantages. This technology stands as a nexus between innovation, education and practical materialization. By enabling the conversion of digital ideas into physical entities, it provides students and researchers with a powerful means for research, innovation and tackling real challenges.

Among the key conclusions derived from these projects, accelerated prototyping stands out, since 3D printing allows researchers and students to create designs in an agile and adaptive manner according to research needs. Furthermore, the cost-benefit ratio is remarkably efficient, enabling the creation of affordable prototypes in short series with minimal investment. The versatility of 3D printing also favors customization, adapting to the specificities of university spaces. One of its outstanding attributes is its interdisciplinary nature, promoting collaboration between different areas of knowledge and stimulating applied learning and the development of digital skills, which are essential in today's engineering degrees. This methodology fosters innovation, allows continuous optimization of processes and solutions to identified challenges. Additionally, these projects promote sustainability, addressing environmental and social challenges and raising awareness of the actions taken. In short, the adoption of this technology in education prepares students for the demands of the modern professional world, equipping them with the skills to face emerging challenges.

Acknowledgments. We would like to acknowledge and thank the following entities for their funding and support to the seed projects that are the subject of this study: the Sustainable UPM RES2+U program, the CEPSA Foundation Chair through the II Call for grants for research projects on Energy and Environment in the ETSIME-UPM, and the UPM ApS Call. In addition, we are grateful for the collaboration of the EELISA-ESCE community of the UPM, Spanish Environmental Club (CEMA), LOEMCO, Testing and Calibration Laboratory of the ETSIME-UPM (LECEM-T) and the Historical Library of the ETSIME-UPM.

References

1. Christensen, C.M., Eyring, H.J.: The Innovative University: Changing the DNA of Higher Education from the Inside Out. Jossey-Bass (2011)
2. Siemens, G., Gašević, D., Dawson, S.: Preparing for the Digital University: A Review of the History and Current State of Distance, Blended, and Online Learning. LINK Research Lab (2015)
3. Barnett, R.: Imagining the University. Routledge, New York (2013)
4. Duderstadt, J.J.: The Future of the Public University in America: Beyond the Crossroads (2014)
5. Goddard, J., Hazelkorn, E., Kempton, L., Vallance, P. (eds.): The Civic University: The Policy and Leadership Challenges (2016)
6. Bessant, J., Tidd, J.: Innovation and Entrepreneurship (2015)
7. Mota, C.: The rise of personal fabrication. In: Proceedings of the 8th ACM Conference on Creativity and Cognition, pp. 279–288 (2011)
8. Blikstein, P.: Digital fabrication and 'making' in education: the democratization of invention. In: FabLabs: Of Machines, Makers and Inventors, pp. 203–221. Transcript Verlag (2013)
9. Gershenfeld, N.: FAB: The Coming Revolution on Your Desktop-From Personal Computers to Personal Fabrication. Basic Books (2005)
10. Mikhak, B., Lyon, C., Gorton, T., Gershenfeld, N., McEnnis, C., Taylor, J.: Fab lab: an alternate model of ICT for development. Development **2**(1), 1–5 (2002)
11. García Pedregal, D.: Desarrollo y estudio de un prototipo modular para la monitorización ambiental basado en tecnología IoT. Trabajo Fin de Grado, ETSIME-UPM (2023)
12. Villa Morán, D.: Monitorización de Partículas PM10 y PM2,5: Evaluación de sensores de Bajo Costó en Ambientes Controlados. Trabajo Fin de Grado, ETSIST-UPM (2023)
13. Presa, L., Rodriguez, J.A., Maroto, J., Martín, D.A., Costafreda, J.L., Álvarez, P.: Monitorización del tiempo de fraguado de probetas de hormigón mediante sensores de temperatura. Póster presentado en el 3er Congreso Anual Internacional de Estudiantes de Doctorado, Universidad Miguel Hernández (2023)

14. Walter-Herrmann, J., Büching, C. (eds.): FabLabs: Of Machines, Makers, and Inventors. Transcript Publishers, Bielefeld (2013)
15. Ecosistema Tellus UPM. https://blogs.upm.es/tellus/
16. Universidad Politécnica de Madrid. El PAS es un eslabón de la comunidad universitaria que en muchas ocasiones presenta un potencial oculto (2023, 16 de marzo). https://www.upm. es/?id=d84de9e7a34e6810VgnVCM10000009c7648a____&prefmt=articulo&fmt=detail
17. Maciá Pérez, F., Berná Martínez, J.V., Sánchez Bernabéu, J.M., Lorenzo Fonseca, I., Fuster Guilló, A.: Smart university: hacia una universidad más abierta. Marcombo (2016)
18. Rodríguez Rama, J.A., García Laso, A., Martín Sanchez, D.A., Maroto Lorenzo, J., García de la Noceda, C., Moraño Rodríguez, A.J.: AulaEnergía ETSIME-UPM: Un espacio colaborativo de difusión, formación tecnológica y desarrollo de la energía: Geotermia. En "GeoEner 2017: IV Congreso de Energía Geotérmica en la Edificación y la Industria", pp. 134–143. Madrid (2017)
19. Rodríguez Rama, J.A., Martín, S.D.A., García, L.A., Maroto, L.J., Godoy, M.C.: Monitorización de espacios urbanos, como herramienta educativa para el apoyo en el cumplimiento de los Objetivos de Desarrollo Sostenible para una Smart University. En Efficient, Sustainable, and Fully Comprehensive Smart Cities. II Ibero-American Congress of Smart Cities (ICSC-CITIES 2019), p. 306 (2019). ISBN 978-958-5583-78-8
20. Kitchin, R.: The Data Revolution: Big Data, Open Data, Data Infrastructures and their Consequences. Sage (2014)
21. IPCC, 2023. Sections. In: Core Writing Team, Lee, H., Romero, J. (eds.). Climate Change 2023: Synthesis Report. Contribution of Working Groups I, II and III to the Sixth Assessment Report of the Intergovernmental Panel on Climate Change, pp. 35–115. IPCC, Geneva (2023). https://doi.org/10.59327/IPCC/AR6-9789291691647
22. Naciones Unidas. Agenda 2030 para el Desarrollo Sostenible. (2015). https://sdgs.un.org/2030agenda
23. Von Munthe Af Morgenstierne, Marina Asuero. Implementación de un techo verde en la ETSIME-UPM. Trabajo Fin de Grado, ETSIME-UPM (2021)
24. González Bescós, Ana. Calibración y trazabilidad de sensores de bajo coste. Caso de estudio: Proyecto MESEME. Trabajo Fin de Grado, ETSIME-UPM (2020)
25. Gordo Pérez, J.A.: Análisis de registros de temperatura con la Transformada de Hilbert-Huang y con redes neuronales. Trabajo Fin de Grado, ETSIME-UPM (2019)
26. Ventola, C.L.: Medical applications for 3D printing: current and projected uses. Pharm. Therapeut. 39(10), 704–711 (2014)
27. Wong, K.V., Hernandez, A.: A review of additive manufacturing. ISRN Mech. Eng. 2012, 208760 (2012)
28. Berman, B.: 3-D printing: the new industrial revolution. Bus. Horiz. 55(2), 155–162 (2012)
29. CanarIoT: proyecto de Internet de las Cosas para hacer de la universidad espacios más sostenibles y resilientes. Revista N° 6. e – Politécnica UPM. https://sostenibilidad.upm.es/eps06-etsime-canariot/
30. Alía, C., Ocaña, R., Caja, J., Maresca, P., Moreno-Díaz, C., Narbón, J.J.: Use of open manufacturing laboratories (Fab Labs) as a new trend in engineering education. Procedia Manufact. 41, 938–943 (2019). https://doi.org/10.1016/j.promfg.2019.10.018
31. Vasilescu, M.D., Ionel, I.: 3D printer FABLAB for students at POLITEHNICA University Timisoara. In: 2017 IEEE 17th International Conference on Advanced Learning Technologies (ICALT), Timisoara, pp. 512–513 (2017). https://doi.org/10.1109/ICALT.2017.106
32. Rodíguez Rama, J.A.: Digitalización de espacios verdes urbanos en un mundo 4.0. En Libro de abstracts del Congreso Anual Internacional de Estudiantes de Doctorado (CAIED). Editorial Electrónica de la Universidad Miguel Hernández de Elche (2023)
33. Álvarez Hervás, Paloma. Transformación digital aplicado en los laboratorios de ensayo: Smart Concrete. Trabajo Fin de Grado, ETSIME-UPM (2023)

34. Barrio-Parra, F., et al.: Proceedings of the Implementation of FabLabs in the Mines and Energy Engineering Studies, pp. 6446–6454 (2020)
35. Plan de Conservación Preventiva de la Biblioteca Histórica de la ETSIME-UPM. Titanio Estudio (2019–2020)
36. PLA Madera. Addnorth. https://filament2print.com/es/madera-piedra/1494-pla-madera-addnorth.html
37. Evaluación del riesgo de transmisión de SARS-CoV-2 mediante aerosoles. Medidas de Prevención y recomendaciones. Ministerio de Sanidad. (18 de noviembre de 2020)
38. Informe Científico sobre vías de transmisión de SARS-CoV-2. Informe para el Ministerio de Ciencia e Innovación de España. (29 de octubre de 2020)
39. Prather, K.A., et al.: Airborne transmission of SARS-CoV-2. Science 70, 303–304 (2020)
40. Editors of Nature. Coronavirus is in the air—there's too much focus on surfaces. Nature (24 de febrero de 2021)
41. Editors of Clinical Infectious Diseases (F.C. Fang et al.): COVID-19—lessons learned and questions remaining. Clin. Infect. Dis. ciaa1654 (2020)
42. US National Academies of Sciences Engineering and Medicine. Airborne Transmission of SARS-CoV-2: Proceedings of a Workshop in Brief. The National Academies Press, Washington, D.C. (2020)
43. Roadmap to improve and ensure good indoor ventilation in the context of COVID-19. Organización Mundial de la Salud (1 de marzo de 2021)
44. Plataforma Aireamos. https://www.aireamos.org/documentacion/
45. PLA i3D Tested Efecto Mármol. https://www.impresoras3d.com/producto/pla-efecto-marmol-impresoras3d-com-1-75-mm/
46. Arduino. (n.d.). MKR WAN 1300. https://docs.arduino.cc/hardware/mkr-wan-1300
47. Sensor Adafruit BME680. https://learn.adafruit.com/adafruit-bme680-humidity-temperature-barometic-pressure-voc-gas
48. Sensor Adafruit LTR390. https://learn.adafruit.com/adafruit-ltr390-uv-sensor
49. Augustin, A., Yi, J., Clausen, T., Townsley, W.M.: A study of LoRa: long range & low power networks for the internet of things. Sensors 16(9), 1466 (2016)
50. Bor, M., Vidler, J., Roedig, U.: LoRa for the internet of things. In: 2016 International Conference on Embedded Wireless Systems and Networks, pp. 361–366. Junction Publishing (2016, June)
51. Filamento ASA FormFutura. https://www.impresoras3d.com/producto/apollox-negro-asa-175-mm/

Innovative Compression Plus Confusion Scheme for Digital Images Used in Smart Cities

J. A. Aboytes-González[1,2] , E. Ibarra-Olivares[2] , M. T. Ramírez-Torres[3] ,
G. Gallegos-García[2]([✉]) , and P. J. Escamilla-Ambrosio[2]

[1] Universidad Politécnica de San Luis Potosí, San Luis Potosí, Mexico
`agustin.aboytes@upslp.edu.mx`
[2] Instituto Politécnico Nacional, Centro de Investigación en Computación, Ciudad de México, Mexico
`{eibarrao2023,ggallegos,pescamilla}@cic.ipn.mx`
[3] Universidad Autónoma de San Luis Potosí, Coordinación Académica Región Altiplano Oeste, San Luis Potosí, Mexico
`tulio.torres@uaslp.mx`

Abstract. In the context of smart cities, where the deployment of surveillance systems and security cameras is becoming increasingly ubiquitous, the efficient management of digital images and their confidentiality has become a critical challenge. In this work, we present an innovative scheme which considers two components: compressive sensing and S-Boxes for image compression and confusion property in the Shannon's information theory context, respectively. The integration of these two building blocks provides a comprehensive solution for the efficient and secure transmission of image data in urban environments. Our scheme expands the compressed image into a 24-bit RGB image and uses three S-Boxes to replace the information of each color channel. One of the new features is that the S-Boxes evolve based on a key. In this sense, the scheme offers a solution for smart cities aiming to optimize the management of digital image data and simultaneously achieving the security of transmitted information. The processed images have been analyzed, and obtained to show that our scheme brings perceptual and cryptographic security to digital images, without compromising the recovered image. Its implementation can significantly contribute to efficiency and security, in the use of surveillance cameras in modern urban environments of smart cities.

Keywords: Compressive sensing · S-Boxes · Smart cities

1 Introduction

Today, the widespread use of smartphones and other types of smart devices has made digital images one of the most important information exchange formats

Supported by SIP-IPN and CONAHCYT.

S. Nesmachnow and L. Hernández Callejo (Eds.): ICSC-Cities 2023, CCIS 1938, pp. 277–290, 2024.
https://doi.org/10.1007/978-3-031-52517-9_19

in the daily life of people. Likewise, the development and design of smart cities demand the use of surveillance cameras in buildings and vehicles, transmitting and storing images and videos. These images can contain sensitive information of different types, such as national security, some particular legal affairs, and/or medical. Hence, according to [27], the unplanned exposure of private images or photos accentuates the importance of image security.

The paradigm of encryption of any type of image, including videos, has its implementation requirements mainly due to its intrinsic characteristics, for example, a bulk data capacity and high redundancy [19]. On the one hand, as the bandwidth in communication channels is increasing, a new challenge arises, as cryptographic solutions must keep up with the large amount of information that should be protected. In addition to that, transmitting large amounts of information needs a form of compression for efficiency. For this, compressive sensing is a technique that has gained significant interest due to its capability to realize simultaneous sampling and compression. It requires a lower sampling frequency than the Nyquist frequency [12] and has been employed in wireless communications and other applications, as magnetic resonance imaging and image classification, among others [9,10,26].

Furthermore, substitution boxes, known as S-Boxes, are a fundamental element in symmetric encryption algorithms, achieving confusion of data in the Shannon's theory context. Their purpose is to substitute blocks of a specified size, making a non-linear substitution. To design and obtain these boxes, there are several methods [23], which are based on different approaches. Taking a step further in substitution boxes, there are the so-called dynamic substitution boxes, which allow the generation or use of multiple substitution boxes within an encryption algorithm. This enables algorithms to have a less predictable behavior since, with fixed substitution boxes, attackers could have a clue about the encryption process.

Therefore, in this research, we are proposing a scheme that combines both techniques, compressive sensing and substitution boxes. This proposal, in a numerical implementation, shows a good performance in its initial stage and achieves a satisfactory level of recovery of the compressed image. The confusion quality is measured using various statistical tests, which leads us to conclude that it is an appeal proposal for using in images. Furthermore, since the compression stage can help to save memory and bandwidth, this scheme could be used in smart cities in their video surveillance service. The article is structured as follows: Sect. 2 discusses the related works concerning the proposed scheme. Section 3 provides an overview of the background. Sections 4 and 5 introduce the proposal and the results of its statistical analysis in different tests. Lastly, Sect. 6 presents a discussion and a brief conclusion to this work.

2 Related Work

Different works have been proposed in the context of mixing compressive sensing and the design of S-Boxes to reduce the amount of data that needs to be encrypted while still ensuring security. Such works can be divided into symmetric and asymmetric techniques.

In the symmetric setting, the work in [24] presents a proposal for digital images that considers two algorithms. The first one focuses on scrambling and the other one to have two-way diffusion, both of them to encrypt a measured value matrix. The work in [4] pays attention in the measurement matrix, which is generated using a three-dimensional chaotic system. For further encryption, the paper proposes a pixel scrambling process by using a one-dimensional chaotic system to generate a scrambling vector. In [15], the authors achieve a good performance of image compression by 2D sparse recovery. The sparse representation is scrambled by using chaotic confusion. The work in [21] proposes a new 1D-chaotic map that is used to construct an incoherence rotated chaotic measurement matrix. The linear measurements obtained are confused and diffused using the chaotic sequence generated using the proposed map. In [8], a proposal for simultaneous image encryption and compression is presented. The authors propose using different techniques such as: compressed sensing considering a structurally random matrix and permutation-diffusion architecture for encryption. In addition, a three-dimensional cat map is introduced for key stream generation. The work in [13] combines compressed sensing and Secret Image Sharing (SIS) to propose a certifiable visually secure image selection encryption. To distinguish and encrypt the information of the plain image, a selective encryption based on a multi-task convolutional neural network is used. Finally, the work in [28] proposes an image encryption algorithm based on compressive sensing and information-hiding technology. The authors use the discrete wavelet transform to sparse the plain image. Then, a confusion operation on pixel positions is made using a logistic-tent map to produce a confusion sequence.

In the asymmetric setting, we can find the references [16,17]. In [16] a new improved 3-dimensional continuous chaotic system is designed, which is used to propose a double image encryption algorithm based on compressive sensing and an elliptic curve cryptographic construction. In [17] an image encryption algorithm based on compressive sensing and integer wavelet transformation is proposed. The RSA algorithm is considered to encrypt the initial values of the chaotic system. The proposed algorithm is resistant to known-plaintext attacks and chosen-plaintext attacks.

3   Compressive Sensing and S-Boxes

As mentioned earlier, in the context of smart cities, the role of images in facilitating information exchange among residents is significant. To enhance their quality of life, the introduction of advanced algorithms for image applications is crucial. In the absence of a secure method for sharing images, the well-being and privacy of residents may be compromised. Therefore, ensuring a secure and efficient transmission of images remains a critical aspect for the development of smart cities [18]. Compressive sensing and S-boxes are two building blocks that seem to be useful to ensure image transmission.

3.1   Compressive Sensing

Compressive Sensing (CS) [5,7] is an innovative method of acquiring signals, which surpasses the limitations of the traditional Shannon-Nyquist theory by merging signal sampling and data compression. It can be likened to a symmetric cryptography encryption model and was initially introduced as a significant advancement in signal processing. The research in [6] demonstrates that a sparse or compressible signal can be accurately computed using specific reconstruction algorithms, as discussed in subsequent studies [5,11,14].

Consider x as a signal to be detected $x \in R^{N \times 1}$. As per the principles of Compressive Sensing (CS), the signal x needs to exhibit sparsity or compressibility on an orthogonal basis $\psi \in R^{N \times N}$. The CS measurement is conducted using the matrix $\phi \in R^{M \times N}$, leading to a measurement outcome $y \in R^{M \times 1}$. Expressible as $y = \phi x = \phi \psi' \theta = A\theta$, where $A \in R^{M \times N}$ denotes the sensing or recovery matrix. The measurement count M is associated with K. The data compression is accomplished due to the condition $M \ll N$.

In this sense, we can say CS is capable of recovering the original signal x from y. It is possible given that the transformation of the signal x (i.e., θ) is K-sparse or K-compressible, θ can be restored from $\hat{\theta} = argmin \parallel \theta \parallel_0$, subject to $y = A\theta$. The minimization of $\parallel \theta \parallel_0$ represents a classical L_0 problem. Since the L_0-norm function is non-convex, non-smooth, discontinuous, and globally non-differentiable, solving $min \parallel \theta \parallel_0$ is challenging. In practice, it can be approximated as an L_1 problem, i.e., $min \parallel \theta \parallel_1$.

The concept of CS-Based Encryption was initially introduced in [20], which leverages the stochastic properties of the Gauss matrix to achieve data confidentiality.

3.2   S-Box

An S-Box plays a crucial role in contemporary block encryption algorithms, facilitating the creation of encrypted text from any given plaintext. Integrating an S-Box into an encryption algorithm results in a non-linear mapping between input and output data, introducing the confusion property from the Shannon's theory context [3]. The effectiveness of the S-Box in a block cipher's security is directly correlated with the level of confusion it creates. Consequently, in many block encryption algorithms, the strength against potential attacks depends significantly on the security provided by one or more S-Boxes. While these algorithms might incorporate various components, an S-Box typically serves as the sole non-linear component enhancing the security of sensitive data [25].

4   Our Innovative Image Compression Plus Confusion Scheme

Our scheme was designed with consideration of two key components: Compressive Sensing (CS) and S-Boxes. The incorporation of S-Boxes aims to add another layer of security to enhance the scheme in terms of processing and storage capacity. Our intention in employing S-Boxes to protect CS data is to minimize the increase in computational cost.

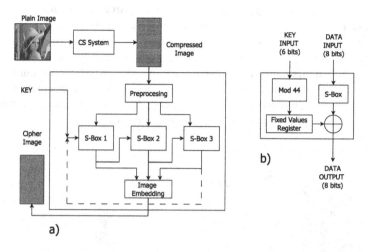

Fig. 1. a). Phases of our innovative image compression plus confusion scheme, b). S-Box module architecture.

The design of our scheme in its confusion building block was carried out in three phases. First, the information was adjusted for processing through the S-Boxes; subsequently, the property of confusion was introduced to the information, and finally, the storage of the data. Figure 1(a) illustrates our proposed scheme. The initial block, labeled 'CS System' represents the compression scheme used, with its output serving as input for our confusion scheme. In the first phase, the preprocessing block adjusts the information. Outputs from this block enter the S-Boxes section, introducing confusion into the information. The S-Boxes used in our design are enhanced versions of an S-Box modified by a correction algorithm using basic operations. The structure of these S-Boxes is shown in Fig. 1(b). Finally, all outputs from the S-Boxes converge in the storage block, utilizing the structure of an RGB image and generating an output image that integrates both compression and security layers.

This approach not only strengthens the security and confidentiality of data but also ensures efficient information processing, creating a comprehensive and effective scheme for image compression and protection.

4.1   Preprocessing Phase

To support our proposal, we conducted a comprehensive statistical study of the values present in various images resulting from the CS scheme. The results indicated that the values were limited in the range of -700 to 700 for the analyzed images, with an average value of -0.575. Based on these findings, the first step is to preprocess the information to give it a proper structure, enabling its treatment with S-Boxes as a traditional image using 8-bit blocks.

To illustrate this action, we take the output image of the CS scheme as an example, as seen in Fig. 2(a), where it is apparent that this image is not perceptible or identifiable. However, it exhibits certain patterns that an attacker could exploit to compromise the security of the image. Observing its histogram shown in Fig. 2(b), we note that indeed the pixel values of the output images from the CS scheme fall within the range of -700 to 700. Furthermore, the histogram reveals that a significant number of pixels are concentrated on the range of -1 to 1. Therefore, failing to process these values correctly poses the risk of losing crucial information for recovering the original data.

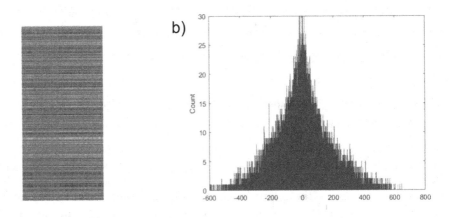

Fig. 2. a). Output image of the CS technique, b). Histogram of the output image.

When handling both high and small values within a single image, the challenge lies in finding a method to standardize the information without losing details for image retrieval. The proposal involves using the RGB image format, which consists of 3 channels of 8 bits each. This implies that the value of a pixel in the output image of the CS scheme must be converted to a total of 24 bits. The best approach to this problem is to scale the information of each pixel by multiplying it by a high-value constant. In our case, the selected variable is $1E4$ or 10,000. This way, the image limits would change to $-7,000,000$ and $7,000,000$. For a small value, such as the mean of -0.575, when scaled, it would change to -5750. Since this number can be represented by multiples of 8 bits, no information would be lost when processing it with S-Boxes.

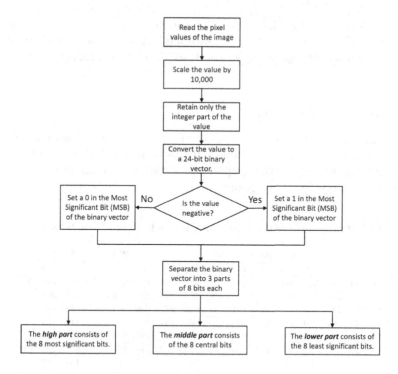

Fig. 3. Flowchart that illustrates the process of prepossessing the information.

In Fig. 3 we can see how the prepossessing phase works and in the first step when the image enters, the pixel values are obtained. The next step is to scale the information by multiplying pixel values by the proposed constant, 10,000. After scaling, the decimal part of the processed data will be removed. This scaling is crucial to prevent the loss of data, which would make it impossible to recover the original information. For example, if a pixel has a value of 0.002563, when scaled, the new value will be 25.63, and by removing the decimal data, the processed value will be 25. In our tests, with this amount of information, it is possible to recover the original image.

After scaling and removing the decimal part, the information is transformed into a 24-bit vector. The most significant bit is used to indicate the sign of the processed value: if the pixel values are negative, this bit has a value of 1, whereas if the value is positive, it is set to 0. The remaining bits represent the scaled pixel value. This number of bits is appropriate since the maximum value that can be represented with 23 bits is 16,777,215. Therefore, the operational range using the 24 bits is between −16,777,215 and 16,777,215, perfectly adapting to the scale of the data used in our proposal.

Finally, the 24-bit vector is divided into 3 subvectors of 8 bits each. These segments are denoted as the high, middle, and low parts, respectively. The 24-bit vector is partitioned as follows: the foremost 8 bits of the most significant segment are allocated to the high part subvector, the subsequent 8 bits are housed within the middle part subvector, and ultimately, the low part encapsulates the concluding 8 bits corresponding to the least significant segment of the 24-bit vector.

4.2 Substitution Bits Phase

In this phase we use the S-Box proposed in [1], which shows high resistance to cryptanalysis and is depicted in Table 1. It has been modified by the affine XOR operation to preserve its cryptographic properties and eliminate vulnerabilities such as fixed or reversed fixed points.

Table 1. Elements of the used S-Box in the form of a 16 × 16 matrix.

0	26	57	121	224	95	64	91	173	14	31	252	160	136	21	179
13	253	73	10	174	180	172	247	159	201	27	67	191	240	155	89
114	146	46	23	167	56	138	17	222	22	169	47	170	19	110	6
123	178	220	133	183	232	105	16	107	226	223	101	5	181	204	41
221	65	112	205	75	30	171	141	142	97	108	251	76	213	164	87
28	143	161	214	235	63	15	53	206	255	39	145	149	116	199	90
128	69	34	32	150	203	139	219	88	166	137	185	186	104	86	40
229	134	79	163	194	227	176	200	100	109	148	168	8	66	245	118
71	35	44	217	216	78	111	77	61	193	51	187	144	103	207	50
190	117	83	115	7	106	11	125	70	234	124	113	238	241	24	184
62	54	94	202	1	129	81	218	131	48	225	239	157	151	74	254
182	243	9	210	60	126	49	153	175	230	188	18	198	211	84	249
93	99	38	119	85	147	80	236	122	140	96	209	192	4	72	196
52	231	228	246	135	177	68	158	156	212	2	120	197	33	189	58
42	43	12	82	152	55	208	132	102	248	195	36	244	37	237	233
242	20	92	165	130	3	29	215	154	250	162	98	59	127	45	25

In our scheme, we use multiple S-Boxes by applying the method proposed in [2] to generate multiple variants from only one S-Box, ensuring that these variants do not have vulnerabilities. This is achieved by using simple logical and arithmetic operations, along with an affine value for each S-Box to be strengthened. For the case of S-Box described in [1], there are 44 affine values that strengthen the S-Box by removing fixed points and inverse fixed points without altering its cryptographic properties, using the XOR operation. These affine values will be stored in a register and will be used by achieving the use of 44 variants from the original S-Box. A list of these related values is shown in Table 2.

The substitution begins with an initial S-box and the lower part. However, the S-Box module will have 2 inputs: the first one, an 8-bit input that contains the data to be processed, and the second one, a 6-bit input where we will enter a value within the range from 0 to 43. It is depicted in Fig. 1(b). It is important to mention that the constant will be responsible for selecting one of the related values that will strengthen the S-Box.

Table 2. All the Fixed Values that enhanced the S-Box.

0	26	57	121	224	95	64	91	173	14	31
13	253	73	10	174	180	172	247	159	201	27
114	146	46	23	167	56	138	17	222	22	169
123	178	220	133	183	232	105	16	107	226	223

Its functionality is as follows: The 6-bit input value in the S-Box is used to select a register element containing the related values. In case such a value exceeds the valid range from 0 to 43, a modulo operation to 44, will be applied to bring it within the allowed range. Once selected, the XOR operation will be performed between each of the S-Box elements and the corresponding affine value. Later, this improved S-Box will process the 8-bit input block.

The next 8-bit block (middle part), corresponding to the central part of the original binary vector, will be processed by a new S-Box based in the initial one. The 8-bit input of this S-Box will handle the data block, while the 6-bit input will connect to the 6 LSBs of the output of the previous S-Box, following the same process. This process is shown in Fig. 1(a).

For the last data block (high part), composed of the 8 Most Significant Bits (MSBs) of the original block, the same procedure will be applied with a third S-Box. The only modification in this third S-Box is that the 6 LSBs of its output will be fed back to the 6-bit input of the first S-Box.

4.3 Storage Phase

After the three 8-bit blocks have been processed by the S-Boxes, the last step is to store them in an RGB image structure. The least significant block will be assigned to the red channel, the middle block to the green channel and finally the most significant block to the blue channel, it is shown in Fig. 4(b), Fig. 4(c) and Fig. 4(d), respectively. The result of our proposal is presented in Fig. 4(a). In Fig. 4(a), it is easy to see that the image does not show perceptible patterns of the original image (Fig. 2(a)), at least at first glance. This procedure is repeated for each pixel in the CS scheme output image.

4.4 Recovery Image Process

For the recovery process, the RGB image becomes input to the decoding block and is separated into its channels. Subsequently, the same steps are followed as the image processing phase, with the difference that the reverse S-Box is used to process the pixel data. Subsequently, the output of each S-Box is placed in the corresponding region of the 24-bit register, in which the red channel is in the least significant part, the green channel is in the central part, and the blue channel is in the most significant part. The number represented in this register is divided by $1E4$ to retrieve the pixel values and store them in an image similar to that original from the compression sensing technique. It can be seen in Fig. 2(b).

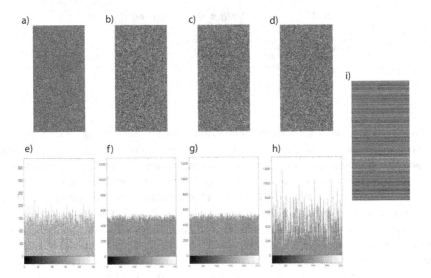

Fig. 4. a). Processed image, b). Red channel of the processed image, c). Green channel of the processed image, d). Blue channel of the processed image, e). Histogram of the processed image, f). Histogram of the red channel of the processed image, g). Histogram of the green channel of the processed image, h). Histogram of blue channel of the processed image, i). Recovery image from our proposal. (Color figure online)

In Fig. 4(i), the image recovered from our proposal is shown, and when is visually compared with the input image in our scheme Fig. 2(b), it can be seen that they are perceptually very similar.

5   Test and Results

To validate the security level of our innovative image compression plus confusion scheme, several tests were carried out. These tests include the analysis of histograms and calculation of entropy and correlation with the original image. All of this, considering the color channels that make up the processed image (Fig. 2(a)).

5.1   Histogram

The histogram analysis involves examining the pixel values of an image and creating a graph that shows how frequently these values occur. In plain-images, it is common to observe that some values tend to be repeated more frequently than others. Therefore, the ideal result of this test for images with a certain level of crypto-security is a uniformly distributed histogram, where all values appear the same number of times [22]. When analyzing the histogram of the image in RGB format Fig. 4(a) , we can see that it is not uniformly distributed.

Fig. 5. Recovery image from CS technique.

However, it does not show a clear trend towards any particular value, which can be considered a satisfactory result. If we examine the histograms of the red and green channels, they both show a uniform distribution, indicating a good level of security in these channels. On the other hand, when we look at the histogram of the blue channel, we notice that it is not uniform due to the presence of multiple peaks. However, like the RGB image histogram, it does not show a clear trend. Therefore, we can say that the security level of our innovative image compression plus confusion scheme is not optimal in this first version. However, the processed images do not reveal patterns of the original image, hence the scheme provides perceptual security.

5.2   Correlation and Entropy

As outlined by [22], the initial phase of statistical scrutiny involved an examination of the correlation between the output image generated by the CS technique and each channel of the processed image. The resultant correlation values, indicative of a discernible absence of correlation, are detailed in Table 3. Computed through Eq. 1, these results demonstrate correlation coefficients (r) consistently below zero, signaling an absence of correlations between the original and encrypted images.

$$r = \frac{N \sum XY - (\sum X \sum Y)}{\sqrt{[N \sum x^2 - (\sum x)^2][N \sum y^2 - (\sum y)^2]}} \tag{1}$$

The correlation coefficient, a crucial metric in statistical analysis, quantifies the strength of the linear relationship between two variables. In this context, it assesses the correlation between the pixels in the input image of our scheme and each channel of the output image.

Table 3. Results of correlation and entropy.

Test	Processed Image Channels			Output CS Scheme
	Red	Green	Blue	
Correlation	−0.0023	−0.000018	0.079	N/A
Entropy	7.999	7.999	5.408	4.726

For the second statistical metric, information entropy is employed to assess the unpredictability in the distribution of gray pixel values in an image. This metric is expressed through the following equation, in accordance with Shannon's theory:

$$H = -\sum_{k=0}^{n} P(r_k) \log_2 P(r_k) \tag{2}$$

where the term $P(r_k)$ represents the probability of symbol r occurring, and n signifies the total number of bits associated with each symbol. Theoretically, the entropy value of a randomly encrypted image is expected to be 8, considering a grayscale image with 256 symbols and 28 possible combinations for pixel data. The entropy values for the analyzed images are detailed in Table 3. Notably, in both the red and green channels, the resulting entropy value is approximately 7.999. This finding indicates that the proposed encryption scheme effectively introduces randomness to the pixel distribution of the original image, preventing attackers from deducing information about the original image based on its encrypted counterpart. However, it is important to say the entropy of the blue channel has a value of 5.408, which indicates that the information lacks disorder.

6   Discussion and Conclusion

As we can see from the perceptual perspective, the results of our innovative compression plus confusion scheme are promising. The patterns that were visible in the output of the compressive sensing scheme disappear completely, giving the confusion property from Shannon's theory context to the processed images. In this sense, the correlation coefficients allow us to conclude that the processed image is independent of the original image. In the entropy and histogram analysis, we could obtain good results for the red and green channels. Hence, in the future, we hope to make modifications that improve the results of the blue channel and also make other tests and attacks to validate this scheme.

Further work also includes testing the proposed approach in a real application environment. For example, for compressing and encrypting the images from surveillance cameras in smart cities applications.

Acknowledgement. Aboytes-González is a postdoctoral fellow of CONAHCYT (México). This work was funded by CONAHCYT under grant 321068 and by SIP-IPN under grants 20232816 and 20230990.

References

1. Aboytes-González, J.A., Murguía, J.S., Mejía-Carlos, M., González-Aguilar, H., Ramírez-Torres, M.T.: Design of a strong s-box based on a matrix approach. Nonl. Dyn. **9**, 2003–2012 (2018). https://doi.org/10.1007/s11071-018-4471-z

2. Aboytes-González, J.A., Soubervielle-Montalvo, C., Campos-Canton, I., Perez-Cham, O.E., Ramírez-Torres, M.T.: Method to improve the cryptographic properties of s-boxes. IEEE Access **11**, 99546–99557 (2023). https://doi.org/10.1109/ACCESS.2023.3313180

3. Ahmad, M., Chugh, H., Goel, A., Singla, P.: A chaos based method for efficient cryptographic s-box design. In: Thampi, S.M., Atrey, P.K., Fan, C.I., Perez, G.M. (eds.) Security in Computing and Communications. CCIS, vol. 377, pp. 130–137. Springer, Heidelberg (2013). https://doi.org/10.1007/978-3-642-40576-1_13

4. Brahim, A.H., Pacha, A.A., Said, N.H.: Image encryption based on compressive sensing and chaos systems. Opt. Laser Technol. **132**, 106489 (2020). https://doi.org/10.1016/j.optlastec.2020.106489

5. Candes, E., Romberg, J., Tao, T.: Robust uncertainty principles: exact signal reconstruction from highly incomplete frequency information. IEEE Trans. Inf. Theory **52**(2), 489–509 (2006). https://doi.org/10.1109/TIT.2005.862083

6. Candes, E.J., Tao, T.: Near-optimal signal recovery from random projections: Universal encoding strategies? IEEE Transactions on Information Theory 52(12), 5406–5425 (2006), https://doi.org/10.1109/TIT.2006.885507

7. Candes, E.J., Wakin, M.B.: An introduction to compressive sampling. IEEE Signal Process. Mag. **25**(2), 21–30 (2008). https://doi.org/10.1109/MSP.2007.914731

8. Chen, J., Zhang, Y., Qi, L., Fu, C., Xu, L.: Exploiting chaos-based compressed sensing and cryptographic algorithm for image encryption and compression. Opt. Laser Technol. **99**, 238–248 (2018). https://doi.org/10.1016/j.optlastec.2017.09.008

9. Choi, J.W., Shim, B., Ding, Y., Rao, B., Kim, D.I.: Compressed sensing for wireless communications: useful tips and tricks. IEEE Commun. Surv. Tutori. **19**(3), 1527–1550 (2017)

10. Della Porta, C.J., Bekit, A.A., Lampe, B.H., Chang, C.I.: Hyperspectral image classification via compressive sensing. IEEE Trans. Geosci. Remote Sens. **57**(10), 8290–8303 (2019)

11. Donoho, D.: Compressed sensing. IEEE Trans. Inf. Theory **52**(4), 1289–1306 (2006). https://doi.org/10.1109/TIT.2006.871582

12. Escamilla-Ambrosio, P.J., Salinas-Rosales, M., Aguirre-Anaya, E., Acosta-Bermejo, R.: Image compressive sensing cryptographic analysis. In: 2016 International Conference on Electronics, Communications and Computers (CONIELECOMP), pp. 81–86. IEEE (2016)

13. Gan, Z., Song, S., Zhou, L., Han, D., Fu, J., Chai, X.: Exploiting compressed sensing and polynomial-based progressive secret image sharing for visually secure image selection encryption with authentication. J. King Saud Univ. Comput. Inf. Sci. **34**(10), 9252–9272 (2022). https://doi.org/10.1016/j.jksuci.2022.09.006

14. Gao, Z., Xiong, C., Ding, L., Zhou, C.: Image representation using block compressive sensing for compression applications. J. Vis. Comun. Image Represent. **24**(7), 885–894 (2013). https://doi.org/10.1016/j.jvcir.2013.06.006

15. Ghaffari, A.: Image compression-encryption method based on two-dimensional sparse recovery and chaotic system. Sci. Rep. **11**(1), 369 (2021). https://doi.org/10.1038/s41598-020-79747-4

16. Guodong, Y., Min, L., Mingfa, W.: Double image encryption algorithm based on compressive sensing and elliptic curve. Alexandria Eng. J. **61**(9), 6785–6795 (2022). https://doi.org/10.1016/j.aej.2021.12.023

17. Huang, X., Dong, Y., Ye, G., Shi, Y.: Meaningful image encryption algorithm based on compressive sensing and integer wavelet transform. Front. Comput. Sci. **17**(3), 173804 (2023). https://doi.org/10.1007/s11704-022-1419-8

18. Jones, L.: Securing the smart city. Eng. Technol. **11**, 30–33 (2016)

19. Lian, S.: Multimedia Content Encryption: Techniques and Applications. CRC Press (2008)

20. Orsdemir, A., Altun, H.O., Sharma, G., Bocko, M.F.: On the security and robustness of encryption via compressed sensing. In: Proceedings of the 2008 IEEE Military Communications Conference (MILCOM 2008), pp. 1–7 (2008). https://doi.org/10.1109/MILCOM.2008.4753187

21. Ponuma, R., Amutha, R.: Compressive sensing based image compression-encryption using novel 1d-chaotic map. Multim. Tools Appl. **77**, 19209–19234 (2018). https://doi.org/10.1007/s11042-017-5378-2

22. Ramírez-Torres, M.T., Murguía, J.S., Mejía-Carlos, M.: Image encryption with an improved cryptosystem based on a matrix approach. Int. J. Mod. Phys. C **25**(10), 14500 (2014). https://doi.org/10.1142/S0129183114500545

23. Siddiqui, N., Khalid, H., Murtaza, F., Ehatisham-Ul-Haq, M., Azam, M.A.: A novel algebraic technique for design of computational substitution-boxes using action of matrices on Galois field. IEEE Access **8**, 197630–197643 (2020)

24. Sun, C., Wang, E., Zhao, B.: Image encryption scheme with compressed sensing based on a new six-dimensional non-degenerate discrete hyperchaotic system and plaintext-related scrambling. Entropy **23**(3), 291 (2021). https://doi.org/10.3390/e23030291

25. Tanyildizi, E., Özkaynak, F.: A new chaotic s-box generation method using parameter optimization of one dimensional chaotic maps. IEEE Access **7**, 117829–117838 (2019). https://doi.org/10.1109/ACCESS.2019.2936447

26. Wu, X., Wang, J., Xu, W., Zhu, Q.: Compressive sensing magnetic resonance imaging reconstruction based on nonlocal autoregressive modeling. In: Tenth International Conference on Digital Image Processing (ICDIP 2018), vol. 10806, pp. 960–967. SPIE (2018)

27. Wu, Y., Yang, G., Jin, H., Noonan, J.P.: Image encryption using the two-dimensional logistic chaotic map. J. Electron. Imaging **21**(1), 013014–013014 (2012)

28. Ye, G., Pan, C., Dong, Y., Shi, Y., Huang, X.: Image encryption and hiding algorithm based on compressive sensing and random numbers insertion. Signal Process. **172**, 107563 (2020). https://doi.org/10.1016/j.sigpro.2020.107563

Author Index

S. Nesmachnow and L. Hernández Callejo (Eds.): ICSC-Cities 2023, CCIS 1938, pp. 291–292, 2024.
https://doi.org/10.1007/978-3-031-52517-9

Printed in the United States
by Baker & Taylor Publisher Services

Printed in the United States
by Baker & Taylor Publisher Services